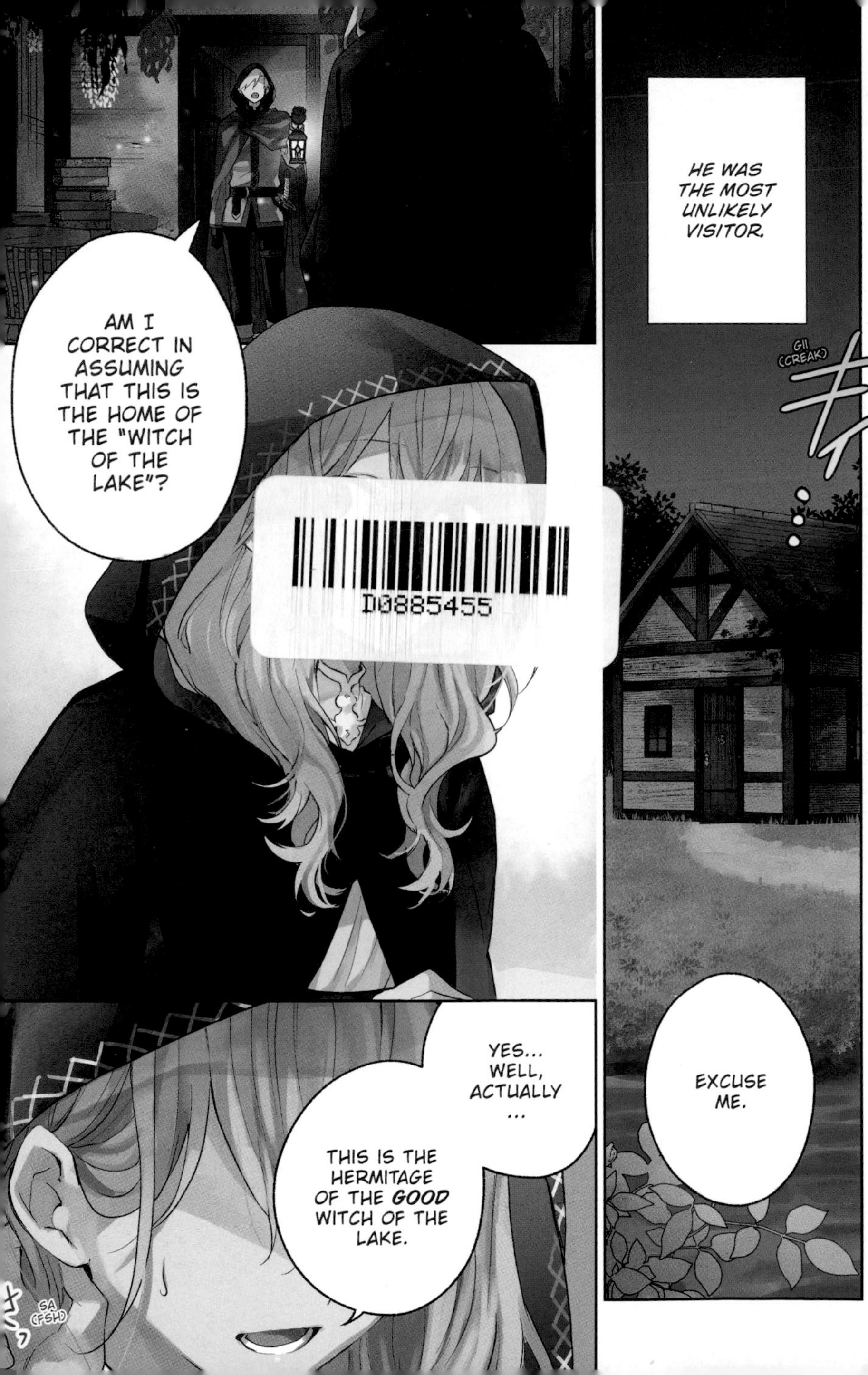
HE WAS THE MOST UNLIKELY VISITOR.
GII (CREAK)
EXCUSE ME.
AM I CORRECT IN ASSUMING THAT THIS IS THE HOME OF THE "WITCH OF THE LAKE"?
YES... WELL, ACTUALLY...
THIS IS THE HERMITAGE OF THE ***GOOD*** WITCH OF THE LAKE.
SA (FSHD)

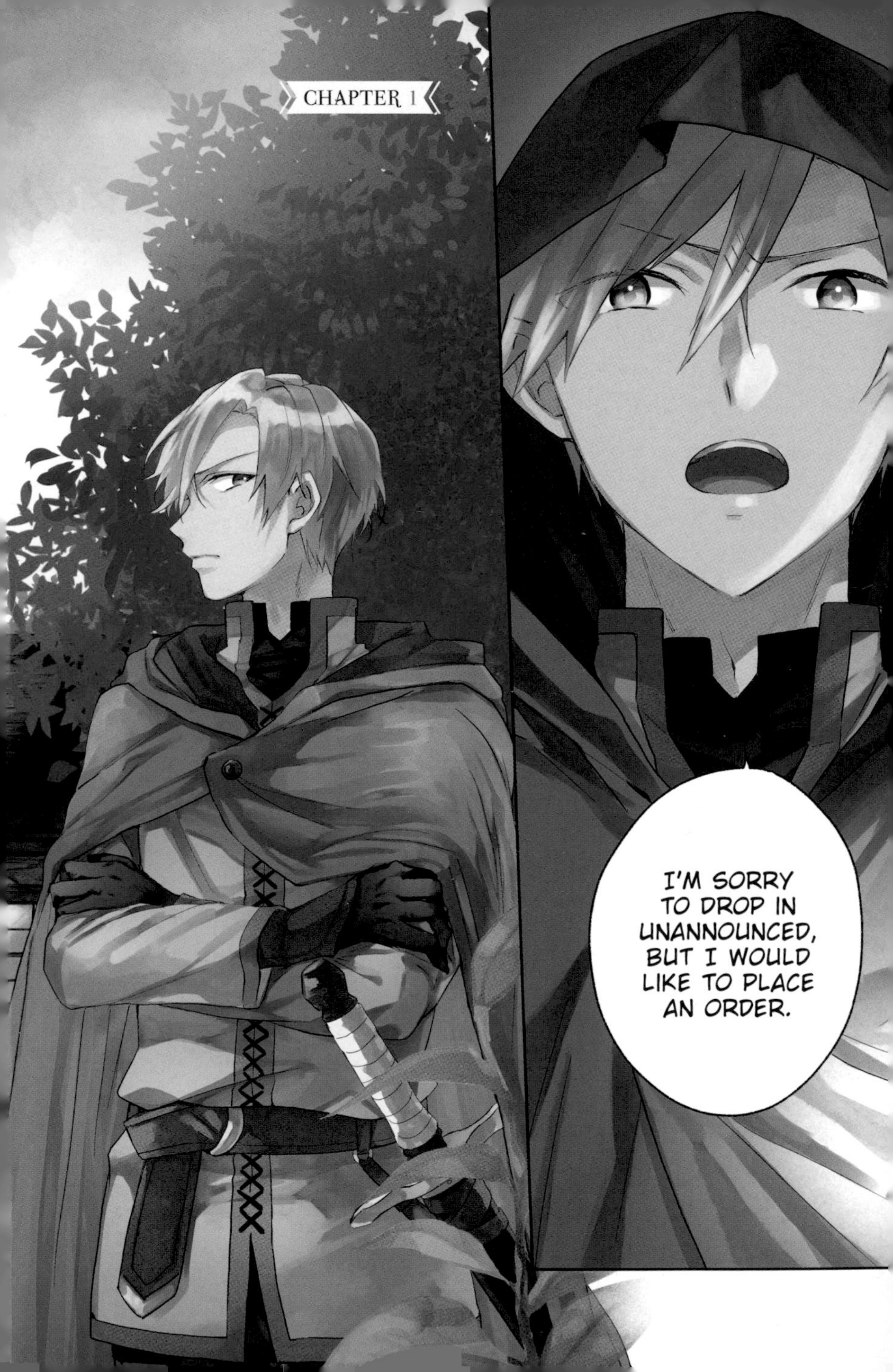
I'M SORRY TO DROP IN UNANNOUNCED, BUT I WOULD LIKE TO PLACE AN ORDER.
CHAPTER 1

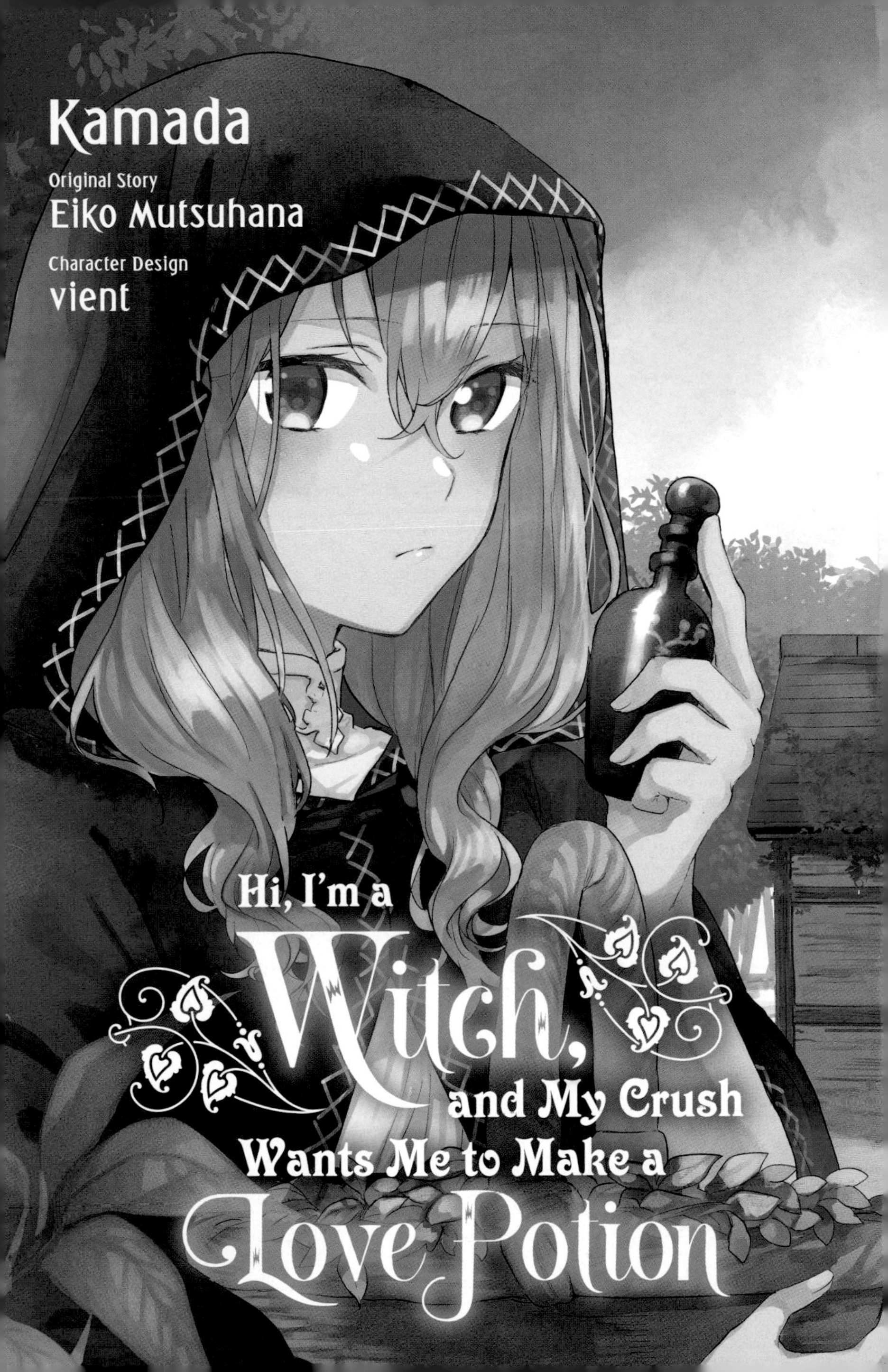
Kamada
Original Story
Eiko Mutsuhana
Character Design
vient
Hi, I'm a Witch, and My Crush Wants Me to Make a Love Potion

Contents

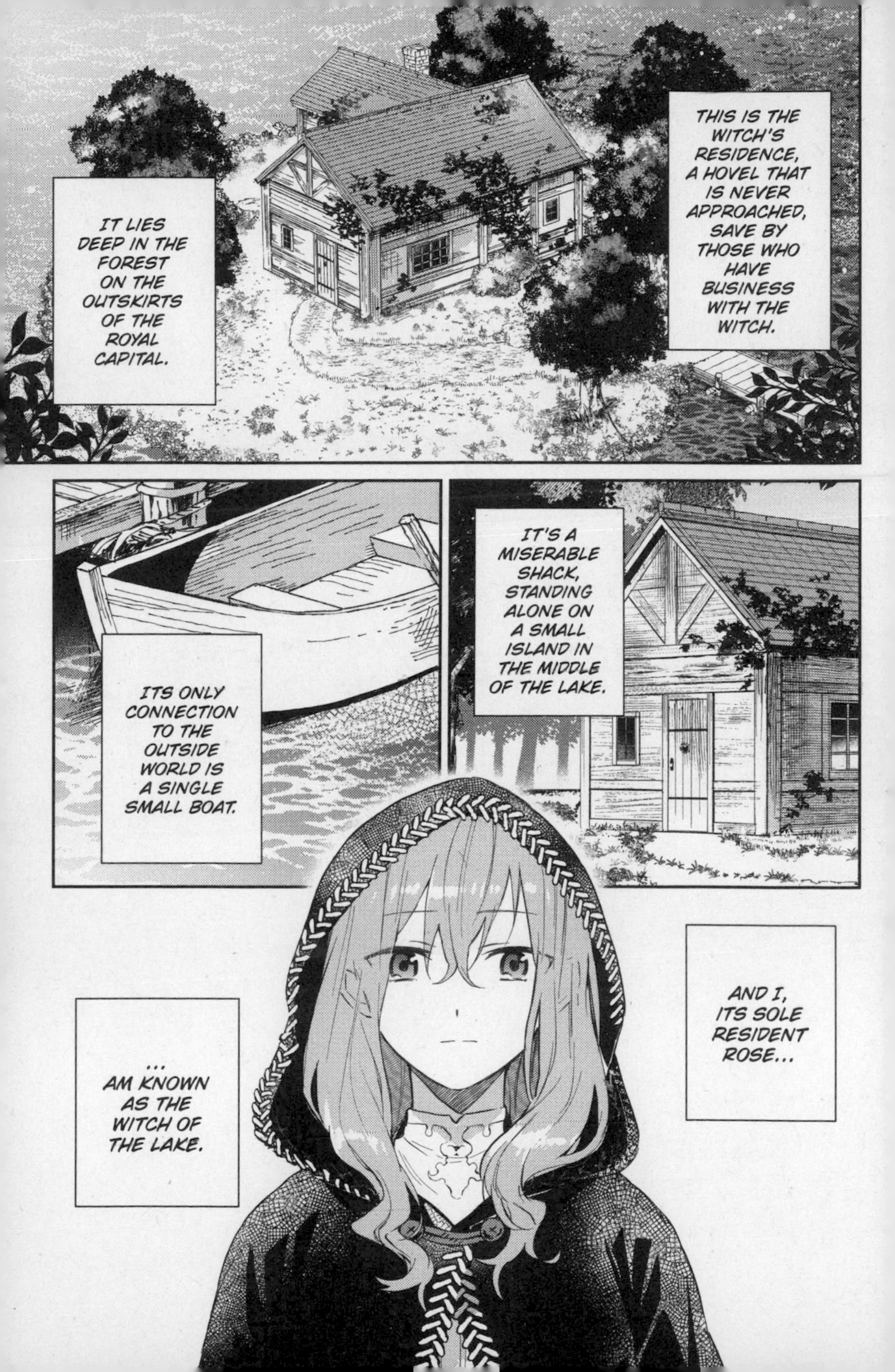
THIS IS THE WITCH'S RESIDENCE, A HOVEL THAT IS NEVER APPROACHED, SAVE BY THOSE WHO HAVE BUSINESS WITH THE WITCH.
IT LIES DEEP IN THE FOREST ON THE OUTSKIRTS OF THE ROYAL CAPITAL.
IT'S A MISERABLE SHACK, STANDING ALONE ON A SMALL ISLAND IN THE MIDDLE OF THE LAKE.
ITS ONLY CONNECTION TO THE OUTSIDE WORLD IS A SINGLE SMALL BOAT.
AND I, ITS SOLE RESIDENT ROSE...
... AM KNOWN AS THE WITCH OF THE LAKE.

MY MOTHER WAS A WITCH, SO I TOO HAVE BEEN ONE SINCE THE DAY I WAS BORN.

MY MOTHER DIED WHEN I WAS VERY YOUNG, SO I WAS RAISED BY MY GRAND-MOTHER.

BUT FOUR YEARS AGO, SHE ALSO RETURNED TO THE EARTH'S EMBRACE, SO NOW I'M ALONE.

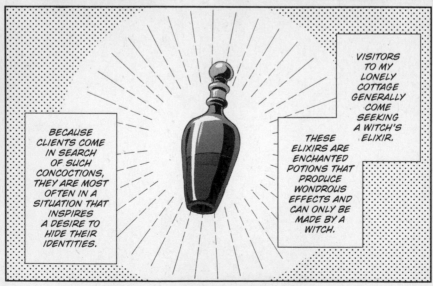

VISITORS TO MY LONELY COTTAGE GENERALLY COME SEEKING A WITCH'S ELIXIR.

THESE ELIXIRS ARE ENCHANTED POTIONS THAT PRODUCE WONDROUS EFFECTS AND CAN ONLY BE MADE BY A WITCH.

BECAUSE CLIENTS COME IN SEARCH OF SUCH CONCOCTIONS, THEY ARE MOST OFTEN IN A SITUATION THAT INSPIRES A DESIRE TO HIDE THEIR IDENTITIES.

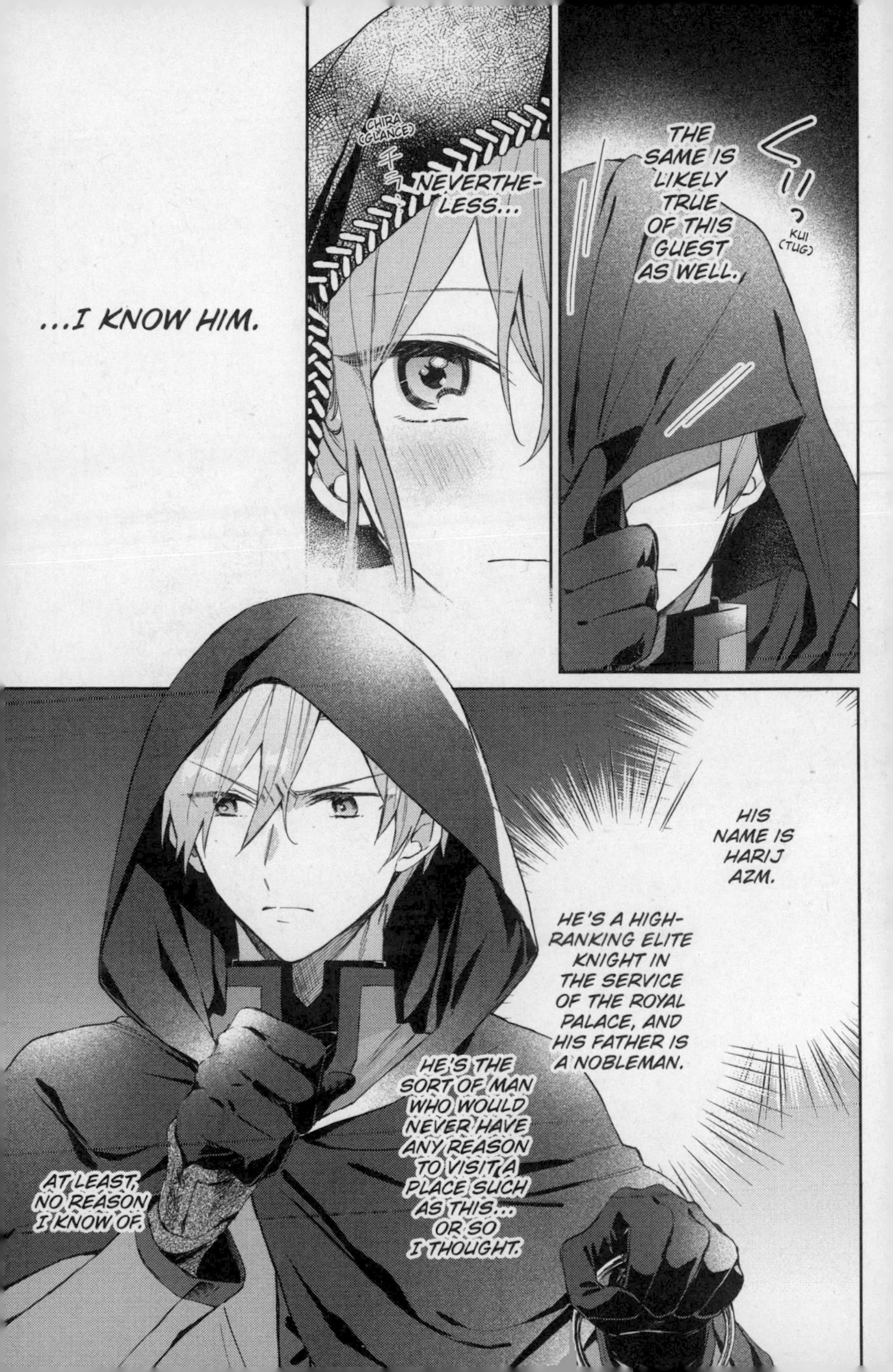
THE SAME IS LIKELY TRUE OF THIS GUEST AS WELL.
くいっ
KUI (TUG)
CHIRA (GLANCE)
チラ
NEVERTHELESS...
...I KNOW HIM.
HIS NAME IS HARIJ AZM.
HE'S A HIGH-RANKING ELITE KNIGHT IN THE SERVICE OF THE ROYAL PALACE, AND HIS FATHER IS A NOBLEMAN.
HE'S THE SORT OF MAN WHO WOULD NEVER HAVE ANY REASON TO VISIT A PLACE SUCH AS THIS... OR SO I THOUGHT.
AT LEAST, NO REASON I KNOW OF.

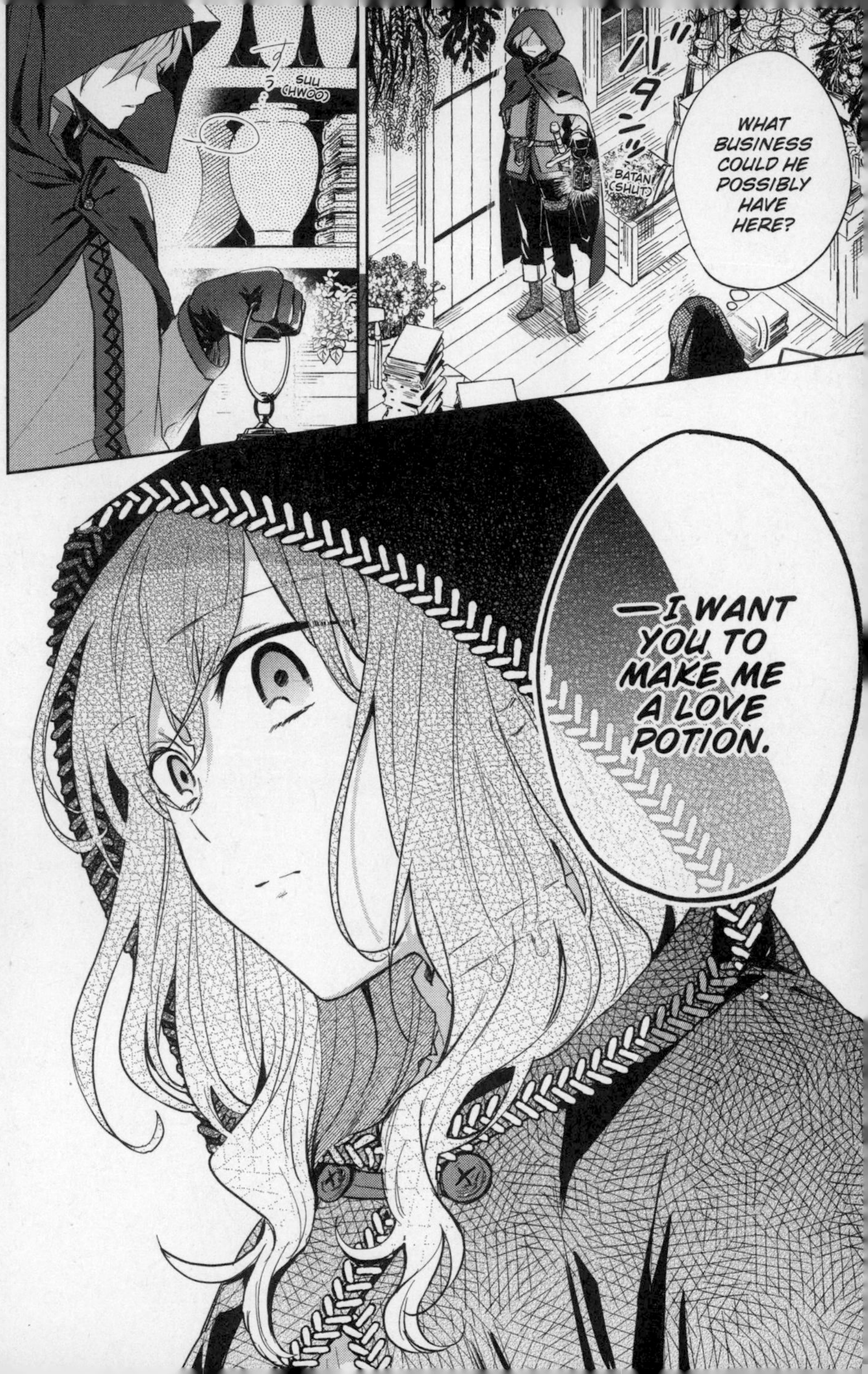
BATAN (SHUT)
WHAT BUSINESS COULD HE POSSIBLY HAVE HERE?
SUU (HWOO)
—I WANT YOU TO MAKE ME A LOVE POTION.

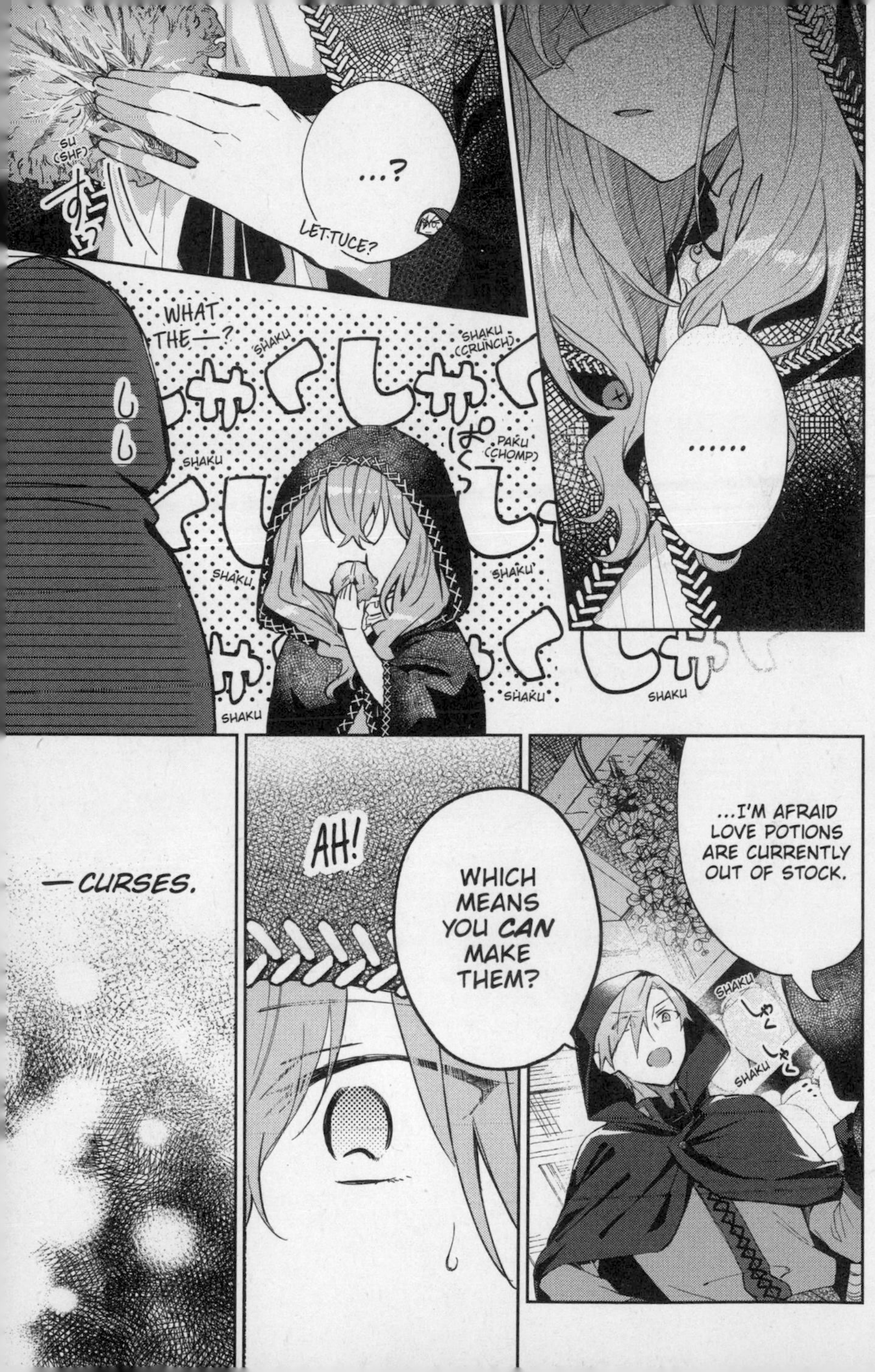
......
...?
LET-TUCE?
SU (SHF)
WHAT THE—?
SHAKU
SHAKU (CRUNCH)
PAKU (CHOMP)
SHAKU
SHAKU
SHAKU
SHAKU
SHAKU
SHAKU
...I'M AFRAID LOVE POTIONS ARE CURRENTLY OUT OF STOCK.
SHAKU
SHAKU
AH!
WHICH MEANS YOU CAN MAKE THEM?
—CURSES.

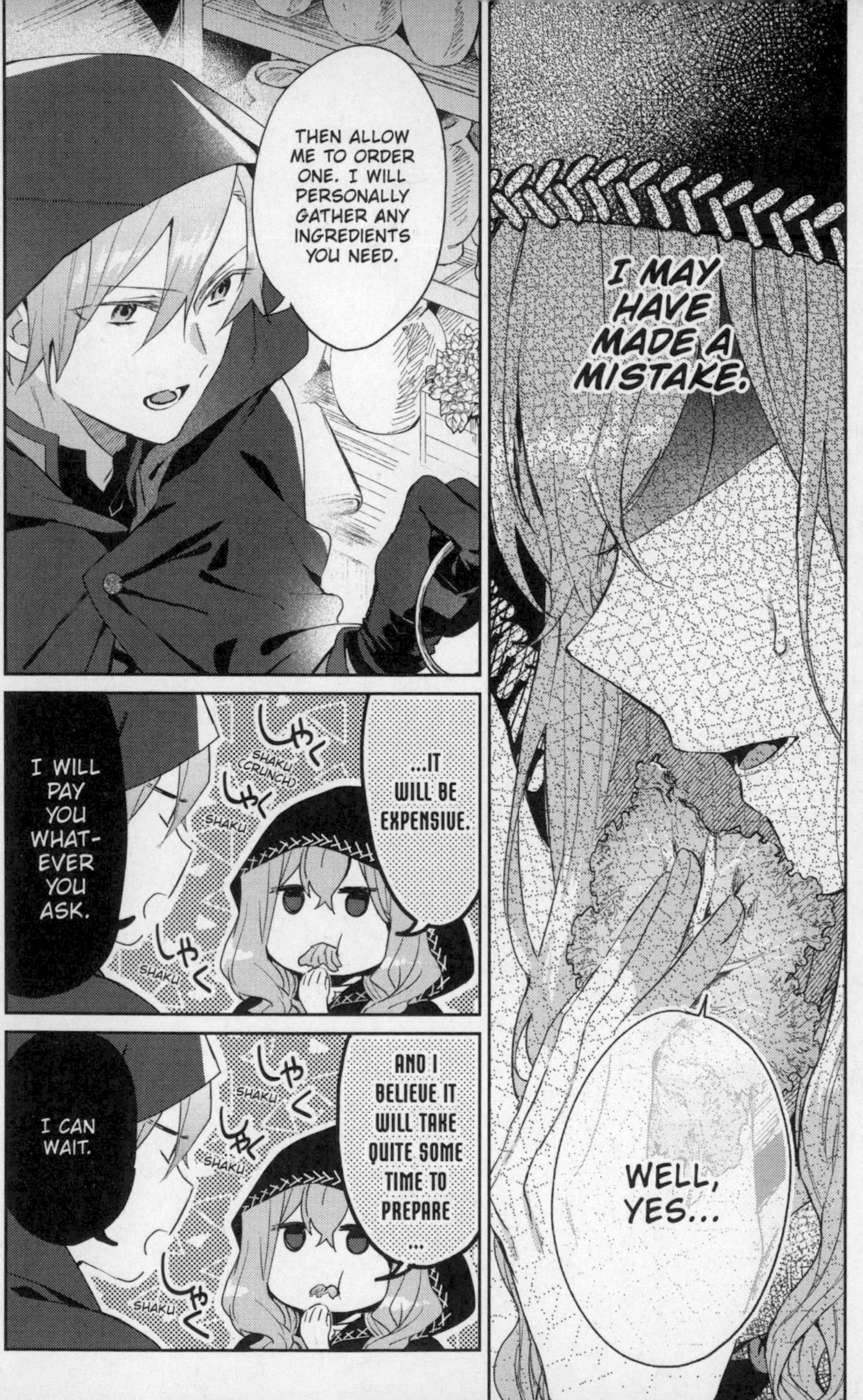
I MAY HAVE MADE A MISTAKE.
WELL, YES...
THEN ALLOW ME TO ORDER ONE. I WILL PERSONALLY GATHER ANY INGREDIENTS YOU NEED.
...IT WILL BE EXPENSIVE.
しゃく
SHAKU (CRUNCH)
しゃく
SHAKU
しゃく
SHAKU
I WILL PAY YOU WHATEVER YOU ASK.
AND I BELIEVE IT WILL TAKE QUITE SOME TIME TO PREPARE ...
しゃく
SHAKU
しゃく
SHAKU
しゃく
SHAKU
I CAN WAIT.

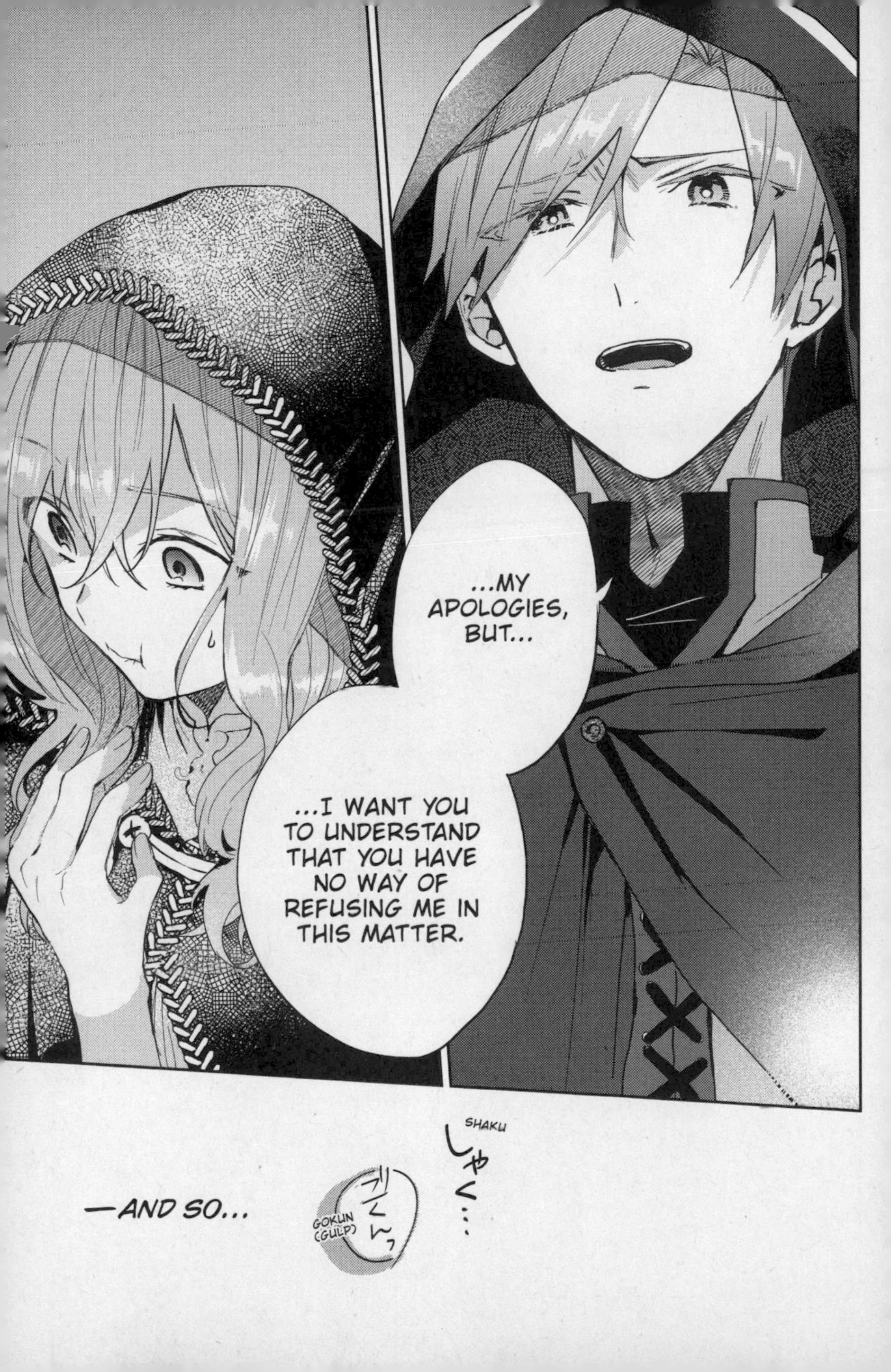
...MY APOLOGIES, BUT...
...I WANT YOU TO UNDERSTAND THAT YOU HAVE NO WAY OF REFUSING ME IN THIS MATTER.
SHAKU
しゃく...
GOKUN (GULP)
ごくんっ
—AND SO...

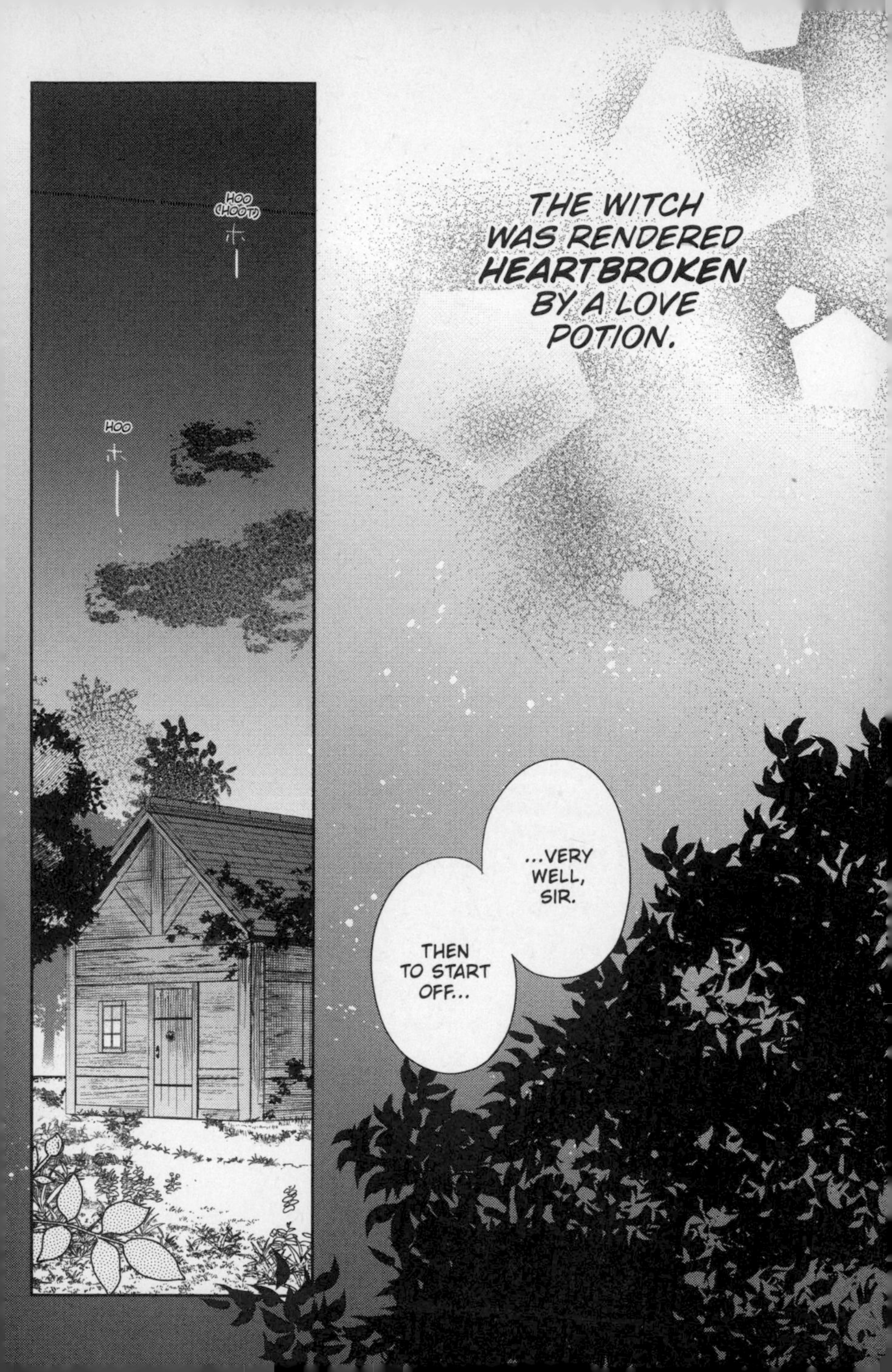
THE WITCH WAS RENDERED HEARTBROKEN BY A LOVE POTION.
...VERY WELL, SIR.
THEN TO START OFF...
HOO (HOOT)
ホー
HOO
ホー

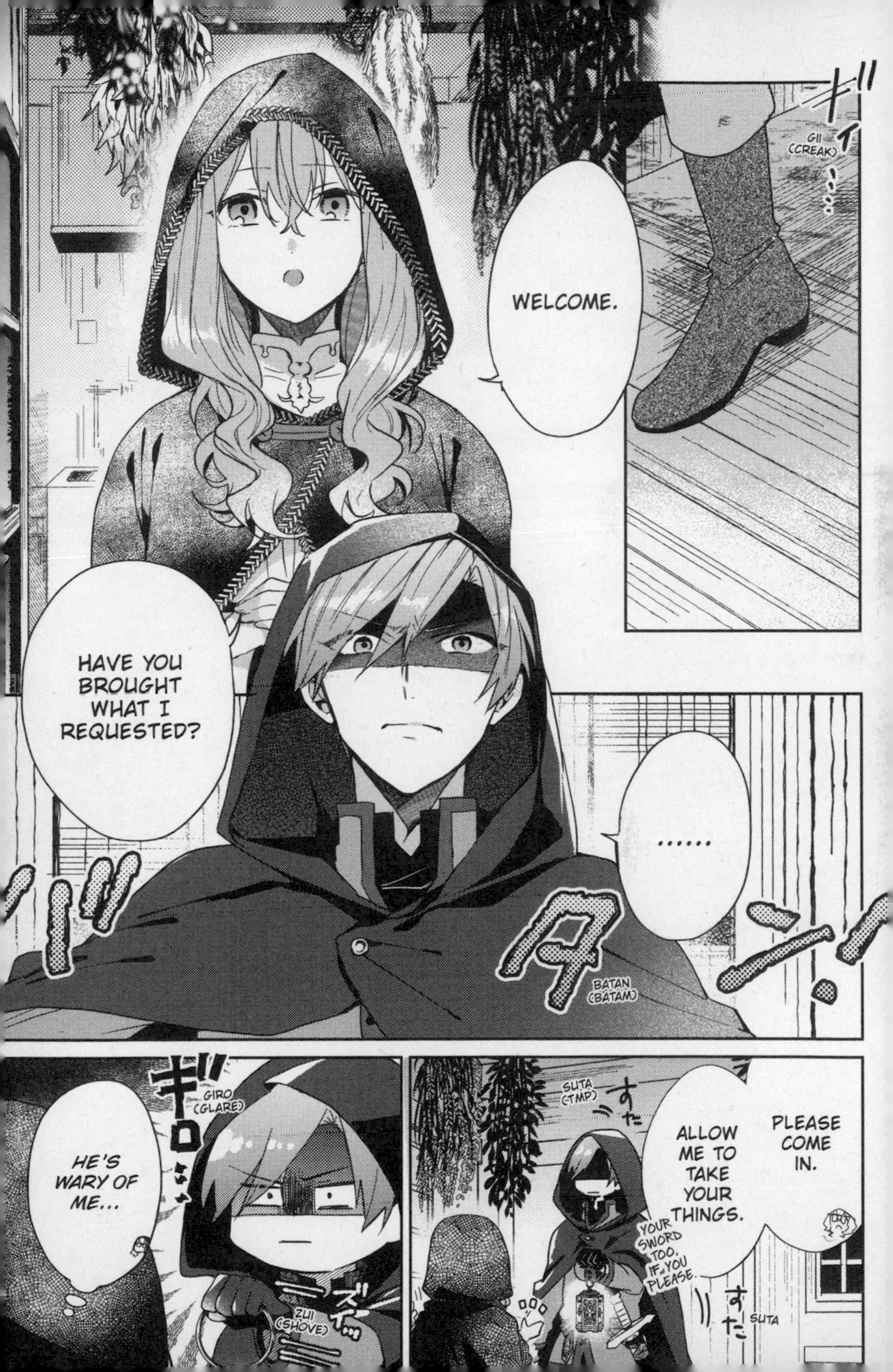
GII (CREAK)
WELCOME.
HAVE YOU BROUGHT WHAT I REQUESTED?
......
BATAN (BATAM)
PLEASE COME IN.
ALLOW ME TO TAKE YOUR THINGS.
SUTA (TMP)
YOUR SWORD TOO, IF YOU PLEASE.
SUTA
GIRO (GLARE)
HE'S WARY OF ME...
ZUII (SHOVE)

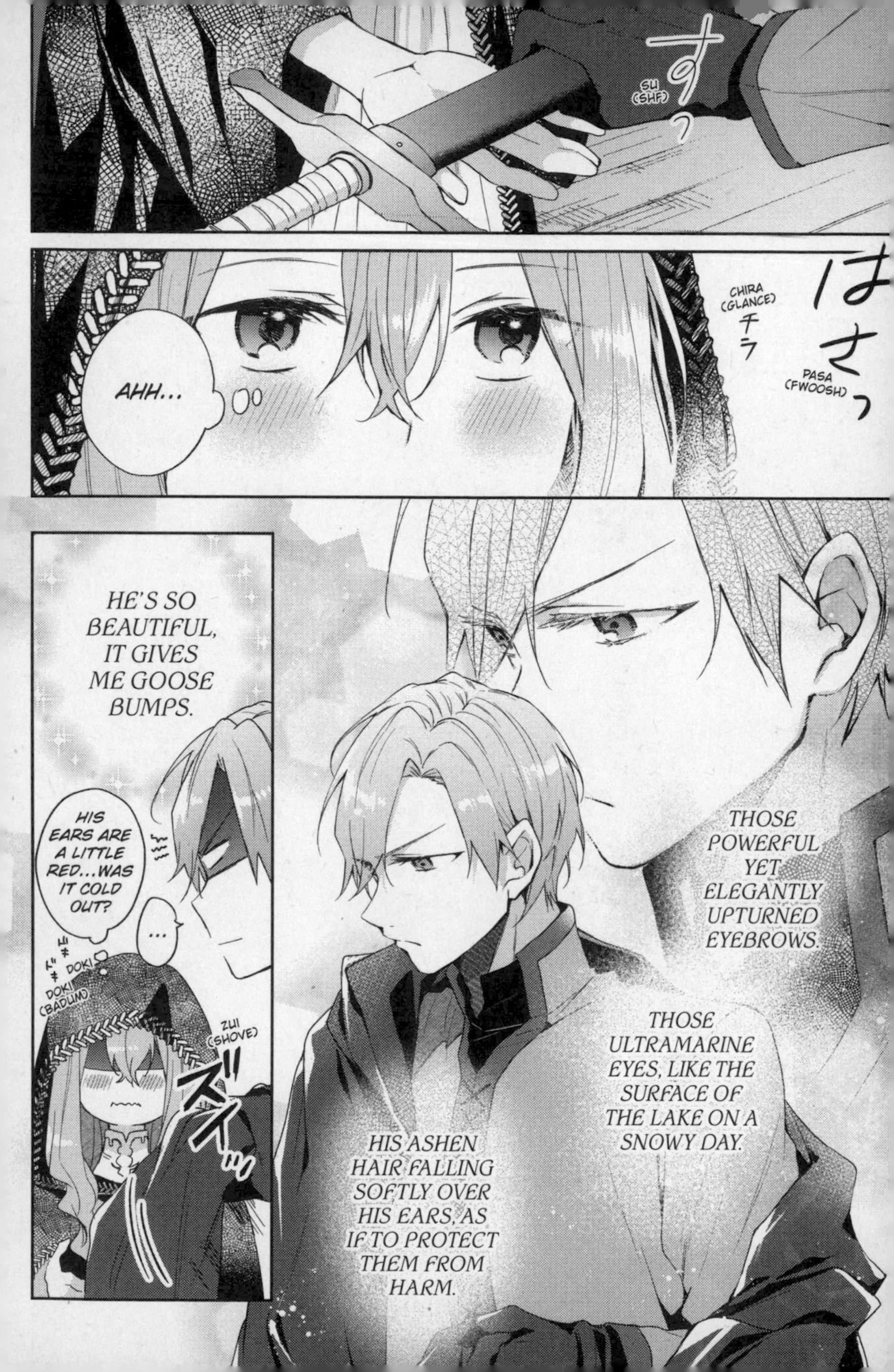
すっ
SU (SHF)
はさっ
PASA (FWOOSH)
チラ
CHIRA (GLANCE)
AHH...
THOSE POWERFUL YET ELEGANTLY UPTURNED EYEBROWS.
THOSE ULTRAMARINE EYES, LIKE THE SURFACE OF THE LAKE ON A SNOWY DAY.
HIS ASHEN HAIR FALLING SOFTLY OVER HIS EARS, AS IF TO PROTECT THEM FROM HARM.
HE'S SO BEAUTIFUL, IT GIVES ME GOOSE BUMPS.
HIS EARS ARE A LITTLE RED...WAS IT COLD OUT?
...
DOKI DOKI (BADUM)
ズイ
ZUI (SHOVE)

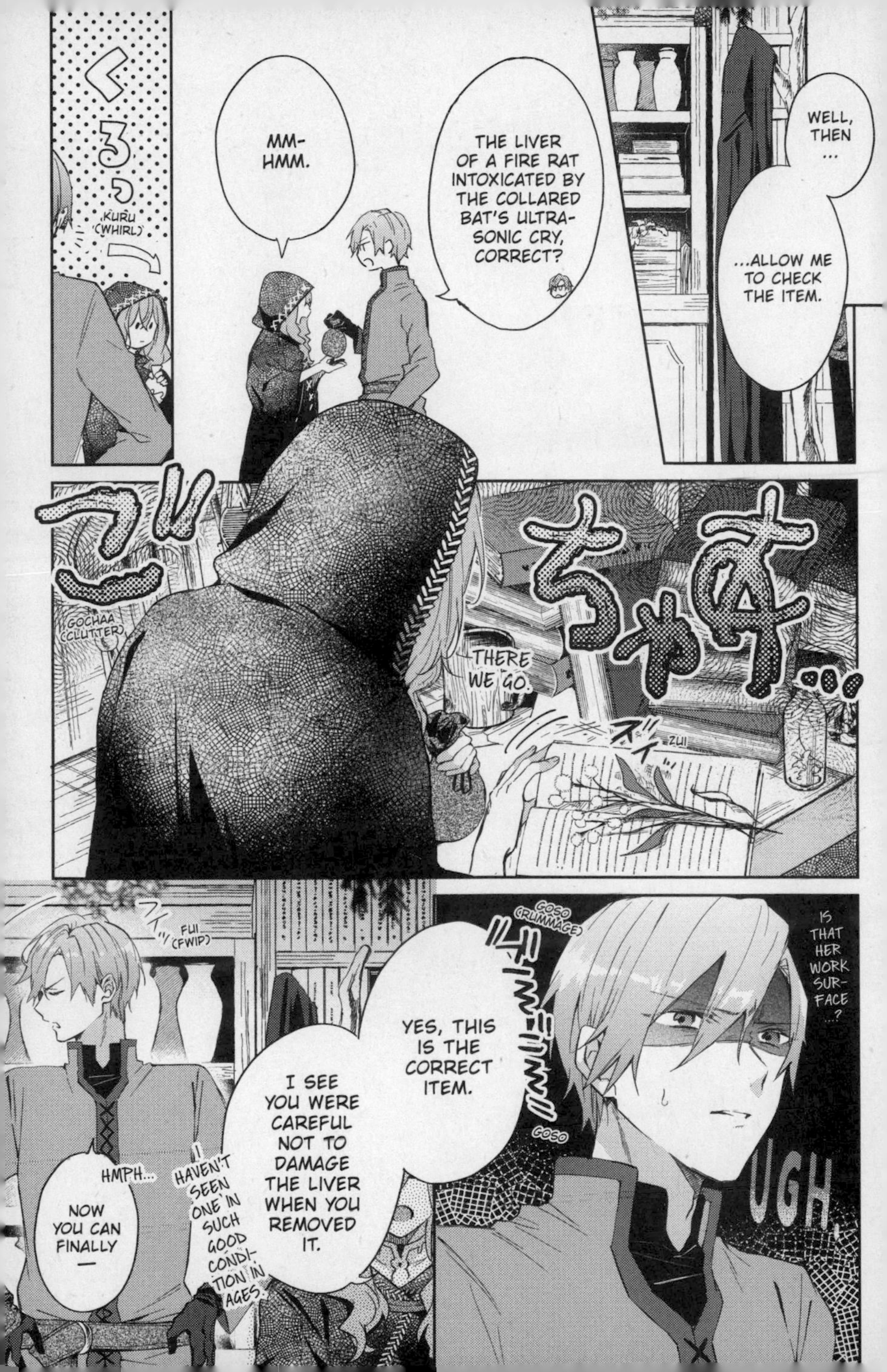
WELL, THEN...
...ALLOW ME TO CHECK THE ITEM.
THE LIVER OF A FIRE RAT INTOXICATED BY THE COLLARED BAT'S ULTRA-SONIC CRY, CORRECT?
MM-HMM.
KURU (WHIRL)
GOCHAA (CLUTTER)
THERE WE GO.
ZUI
IS THAT HER WORK SURFACE...?
GOSO (RUMMAGE)
UGH.
GOSO
FUI (FWIP)
YES, THIS IS THE CORRECT ITEM.
I SEE YOU WERE CAREFUL NOT TO DAMAGE THE LIVER WHEN YOU REMOVED IT.
I HAVEN'T SEEN ONE IN SUCH GOOD CONDITION IN AGES.
HMPH...
NOW YOU CAN FINALLY —

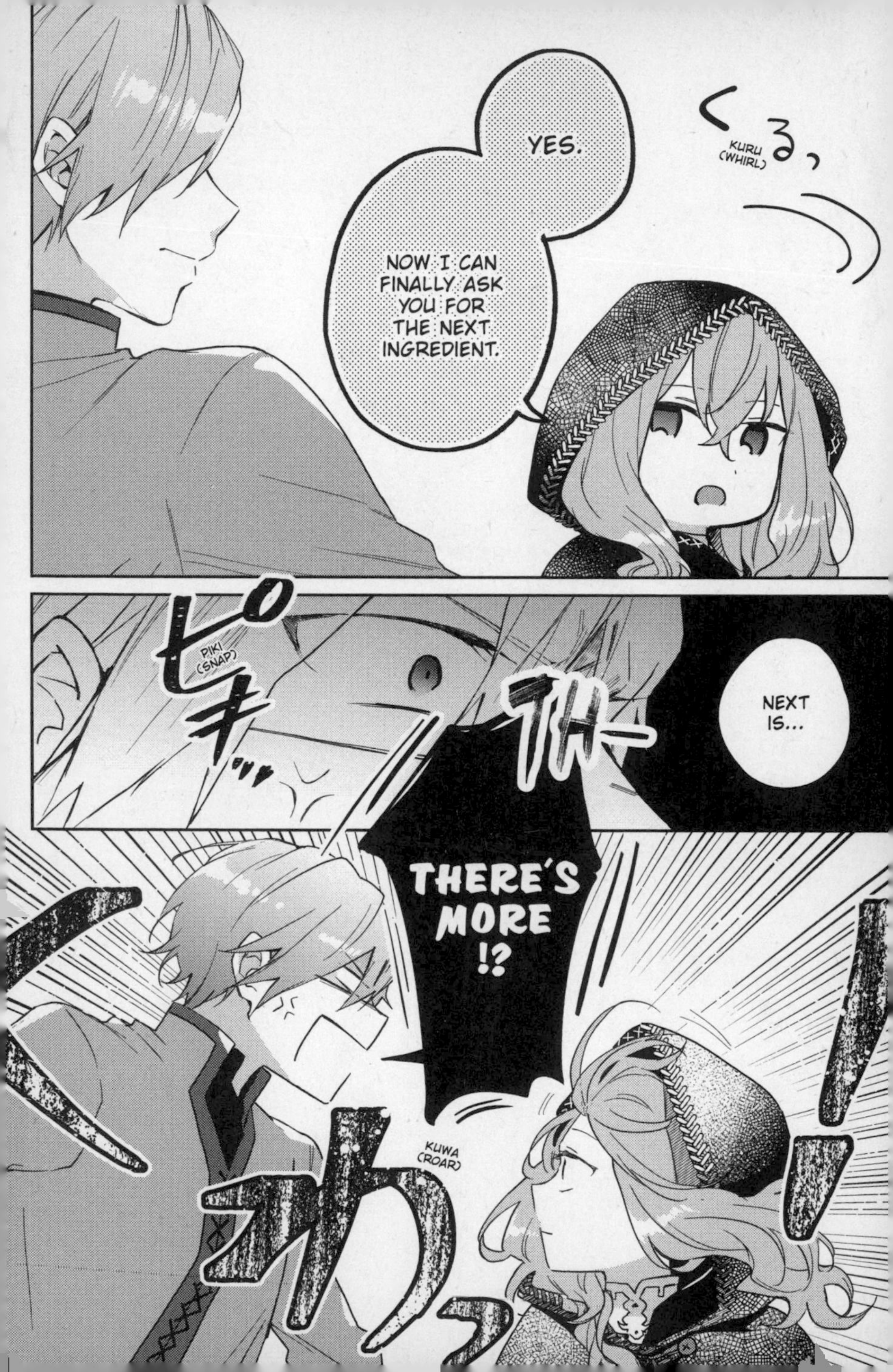
KURU (WHIRL)
YES.
NOW I CAN FINALLY ASK YOU FOR THE NEXT INGREDIENT.
NEXT IS...
TH-
PIKI (SNAP)
THERE'S MORE !?
KUWA (ROAR)

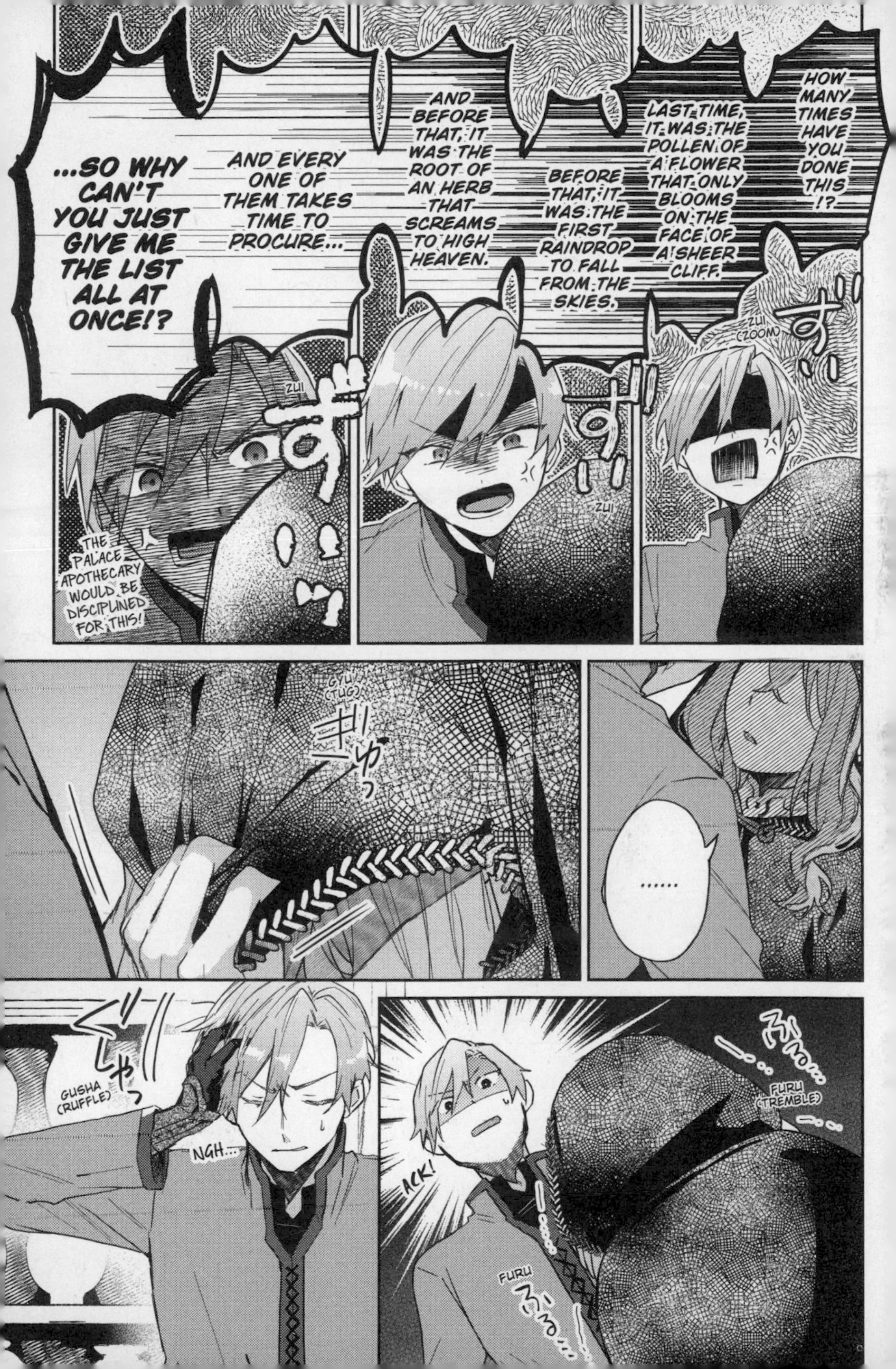
HOW MANY TIMES HAVE YOU DONE THIS!?
LAST TIME, IT WAS THE POLLEN OF A FLOWER THAT ONLY BLOOMS ON THE FACE OF A SHEER CLIFF.
BEFORE THAT, IT WAS THE FIRST RAINDROP TO FALL FROM THE SKIES.
AND BEFORE THAT, IT WAS THE ROOT OF AN HERB THAT SCREAMS TO HIGH HEAVEN.
AND EVERY ONE OF THEM TAKES TIME TO PROCURE...
...SO WHY CAN'T YOU JUST GIVE ME THE LIST ALL AT ONCE!?
ZUI (ZOOM)
ZUI
ZUI
THE PALACE APOTHECARY WOULD BE DISCIPLINED FOR THIS!
......
GYU (TUG)
FURU (TREMBLE)
ACK!
FURU
GUSHA (RUFFLE)
NGH...

...I'M SORRY. I SHOULDN'T HAVE RAISED MY VOICE.

SU? (SHF.)

...NO, IT'S JUST...

FURU (TREMBLE)

AND UP/SO CLOSE...

...SO BLINDINGLY GLORIOUS.

HUH?

FURU (TREMBLE)

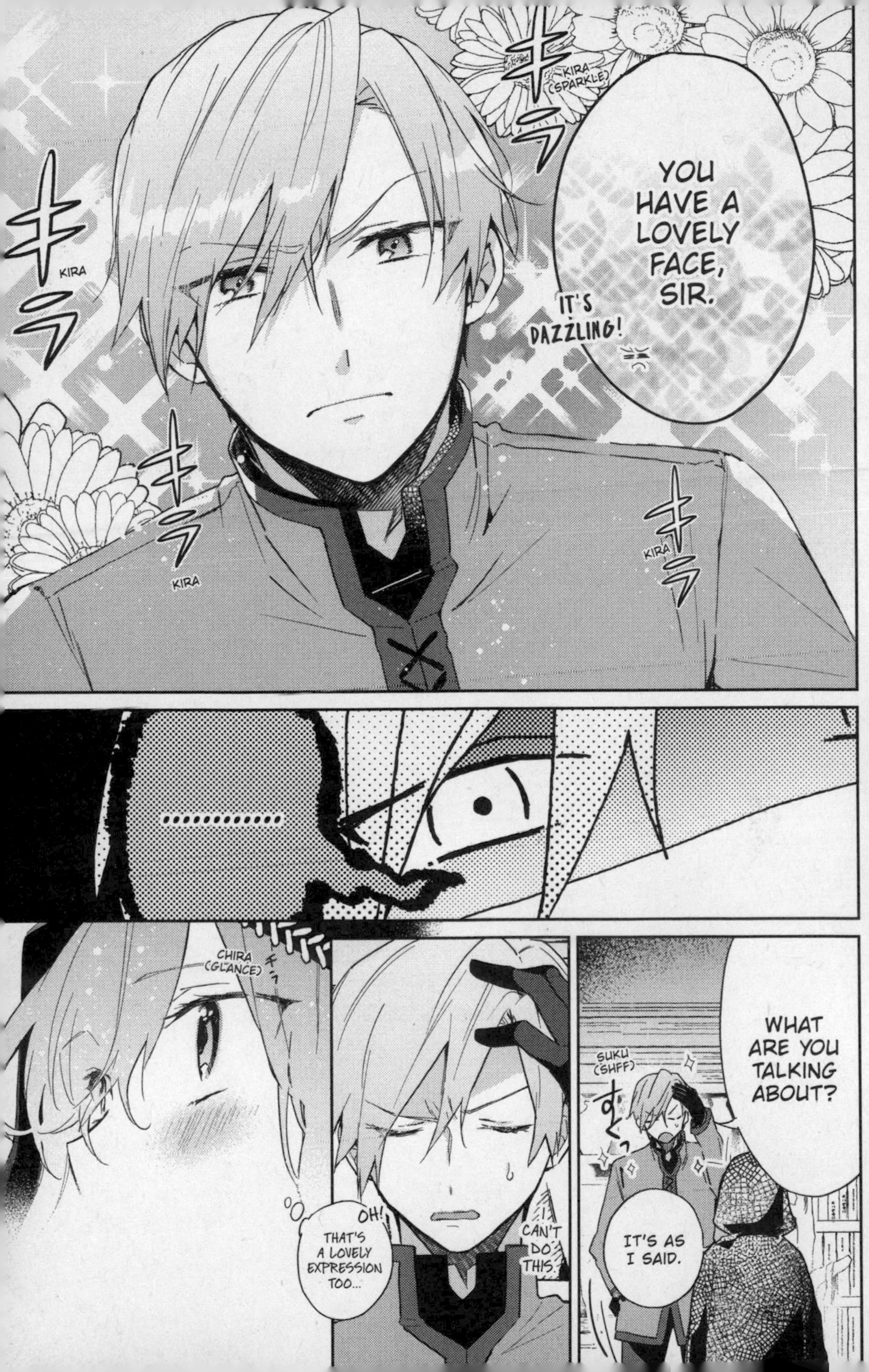
YOU HAVE A LOVELY FACE, SIR.
KIRA (SPARKLE)
IT'S DAZZLING!
KIRA
KIRA
KIRA
....
WHAT ARE YOU TALKING ABOUT?
SUKU (SHFF)
IT'S AS I SAID.
I CAN'T DO THIS.
OH!
THAT'S A LOVELY EXPRESSION TOO...
CHIRA (GLANCE)

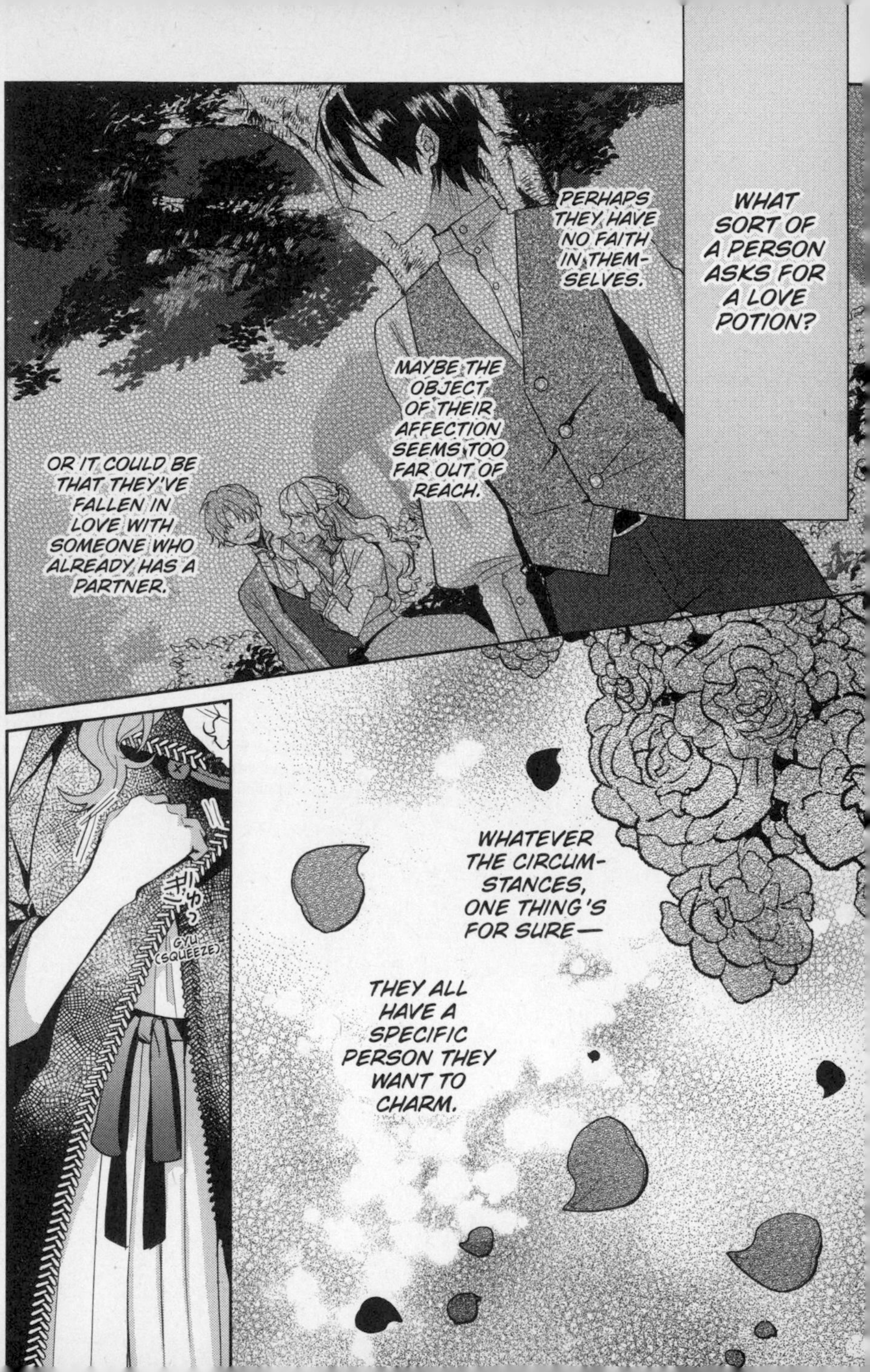
WHAT SORT OF A PERSON ASKS FOR A LOVE POTION?
PERHAPS THEY HAVE NO FAITH IN THEMSELVES.
MAYBE THE OBJECT OF THEIR AFFECTION SEEMS TOO FAR OUT OF REACH.
OR IT COULD BE THAT THEY'VE FALLEN IN LOVE WITH SOMEONE WHO ALREADY HAS A PARTNER.
WHATEVER THE CIRCUMSTANCES, ONE THING'S FOR SURE—
THEY ALL HAVE A SPECIFIC PERSON THEY WANT TO CHARM.
GYU (SQUEEZE)

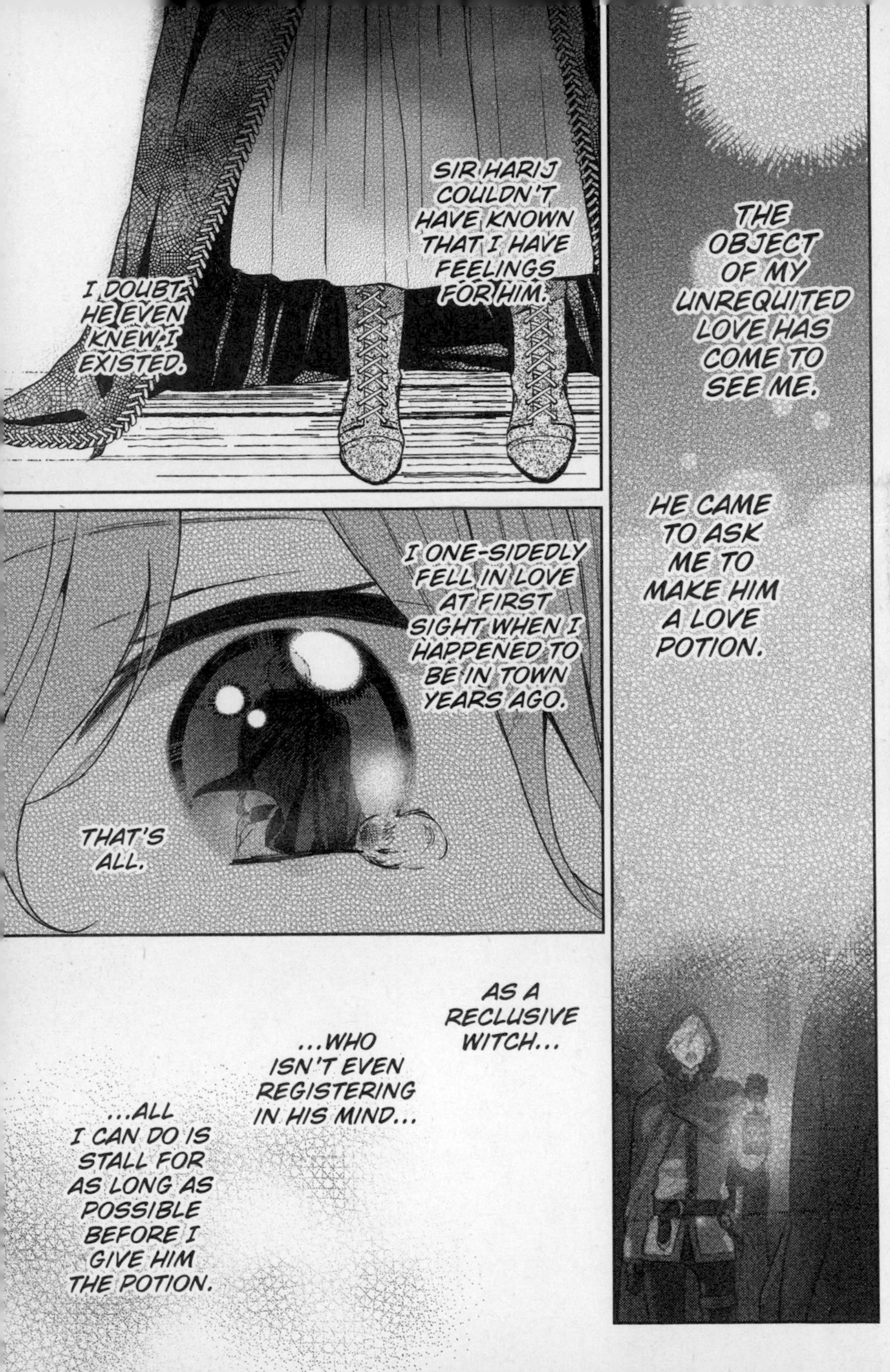
THE OBJECT OF MY UNREQUITED LOVE HAS COME TO SEE ME.
HE CAME TO ASK ME TO MAKE HIM A LOVE POTION.
SIR HARIJ COULDN'T HAVE KNOWN THAT I HAVE FEELINGS FOR HIM.
I DOUBT HE EVEN KNEW I EXISTED.
I ONE-SIDEDLY FELL IN LOVE AT FIRST SIGHT WHEN I HAPPENED TO BE IN TOWN YEARS AGO.
THAT'S ALL.
AS A RECLUSIVE WITCH...
...WHO ISN'T EVEN REGISTERING IN HIS MIND...
...ALL I CAN DO IS STALL FOR AS LONG AS POSSIBLE BEFORE I GIVE HIM THE POTION.

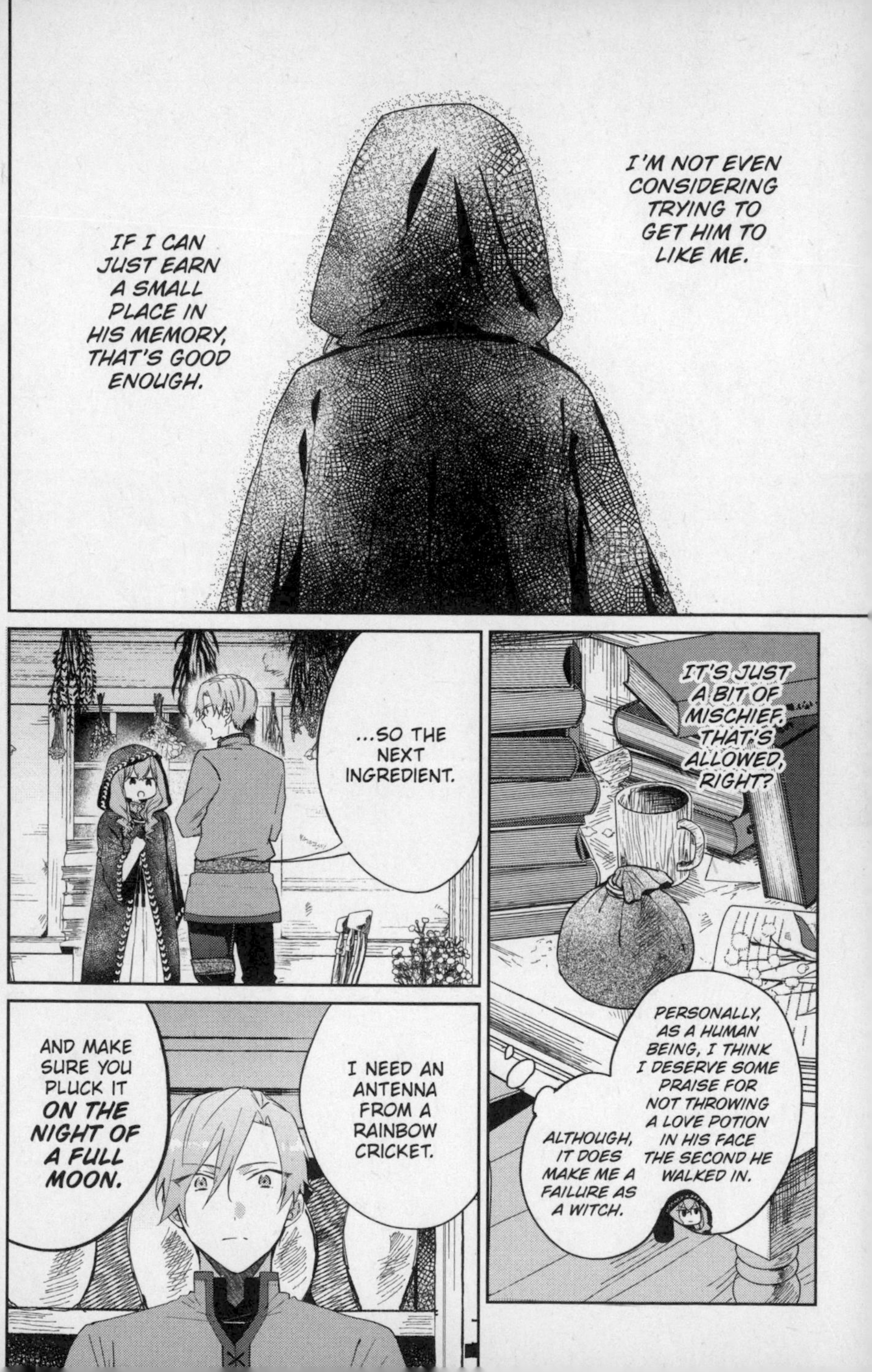
I'M NOT EVEN CONSIDERING TRYING TO GET HIM TO LIKE ME.
IF I CAN JUST EARN A SMALL PLACE IN HIS MEMORY, THAT'S GOOD ENOUGH.
IT'S JUST A BIT OF MISCHIEF. THAT'S ALLOWED, RIGHT?
PERSONALLY, AS A HUMAN BEING, I THINK I DESERVE SOME PRAISE FOR NOT THROWING A LOVE POTION IN HIS FACE THE SECOND HE WALKED IN.
ALTHOUGH, IT DOES MAKE ME A FAILURE AS A WITCH.
...SO THE NEXT INGREDIENT.
I NEED AN ANTENNA FROM A RAINBOW CRICKET.
AND MAKE SURE YOU PLUCK IT ON THE NIGHT OF A FULL MOON.

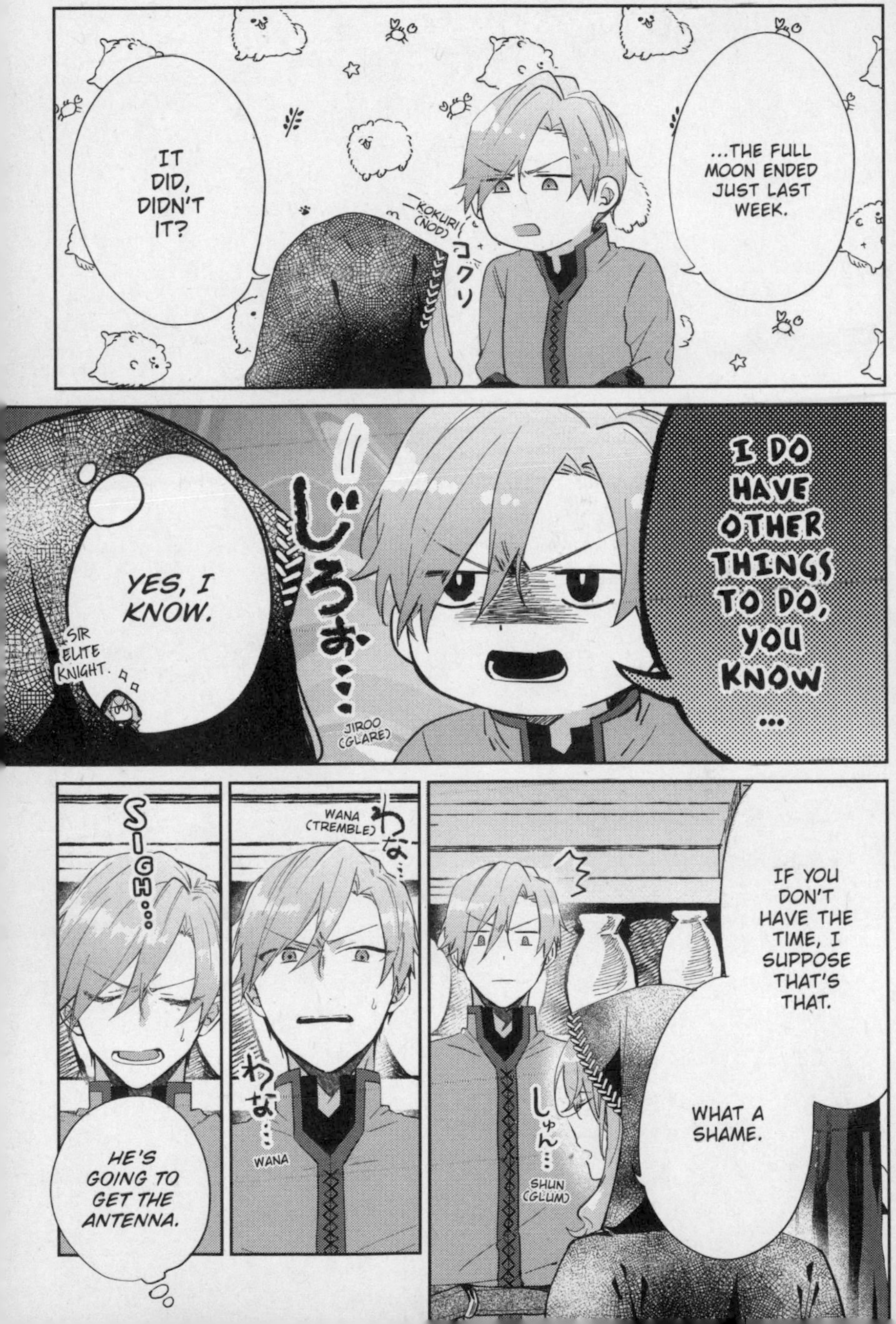
...THE FULL MOON ENDED JUST LAST WEEK.
KOKURI (NOD)
コクリ
IT DID, DIDN'T IT?
I DO HAVE OTHER THINGS TO DO, YOU KNOW...
じろぉ…
JIROO (GLARE)
YES, I KNOW.
SIR ELITE KNIGHT.
IF YOU DON'T HAVE THE TIME, I SUPPOSE THAT'S THAT.
WHAT A SHAME.
しゅん…
SHUN (GLUM)
わな…
WANA (TREMBLE)
わな…
WANA
SIGH...
HE'S GOING TO GET THE ANTENNA.

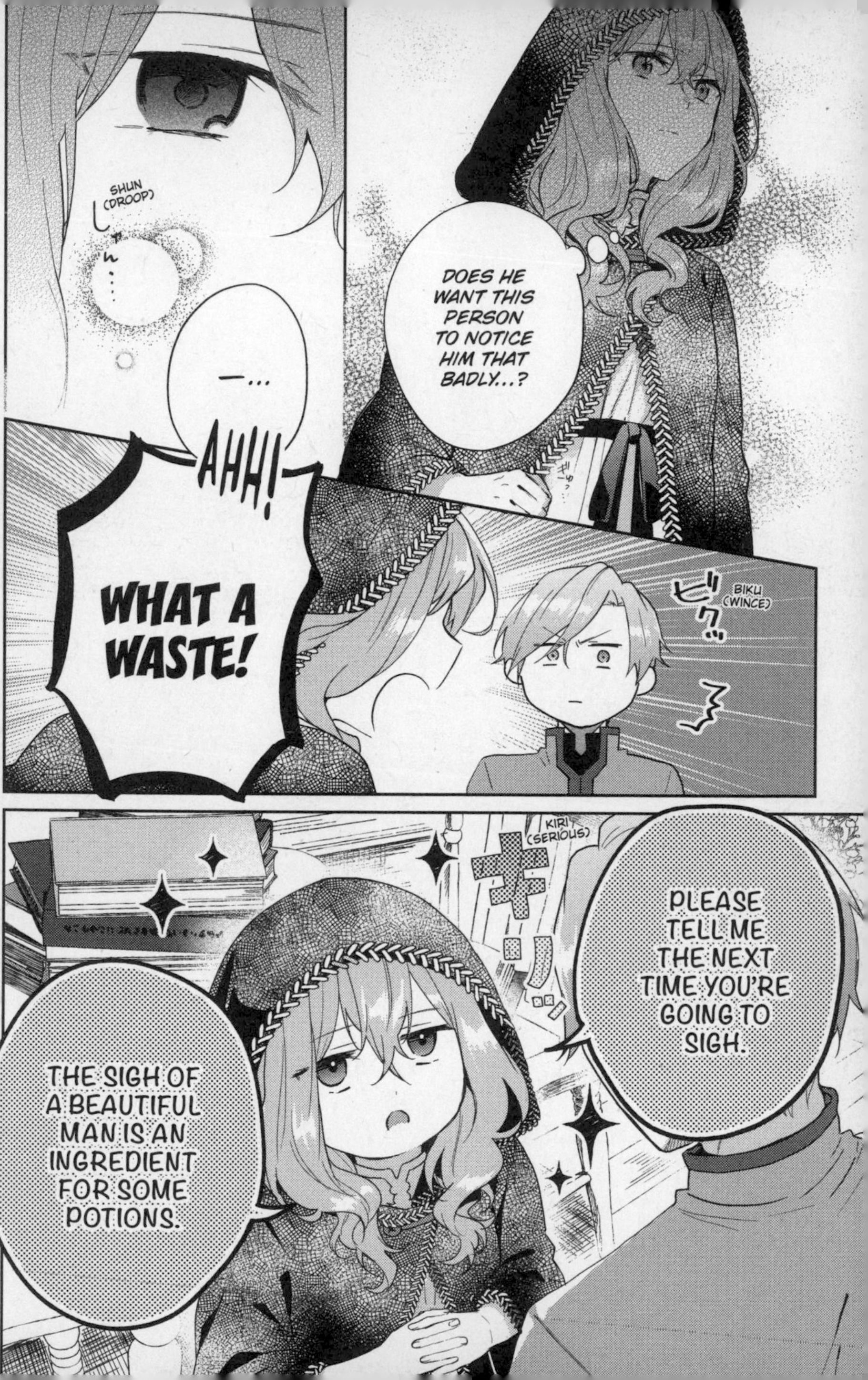

DOES HE WANT THIS PERSON TO NOTICE HIM THAT BADLY...?
SHUN (DROOP)
—...
AHH!
WHAT A WASTE!
BIKU (WINCE)
KIRI (SERIOUS)
PLEASE TELL ME THE NEXT TIME YOU'RE GOING TO SIGH.
THE SIGH OF A BEAUTIFUL MAN IS AN INGREDIENT FOR SOME POTIONS.

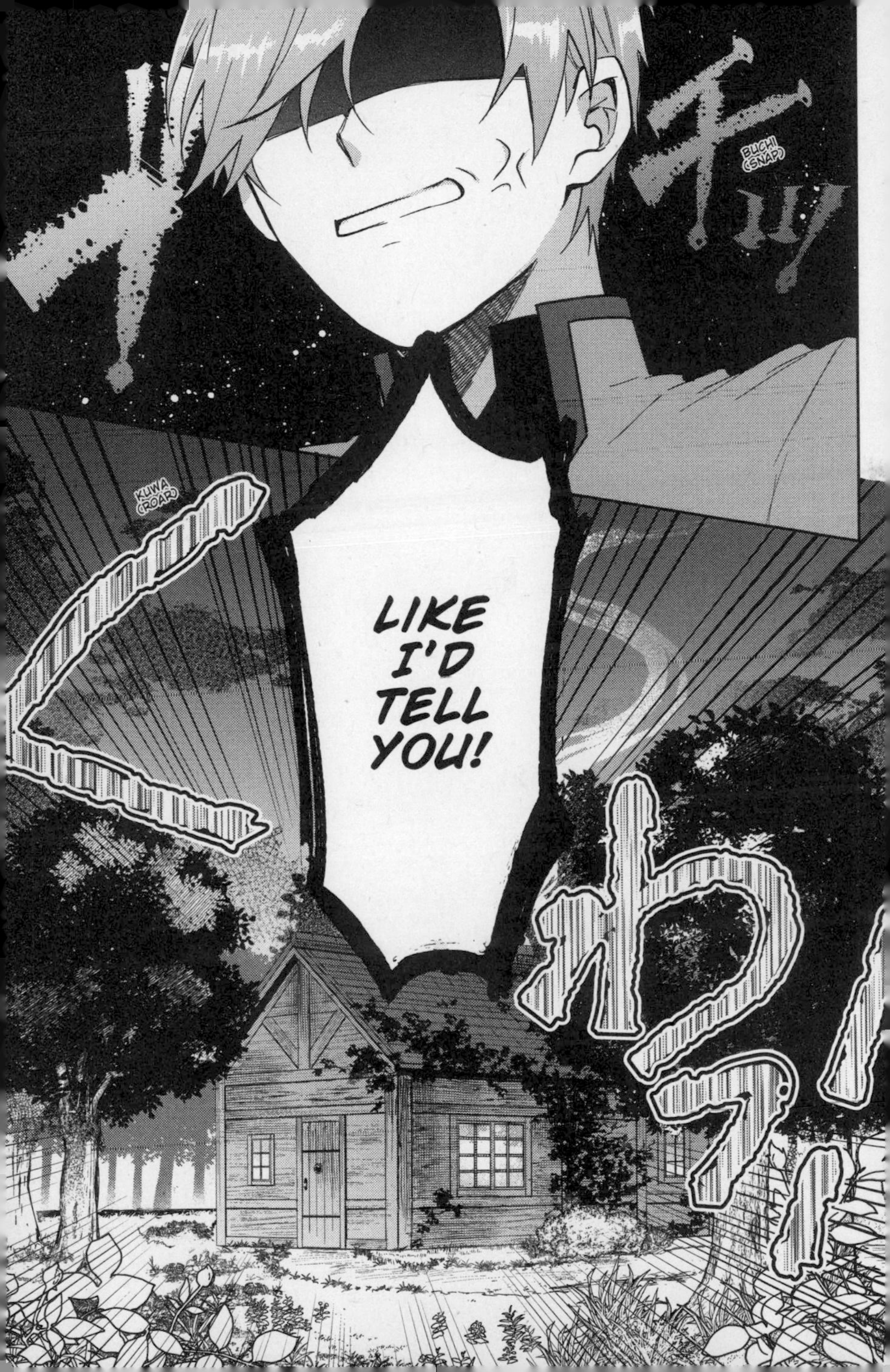
BUCHI (SNAP)
KUWA (ROAR)
LIKE I'D TELL YOU!

Hi, I'm a

Witch,

and My Crush
Wants Me to Make a
Love Potion

CHAPTER 2

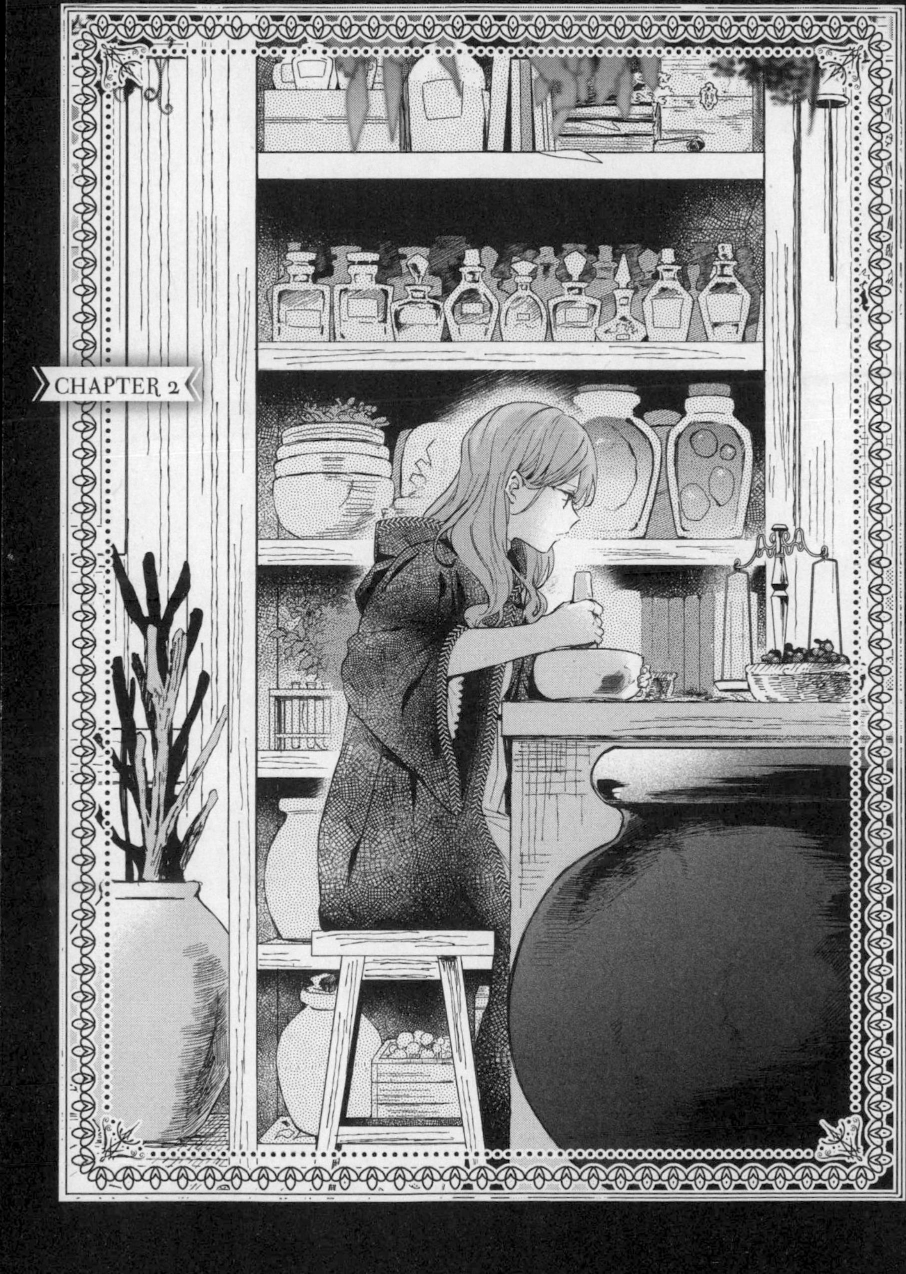

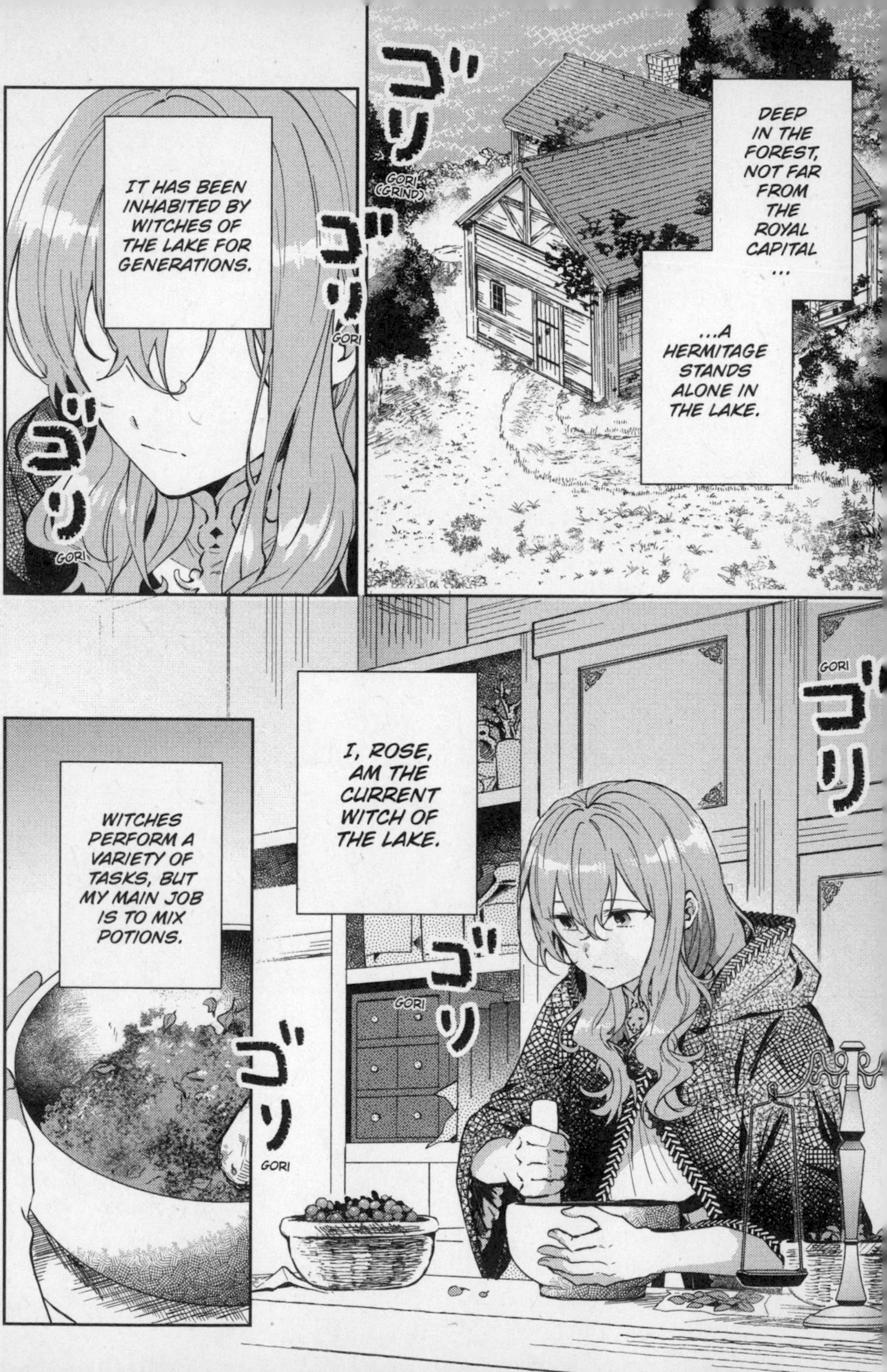
DEEP IN THE FOREST, NOT FAR FROM THE ROYAL CAPITAL...
...A HERMITAGE STANDS ALONE IN THE LAKE.
ゴリ
GORI (GRIND)
IT HAS BEEN INHABITED BY WITCHES OF THE LAKE FOR GENERATIONS.
ゴリ
GORI
ゴリ
GORI
ゴリ
GORI
I, ROSE, AM THE CURRENT WITCH OF THE LAKE.
ゴリ
GORI
WITCHES PERFORM A VARIETY OF TASKS, BUT MY MAIN JOB IS TO MIX POTIONS.
ゴリ
GORI

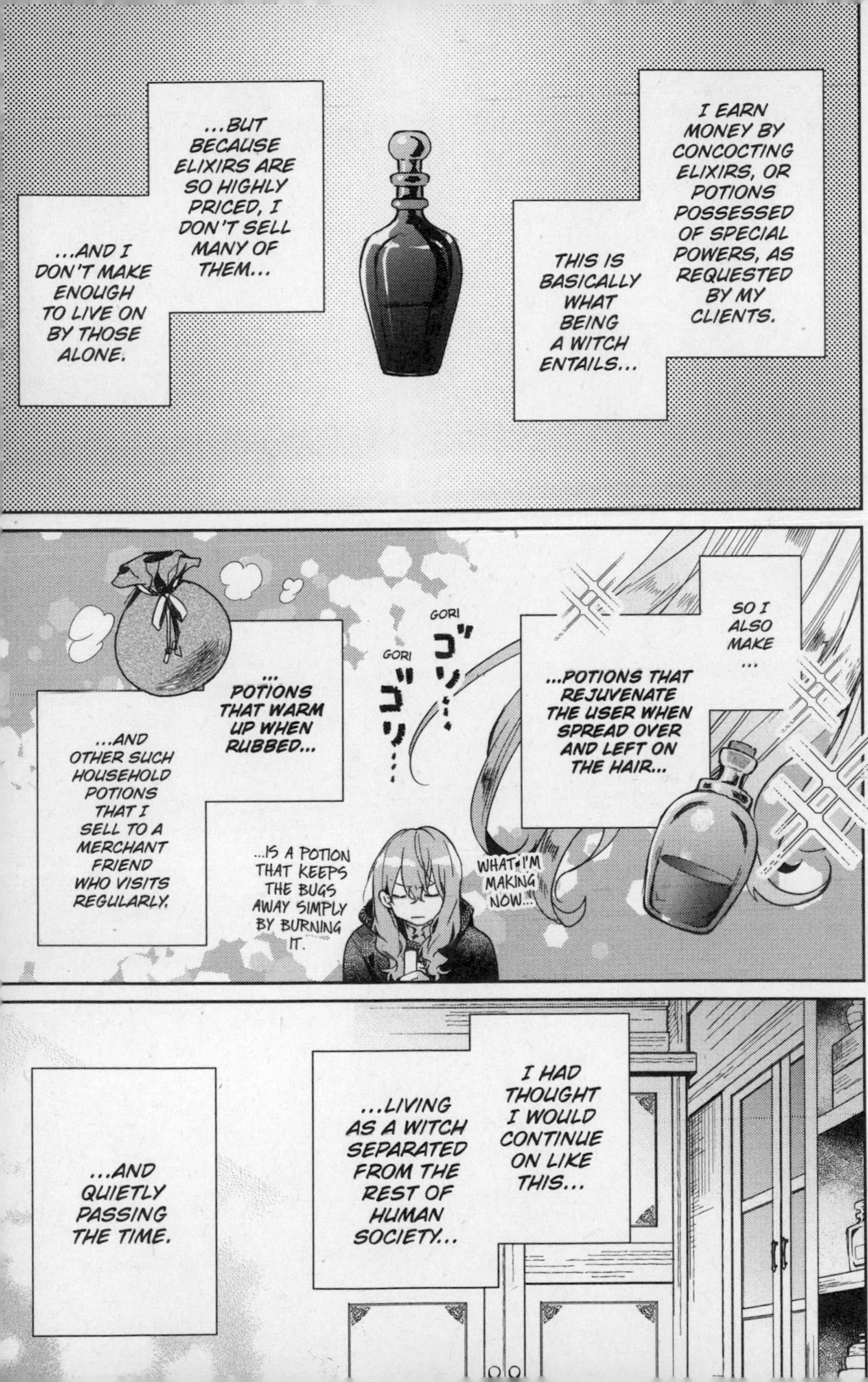
I EARN MONEY BY CONCOCTING ELIXIRS, OR POTIONS POSSESSED OF SPECIAL POWERS, AS REQUESTED BY MY CLIENTS.
THIS IS BASICALLY WHAT BEING A WITCH ENTAILS…
…BUT BECAUSE ELIXIRS ARE SO HIGHLY PRICED, I DON'T SELL MANY OF THEM…
…AND I DON'T MAKE ENOUGH TO LIVE ON BY THOSE ALONE.
SO I ALSO MAKE…
…POTIONS THAT REJUVENATE THE USER WHEN SPREAD OVER AND LEFT ON THE HAIR…
GORI
ゴリ…
GORI
ゴリ…
…POTIONS THAT WARM UP WHEN RUBBED…
…AND OTHER SUCH HOUSEHOLD POTIONS THAT I SELL TO A MERCHANT FRIEND WHO VISITS REGULARLY.
WHAT I'M MAKING NOW…
…IS A POTION THAT KEEPS THE BUGS AWAY SIMPLY BY BURNING IT.
I HAD THOUGHT I WOULD CONTINUE ON LIKE THIS…
…LIVING AS A WITCH SEPARATED FROM THE REST OF HUMAN SOCIETY…
…AND QUIETLY PASSING THE TIME.

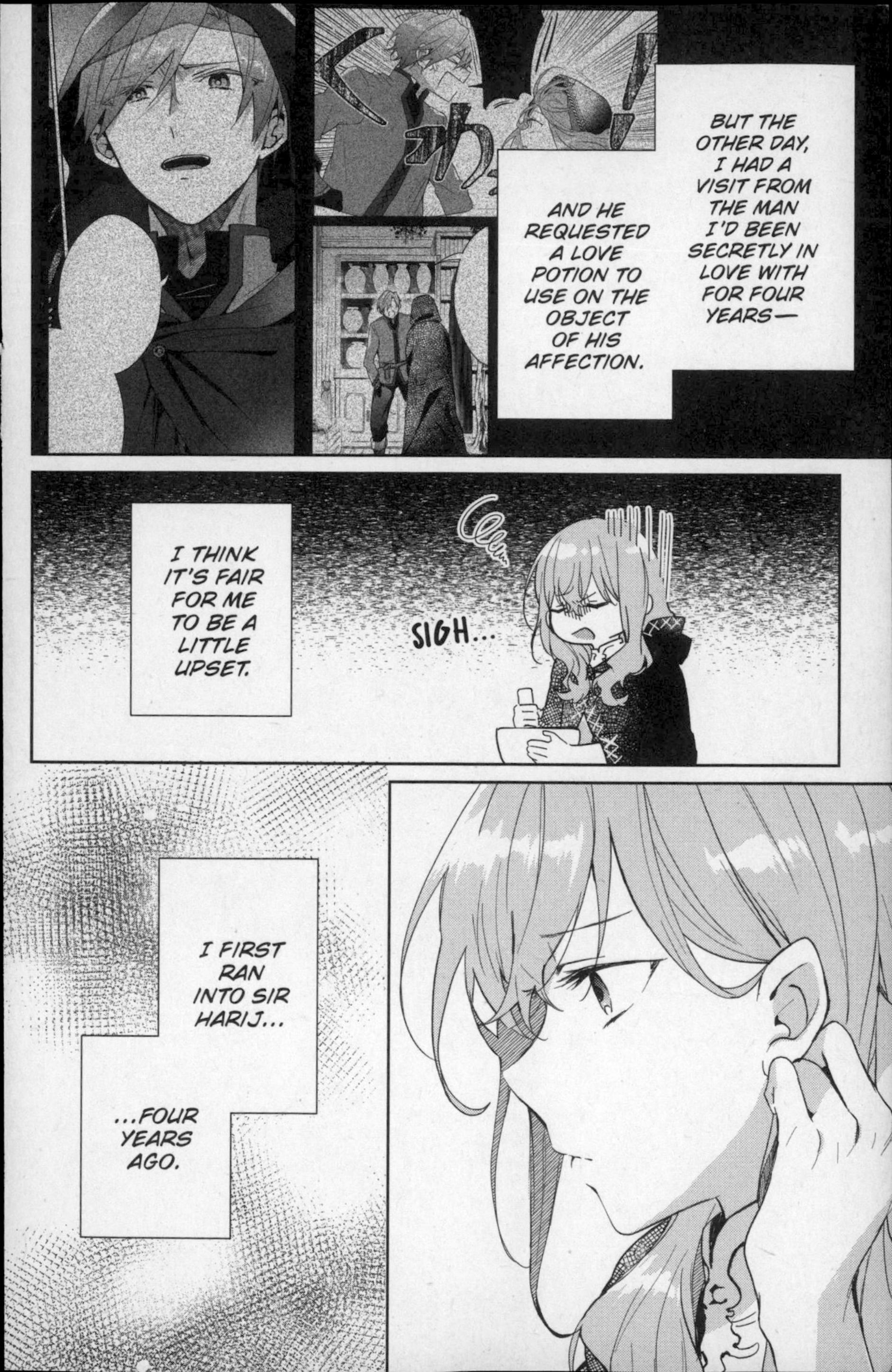
BUT THE OTHER DAY, I HAD A VISIT FROM THE MAN I'D BEEN SECRETLY IN LOVE WITH FOR FOUR YEARS—
AND HE REQUESTED A LOVE POTION TO USE ON THE OBJECT OF HIS AFFECTION.
SIGH...
I THINK IT'S FAIR FOR ME TO BE A LITTLE UPSET.
I FIRST RAN INTO SIR HARIJ...
...FOUR YEARS AGO.

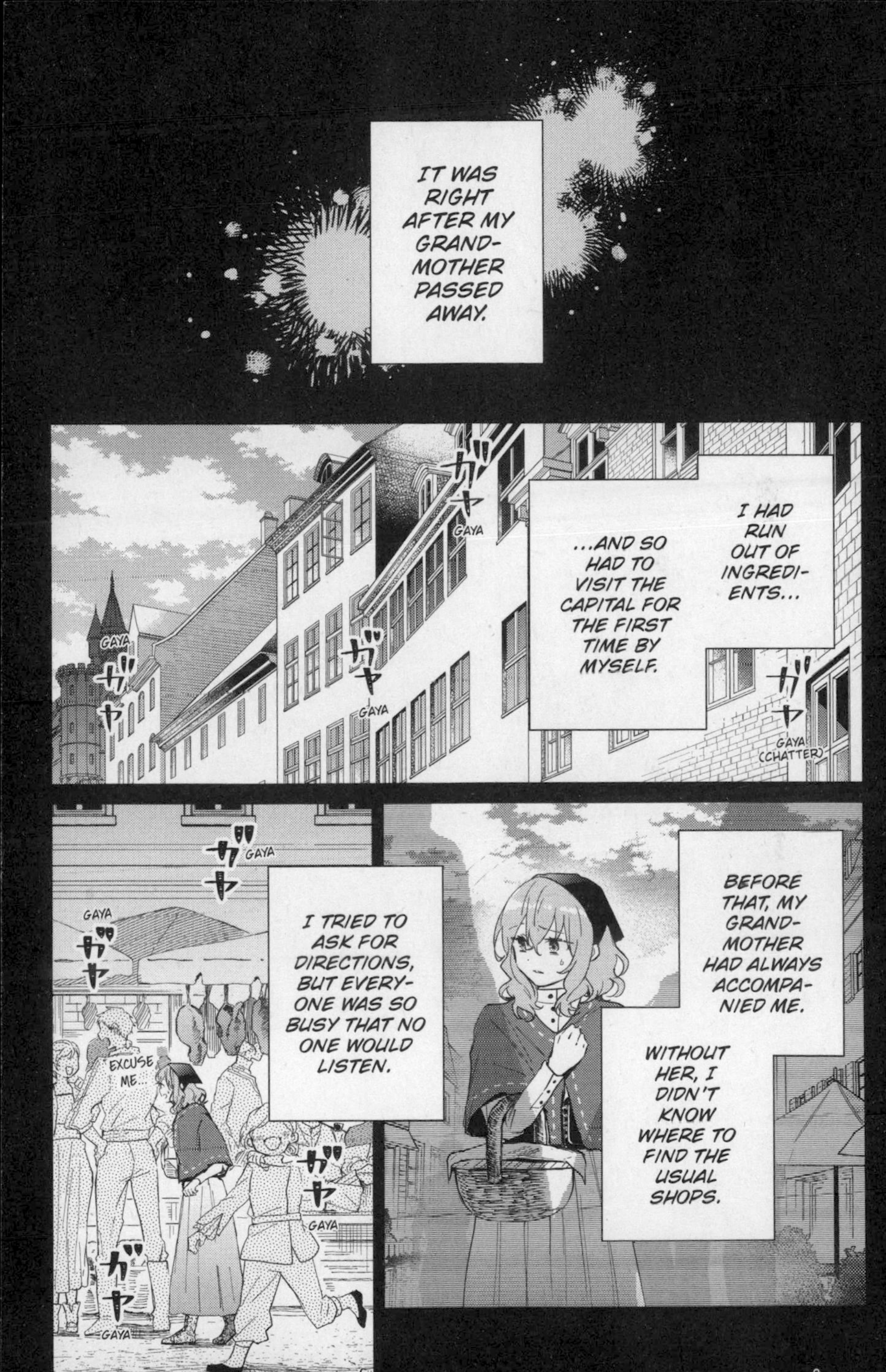
IT WAS RIGHT AFTER MY GRAND-MOTHER PASSED AWAY.
GAYA (CHATTER)
GAYA
I HAD RUN OUT OF INGREDI-ENTS...
...AND SO HAD TO VISIT THE CAPITAL FOR THE FIRST TIME BY MYSELF.
GAYA
GAYA
BEFORE THAT, MY GRAND-MOTHER HAD ALWAYS ACCOMPA-NIED ME.
WITHOUT HER, I DIDN'T KNOW WHERE TO FIND THE USUAL SHOPS.
GAYA
I TRIED TO ASK FOR DIRECTIONS, BUT EVERY-ONE WAS SO BUSY THAT NO ONE WOULD LISTEN.
GAYA
EXCUSE ME...
GAYA
GAYA

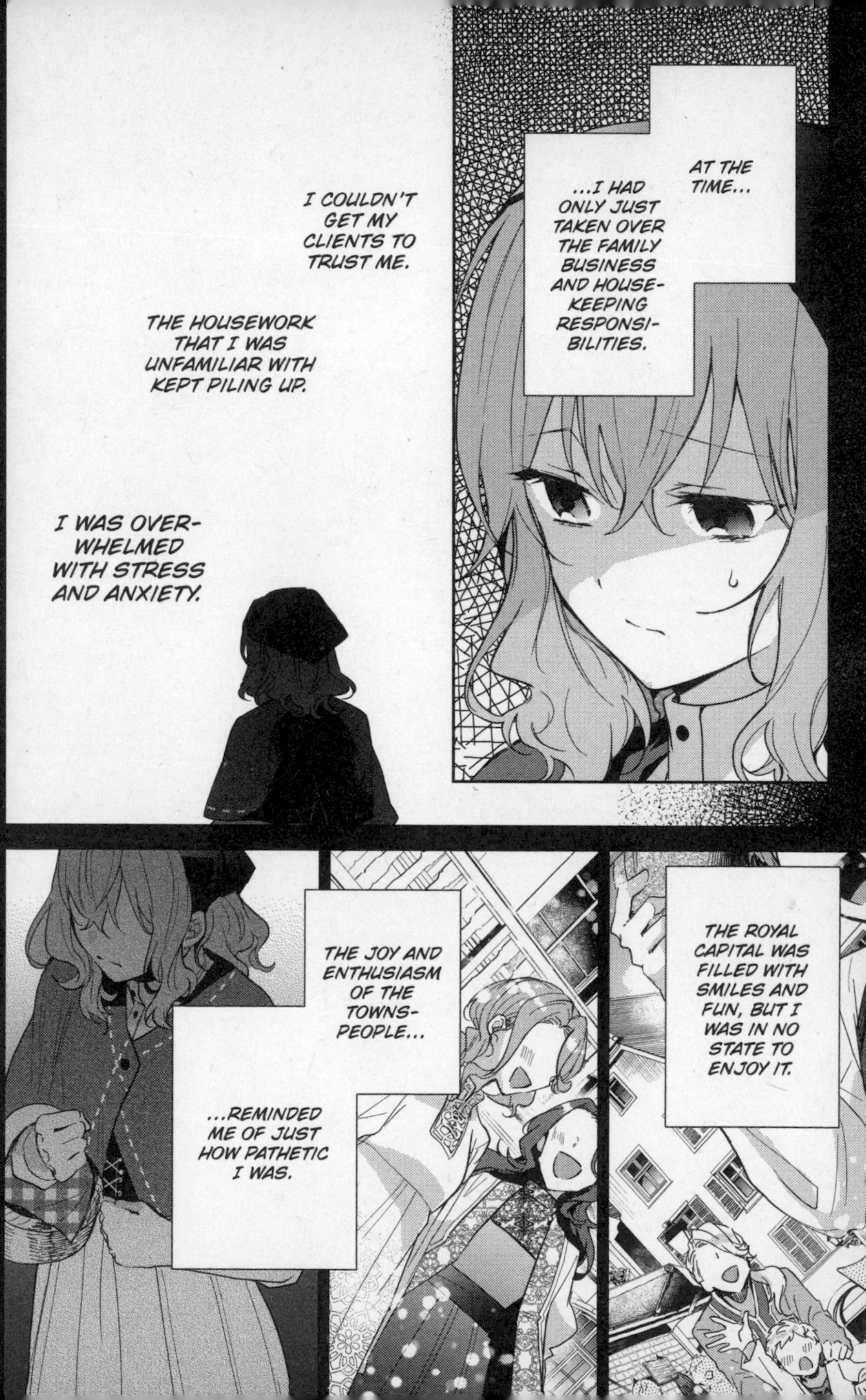
AT THE TIME...
...I HAD ONLY JUST TAKEN OVER THE FAMILY BUSINESS AND HOUSE-KEEPING RESPONSI-BILITIES.
I COULDN'T GET MY CLIENTS TO TRUST ME.
THE HOUSEWORK THAT I WAS UNFAMILIAR WITH KEPT PILING UP.
I WAS OVER-WHELMED WITH STRESS AND ANXIETY.
THE ROYAL CAPITAL WAS FILLED WITH SMILES AND FUN, BUT I WAS IN NO STATE TO ENJOY IT.
THE JOY AND ENTHUSIASM OF THE TOWNS-PEOPLE...
...REMINDED ME OF JUST HOW PATHETIC I WAS.

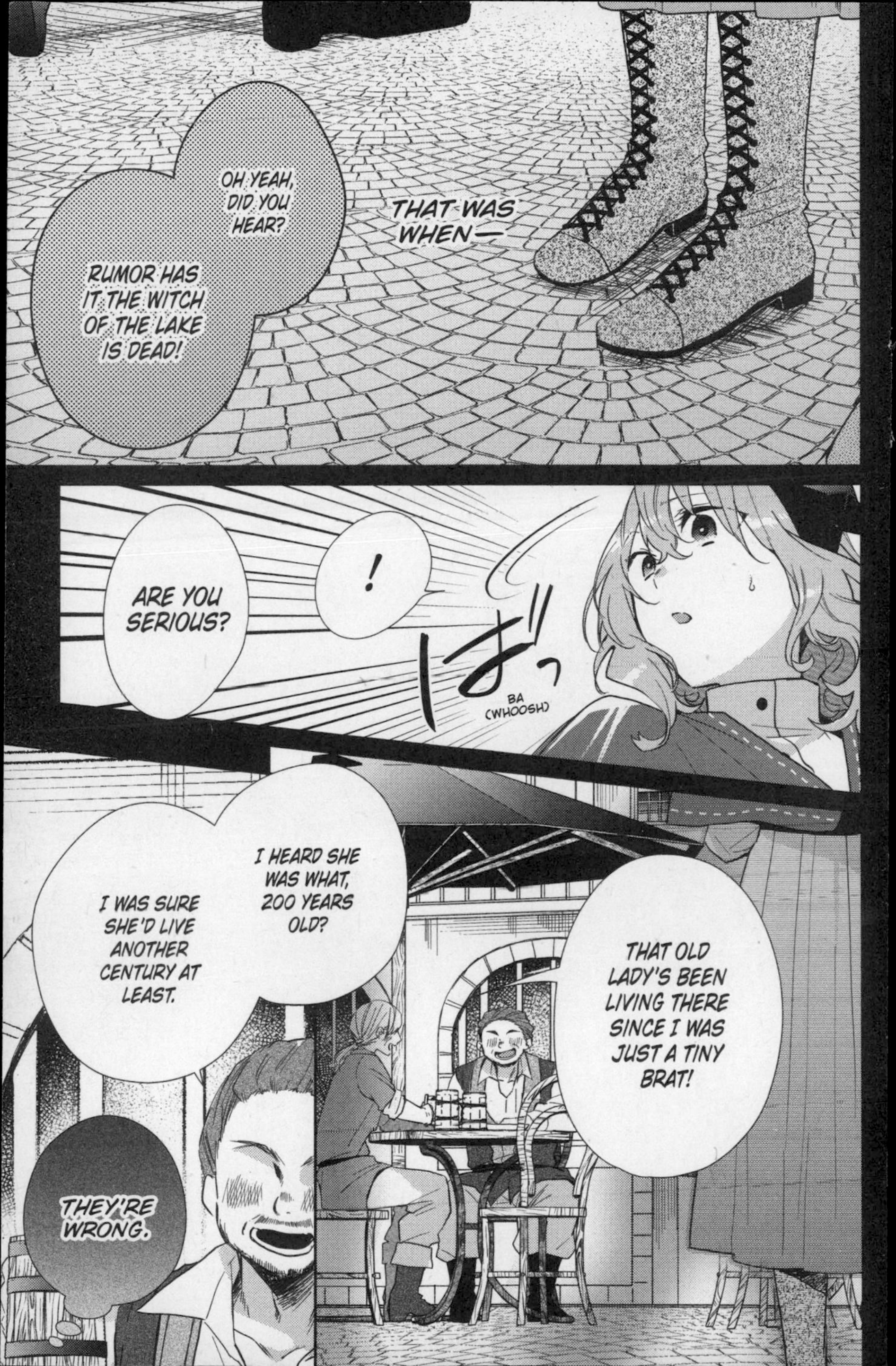
THAT WAS WHEN—
OH YEAH, DID YOU HEAR?
RUMOR HAS IT THE WITCH OF THE LAKE IS DEAD!
!
ばっ
BA (WHOOSH)
ARE YOU SERIOUS?
THAT OLD LADY'S BEEN LIVING THERE SINCE I WAS JUST A TINY BRAT!
I HEARD SHE WAS WHAT, 200 YEARS OLD?
I WAS SURE SHE'D LIVE ANOTHER CENTURY AT LEAST.
THEY'RE WRONG.

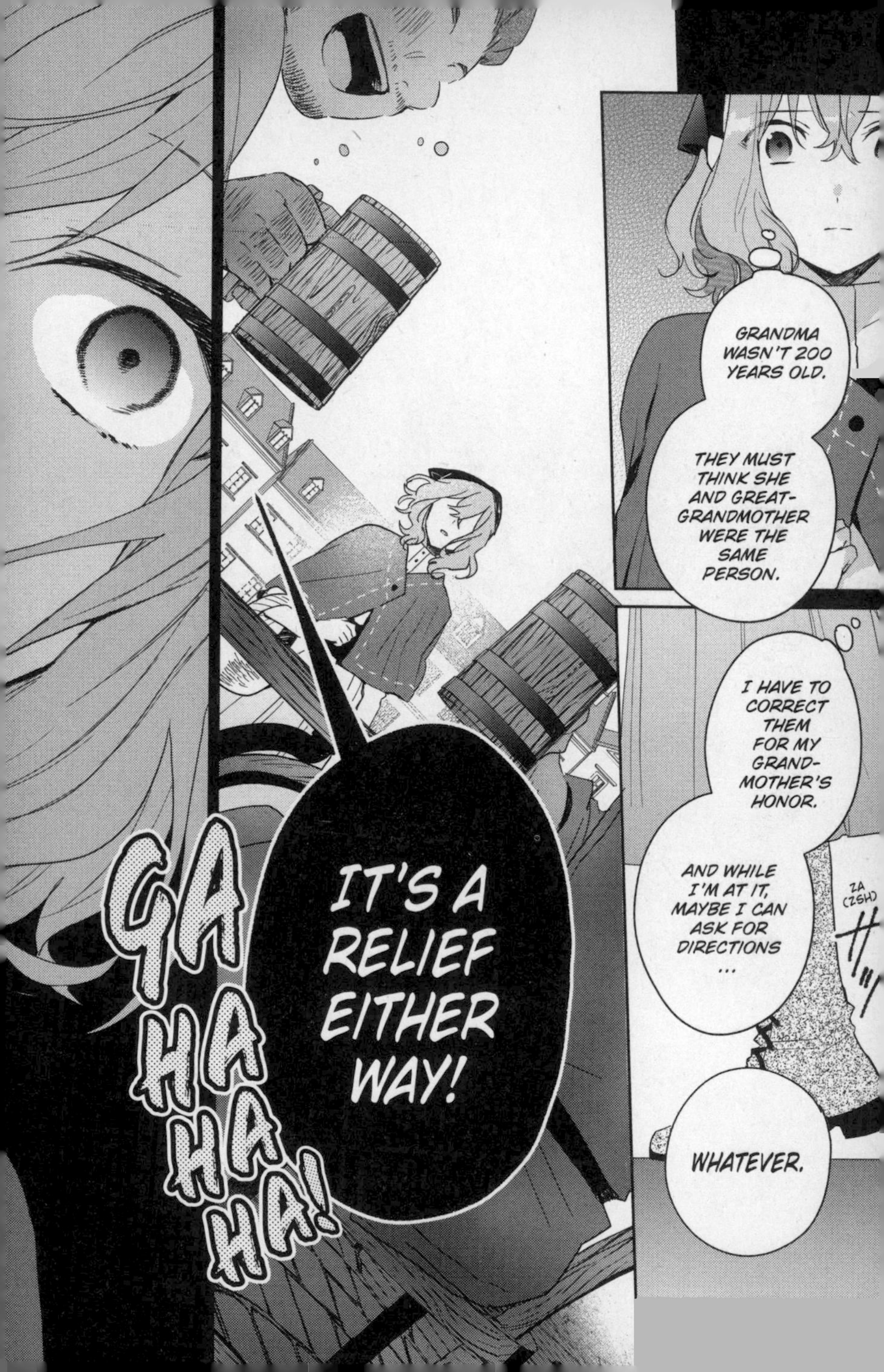
GRANDMA WASN'T 200 YEARS OLD.
THEY MUST THINK SHE AND GREAT-GRANDMOTHER WERE THE SAME PERSON.
I HAVE TO CORRECT THEM FOR MY GRAND-MOTHER'S HONOR.
AND WHILE I'M AT IT, MAYBE I CAN ASK FOR DIRECTIONS...
ZA (ZSH)
WHATEVER.
IT'S A RELIEF EITHER WAY!
GAHAHAHA!

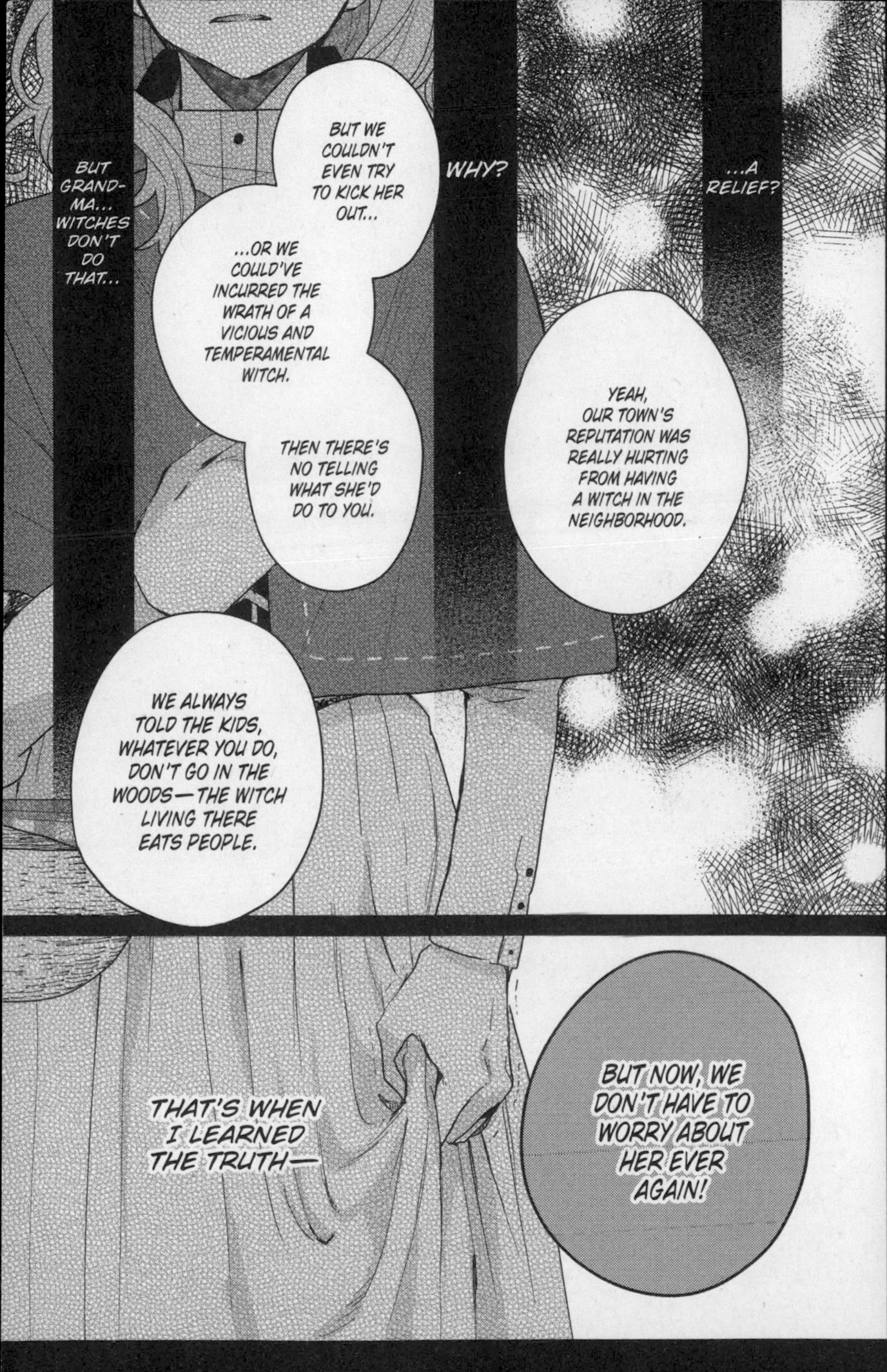
...A RELIEF?
WHY?
YEAH, OUR TOWN'S REPUTATION WAS REALLY HURTING FROM HAVING A WITCH IN THE NEIGHBORHOOD.
BUT WE COULDN'T EVEN TRY TO KICK HER OUT...
...OR WE COULD'VE INCURRED THE WRATH OF A VICIOUS AND TEMPERAMENTAL WITCH.
THEN THERE'S NO TELLING WHAT SHE'D DO TO YOU.
WE ALWAYS TOLD THE KIDS, WHATEVER YOU DO, DON'T GO IN THE WOODS—THE WITCH LIVING THERE EATS PEOPLE.
BUT GRAND-MA... WITCHES DON'T DO THAT...
BUT NOW, WE DON'T HAVE TO WORRY ABOUT HER EVER AGAIN!
THAT'S WHEN I LEARNED THE TRUTH—

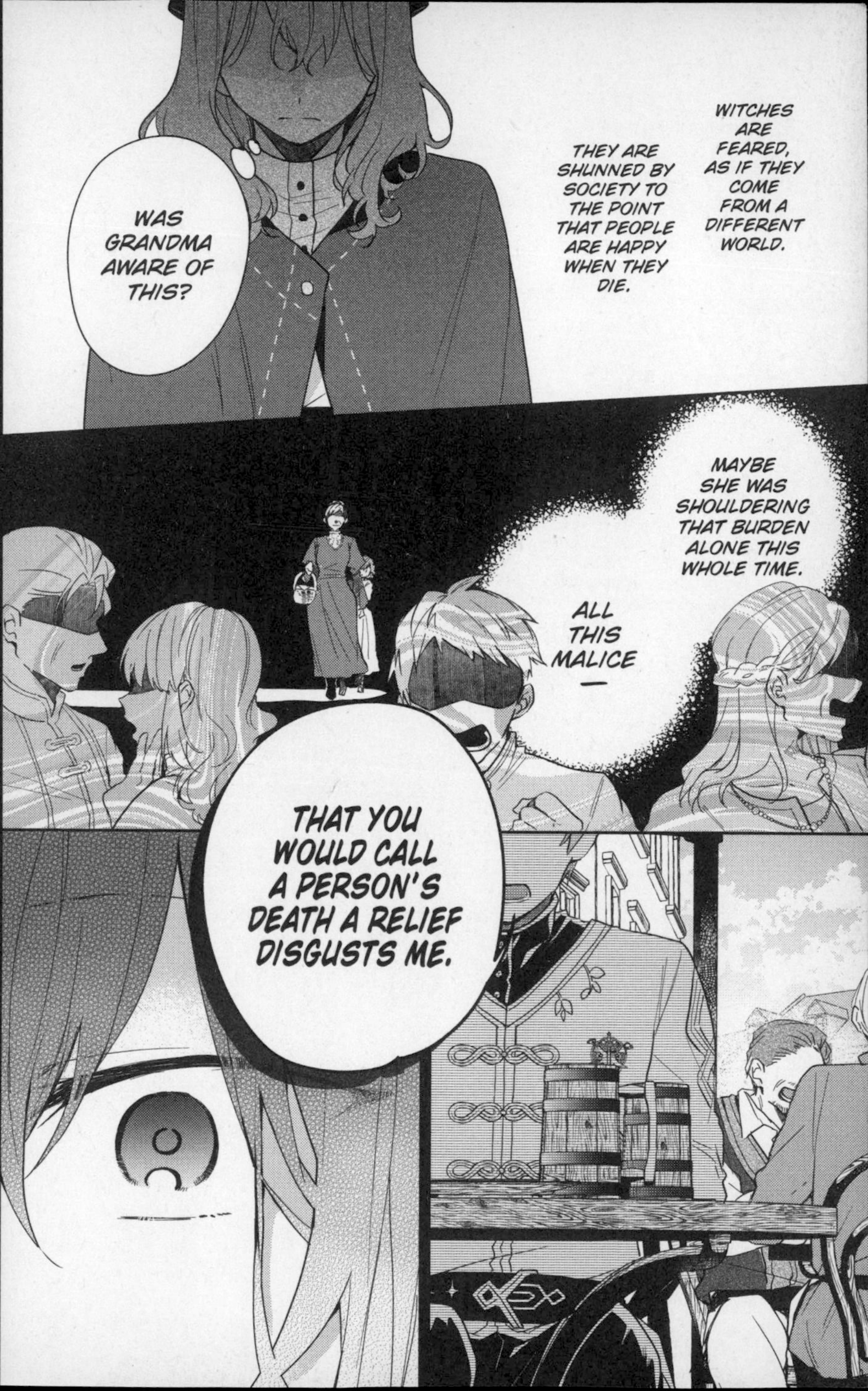
WITCHES ARE FEARED, AS IF THEY COME FROM A DIFFERENT WORLD.
THEY ARE SHUNNED BY SOCIETY TO THE POINT THAT PEOPLE ARE HAPPY WHEN THEY DIE.
WAS GRANDMA AWARE OF THIS?
MAYBE SHE WAS SHOULDERING THAT BURDEN ALONE THIS WHOLE TIME.
ALL THIS MALICE —
THAT YOU WOULD CALL A PERSON'S DEATH A RELIEF DISGUSTS ME.

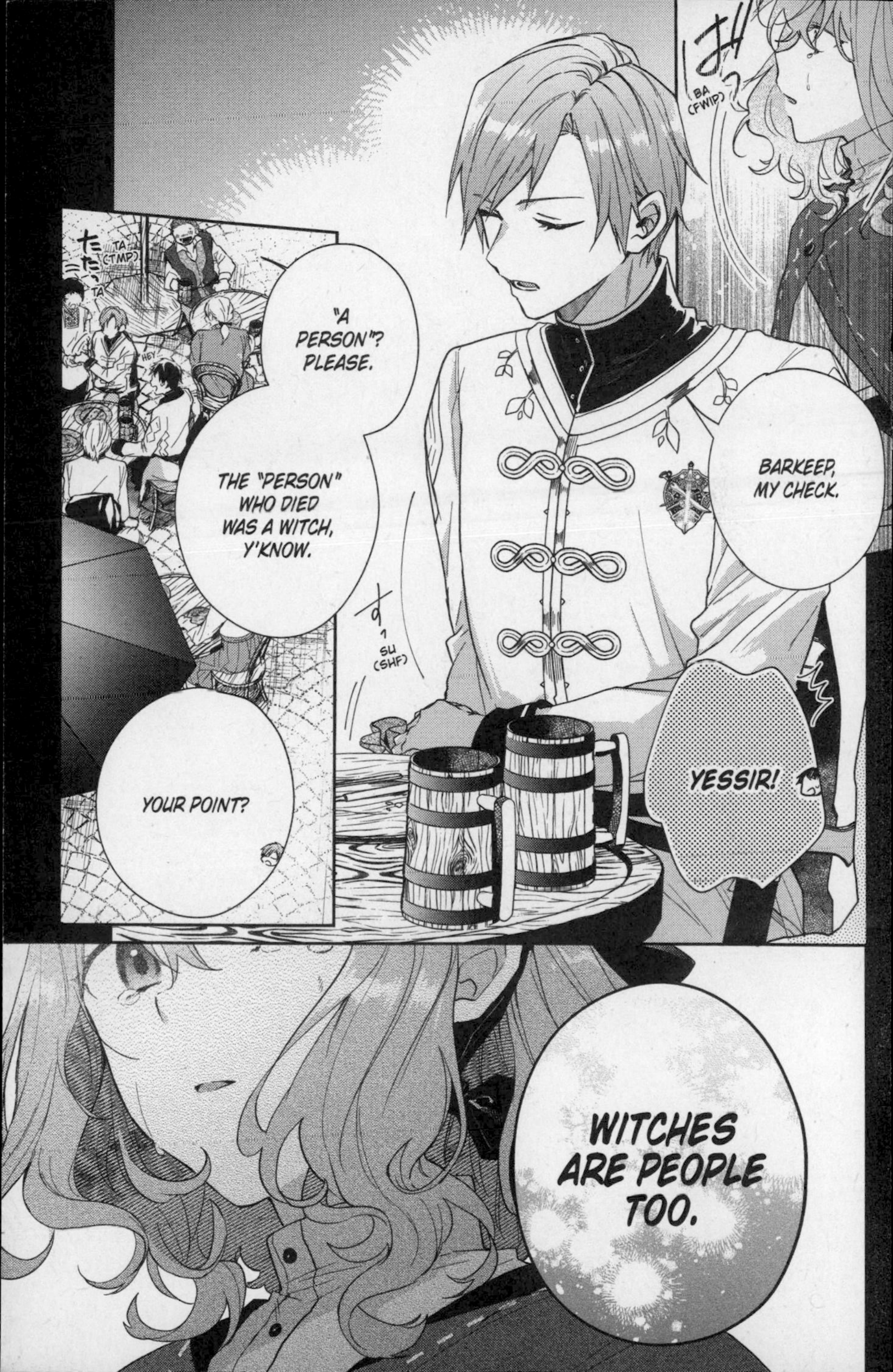
BA (FWIP)
"A PERSON"? PLEASE.
THE "PERSON" WHO DIED WAS A WITCH, Y'KNOW.
SU (SHF)
BARKEEP, MY CHECK.
YESSIR!
TA (TMP) TA
HEY
YOUR POINT?
WITCHES ARE PEOPLE TOO.

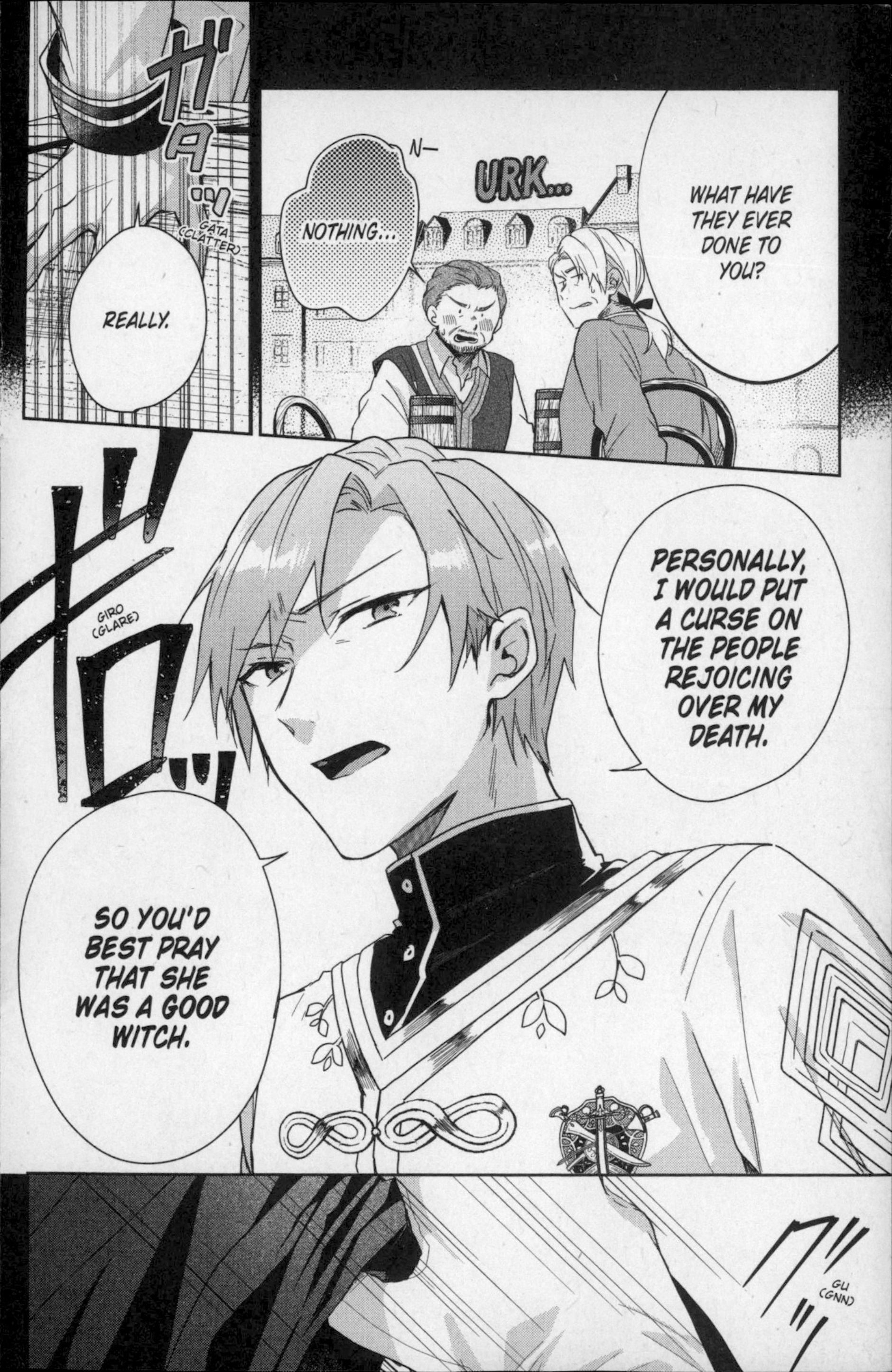
WHAT HAVE THEY EVER DONE TO YOU?
URK...
N—
NOTHING...
GATA (CLATTER)
REALLY.
PERSONALLY, I WOULD PUT A CURSE ON THE PEOPLE REJOICING OVER MY DEATH.
GIRO (GLARE)
SO YOU'D BEST PRAY THAT SHE WAS A GOOD WITCH.
GU (GNN)

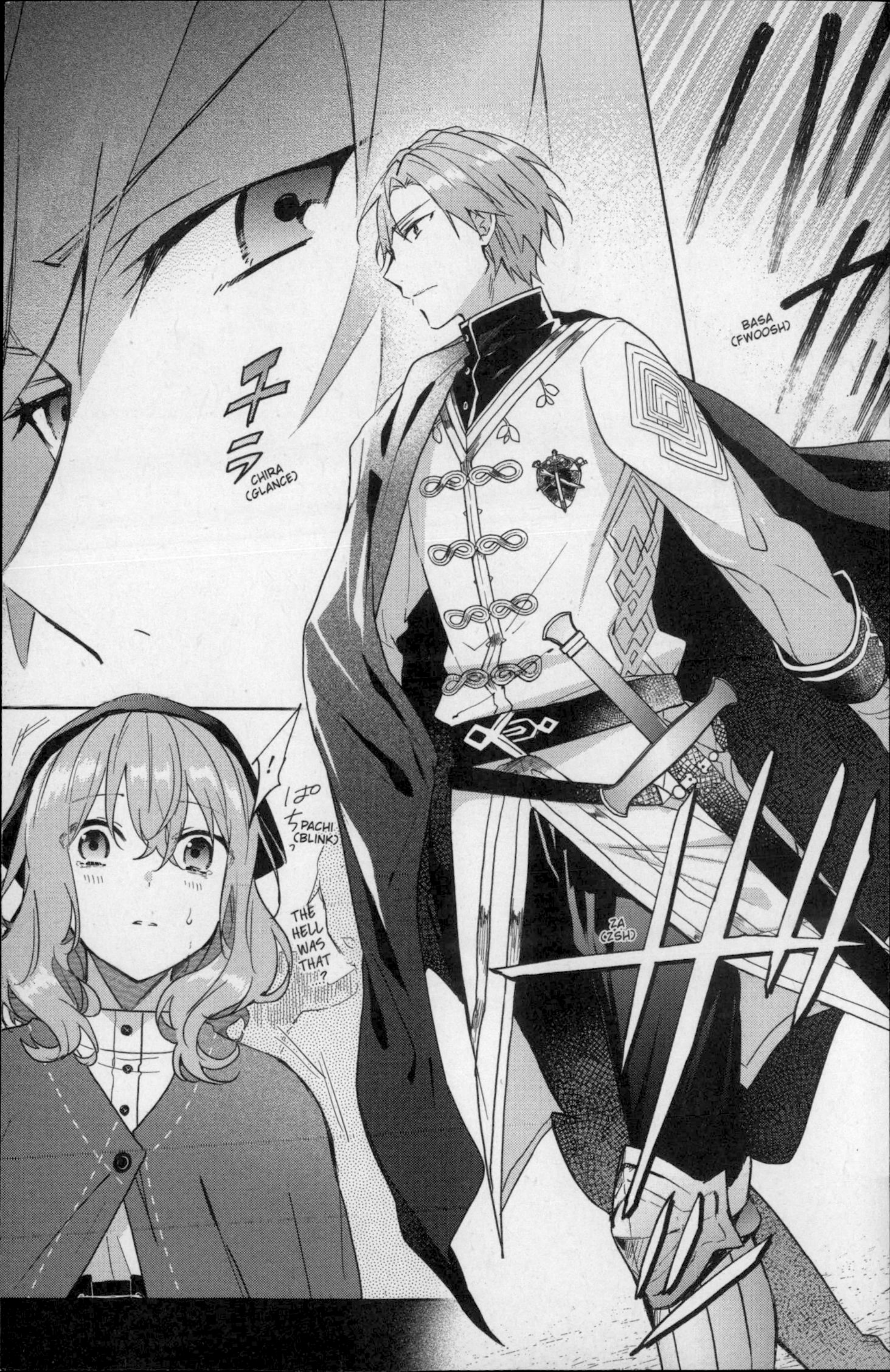

BASA (FWOOSH)
ZA (ZSH)
チラ
CHIRA (GLANCE)
!
ぱち
PACHI (BLINK)
THE HELL WAS THAT?

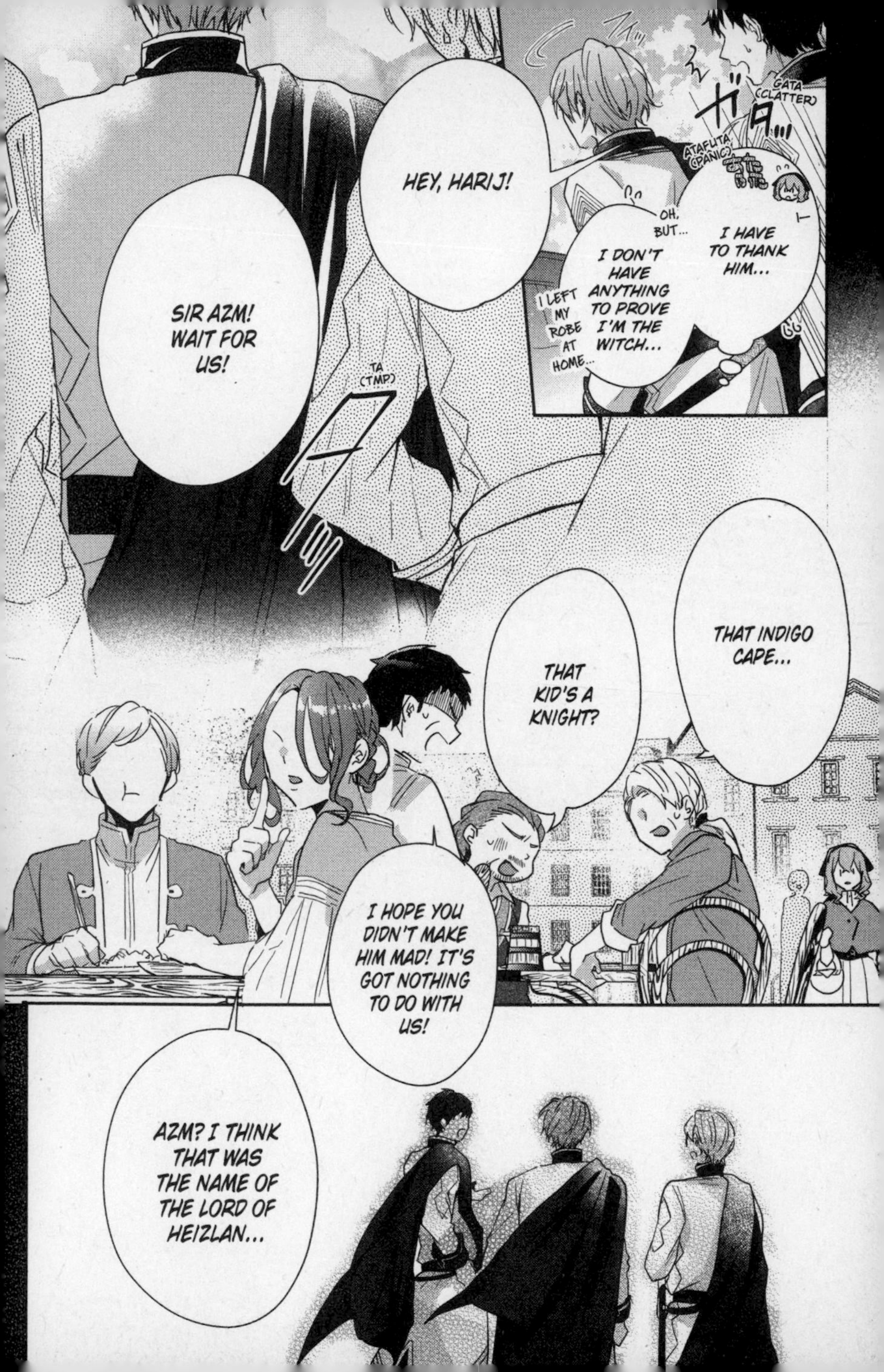
GATA (CLATTER)
ATAFUTA (PANIC)
I HAVE TO THANK HIM...
OH, BUT... I DON'T HAVE ANYTHING TO PROVE I'M THE WITCH...
I LEFT MY ROBE AT HOME...
HEY, HARIJ!
TA (TMP)
SIR AZM! WAIT FOR US!
THAT INDIGO CAPE...
THAT KID'S A KNIGHT?
I HOPE YOU DIDN'T MAKE HIM MAD! IT'S GOT NOTHING TO DO WITH US!
AZM? I THINK THAT WAS THE NAME OF THE LORD OF HEIZLAN...

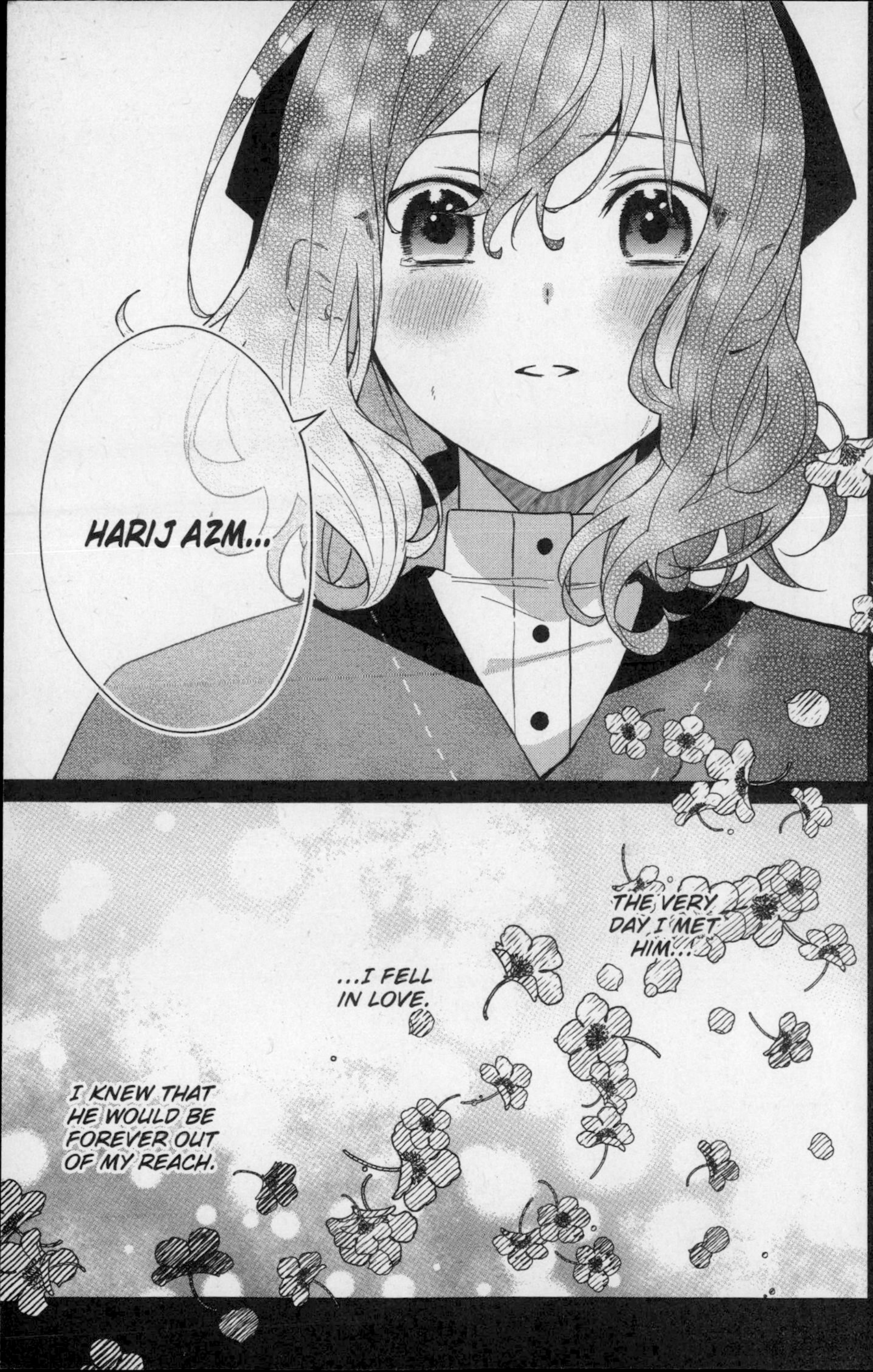
HARIJ AZM...
THE VERY DAY I MET HIM...
...I FELL IN LOVE.
I KNEW THAT HE WOULD BE FOREVER OUT OF MY REACH.

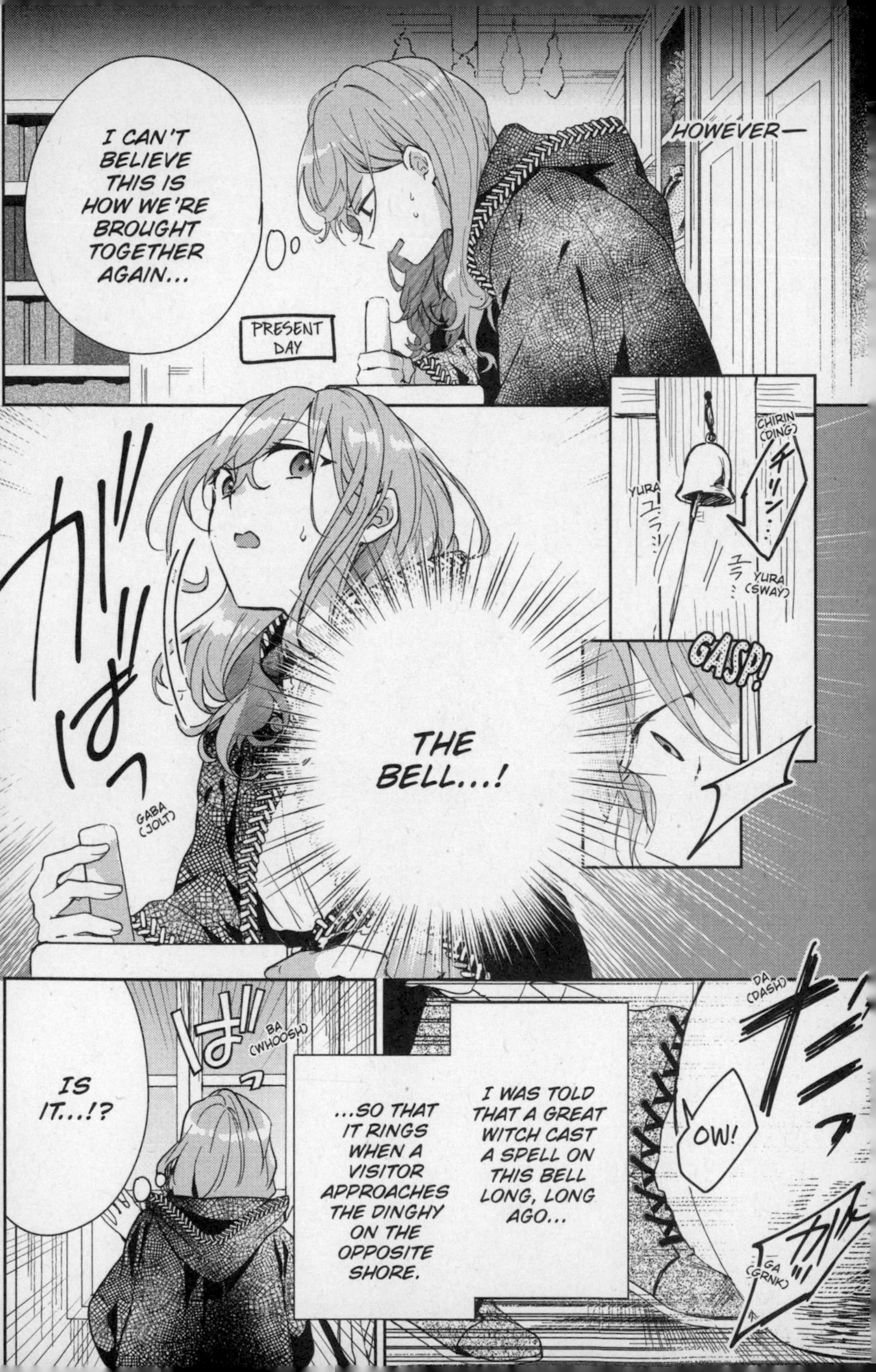
HOWEVER—
I CAN'T BELIEVE THIS IS HOW WE'RE BROUGHT TOGETHER AGAIN...
PRESENT DAY
CHIRIN (DING)
YURA
YURA (SWAY)
GASP!
THE BELL...!
GABA (JOLT)
DA (DASH)
OW!
GA (GRNK)
I WAS TOLD THAT A GREAT WITCH CAST A SPELL ON THIS BELL LONG, LONG AGO...
...SO THAT IT RINGS WHEN A VISITOR APPROACHES THE DINGHY ON THE OPPOSITE SHORE.
BA (WHOOSH)
IS IT...!?

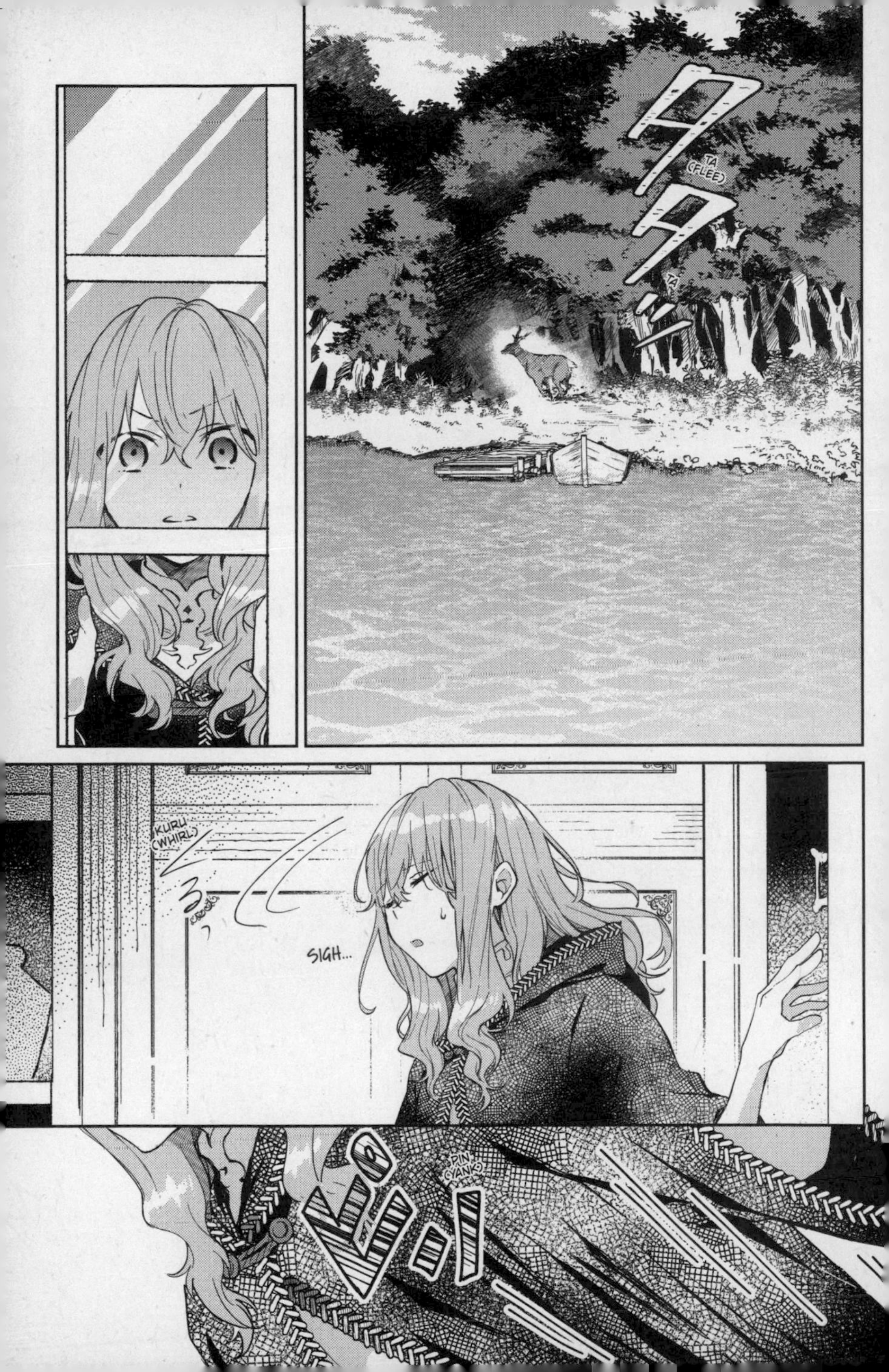
TA (FLEE)
TA
KURU (WHIRL)
SIGH...
PIN (YANK)

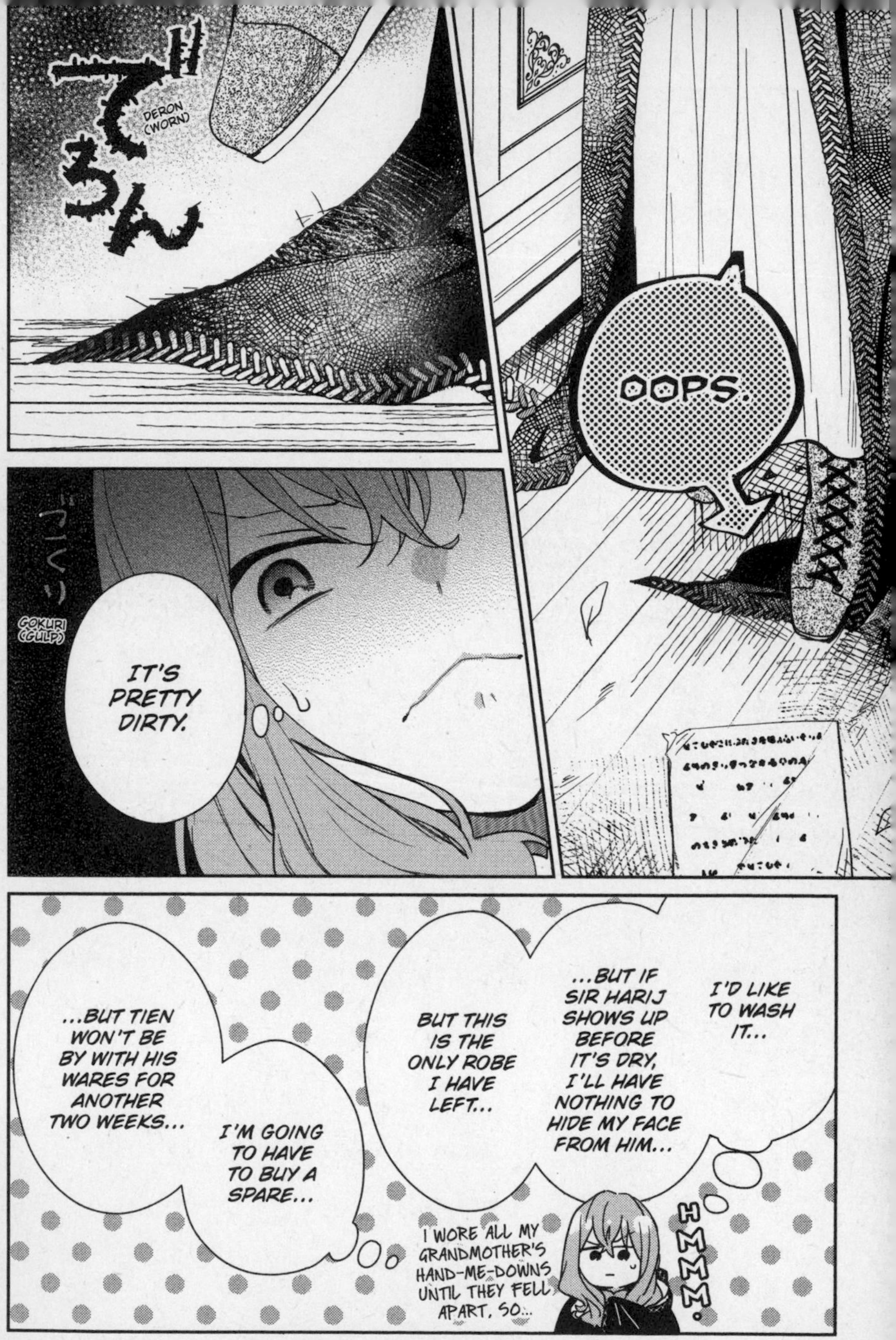
OOPS.
でろん
DERON (WORN)
ごくり
GOKURI (GULP)
IT'S PRETTY DIRTY.
I'D LIKE TO WASH IT...
...BUT IF SIR HARIJ SHOWS UP BEFORE IT'S DRY, I'LL HAVE NOTHING TO HIDE MY FACE FROM HIM...
BUT THIS IS THE ONLY ROBE I HAVE LEFT...
I'M GOING TO HAVE TO BUY A SPARE...
...BUT TIEN WON'T BE BY WITH HIS WARES FOR ANOTHER TWO WEEKS...
HMMM.
I WORE ALL MY GRANDMOTHER'S HAND-ME-DOWNS UNTIL THEY FELL APART, SO...

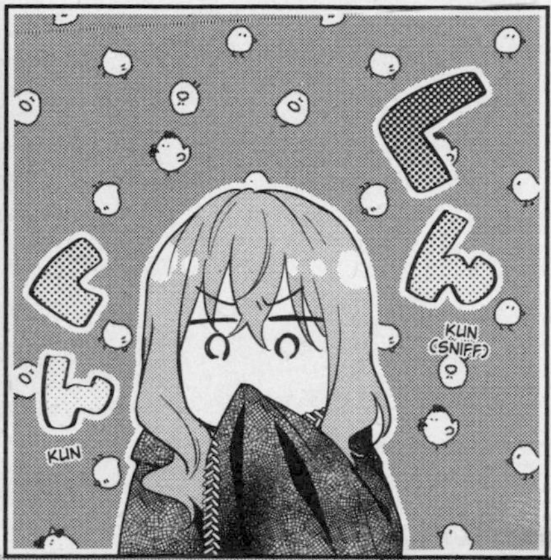
くん
KUN (SNIFF)
くん
KUN

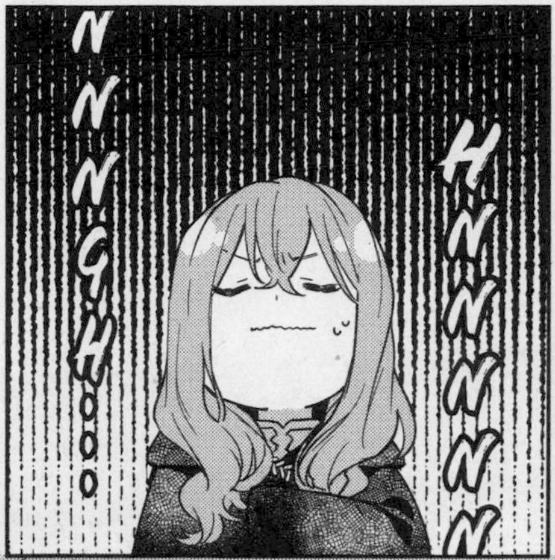
HNNNNNNN
NNNGHOOO

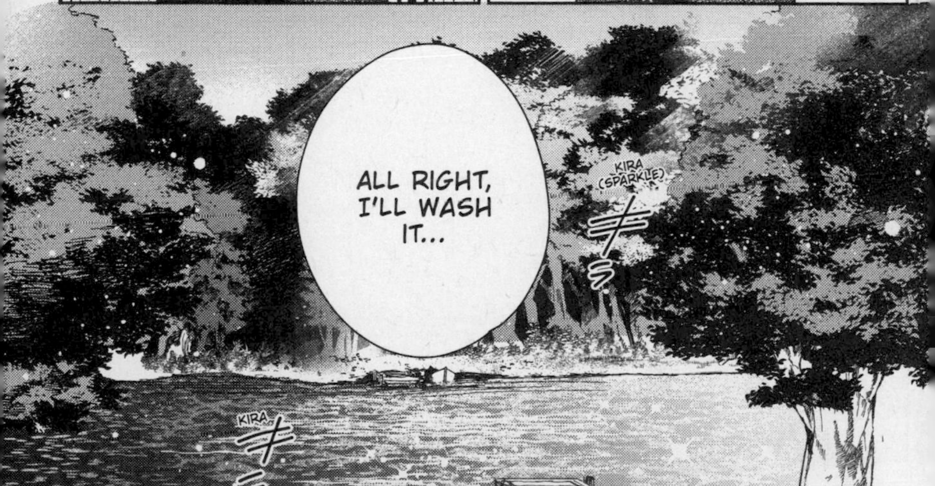
ALL RIGHT, I'LL WASH IT...
KIRA (SPARKLE)
キラ
KIRA
キラ

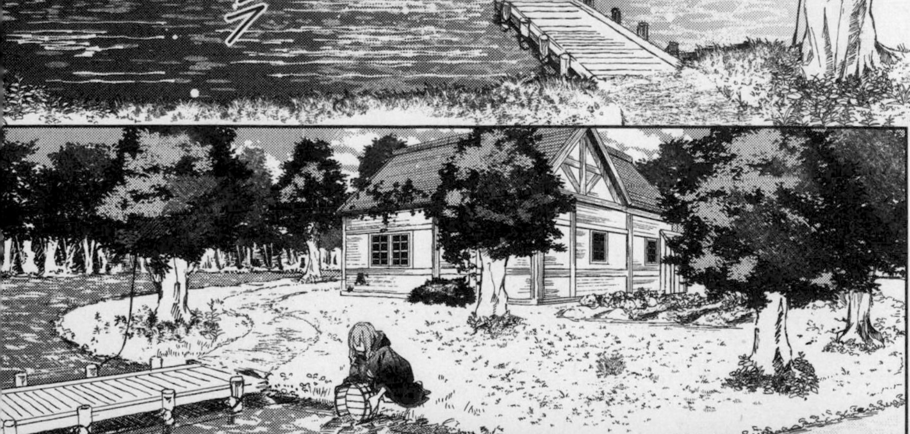

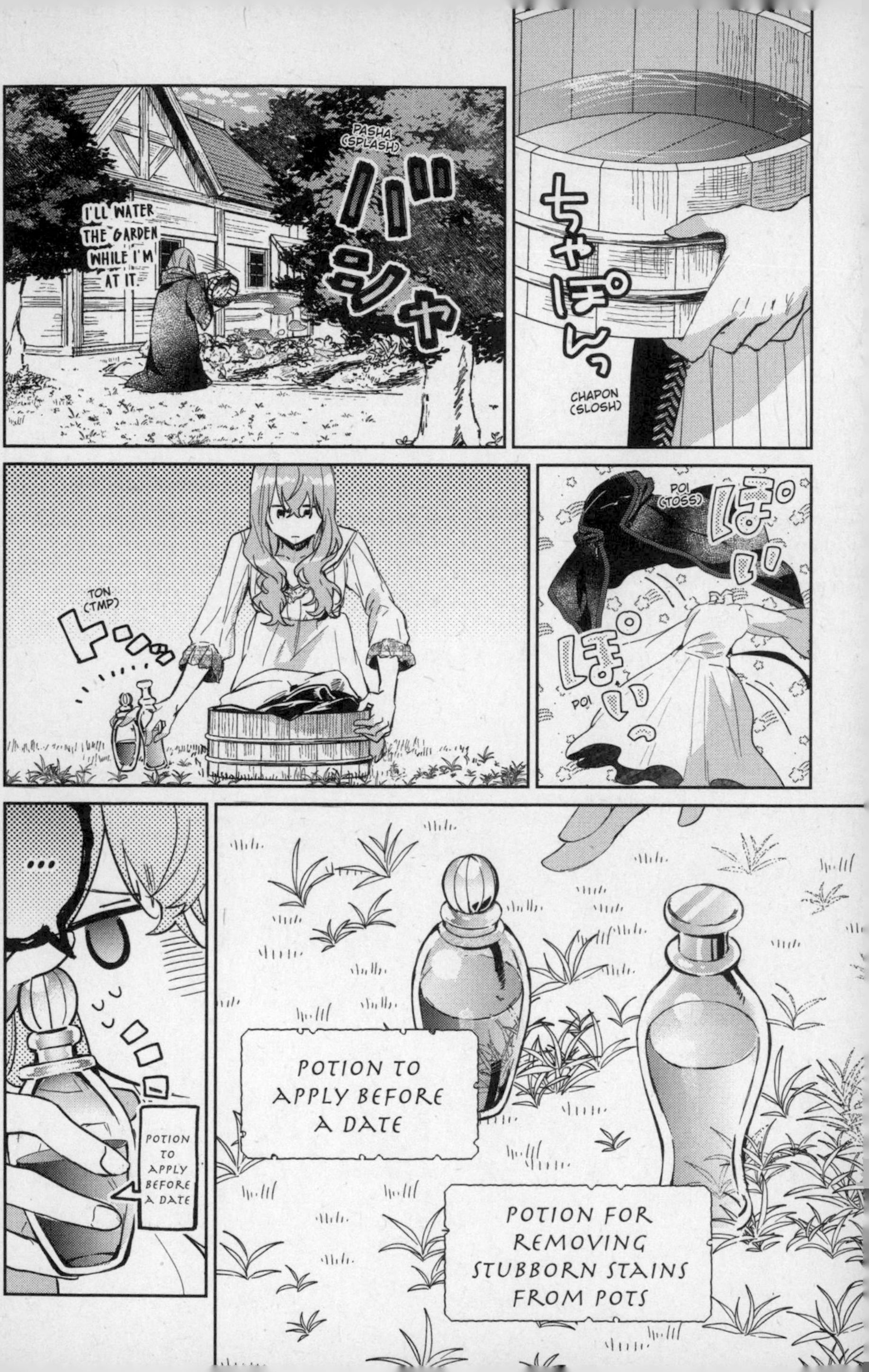
ちゃぽんっ
CHAPON (SLOSH)
PASHA (SPLASH)
バシャ
I'LL WATER THE GARDEN WHILE I'M AT IT.
POI (TOSS)
ぽい
ぽいっ
POI
TON (TMP)
ト…ン
POTION TO APPLY BEFORE A DATE
POTION FOR REMOVING STUBBORN STAINS FROM POTS
...
POTION TO APPLY BEFORE A DATE

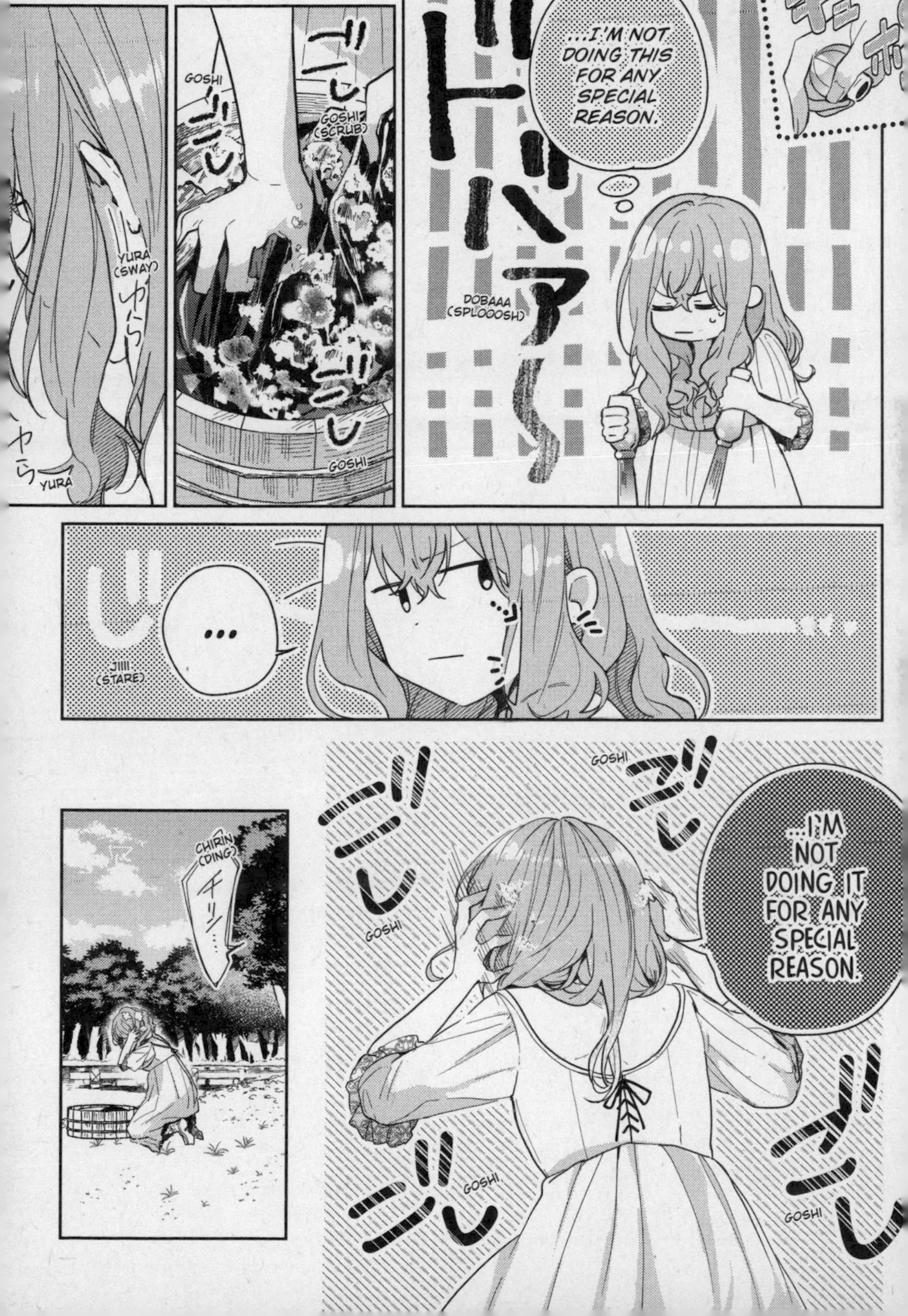
KYUPO (POP)
...I'M NOT DOING THIS FOR ANY SPECIAL REASON.
DOBAAA (SPLOOOSH)
GOSHI
GOSHI (SCRUB)
GOSHI
YURA (SWAY)
YURA
...
JIIII (STARE)
GOSHI
...I'M NOT DOING IT FOR ANY SPECIAL REASON.
GOSHI
GOSHI
GOSHI
CHIRIN (DING)

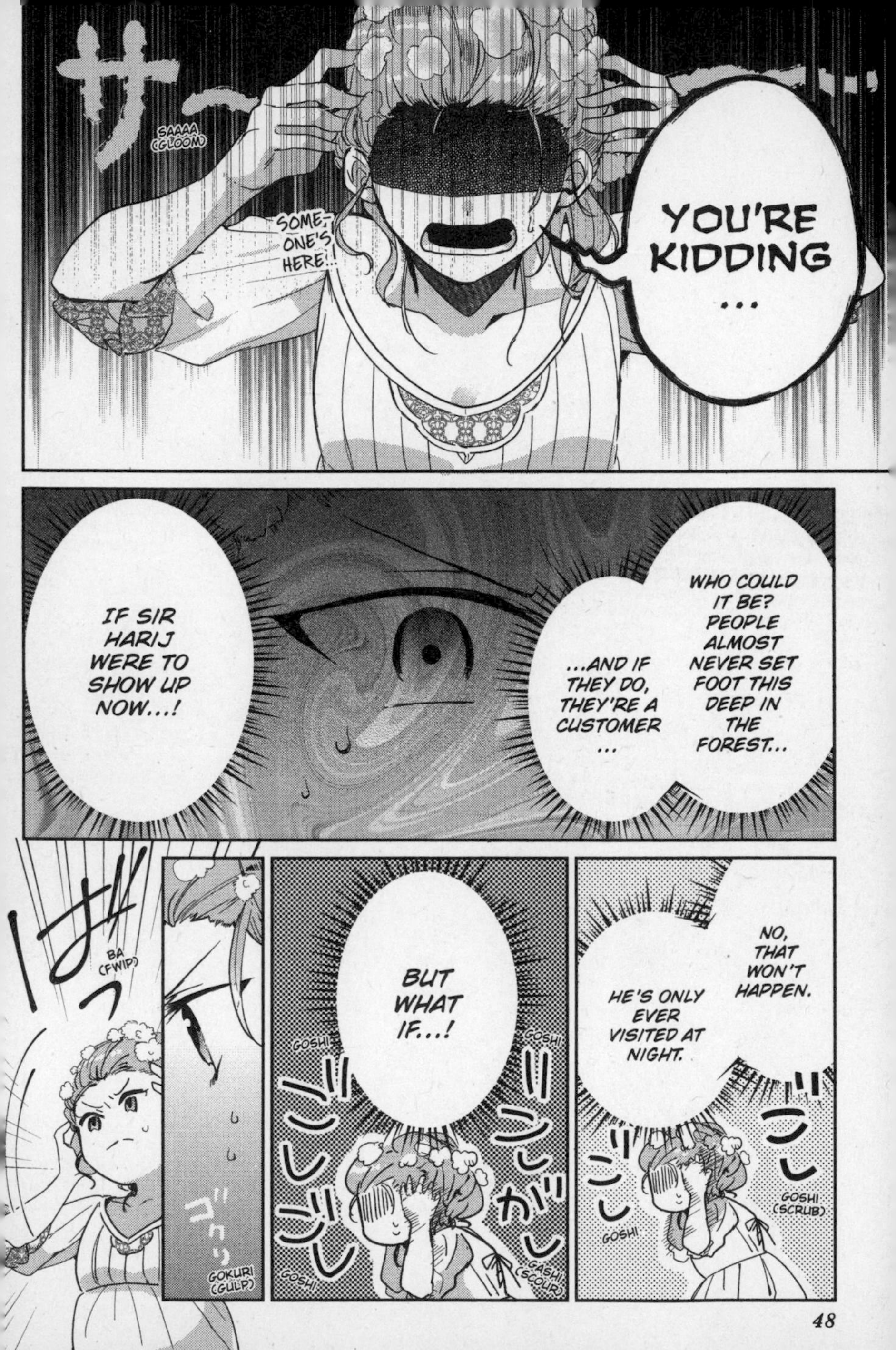

YOU'RE KIDDING ...
SOME-ONE'S HERE!!
SAAAA (GLOOM)
WHO COULD IT BE? PEOPLE ALMOST NEVER SET FOOT THIS DEEP IN THE FOREST...
...AND IF THEY DO, THEY'RE A CUSTOMER ...
IF SIR HARIJ WERE TO SHOW UP NOW...!
NO, THAT WON'T HAPPEN.
HE'S ONLY EVER VISITED AT NIGHT.
GOSHI (SCRUB)
GOSHI
BUT WHAT IF...!
GOSHI
GOSHI
GASHI (SCOUR)
GOSHI
GOKURI (GULP)
BA (FWIP)

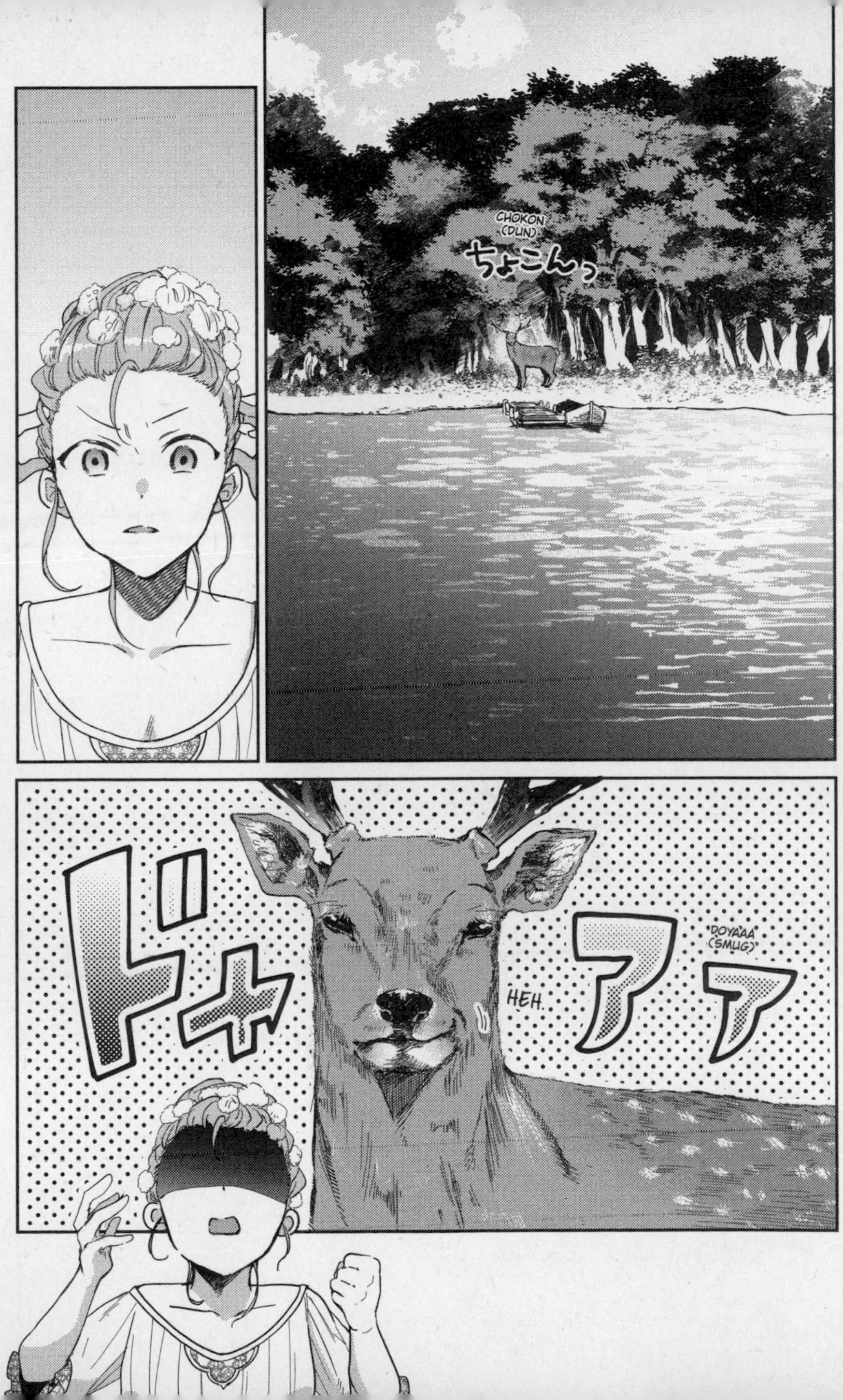
CHOKON (DUN)
ちょこんっ
DOYAAA (SMUG)
ドャアァ
HEH.

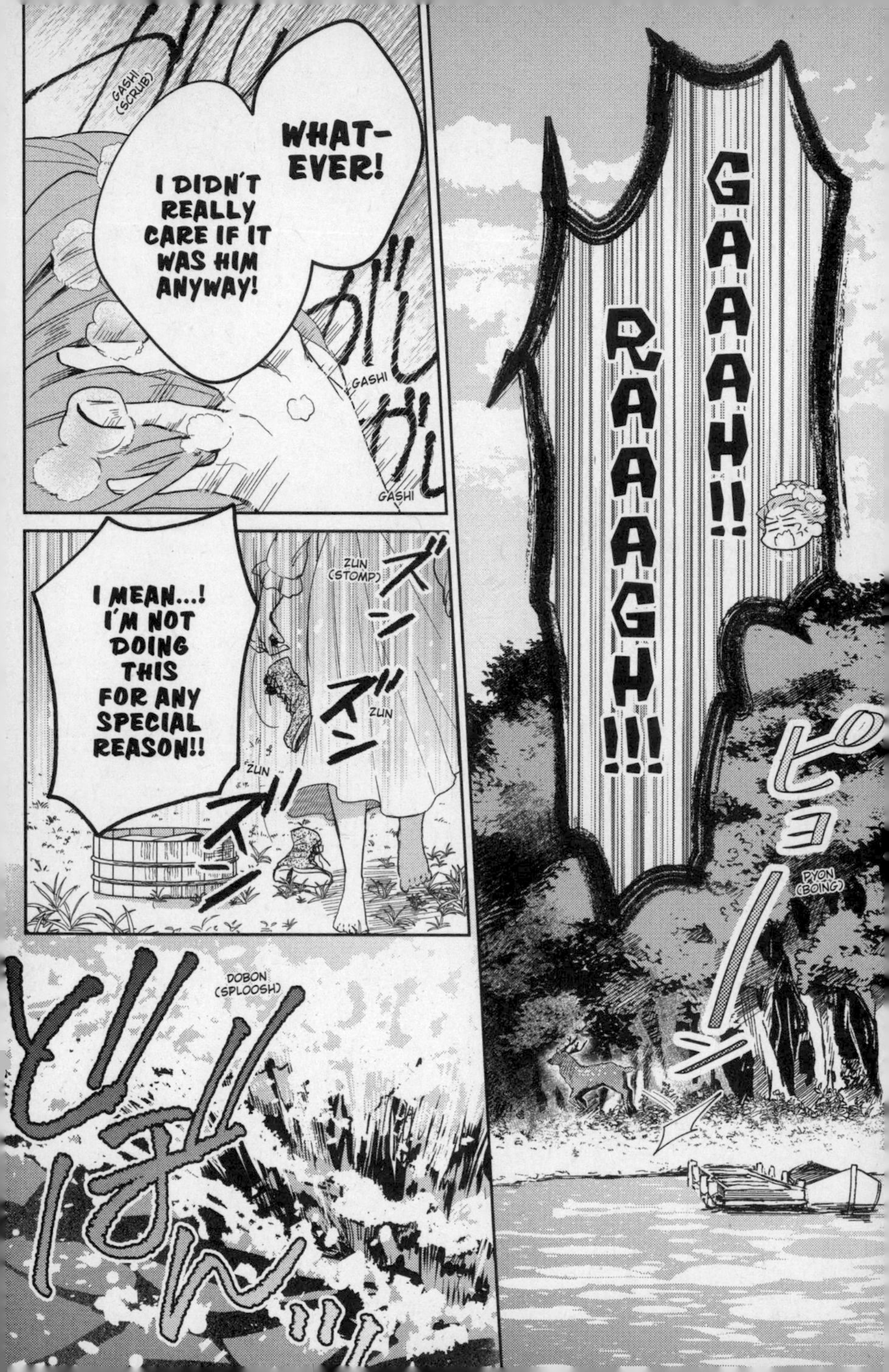
GAAAH!!
RAAAAGH!!!
PYON (BOING)
GASHI (SCRUB)
WHAT-EVER!
I DIDN'T REALLY CARE IF IT WAS HIM ANYWAY!
GASHI
GASHI
I MEAN...! I'M NOT DOING THIS FOR ANY SPECIAL REASON!!
ZUN (STOMP)
ZUN
ZUN
DOBON (SPLOOSH)

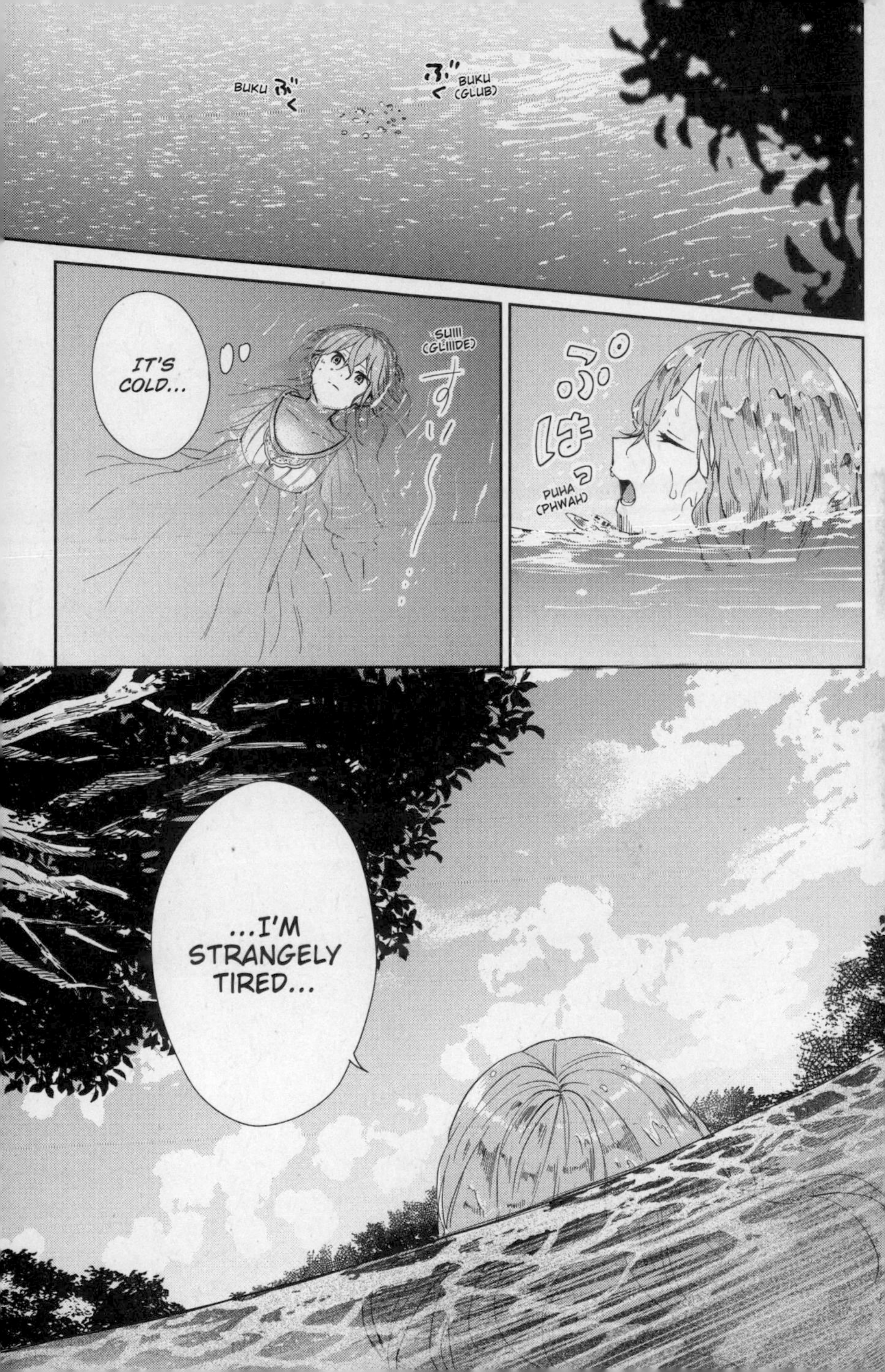
ぶく
BUKU (GLUB)
BUKU
ぶく
ぷはっ
PUHA (PHWAH)
SUIII (GLIIIDE)
すい~
IT'S COLD...
...I'M STRANGELY TIRED...

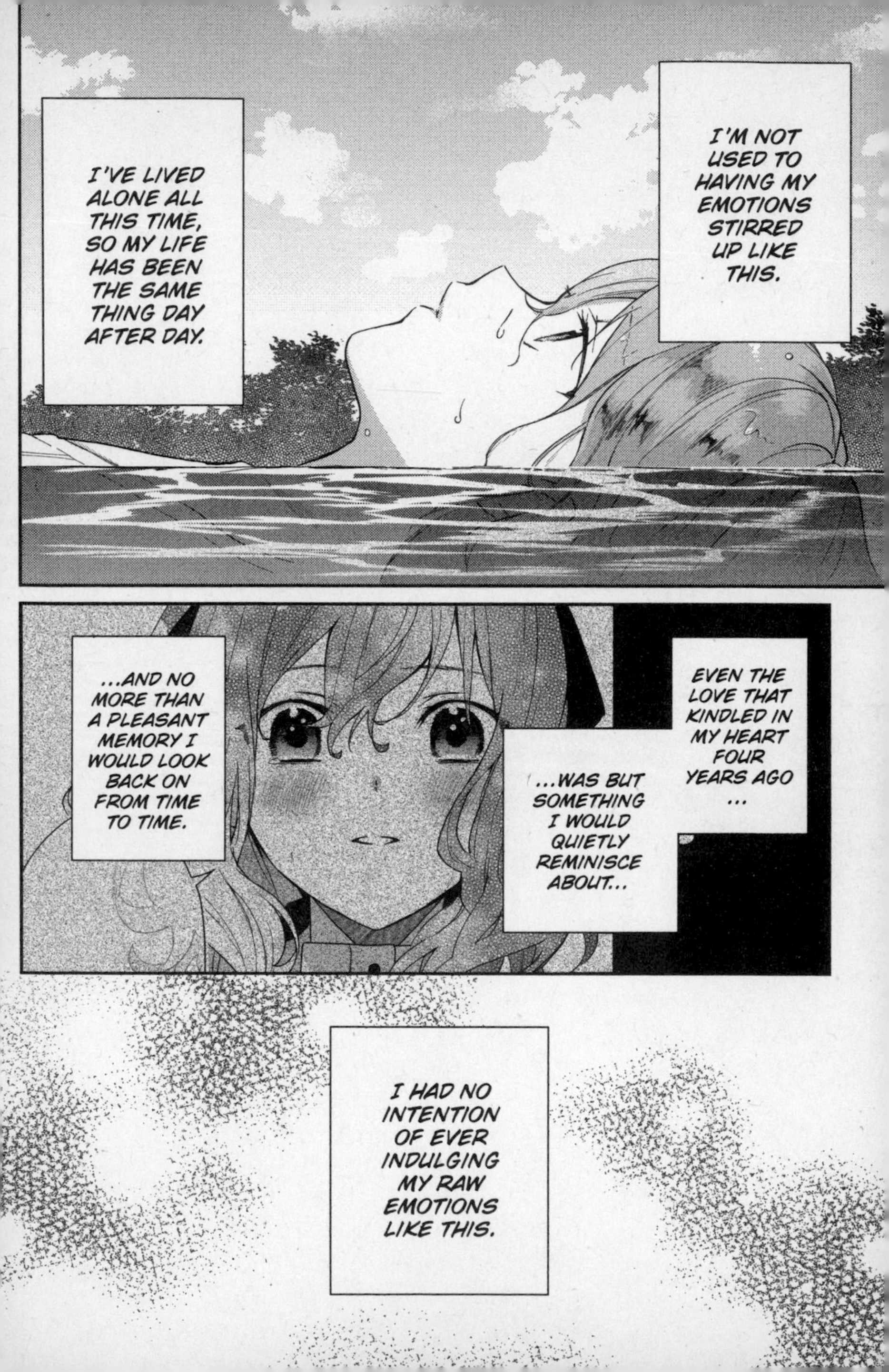
I'M NOT USED TO HAVING MY EMOTIONS STIRRED UP LIKE THIS.
I'VE LIVED ALONE ALL THIS TIME, SO MY LIFE HAS BEEN THE SAME THING DAY AFTER DAY.
EVEN THE LOVE THAT KINDLED IN MY HEART FOUR YEARS AGO…
…WAS BUT SOMETHING I WOULD QUIETLY REMINISCE ABOUT…
…AND NO MORE THAN A PLEASANT MEMORY I WOULD LOOK BACK ON FROM TIME TO TIME.
I HAD NO INTENTION OF EVER INDULGING MY RAW EMOTIONS LIKE THIS.

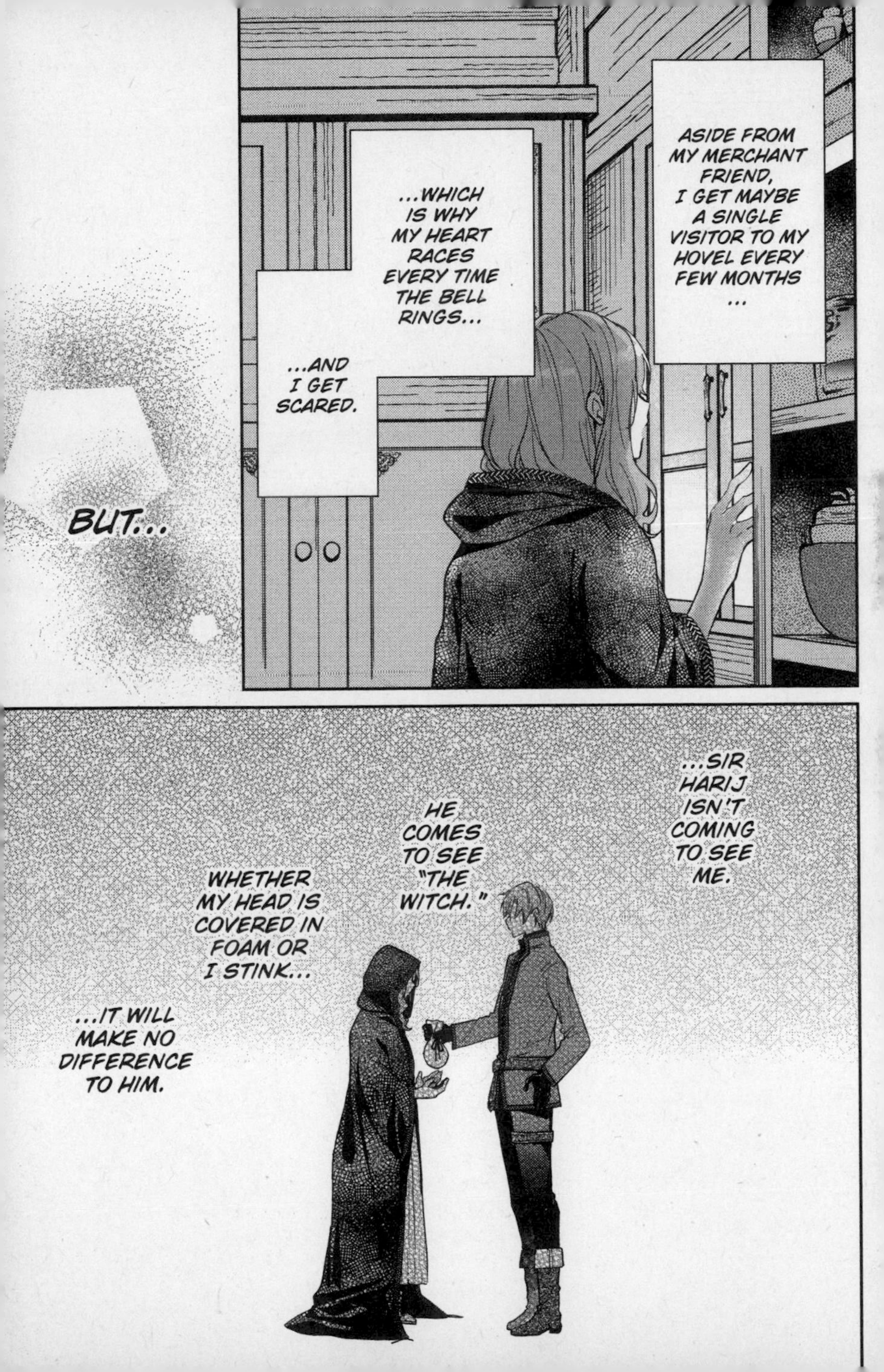
ASIDE FROM MY MERCHANT FRIEND, I GET MAYBE A SINGLE VISITOR TO MY HOVEL EVERY FEW MONTHS ...
...WHICH IS WHY MY HEART RACES EVERY TIME THE BELL RINGS...
...AND I GET SCARED.
BUT...
...SIR HARIJ ISN'T COMING TO SEE ME.
HE COMES TO SEE "THE WITCH."
WHETHER MY HEAD IS COVERED IN FOAM OR I STINK...
...IT WILL MAKE NO DIFFERENCE TO HIM.

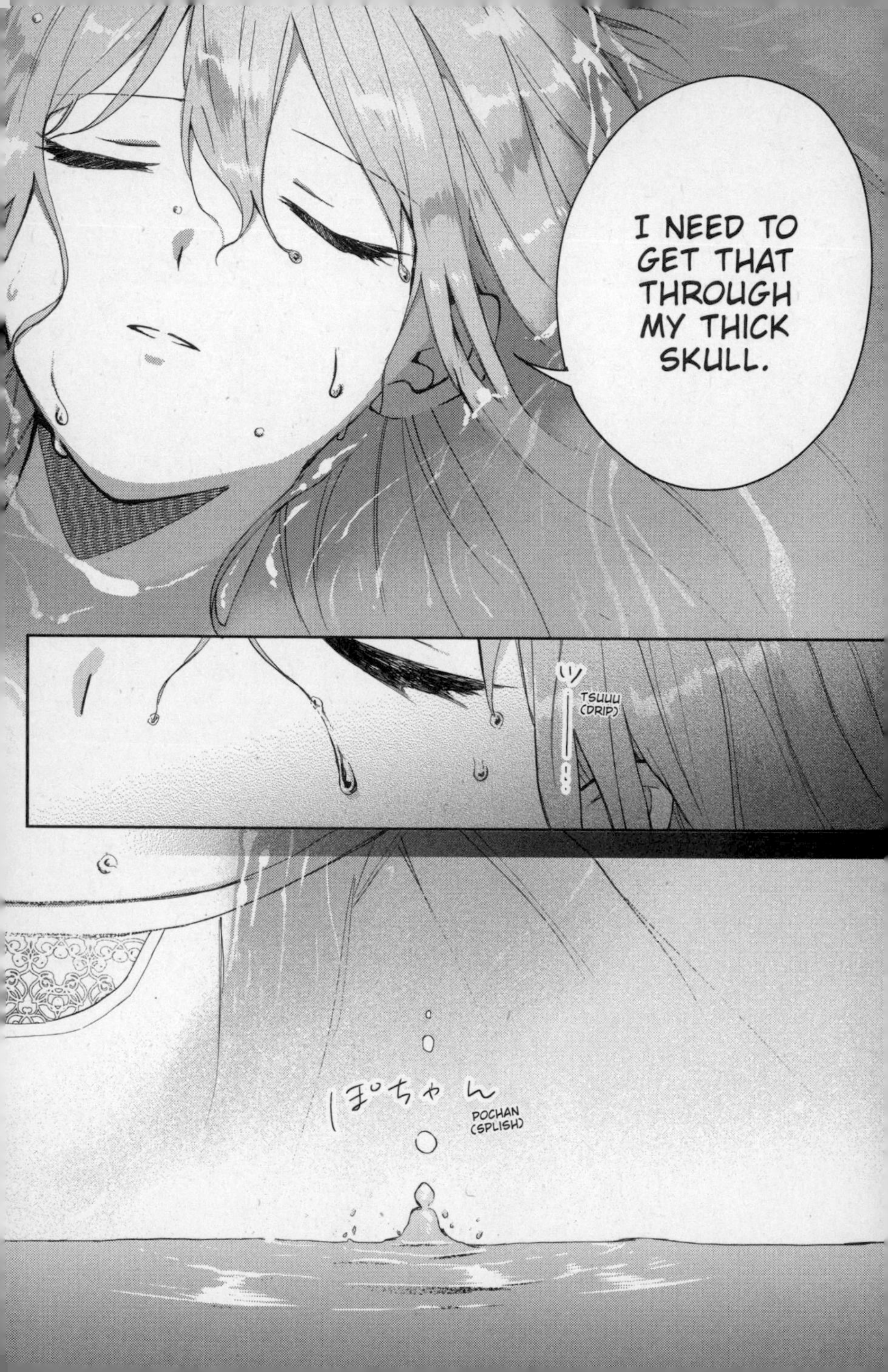
I NEED TO GET THAT THROUGH MY THICK SKULL.
ツー…
TSUUU (DRIP)
ぽちゃん
POCHAN (SPLISH)

Hi, I'm a

Witch,

and My Crush

Wants Me to Make a

Love Potion

Hi, I'm a

Witch,

and My Crush
Wants Me to Make a
Love Potion

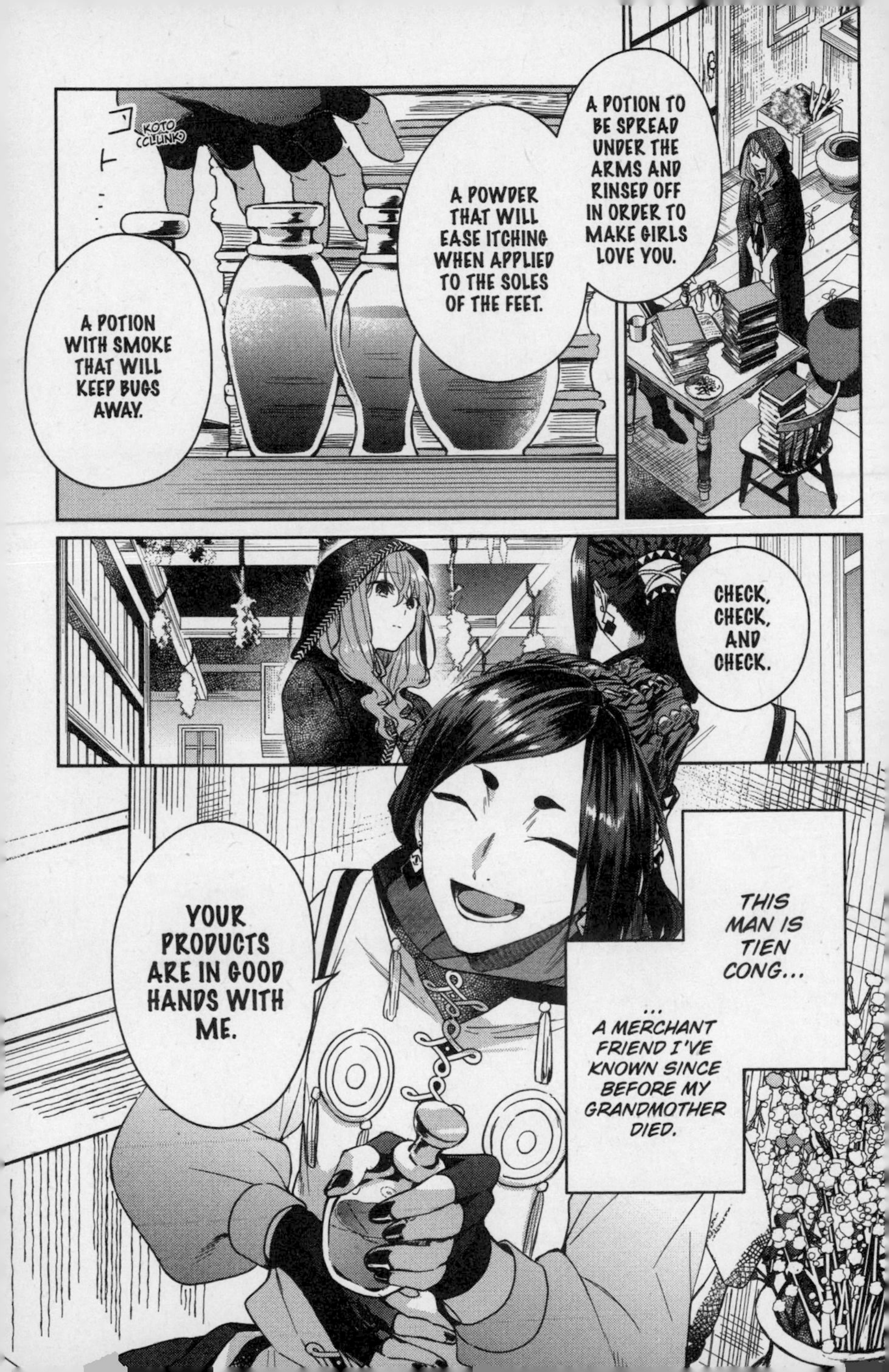

A POTION TO BE SPREAD UNDER THE ARMS AND RINSED OFF IN ORDER TO MAKE GIRLS LOVE YOU.
A POWDER THAT WILL EASE ITCHING WHEN APPLIED TO THE SOLES OF THE FEET.
KOTO (CLINK)
A POTION WITH SMOKE THAT WILL KEEP BUGS AWAY.
CHECK, CHECK, AND CHECK.
THIS MAN IS TIEN CONG...
...A MERCHANT FRIEND I'VE KNOWN SINCE BEFORE MY GRANDMOTHER DIED.
YOUR PRODUCTS ARE IN GOOD HANDS WITH ME.

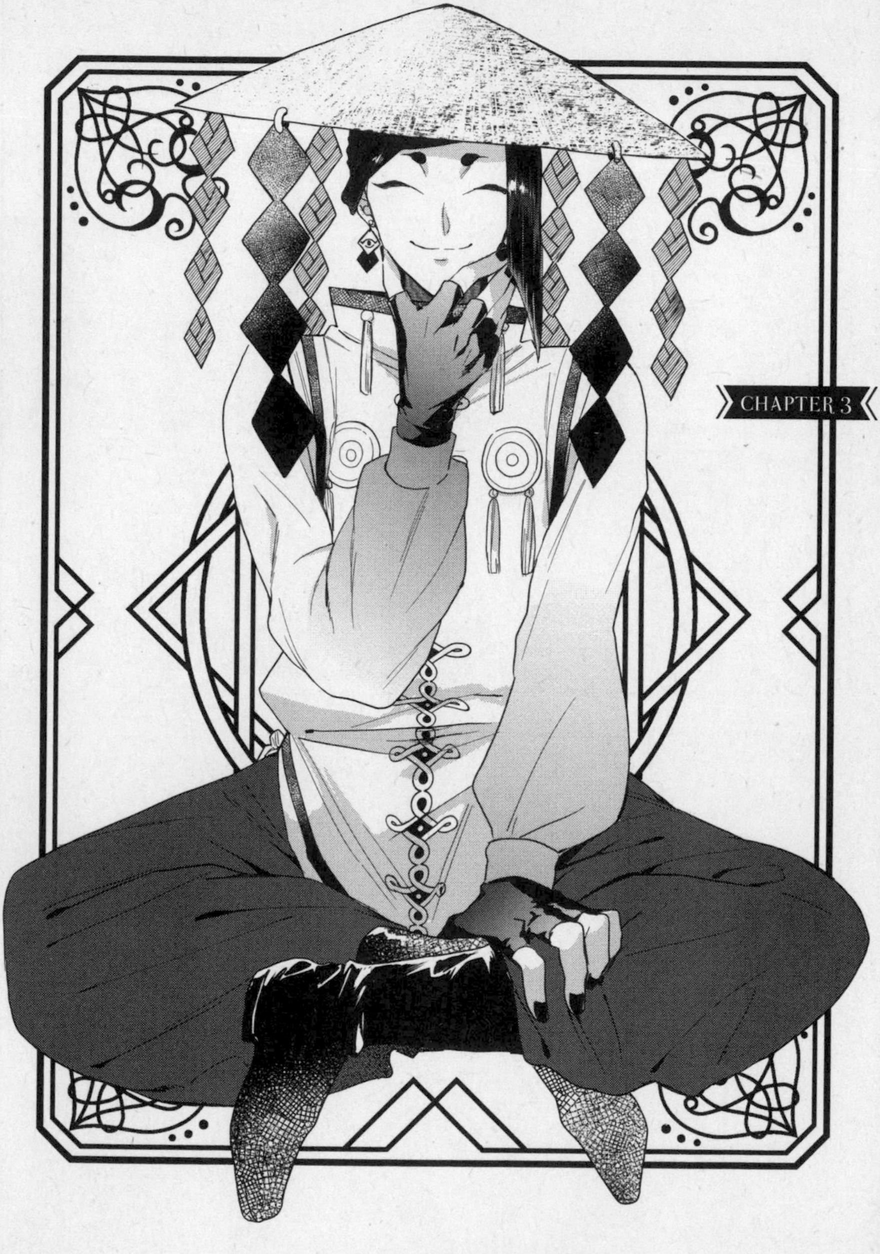

CHAPTER 3

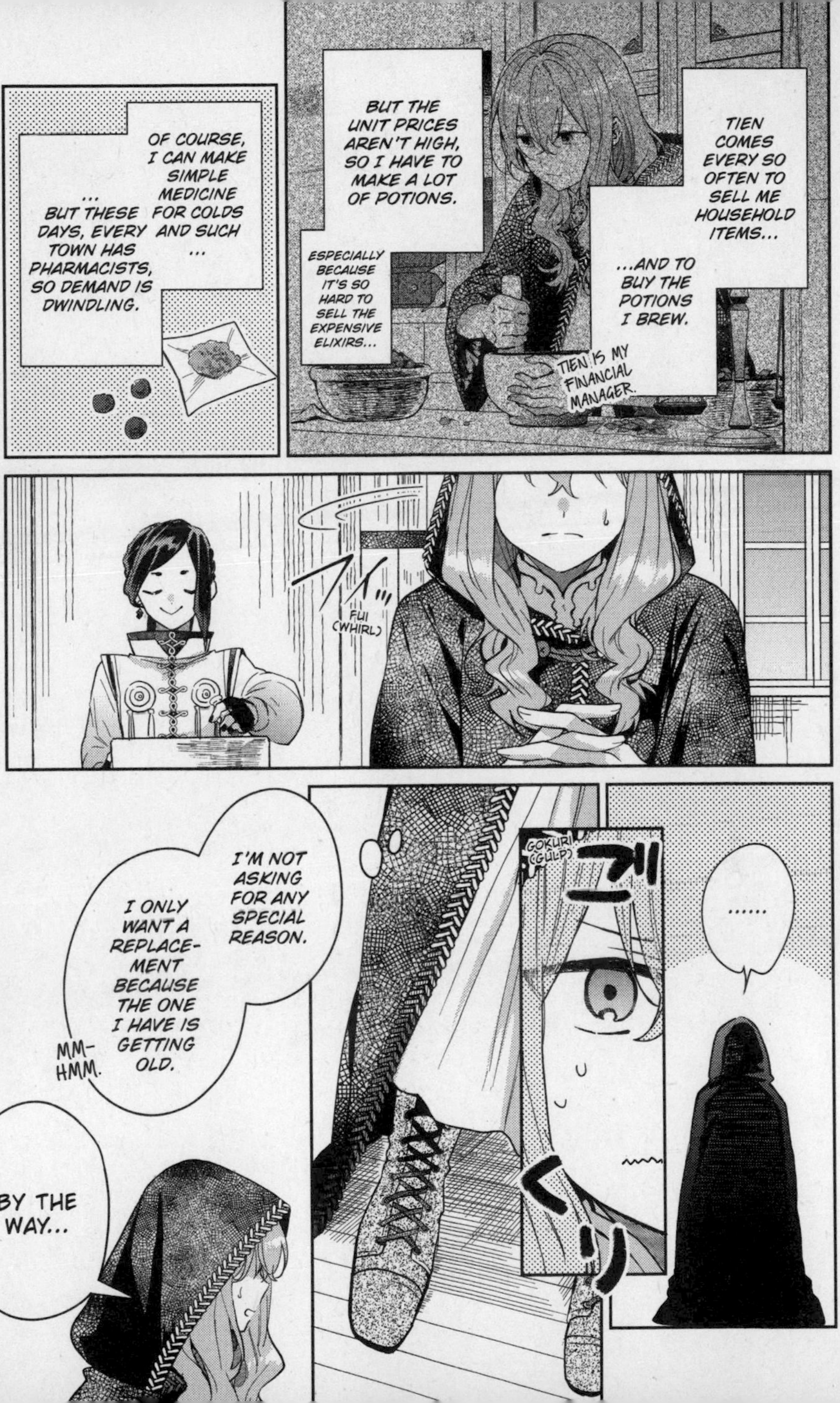
TIEN COMES EVERY SO OFTEN TO SELL ME HOUSEHOLD ITEMS...
...AND TO BUY THE POTIONS I BREW.
TIEN IS MY FINANCIAL MANAGER.
BUT THE UNIT PRICES AREN'T HIGH, SO I HAVE TO MAKE A LOT OF POTIONS.
ESPECIALLY BECAUSE IT'S SO HARD TO SELL THE EXPENSIVE ELIXIRS...
OF COURSE, I CAN MAKE SIMPLE MEDICINE FOR COLDS AND SUCH...
...BUT THESE DAYS, EVERY TOWN HAS PHARMACISTS, SO DEMAND IS DWINDLING.
FUI (WHIRL)
GOKURI (GULP)
......
I'M NOT ASKING FOR ANY SPECIAL REASON.
I ONLY WANT A REPLACEMENT BECAUSE THE ONE I HAVE IS GETTING OLD.
MM-HMM.
BY THE WAY...

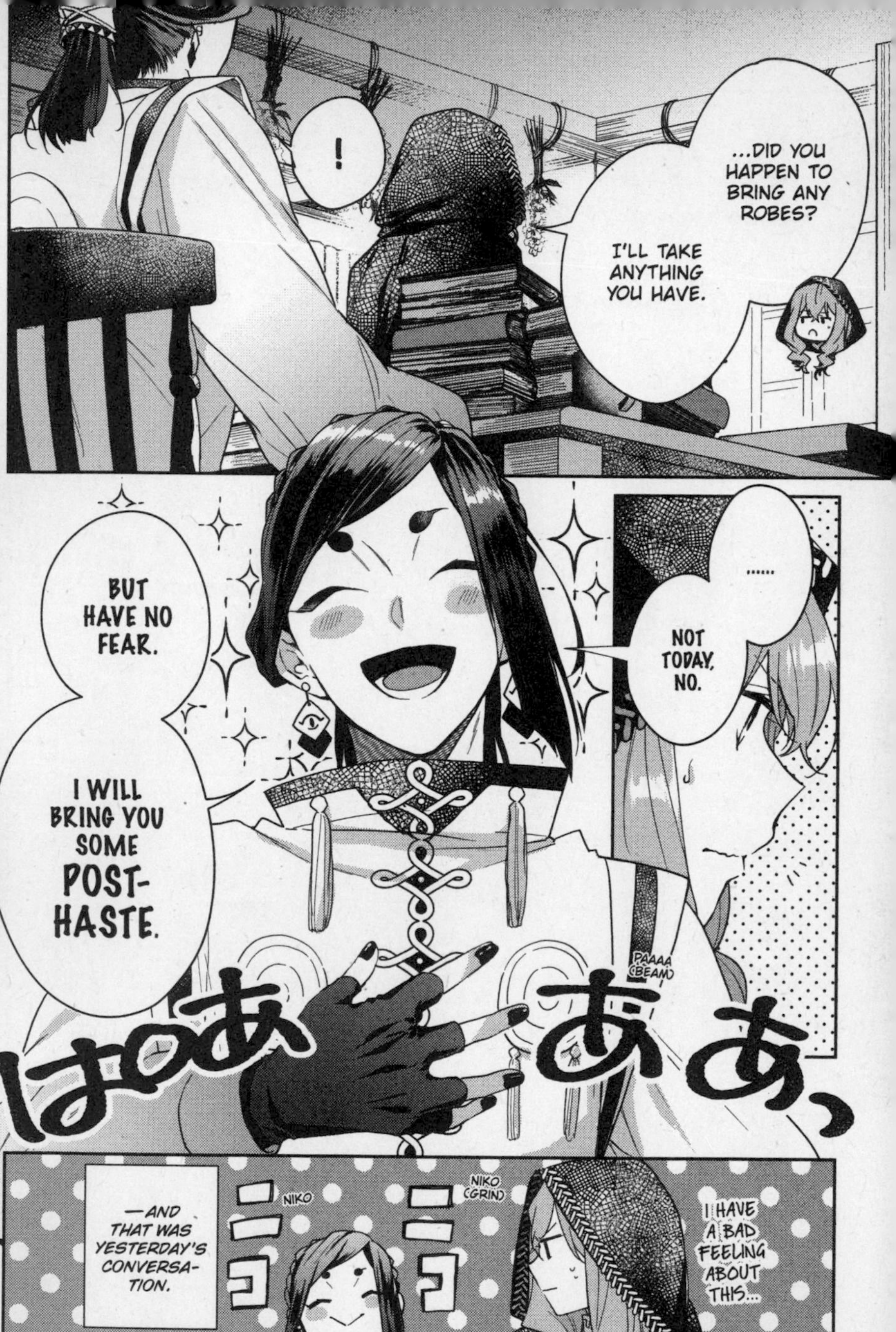
...DID YOU HAPPEN TO BRING ANY ROBES?
I'LL TAKE ANYTHING YOU HAVE.
!
......
NOT TODAY, NO.
BUT HAVE NO FEAR.
I WILL BRING YOU SOME POST-HASTE.
PAAAA (BEAM)
はぁああああっ
I HAVE A BAD FEELING ABOUT THIS...
NIKO (GRIN)
ニコ
NIKO
ニコ
—AND THAT WAS YESTERDAY'S CONVERSATION.

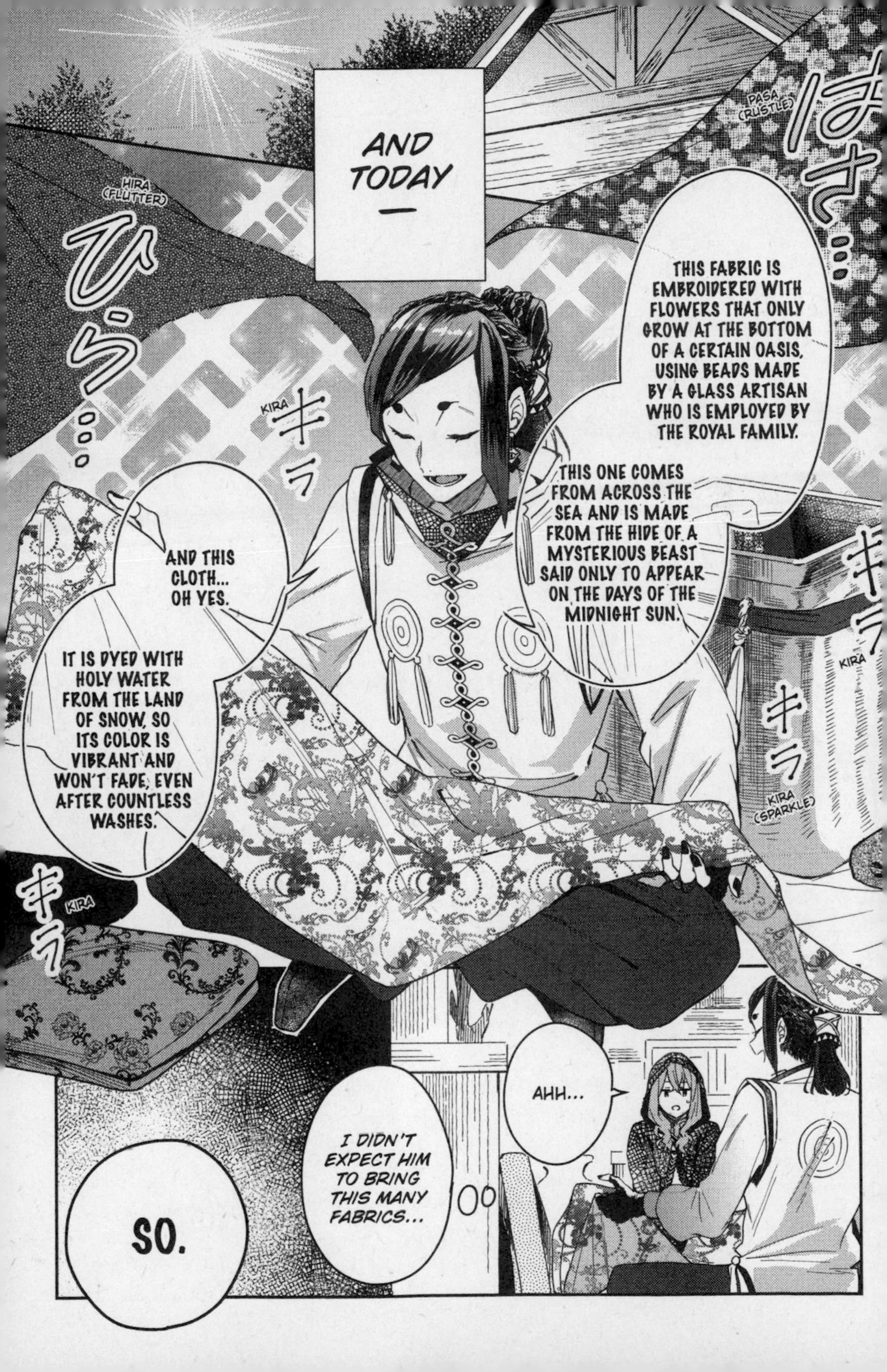
AND TODAY —
PASA (RUSTLE)
HIRA (FLUTTER)
THIS FABRIC IS EMBROIDERED WITH FLOWERS THAT ONLY GROW AT THE BOTTOM OF A CERTAIN OASIS, USING BEADS MADE BY A GLASS ARTISAN WHO IS EMPLOYED BY THE ROYAL FAMILY.
KIRA
THIS ONE COMES FROM ACROSS THE SEA AND IS MADE FROM THE HIDE OF A MYSTERIOUS BEAST SAID ONLY TO APPEAR ON THE DAYS OF THE MIDNIGHT SUN.
AND THIS CLOTH... OH YES.
KIRA
KIRA (SPARKLE)
IT IS DYED WITH HOLY WATER FROM THE LAND OF SNOW, SO ITS COLOR IS VIBRANT AND WON'T FADE, EVEN AFTER COUNTLESS WASHES.
KIRA
AHH...
I DIDN'T EXPECT HIM TO BRING THIS MANY FABRICS...
SO.

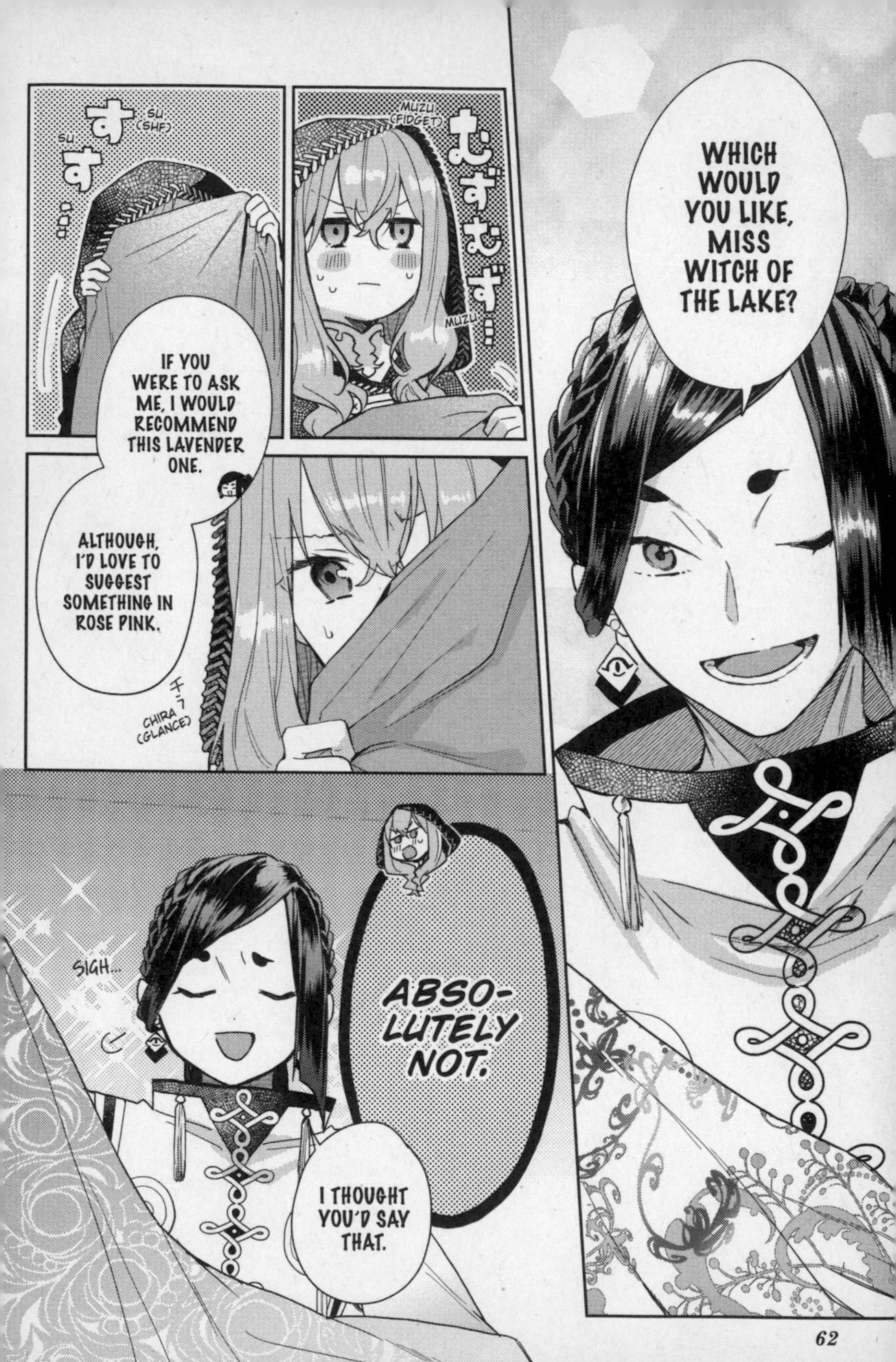
WHICH WOULD YOU LIKE, MISS WITCH OF THE LAKE?
むずむず
MUZU (FIDGET)
MUZU
すす
SU (SHF)
SU
IF YOU WERE TO ASK ME, I WOULD RECOMMEND THIS LAVENDER ONE.
ALTHOUGH, I'D LOVE TO SUGGEST SOMETHING IN ROSE PINK.
チラ
CHIRA (GLANCE)
SIGH...
ABSO-LUTELY NOT.
I THOUGHT YOU'D SAY THAT.

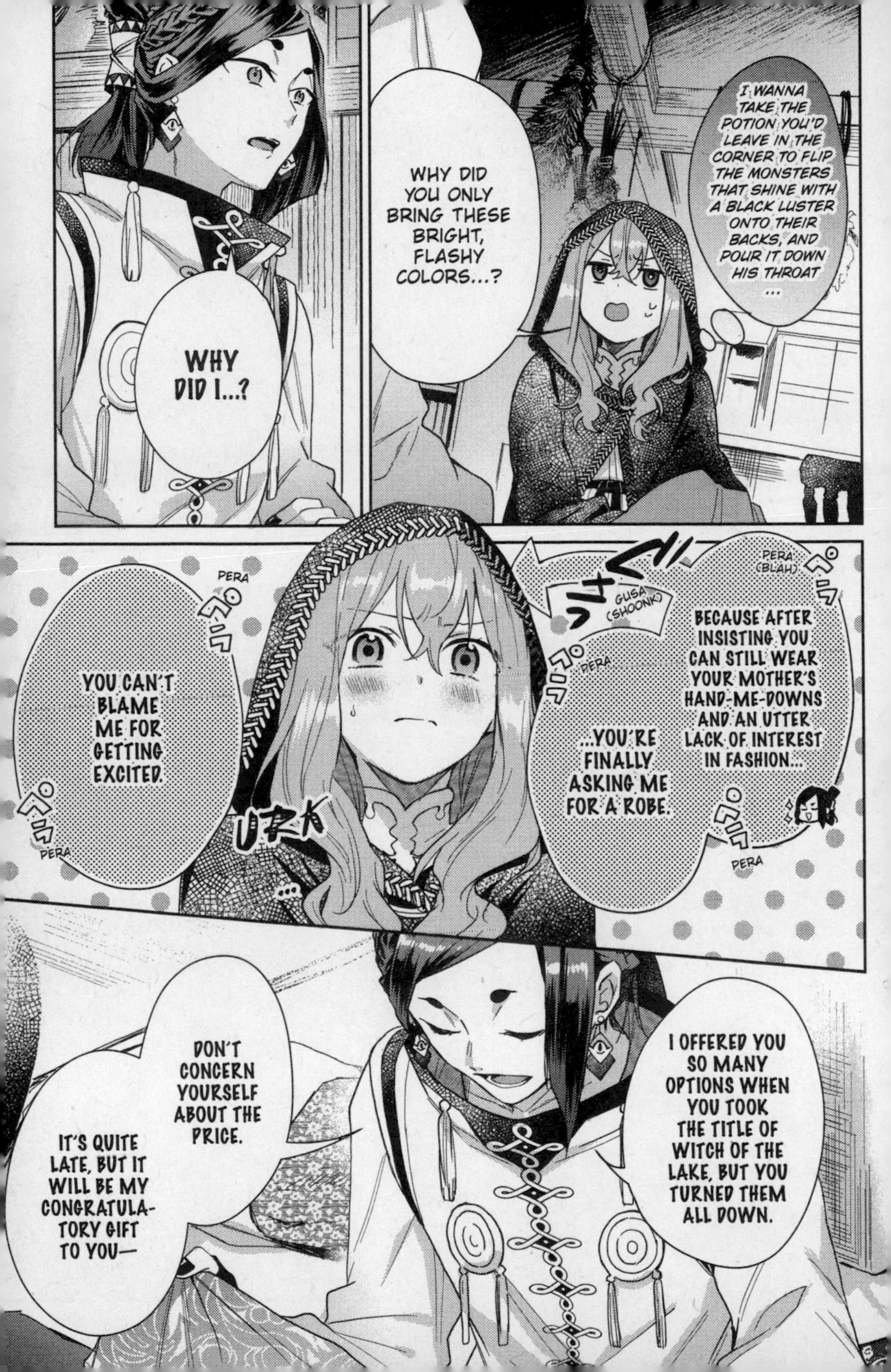
I WANNA TAKE THE POTION YOU'D LEAVE IN THE CORNER TO FLIP THE MONSTERS THAT SHINE WITH A BLACK LUSTER ONTO THEIR BACKS, AND POUR IT DOWN HIS THROAT ...
WHY DID YOU ONLY BRING THESE BRIGHT, FLASHY COLORS...?
WHY DID I...?
PERA (BLAH)
GUSA (SHOONK)
BECAUSE AFTER INSISTING YOU CAN STILL WEAR YOUR MOTHER'S HAND-ME-DOWNS AND AN UTTER LACK OF INTEREST IN FASHION...
PERA
...YOU'RE FINALLY ASKING ME FOR A ROBE.
PERA
URK
PERA
YOU CAN'T BLAME ME FOR GETTING EXCITED.
PERA
I OFFERED YOU SO MANY OPTIONS WHEN YOU TOOK THE TITLE OF WITCH OF THE LAKE, BUT YOU TURNED THEM ALL DOWN.
DON'T CONCERN YOURSELF ABOUT THE PRICE.
IT'S QUITE LATE, BUT IT WILL BE MY CONGRATULATORY GIFT TO YOU—

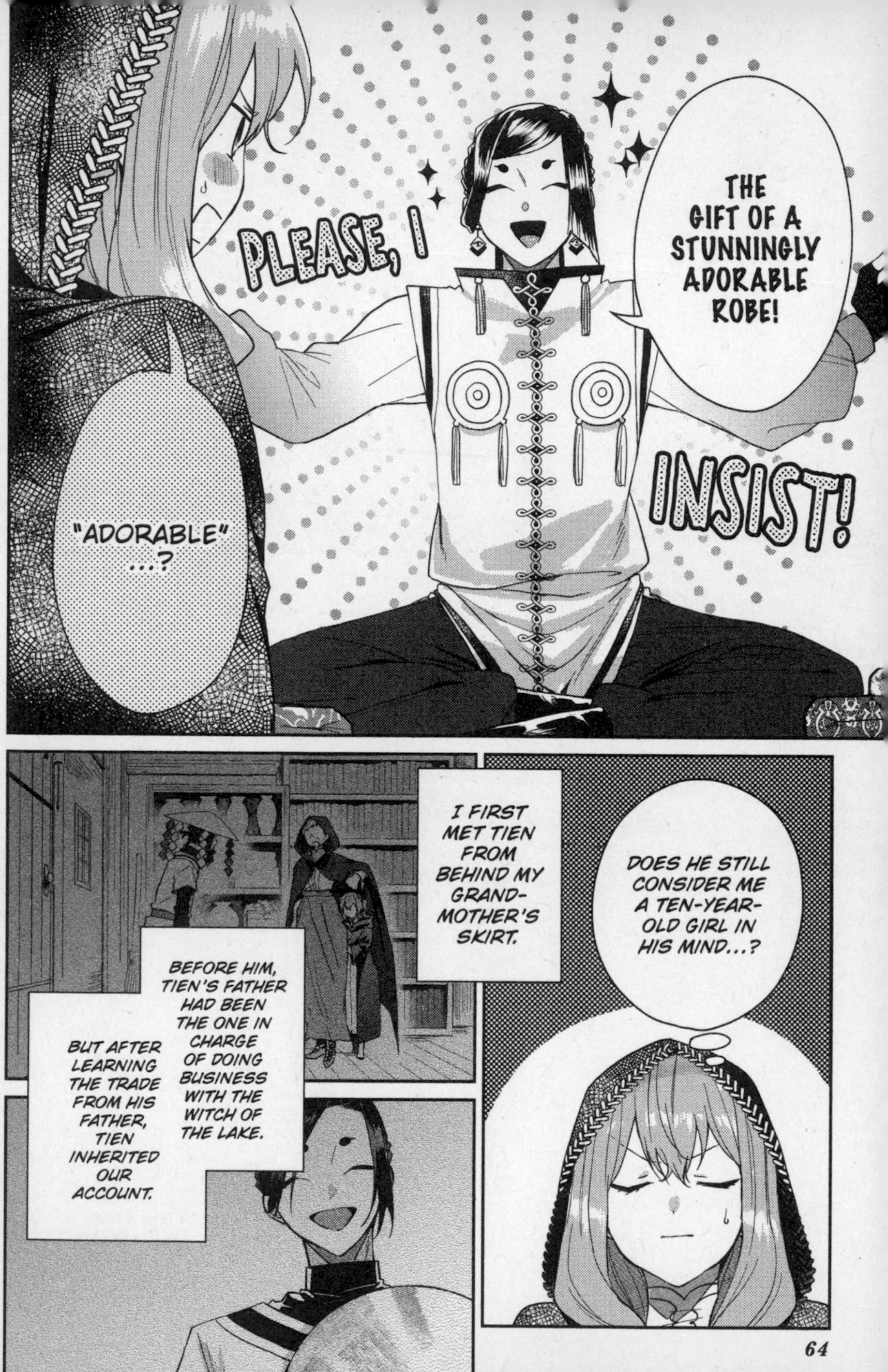
THE GIFT OF A STUNNINGLY ADORABLE ROBE!
PLEASE, I
INSIST!
"ADORABLE" ...?
DOES HE STILL CONSIDER ME A TEN-YEAR-OLD GIRL IN HIS MIND...?
I FIRST MET TIEN FROM BEHIND MY GRAND-MOTHER'S SKIRT.
BEFORE HIM, TIEN'S FATHER HAD BEEN THE ONE IN CHARGE OF DOING BUSINESS WITH THE WITCH OF THE LAKE.
BUT AFTER LEARNING THE TRADE FROM HIS FATHER, TIEN INHERITED OUR ACCOUNT.

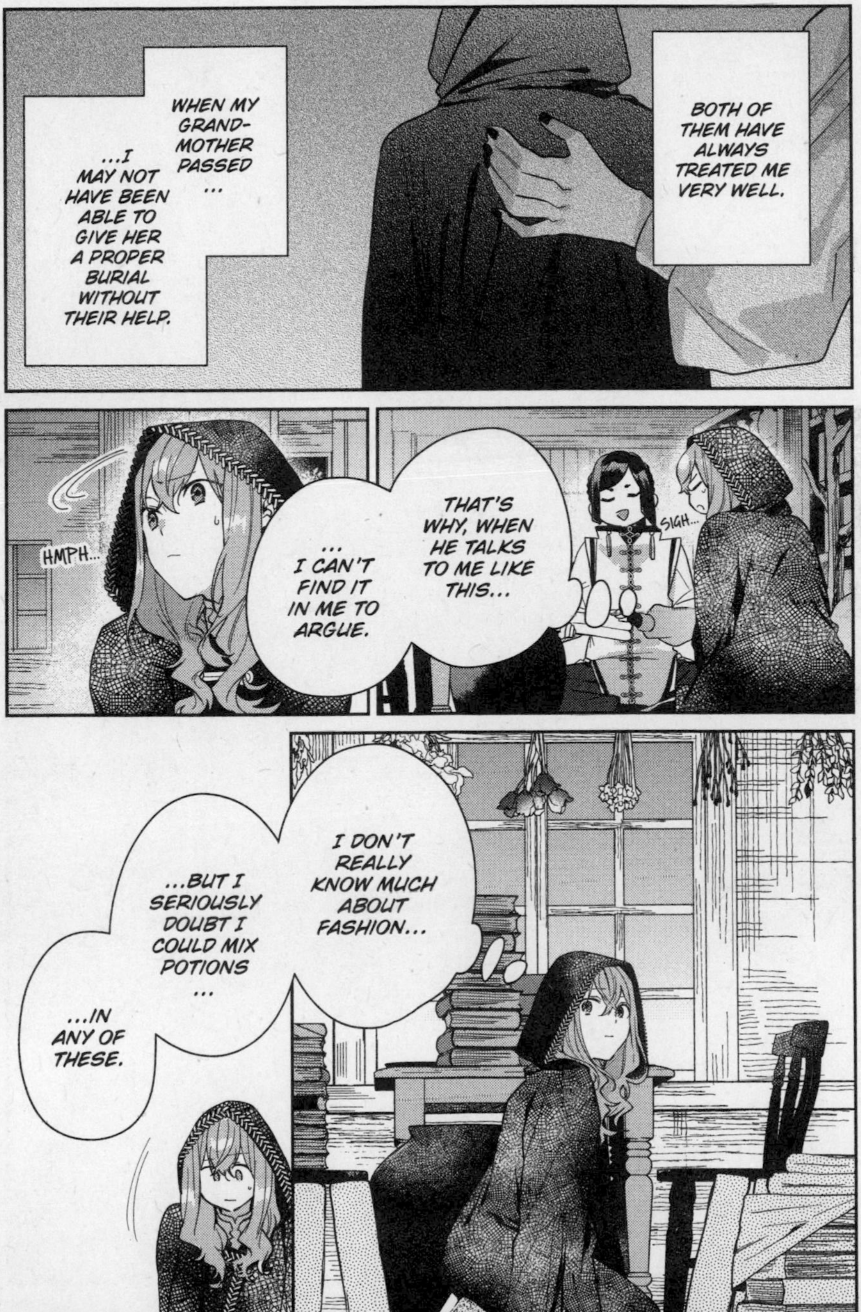
BOTH OF THEM HAVE ALWAYS TREATED ME VERY WELL.
WHEN MY GRAND-MOTHER PASSED ...
...I MAY NOT HAVE BEEN ABLE TO GIVE HER A PROPER BURIAL WITHOUT THEIR HELP.
SIGH...
THAT'S WHY, WHEN HE TALKS TO ME LIKE THIS...
... I CAN'T FIND IT IN ME TO ARGUE.
HMPH...
I DON'T REALLY KNOW MUCH ABOUT FASHION...
...BUT I SERIOUSLY DOUBT I COULD MIX POTIONS ...
...IN ANY OF THESE.

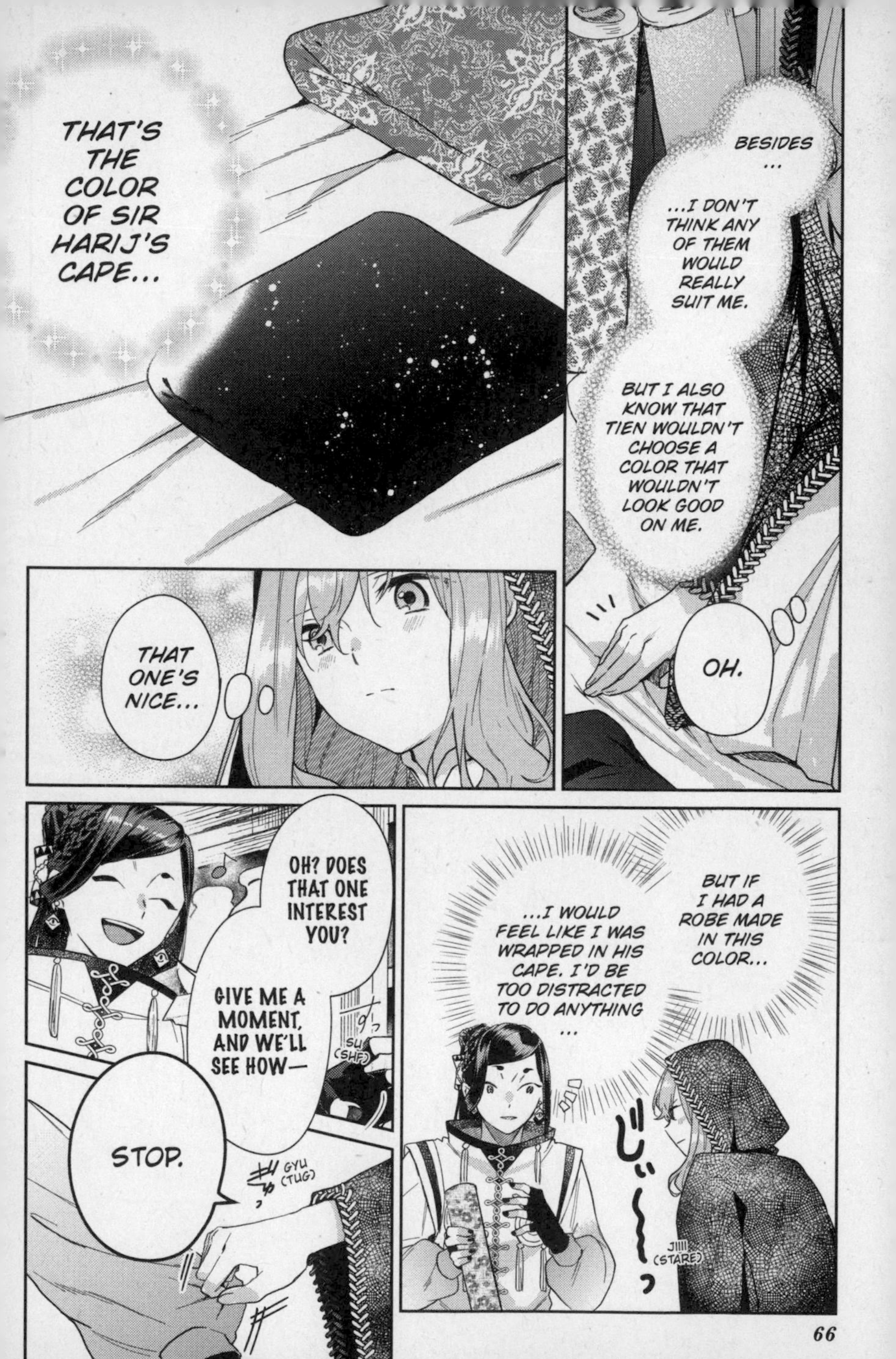
BESIDES...
...I DON'T THINK ANY OF THEM WOULD REALLY SUIT ME.
BUT I ALSO KNOW THAT TIEN WOULDN'T CHOOSE A COLOR THAT WOULDN'T LOOK GOOD ON ME.
OH.
THAT'S THE COLOR OF SIR HARIJ'S CAPE...
THAT ONE'S NICE...
BUT IF I HAD A ROBE MADE IN THIS COLOR...
...I WOULD FEEL LIKE I WAS WRAPPED IN HIS CAPE. I'D BE TOO DISTRACTED TO DO ANYTHING...
JIIII (STARE)
OH? DOES THAT ONE INTEREST YOU?
GIVE ME A MOMENT, AND WE'LL SEE HOW—
SU (SHF)
STOP.
GYU (TUG)

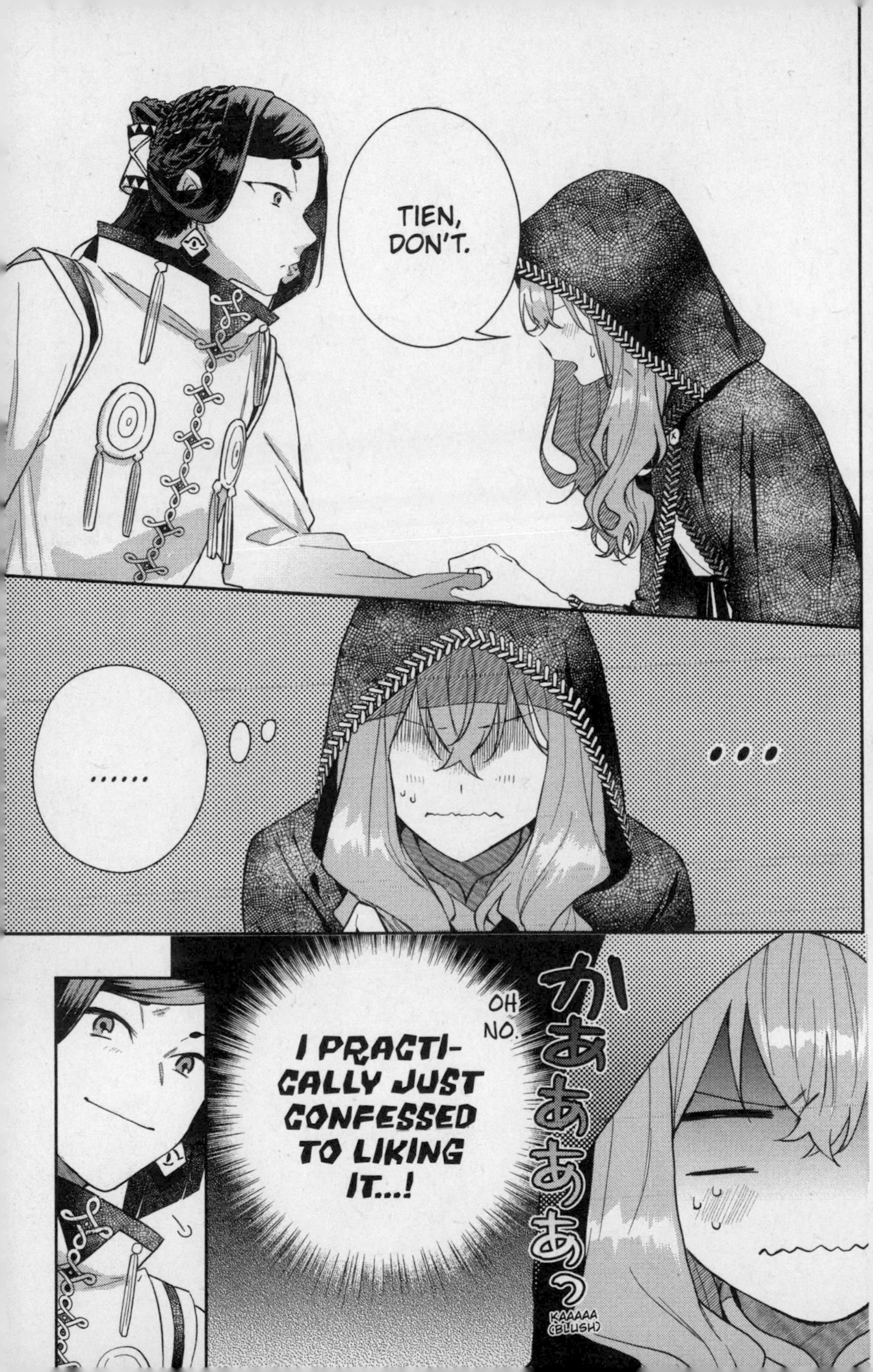
TIEN, DON'T.
• • •
......
かああああっ
KAAAAA (BLUSH)
OH NO.
I PRACTI-CALLY JUST CONFESSED TO LIKING IT...!

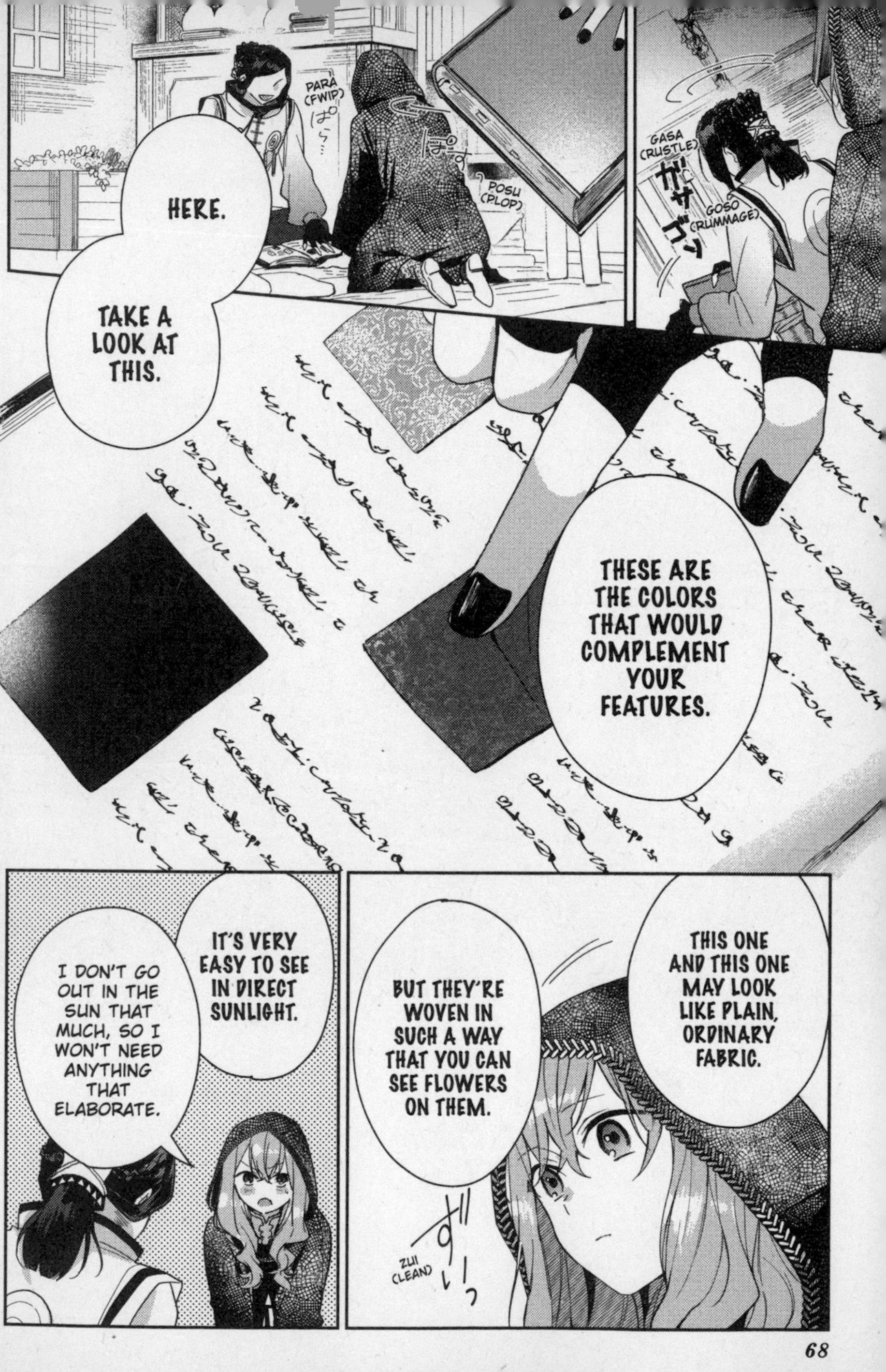
GASA (RUSTLE)
ガサ
GOSO (RUMMAGE)
ゴソッ
PARA (FWIP)
ぱら…
ぽす
POSU (PLOP)
HERE.
TAKE A LOOK AT THIS.
THESE ARE THE COLORS THAT WOULD COMPLEMENT YOUR FEATURES.
THIS ONE AND THIS ONE MAY LOOK LIKE PLAIN, ORDINARY FABRIC.
BUT THEY'RE WOVEN IN SUCH A WAY THAT YOU CAN SEE FLOWERS ON THEM.
ずいっ
ZUI CLEAND
IT'S VERY EASY TO SEE IN DIRECT SUNLIGHT.
I DON'T GO OUT IN THE SUN THAT MUCH, SO I WON'T NEED ANYTHING THAT ELABORATE.

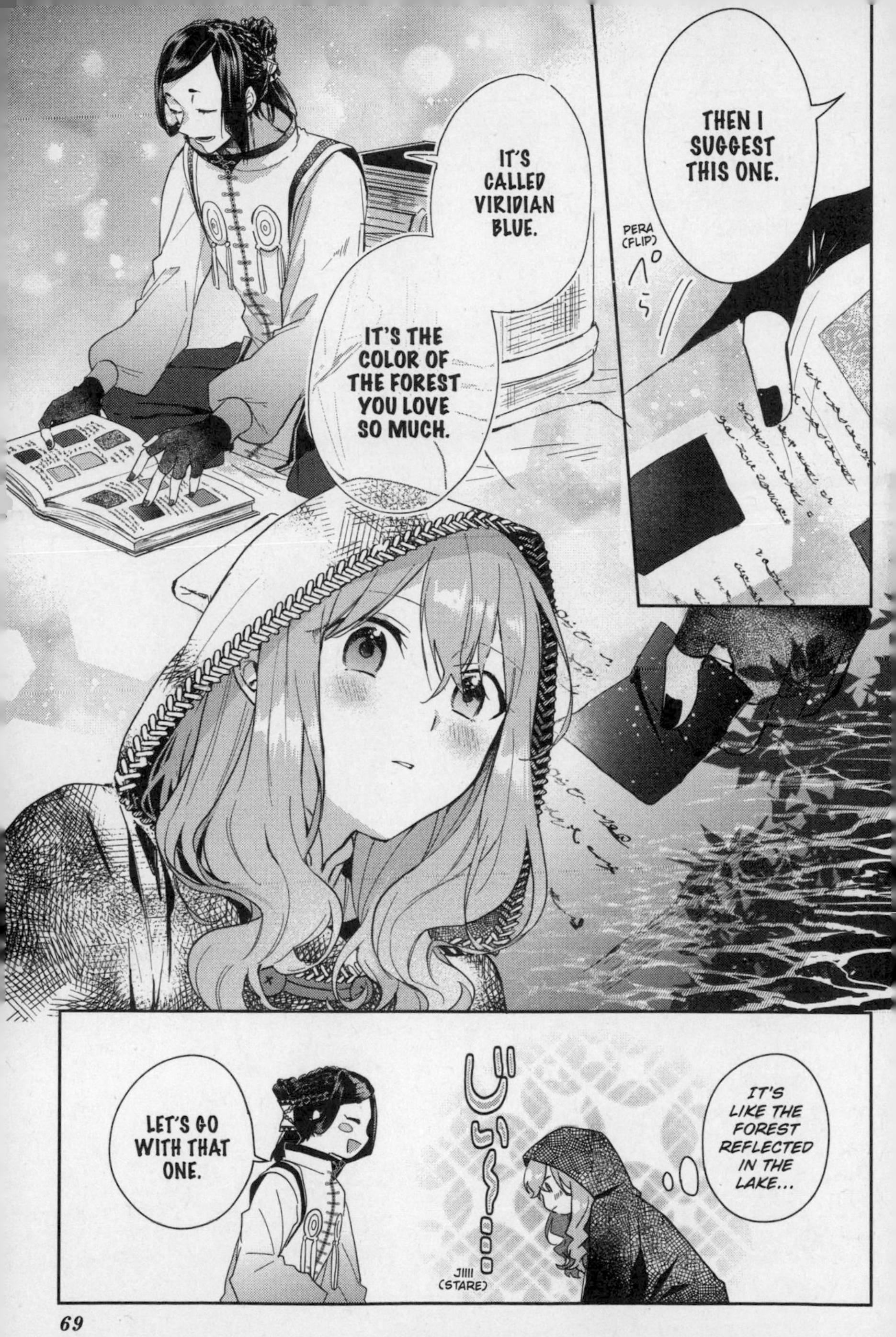
THEN I SUGGEST THIS ONE.
PERA (FLIP)
IT'S CALLED VIRIDIAN BLUE.
IT'S THE COLOR OF THE FOREST YOU LOVE SO MUCH.
IT'S LIKE THE FOREST REFLECTED IN THE LAKE...
JIIII (STARE)
LET'S GO WITH THAT ONE.

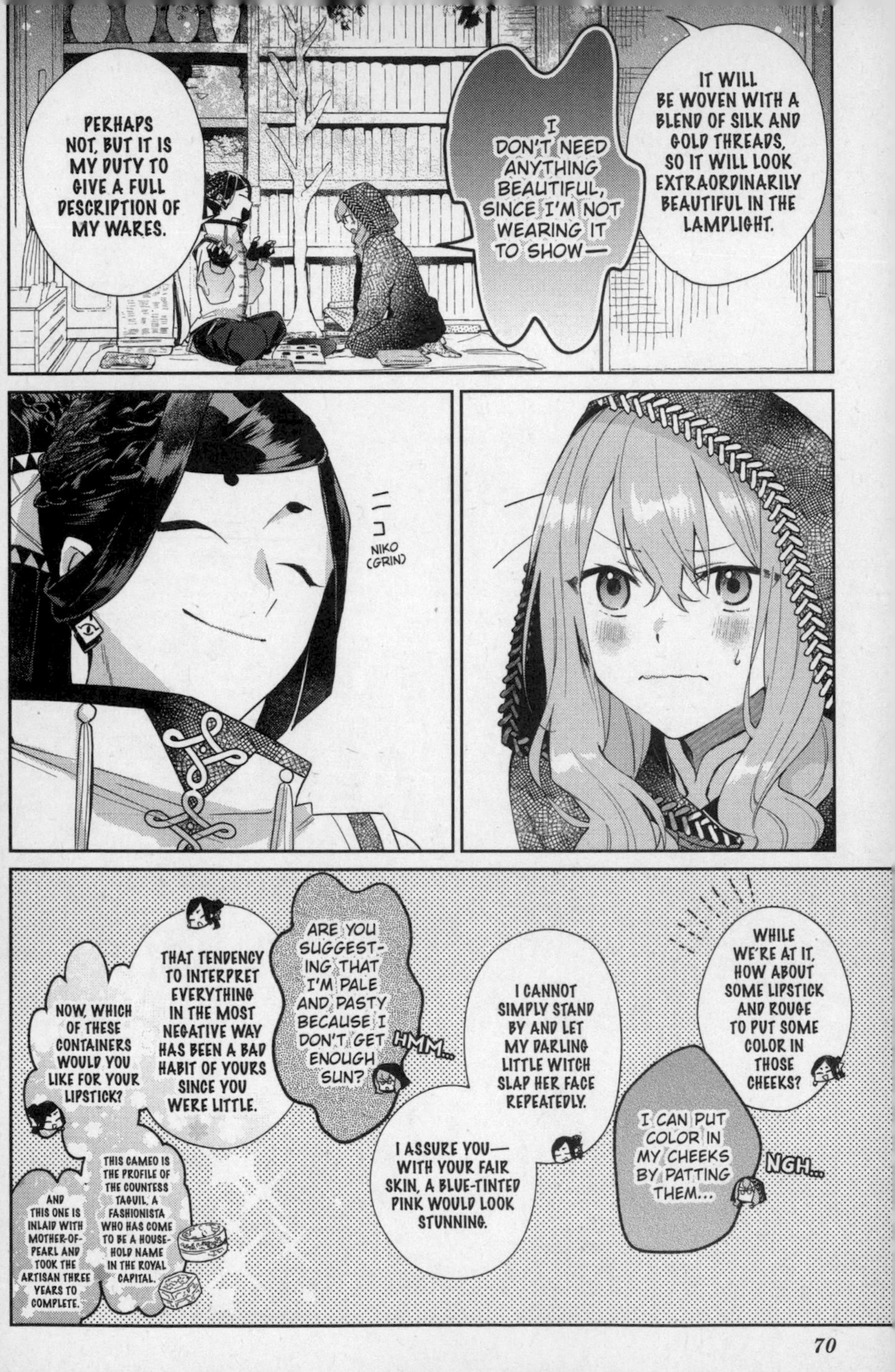
IT WILL BE WOVEN WITH A BLEND OF SILK AND GOLD THREADS, SO IT WILL LOOK EXTRAORDINARILY BEAUTIFUL IN THE LAMPLIGHT.
I DON'T NEED ANYTHING BEAUTIFUL, SINCE I'M NOT WEARING IT TO SHOW—
PERHAPS NOT, BUT IT IS MY DUTY TO GIVE A FULL DESCRIPTION OF MY WARES.
NIKO (GRIN)
WHILE WE'RE AT IT, HOW ABOUT SOME LIPSTICK AND ROUGE TO PUT SOME COLOR IN THOSE CHEEKS?
I CAN PUT COLOR IN MY CHEEKS BY PATTING THEM...
NGH...
I CANNOT SIMPLY STAND BY AND LET MY DARLING LITTLE WITCH SLAP HER FACE REPEATEDLY.
I ASSURE YOU—WITH YOUR FAIR SKIN, A BLUE-TINTED PINK WOULD LOOK STUNNING.
ARE YOU SUGGESTING THAT I'M PALE AND PASTY BECAUSE I DON'T GET ENOUGH SUN?
HMM...
THAT TENDENCY TO INTERPRET EVERYTHING IN THE MOST NEGATIVE WAY HAS BEEN A BAD HABIT OF YOURS SINCE YOU WERE LITTLE.
NOW, WHICH OF THESE CONTAINERS WOULD YOU LIKE FOR YOUR LIPSTICK?
THIS CAMEO IS THE PROFILE OF THE COUNTESS TAGUIL, A FASHIONISTA WHO HAS COME TO BE A HOUSEHOLD NAME IN THE ROYAL CAPITAL.
AND THIS ONE IS INLAID WITH MOTHER-OF-PEARL AND TOOK THE ARTISAN THREE YEARS TO COMPLETE.

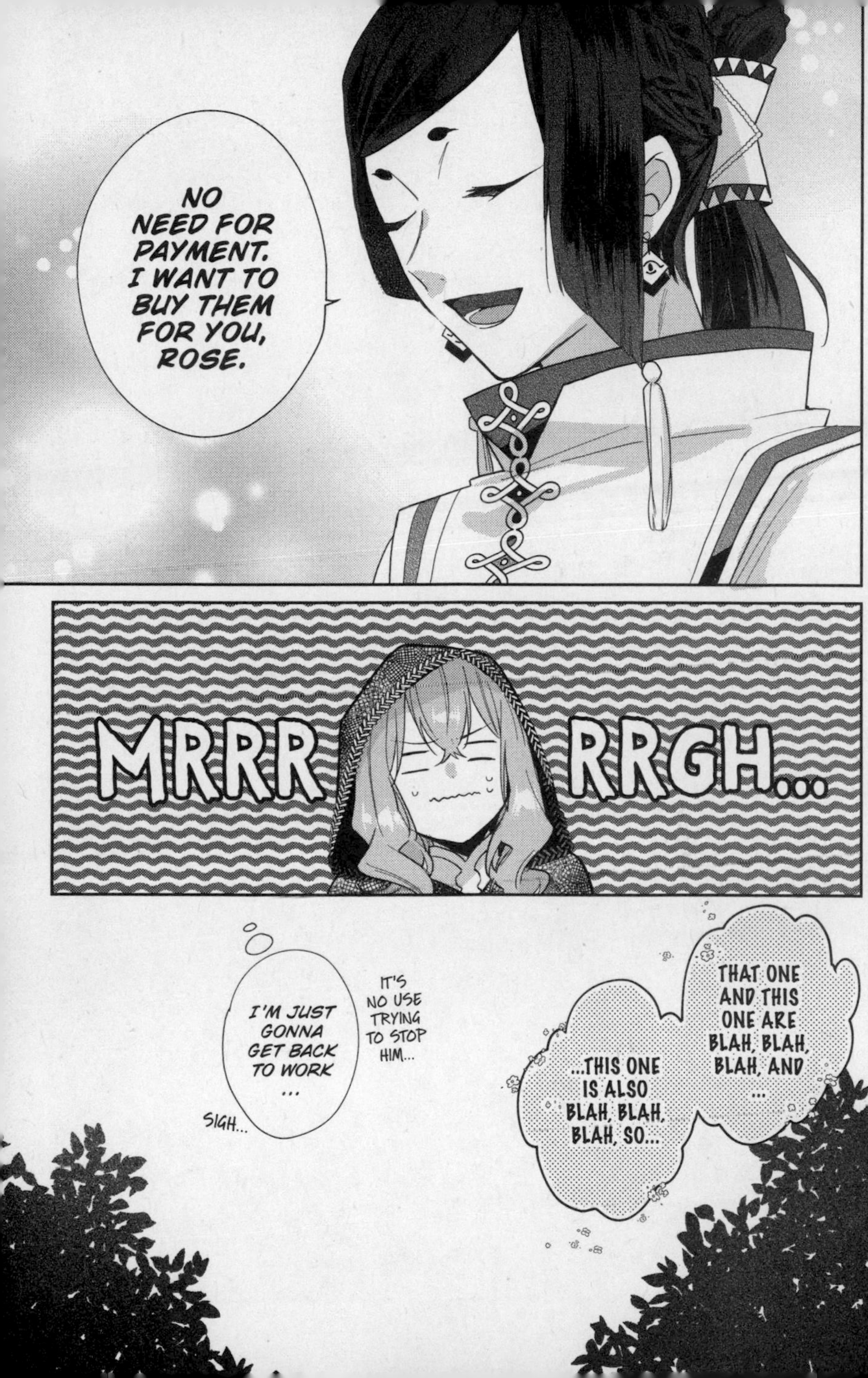
NO NEED FOR PAYMENT. I WANT TO BUY THEM FOR YOU, ROSE.
MRRR RRGH...
THAT ONE AND THIS ONE ARE BLAH, BLAH, BLAH, AND ...
...THIS ONE IS ALSO BLAH, BLAH, BLAH, SO...
IT'S NO USE TRYING TO STOP HIM...
I'M JUST GONNA GET BACK TO WORK ...
SIGH...

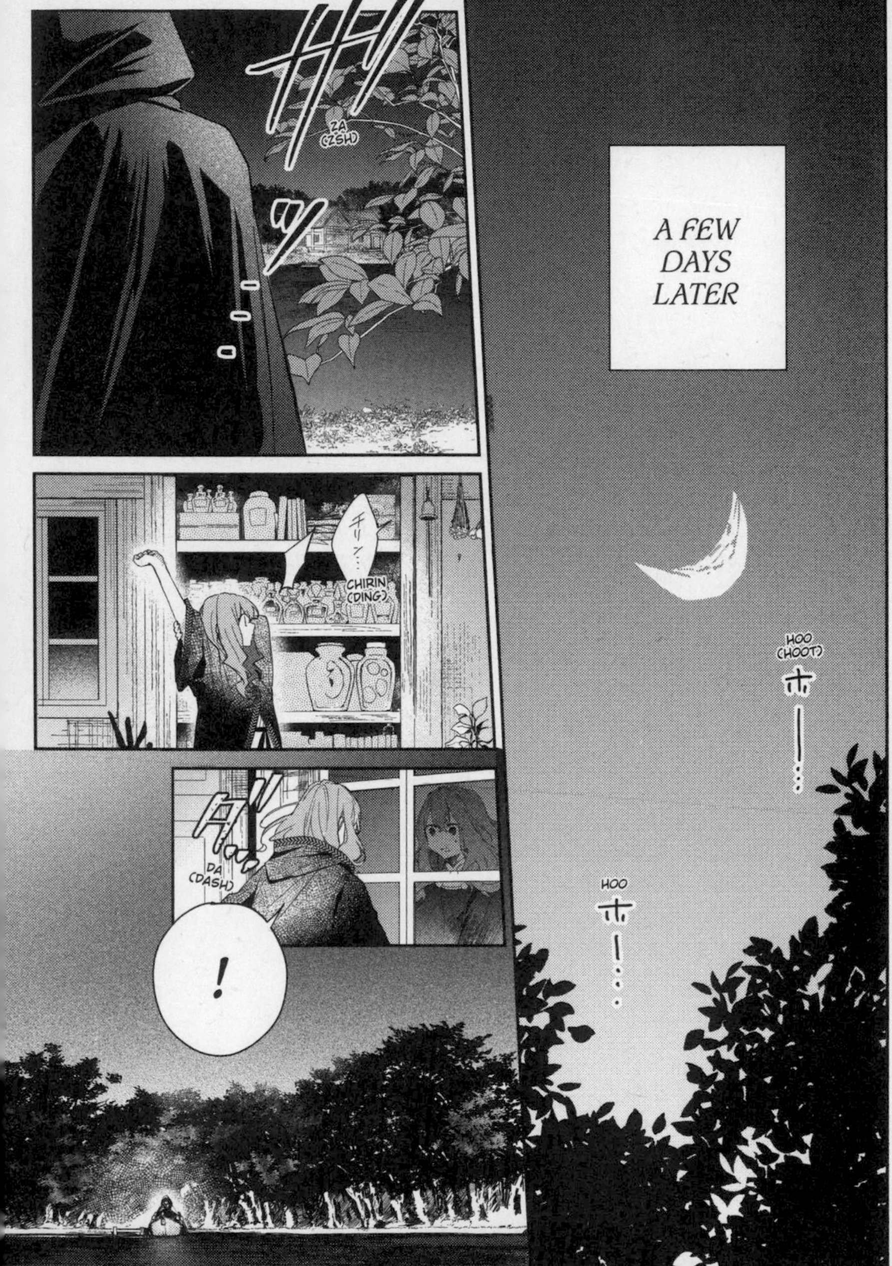
A FEW DAYS LATER
HOO (HOOT)
ホー…
HOO
ホー…
ZA (ZSH)
チリン…
CHIRIN (DING)
DA (DASH)
!

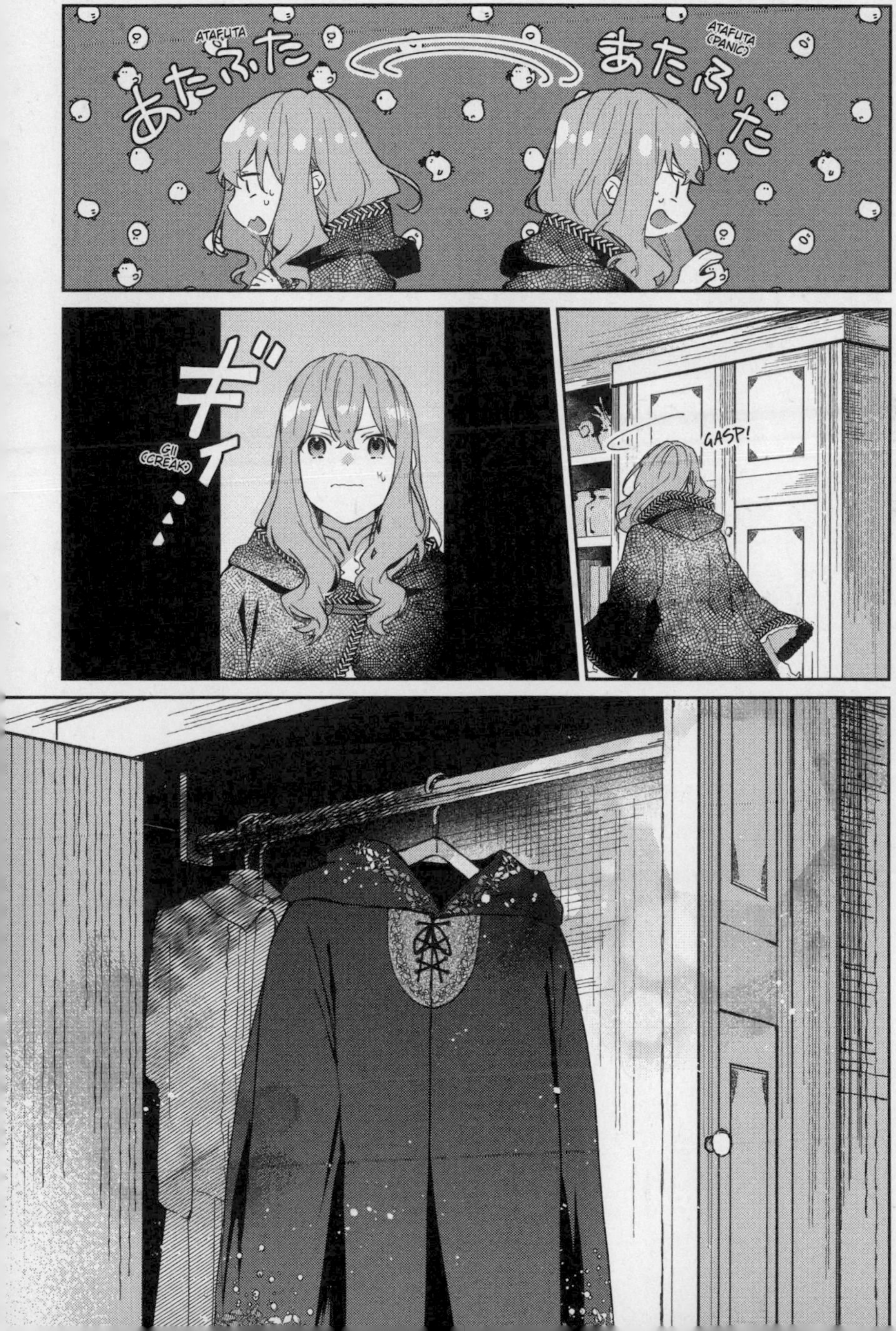
あたふた
ATAFUTA (PANIC)
あたふた
ATAFUTA
GASP!
ギイ…
GII (CREAK)

SAWA
(BRUSH)

ギュ
GYU
(SQUEEZE)

SIGH...

NOW THAT I THINK ABOUT IT, IF I SUDDENLY APPEARED IN A BRAND-NEW ROBE...

...IT WOULD BE LIKE TELLING HIM, "YES, I DID GET A NEW ROBE BECAUSE I KNEW YOU WERE COMING."

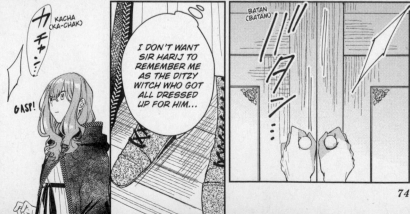

KACHA
(KA-CHAK)

GASP!

I DON'T WANT SIR HARIJ TO REMEMBER ME AS THE DITZY WITCH WHO GOT ALL DRESSED UP FOR HIM...

BATAN
(BATAM)

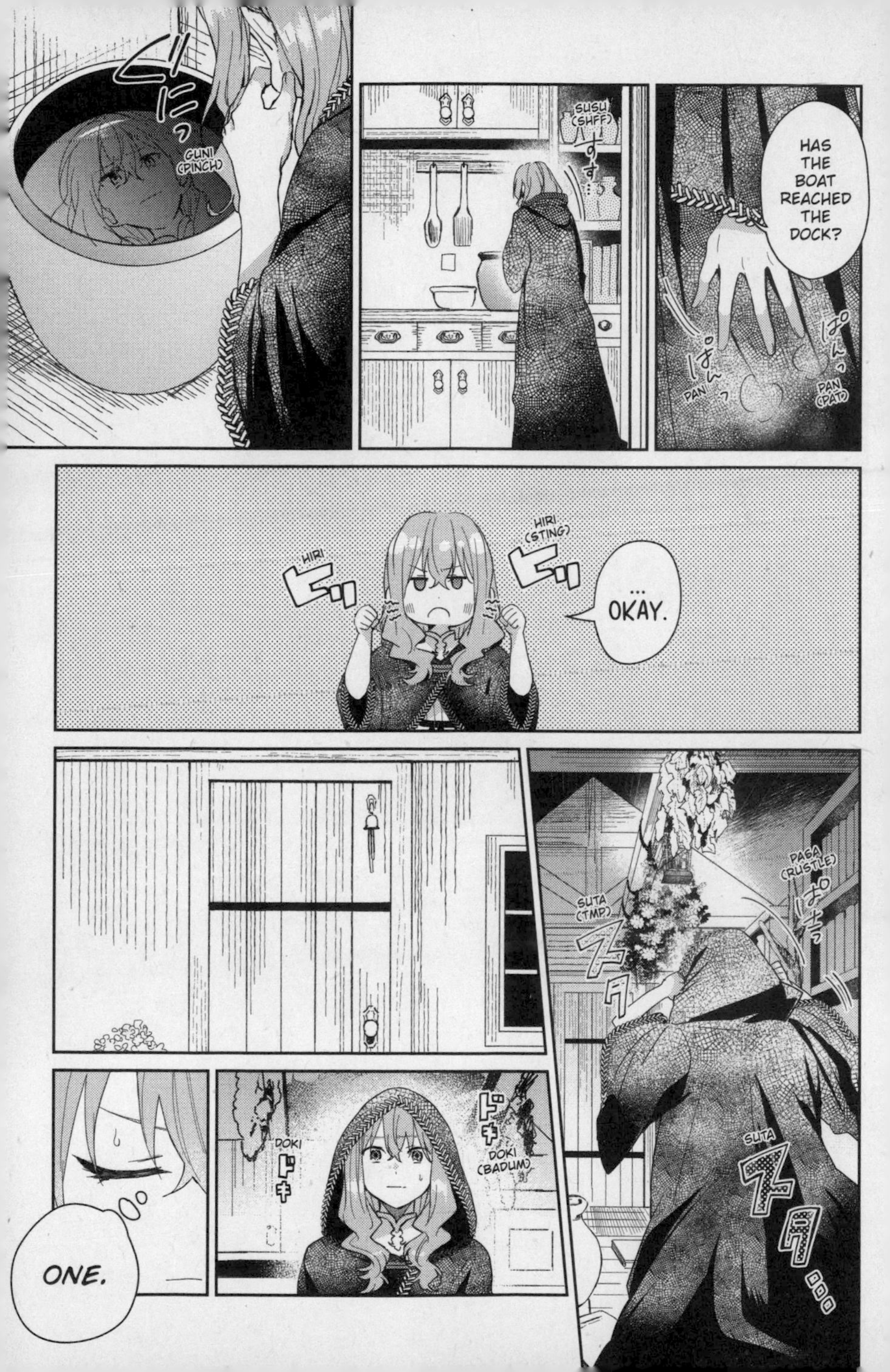
HAS THE BOAT REACHED THE DOCK?
PAN (PAT)
PAN
SUSU (SHFF)
すす
GUNI (PINCH)
... OKAY.
HIRI (STING)
HIRI
PAGA (RUSTLE)
SUTA (TMP)
SUTA
スタ...
DOKI (BADUM)
ドキ
DOKI
ドキ
ONE.

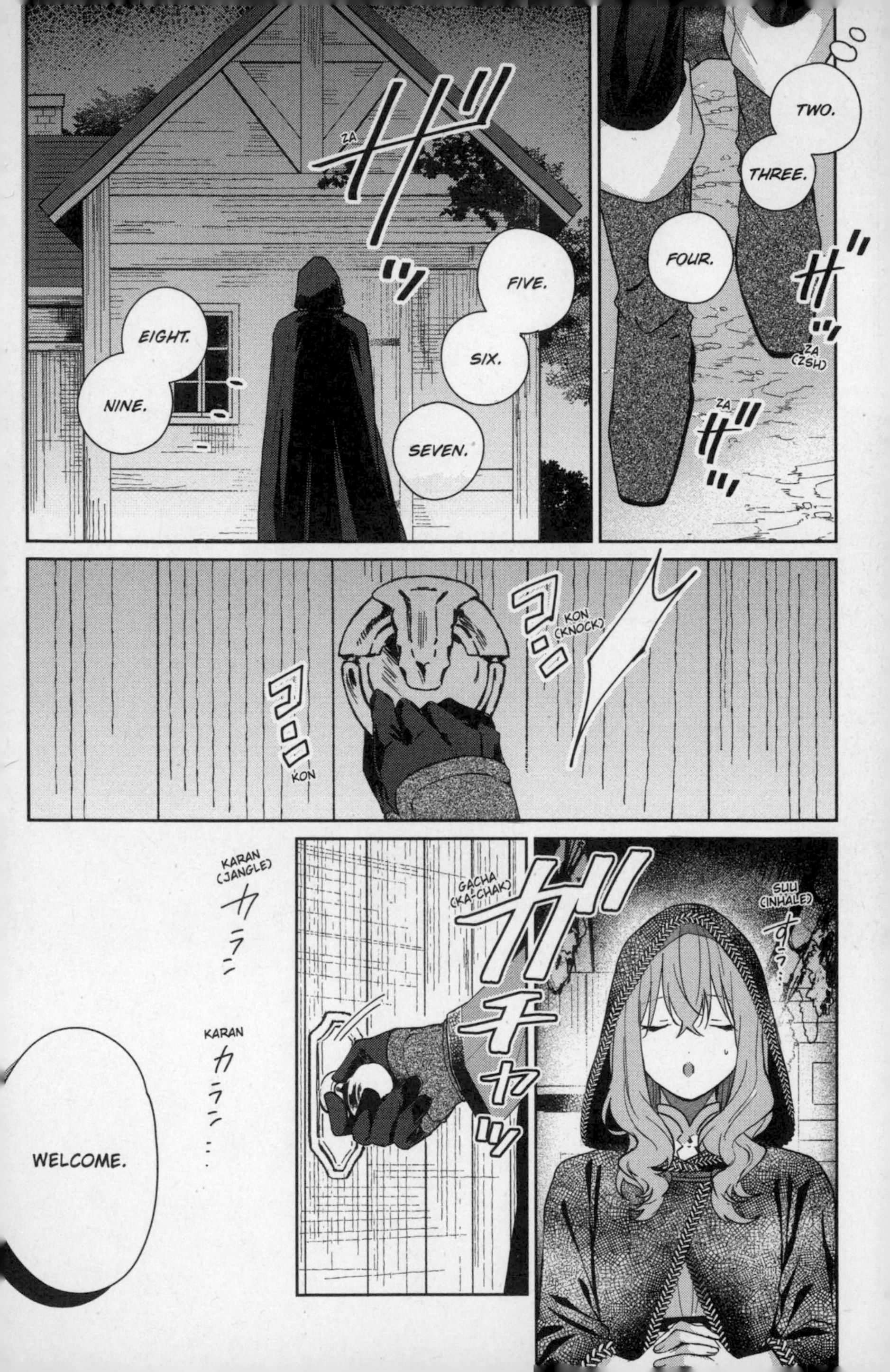
TWO.
THREE.
FOUR.
ZA (ZSH)
ZA
ZA
FIVE.
SIX.
SEVEN.
EIGHT.
NINE.
KON (KNOCK)
KON
SUU (INHALE)
GACHA (KA-CHAK)
KARAN (JANGLE)
KARAN
WELCOME.

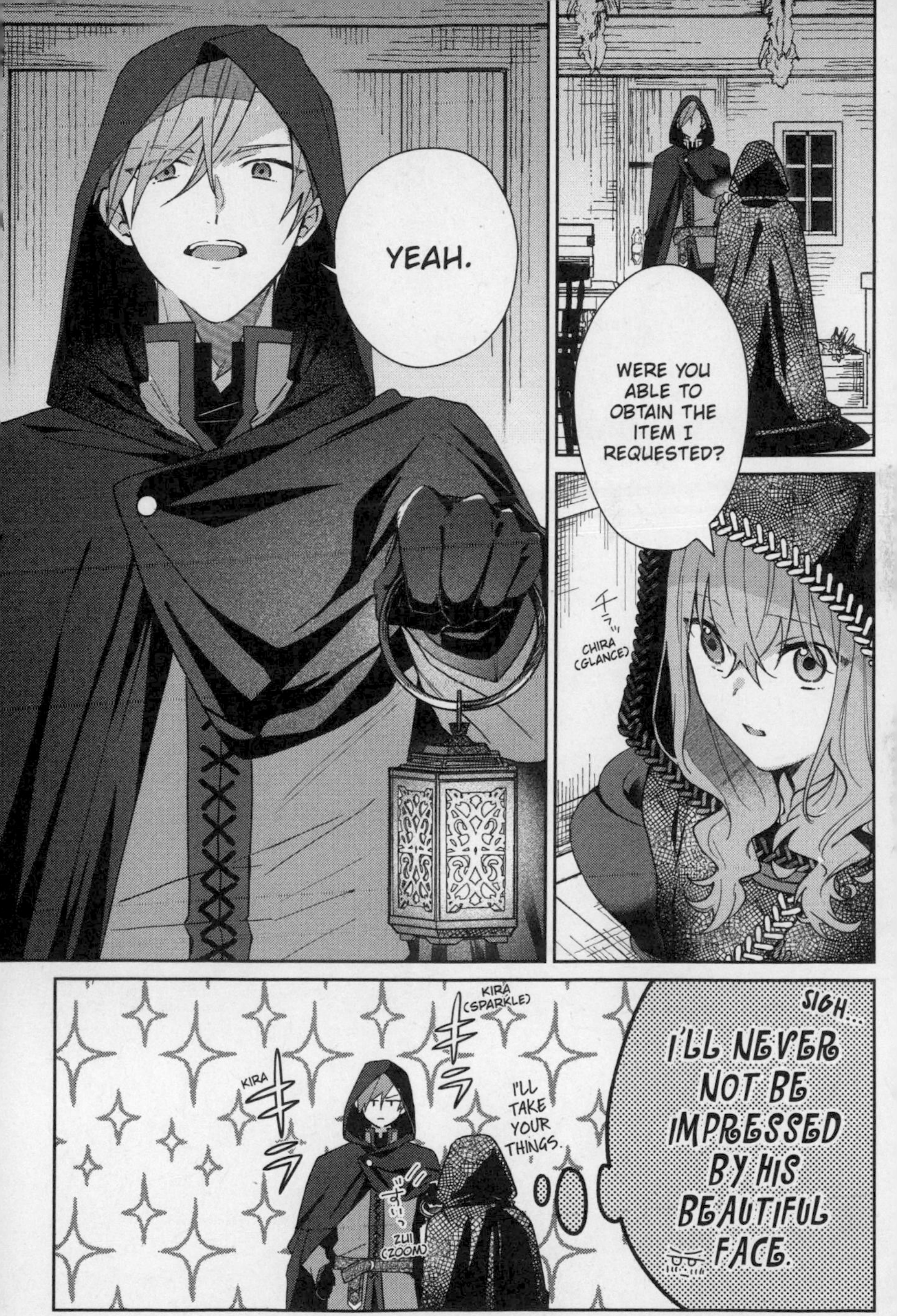
WERE YOU ABLE TO OBTAIN THE ITEM I REQUESTED?
CHIRA (GLANCE)
YEAH.
SIGH...
I'LL NEVER NOT BE IMPRESSED BY HIS BEAUTIFUL FACE.
I'LL TAKE YOUR THINGS.
KIRA (SPARKLE)
KIRA
ZUI (ZOOM)

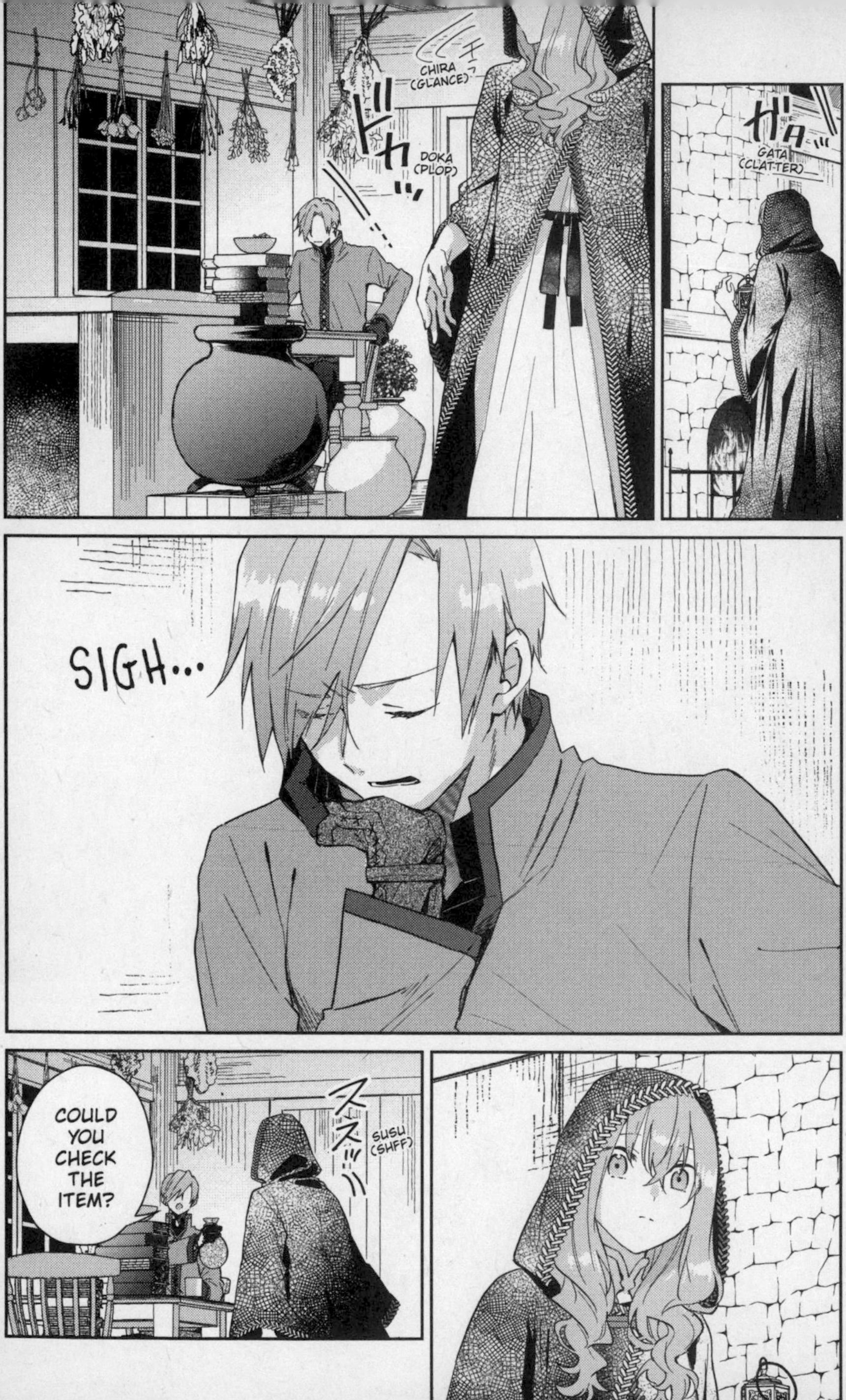
ガタッ
GATA (CLATTER)
CHIRA (GLANCE)
ドカッ
DOKA (PLOP)
SIGH...
SUSU (SHFF)
COULD YOU CHECK THE ITEM?

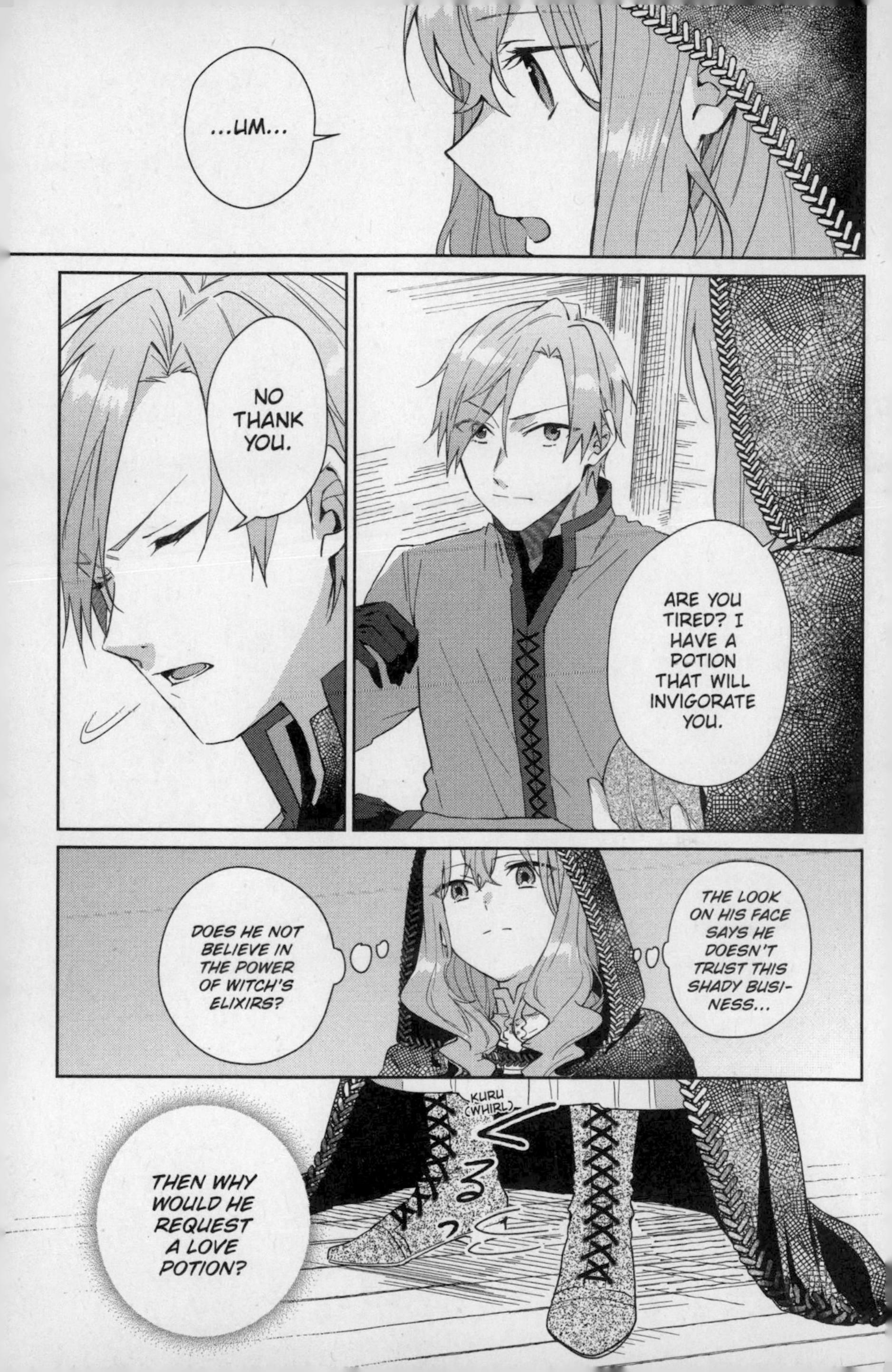
...UM...
ARE YOU TIRED? I HAVE A POTION THAT WILL INVIGORATE YOU.
NO THANK YOU.
THE LOOK ON HIS FACE SAYS HE DOESN'T TRUST THIS SHADY BUSINESS...
DOES HE NOT BELIEVE IN THE POWER OF WITCH'S ELIXIRS?
KURU (WHIRL)
THEN WHY WOULD HE REQUEST A LOVE POTION?

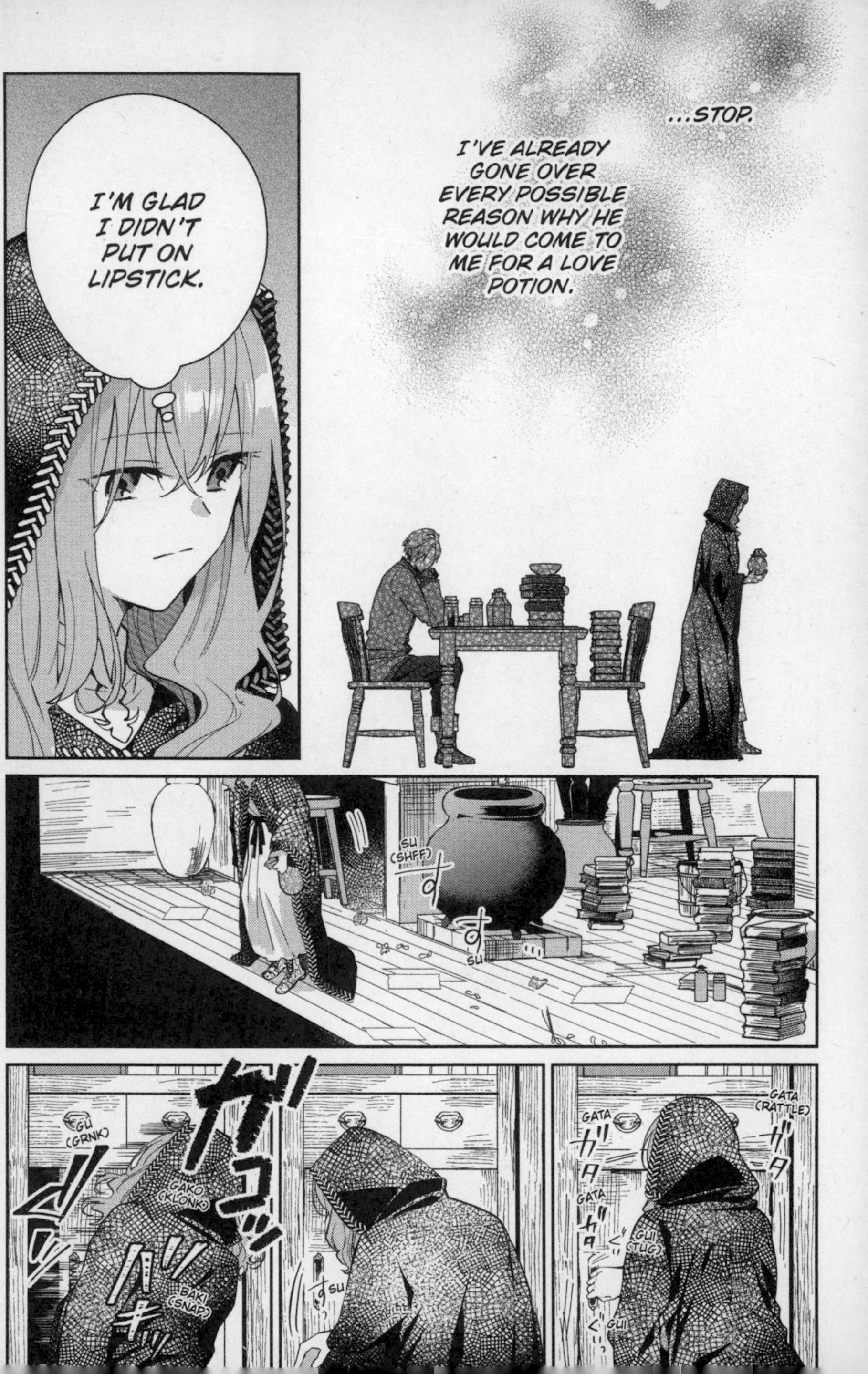
...STOP.
I'VE ALREADY GONE OVER EVERY POSSIBLE REASON WHY HE WOULD COME TO ME FOR A LOVE POTION.
I'M GLAD I DIDN'T PUT ON LIPSTICK.
SU (SHFF)
SU
GATA (RATTLE)
GATA
GATA
GUI (TUG)
GUI
SU
GU (GRNK)
GAKO (KLONK)
BAKI (SNAP)

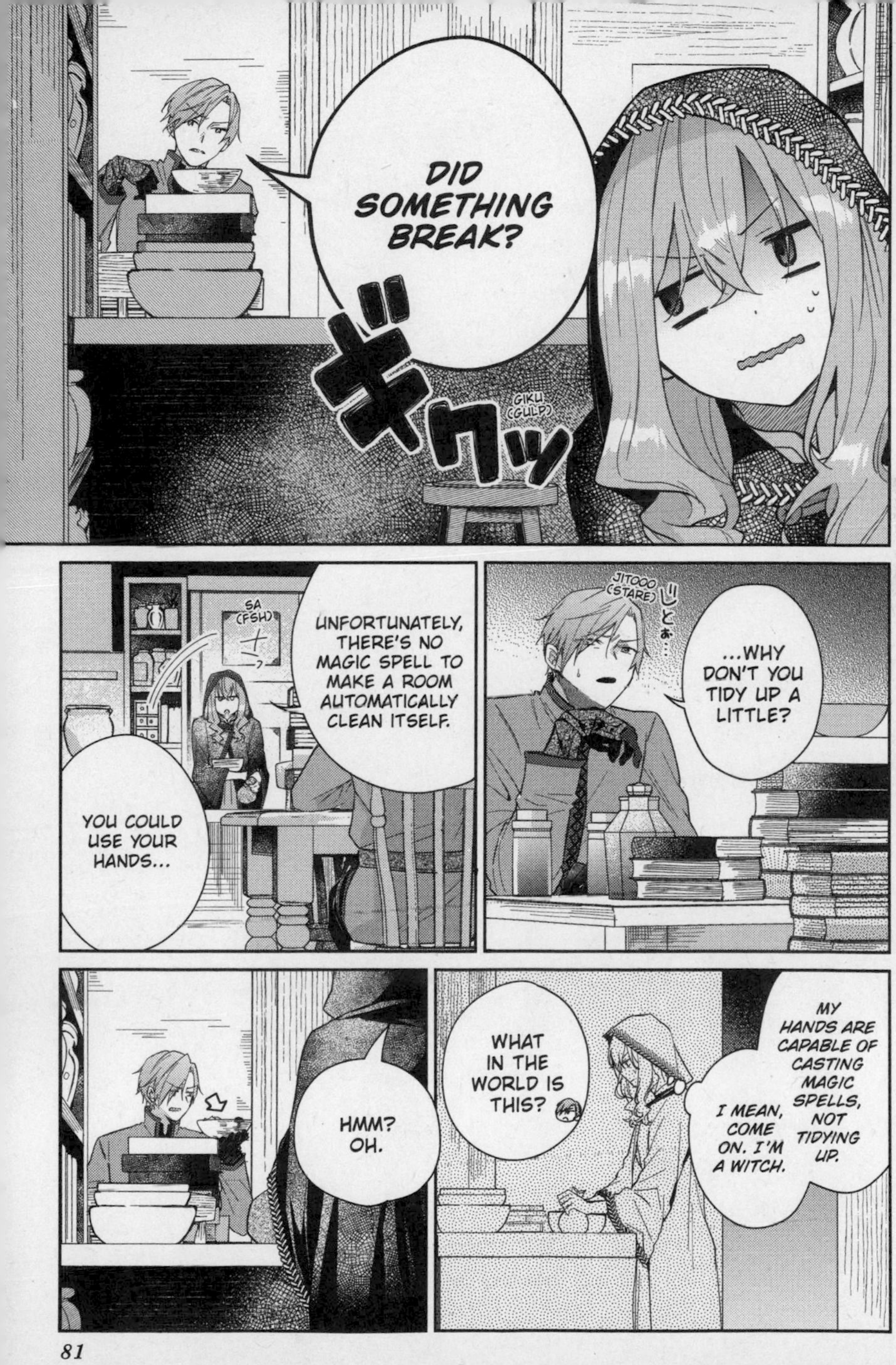
DID SOMETHING BREAK?
GIKU (GULP)
JITOOO (STARE)
...WHY DON'T YOU TIDY UP A LITTLE?
UNFORTUNATELY, THERE'S NO MAGIC SPELL TO MAKE A ROOM AUTOMATICALLY CLEAN ITSELF.
SA (FSH)
YOU COULD USE YOUR HANDS...
MY HANDS ARE CAPABLE OF CASTING MAGIC SPELLS, NOT TIDYING UP.
I MEAN, COME ON. I'M A WITCH.
WHAT IN THE WORLD IS THIS?
HMM? OH.

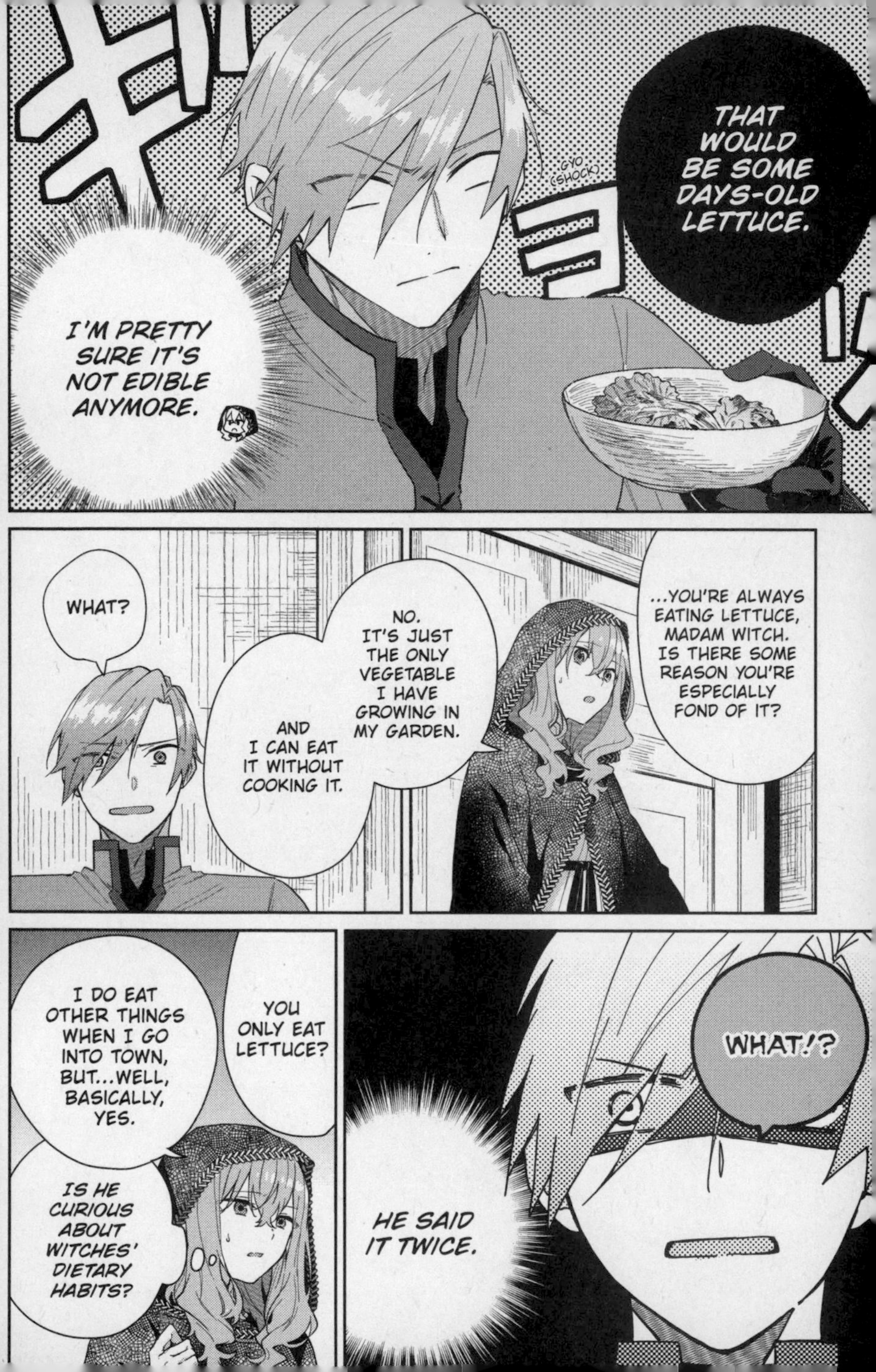
THAT WOULD BE SOME DAYS-OLD LETTUCE.
GYO (SHOCK)
I'M PRETTY SURE IT'S NOT EDIBLE ANYMORE.
...YOU'RE ALWAYS EATING LETTUCE, MADAM WITCH. IS THERE SOME REASON YOU'RE ESPECIALLY FOND OF IT?
NO. IT'S JUST THE ONLY VEGETABLE I HAVE GROWING IN MY GARDEN.
AND I CAN EAT IT WITHOUT COOKING IT.
WHAT?
WHAT!?
HE SAID IT TWICE.
YOU ONLY EAT LETTUCE?
I DO EAT OTHER THINGS WHEN I GO INTO TOWN, BUT...WELL, BASICALLY, YES.
IS HE CURIOUS ABOUT WITCHES' DIETARY HABITS?

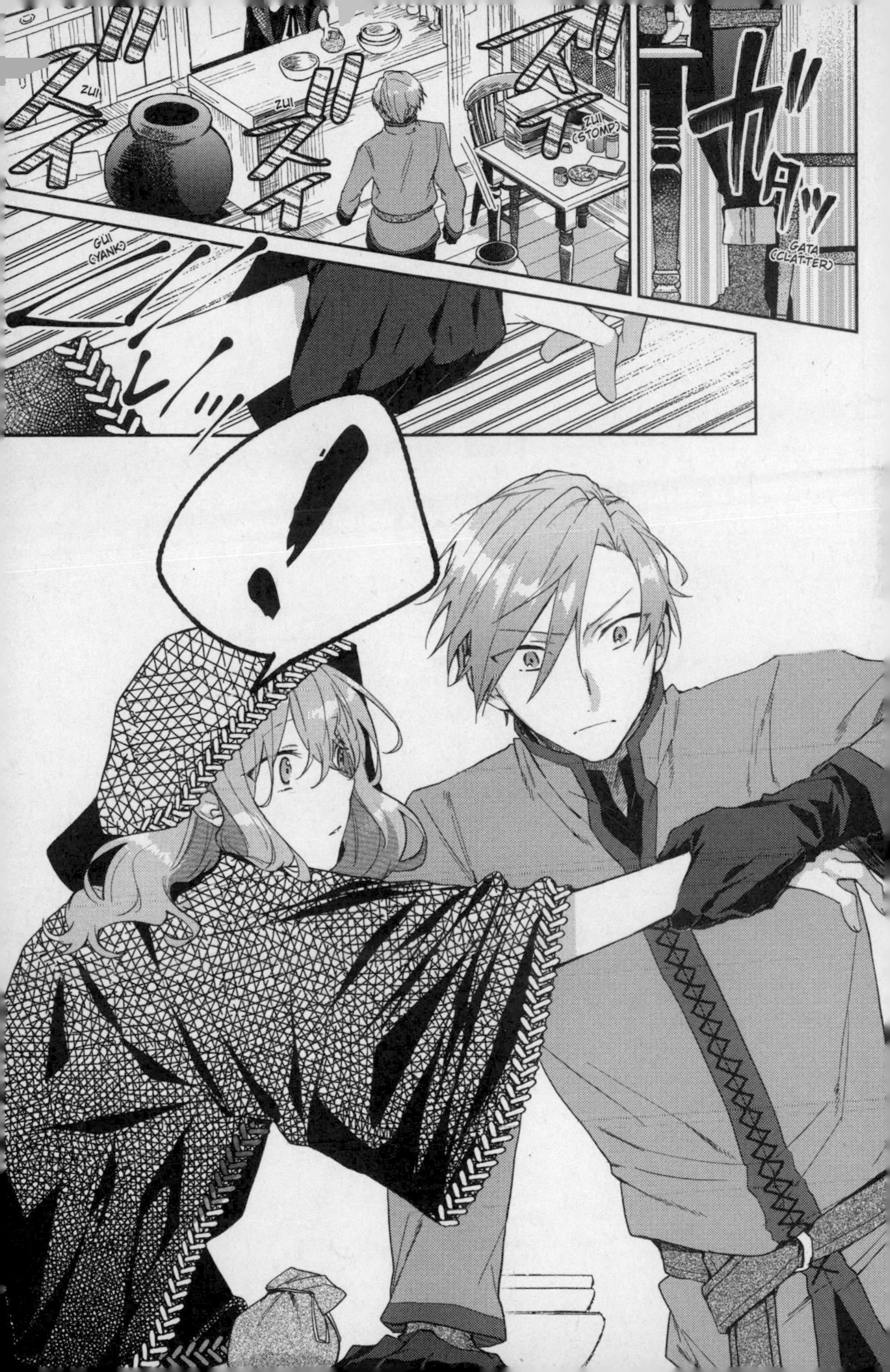
GATA
(CLATTER)
ZUI
(STOMP)
ZUI
ZUI
GUI
(YANK)
!

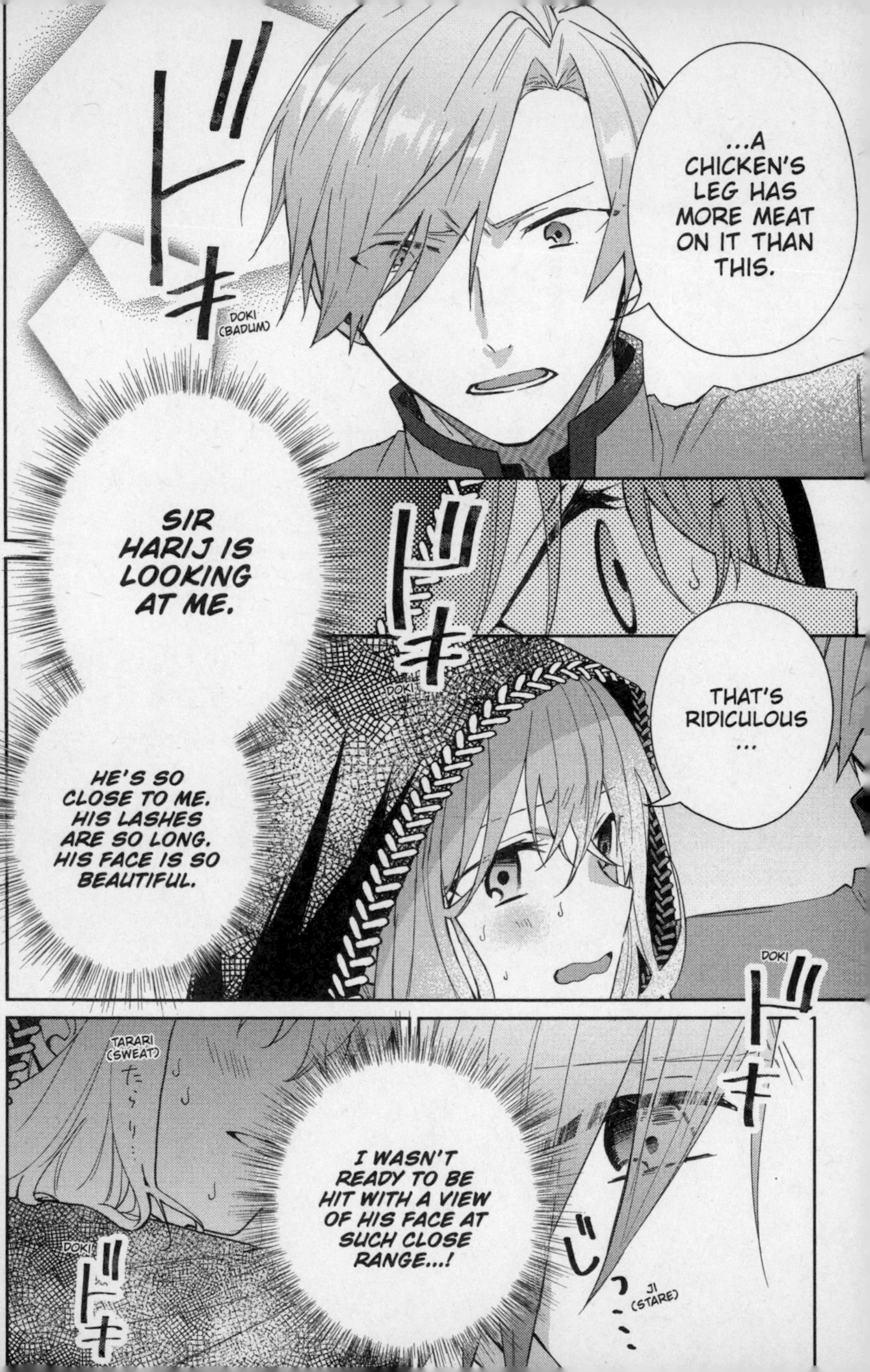
...A CHICKEN'S LEG HAS MORE MEAT ON IT THAN THIS.
DOKI (BADUM)
SIR HARIJ IS LOOKING AT ME.
THAT'S RIDICULOUS...
DOKI
HE'S SO CLOSE TO ME. HIS LASHES ARE SO LONG. HIS FACE IS SO BEAUTIFUL.
DOKI
JI (STARE)
I WASN'T READY TO BE HIT WITH A VIEW OF HIS FACE AT SUCH CLOSE RANGE...!
TARARI (SWEAT)
DOKI

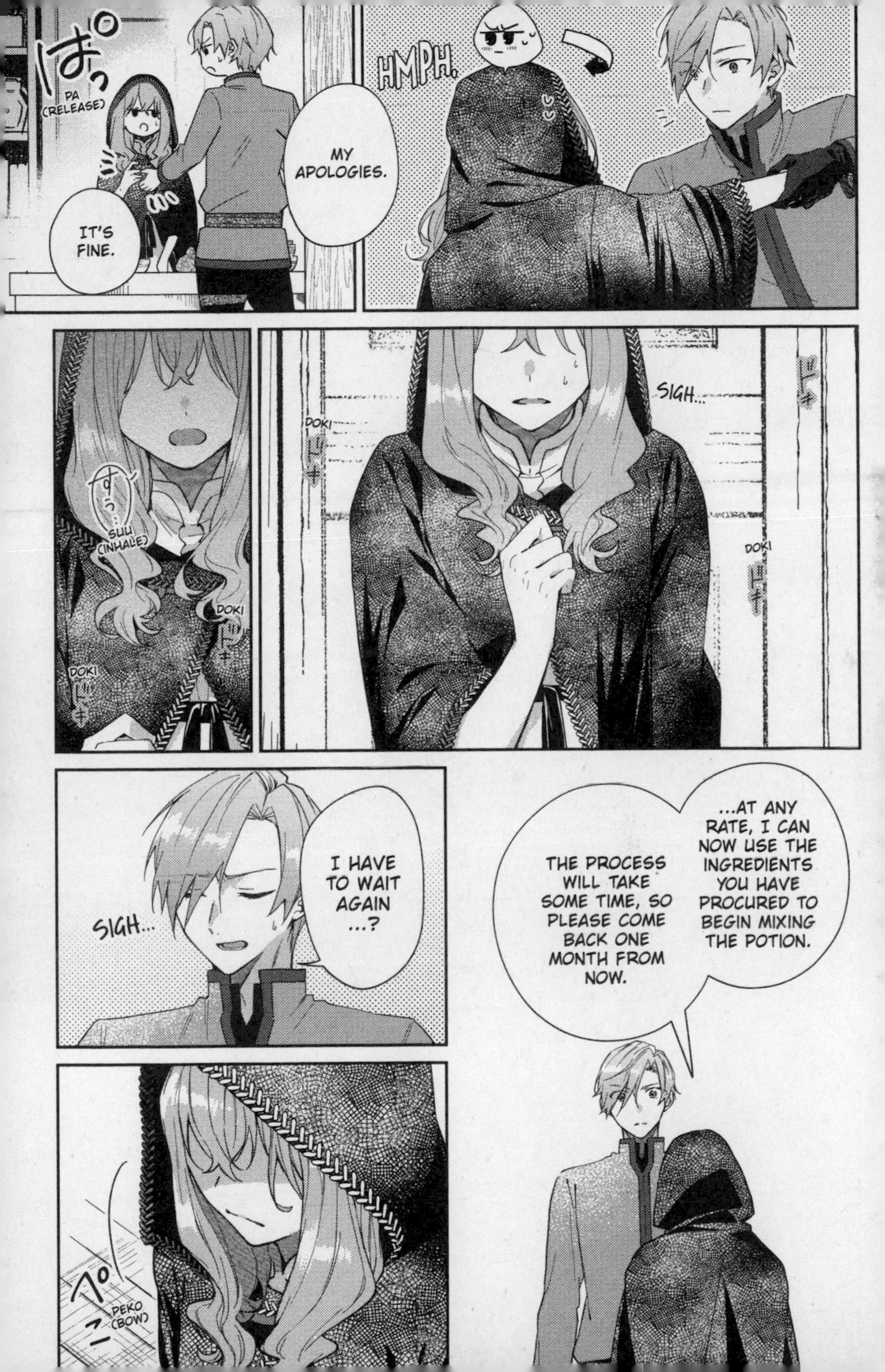
HMPH.
MY APOLOGIES.
ぱっ
PA (RELEASE)
IT'S FINE.
SIGH...
DOKI
DOKI
すぅ…
SUU (INHALE)
DOKI
DOKI
...AT ANY RATE, I CAN NOW USE THE INGREDIENTS YOU HAVE PROCURED TO BEGIN MIXING THE POTION.
THE PROCESS WILL TAKE SOME TIME, SO PLEASE COME BACK ONE MONTH FROM NOW.
I HAVE TO WAIT AGAIN ...?
SIGH...
ペこ
PEKO (BOW)

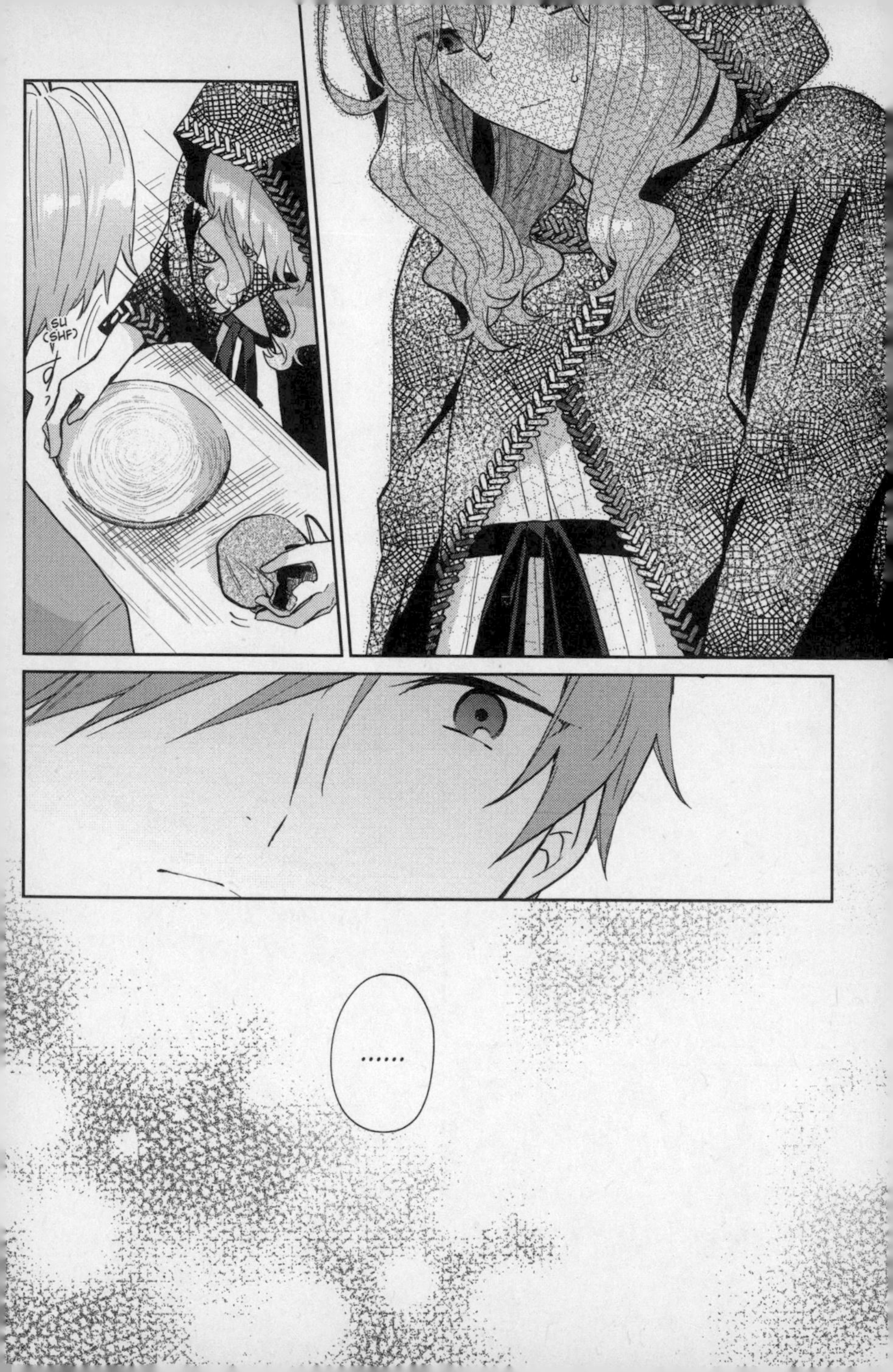
SU (SHF)
......

Hi, I'm a

Witch,
and My Crush
Wants Me to Make a
Love Potion

Hi, I'm a Witch, and My Crush Wants Me to Make a Love Potion

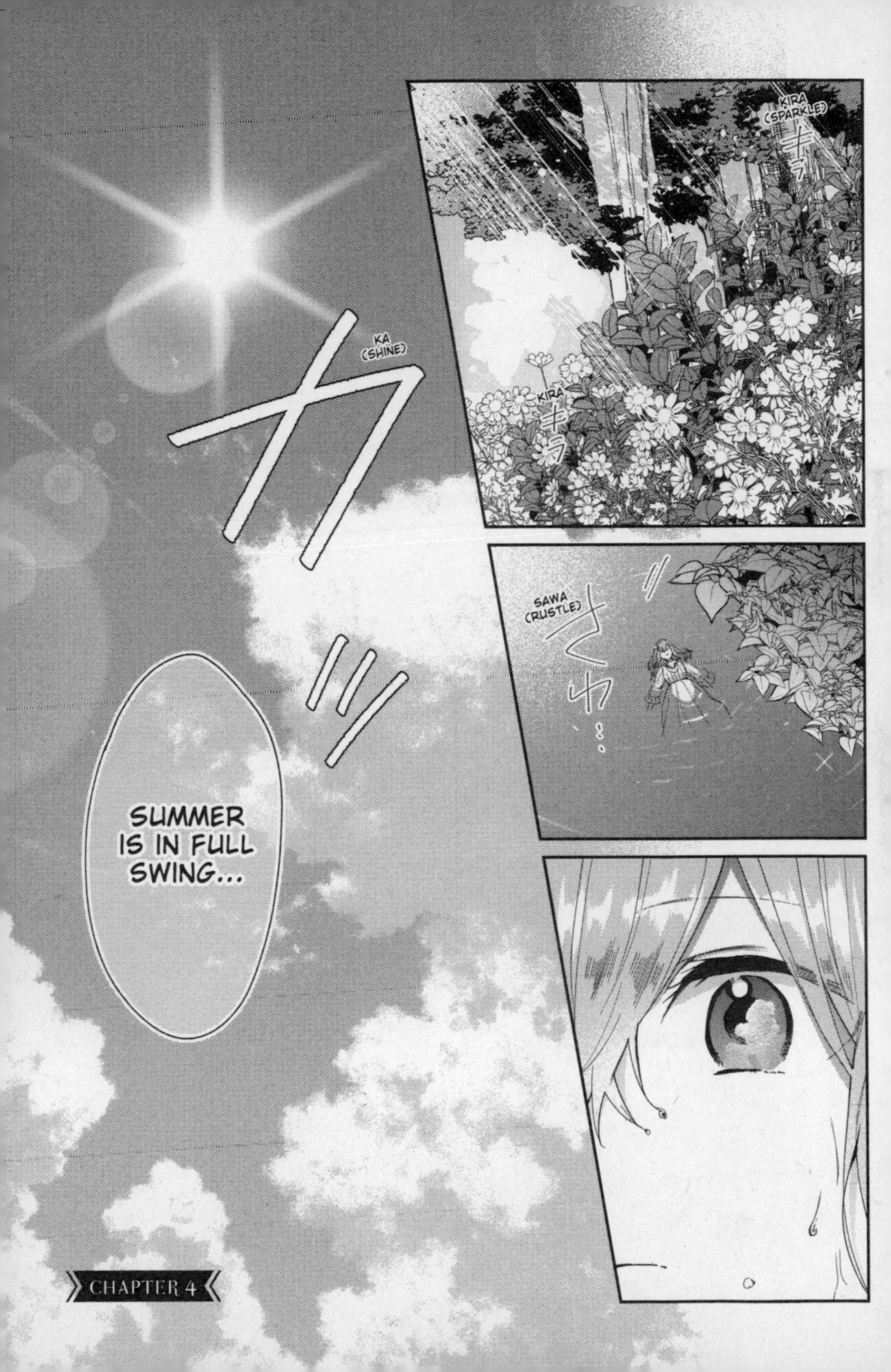
KIRA (SPARKLE)
キラ
KIRA
キラ
SAWA (RUSTLE)
さわ…
KA (SHINE)
カッ
SUMMER IS IN FULL SWING…
CHAPTER 4

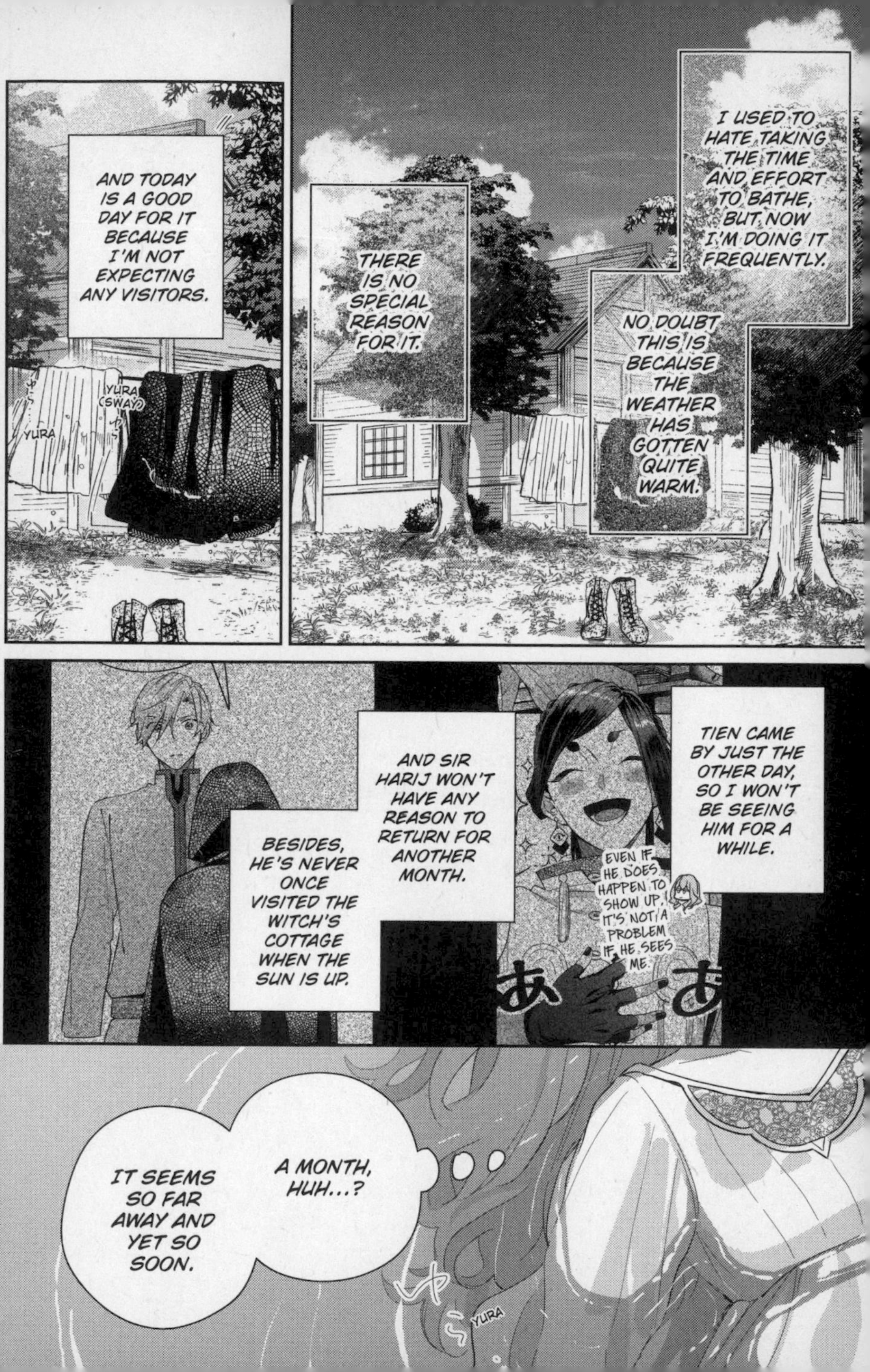

I USED TO HATE TAKING THE TIME AND EFFORT TO BATHE, BUT NOW I'M DOING IT FREQUENTLY.
NO DOUBT THIS IS BECAUSE THE WEATHER HAS GOTTEN QUITE WARM.
THERE IS NO SPECIAL REASON FOR IT.
AND TODAY IS A GOOD DAY FOR IT BECAUSE I'M NOT EXPECTING ANY VISITORS.
YURA (SWAY)
YURA
TIEN CAME BY JUST THE OTHER DAY, SO I WON'T BE SEEING HIM FOR A WHILE.
EVEN IF HE DOES HAPPEN TO SHOW UP, IT'S NOT A PROBLEM IF HE SEES ME.
AND SIR HARIJ WON'T HAVE ANY REASON TO RETURN FOR ANOTHER MONTH.
BESIDES, HE'S NEVER ONCE VISITED THE WITCH'S COTTAGE WHEN THE SUN IS UP.
A MONTH, HUH...?
IT SEEMS SO FAR AWAY AND YET SO SOON.
YURA

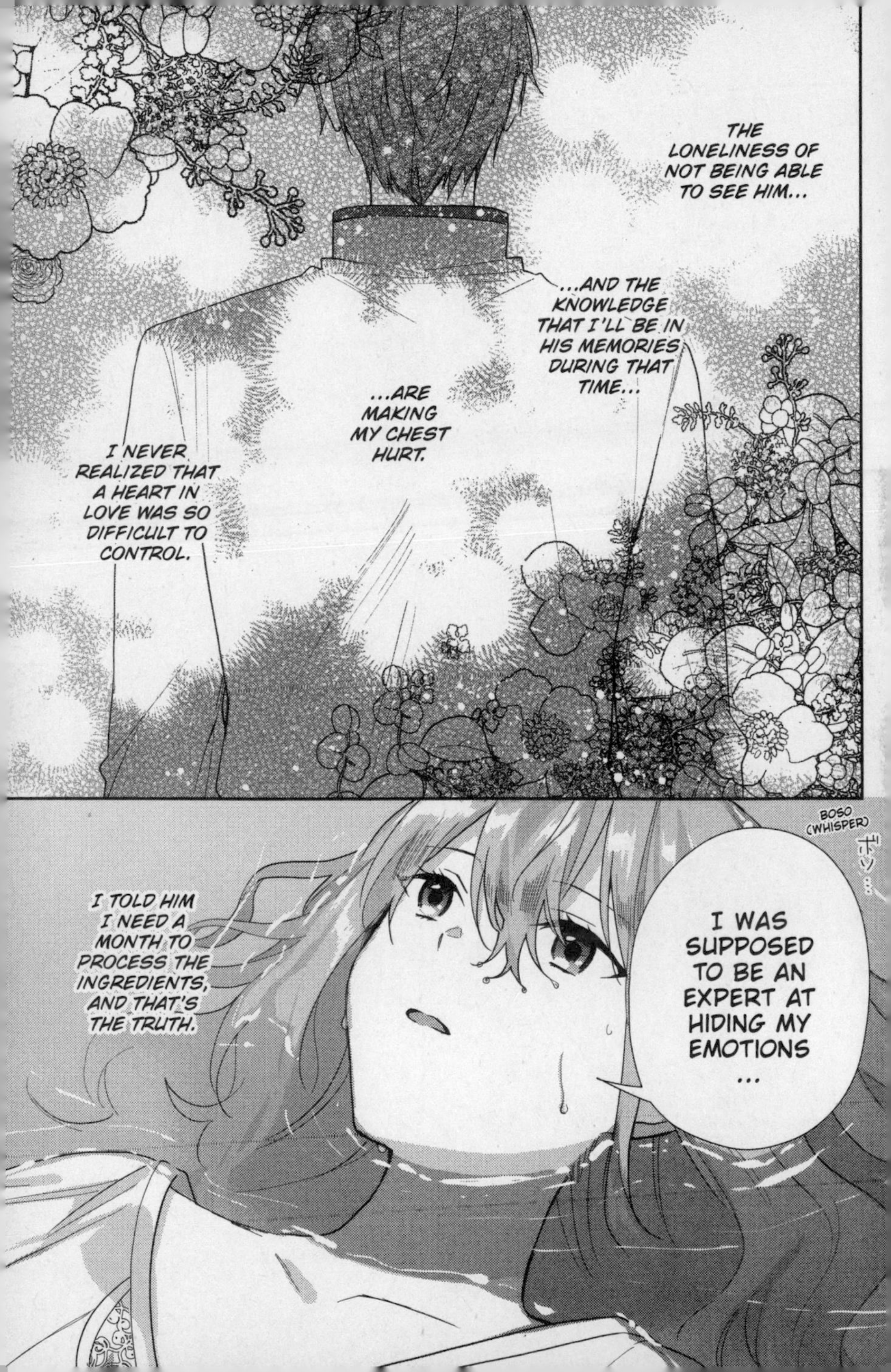
THE LONELINESS OF NOT BEING ABLE TO SEE HIM...
...AND THE KNOWLEDGE THAT I'LL BE IN HIS MEMORIES DURING THAT TIME...
...ARE MAKING MY CHEST HURT.
I NEVER REALIZED THAT A HEART IN LOVE WAS SO DIFFICULT TO CONTROL.
BOSO (WHISPER)
ボソ...
I WAS SUPPOSED TO BE AN EXPERT AT HIDING MY EMOTIONS ...
I TOLD HIM I NEED A MONTH TO PROCESS THE INGREDIENTS, AND THAT'S THE TRUTH.

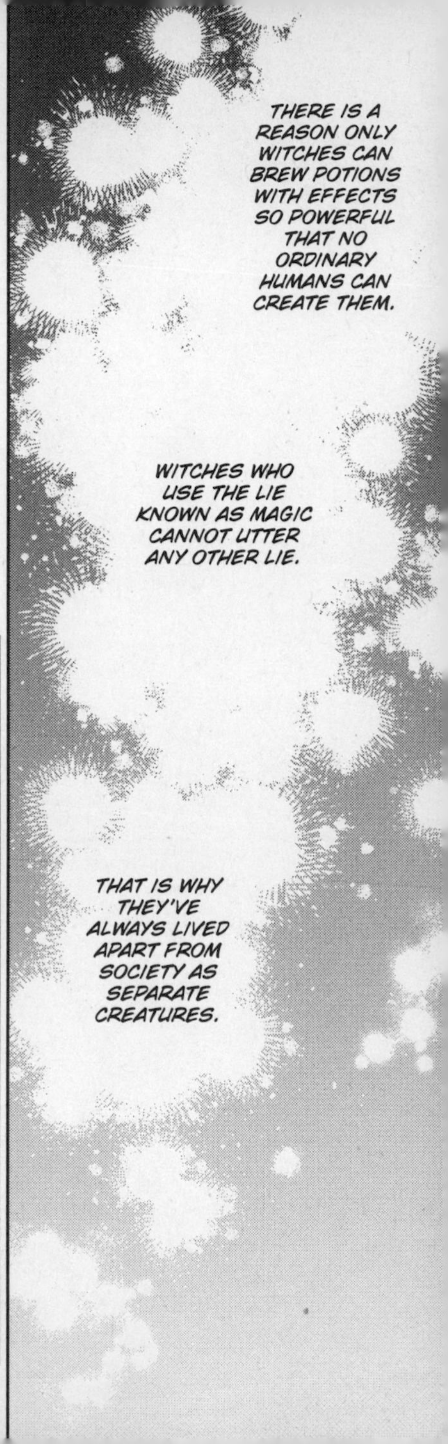
THERE IS A REASON ONLY WITCHES CAN BREW POTIONS WITH EFFECTS SO POWERFUL THAT NO ORDINARY HUMANS CAN CREATE THEM.
WITCHES WHO USE THE LIE KNOWN AS MAGIC CANNOT UTTER ANY OTHER LIE.
THAT IS WHY THEY'VE ALWAYS LIVED APART FROM SOCIETY AS SEPARATE CREATURES.

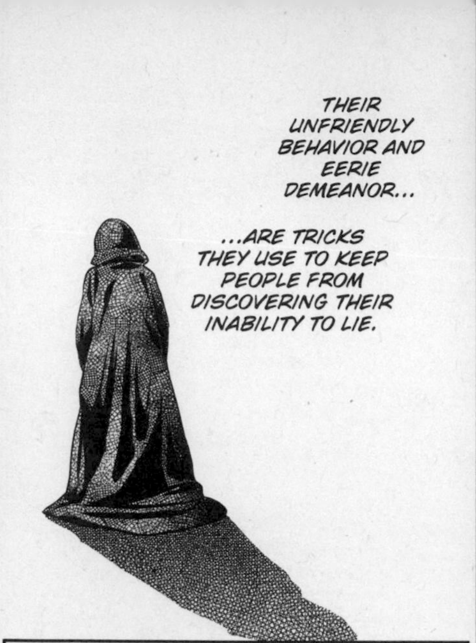
THEIR UNFRIENDLY BEHAVIOR AND EERIE DEMEANOR...
...ARE TRICKS THEY USE TO KEEP PEOPLE FROM DISCOVERING THEIR INABILITY TO LIE.

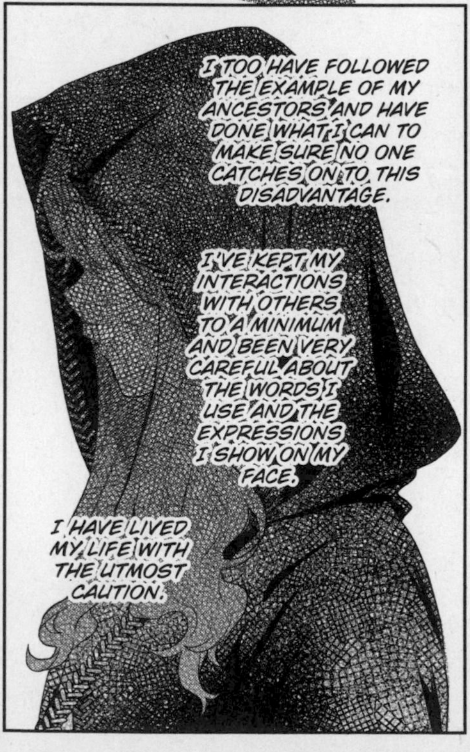
I TOO HAVE FOLLOWED THE EXAMPLE OF MY ANCESTORS AND HAVE DONE WHAT I CAN TO MAKE SURE NO ONE CATCHES ON TO THIS DISADVANTAGE.
I'VE KEPT MY INTERACTIONS WITH OTHERS TO A MINIMUM AND BEEN VERY CAREFUL ABOUT THE WORDS I USE AND THE EXPRESSIONS I SHOW ON MY FACE.
I HAVE LIVED MY LIFE WITH THE UTMOST CAUTION.

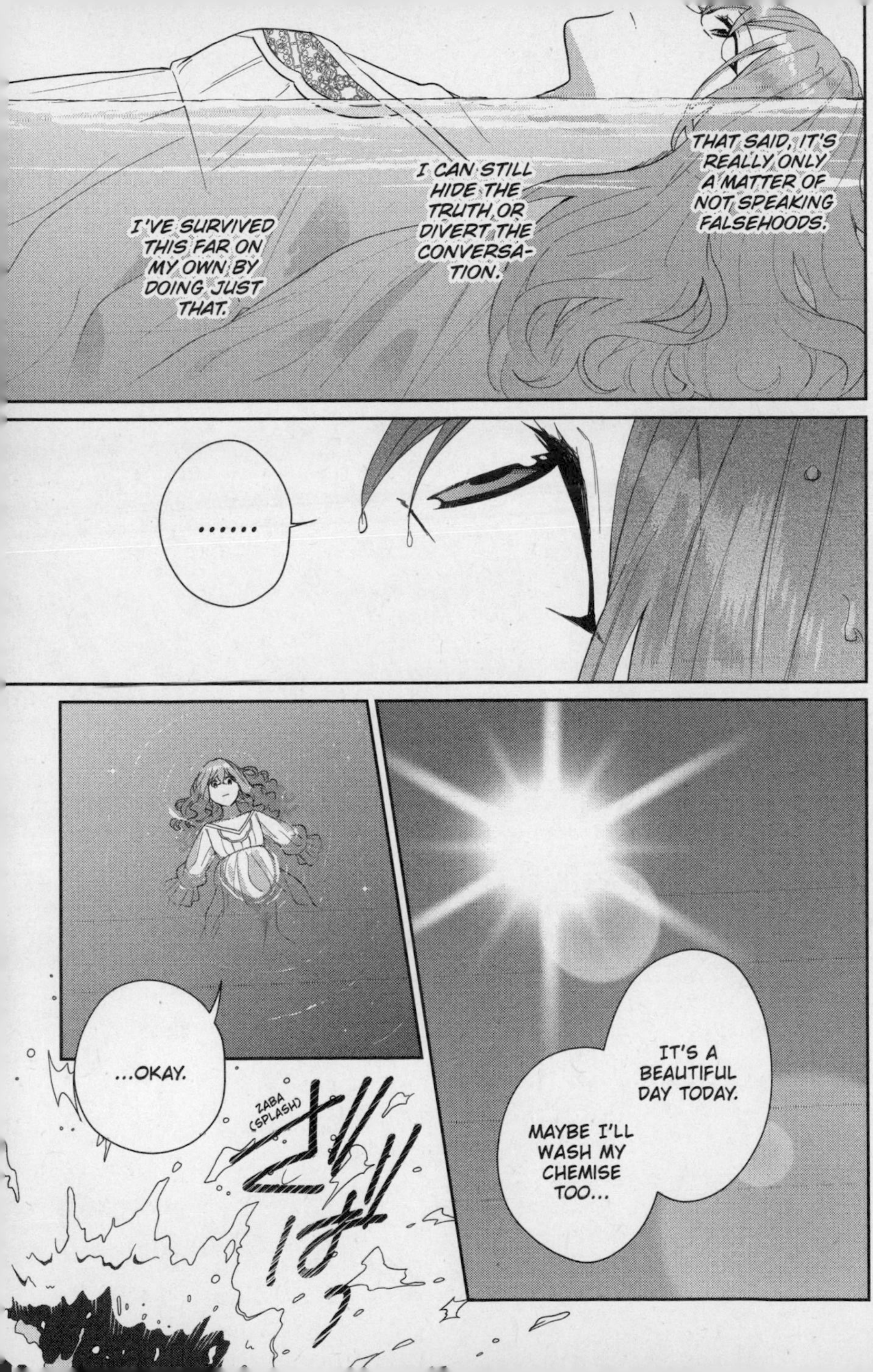
THAT SAID, IT'S REALLY ONLY A MATTER OF NOT SPEAKING FALSEHOODS.
I CAN STILL HIDE THE TRUTH OR DIVERT THE CONVERSA-TION.
I'VE SURVIVED THIS FAR ON MY OWN BY DOING JUST THAT.
......
IT'S A BEAUTIFUL DAY TODAY.
MAYBE I'LL WASH MY CHEMISE TOO...
...OKAY.
ZABA (SPLASH)
ざばっ

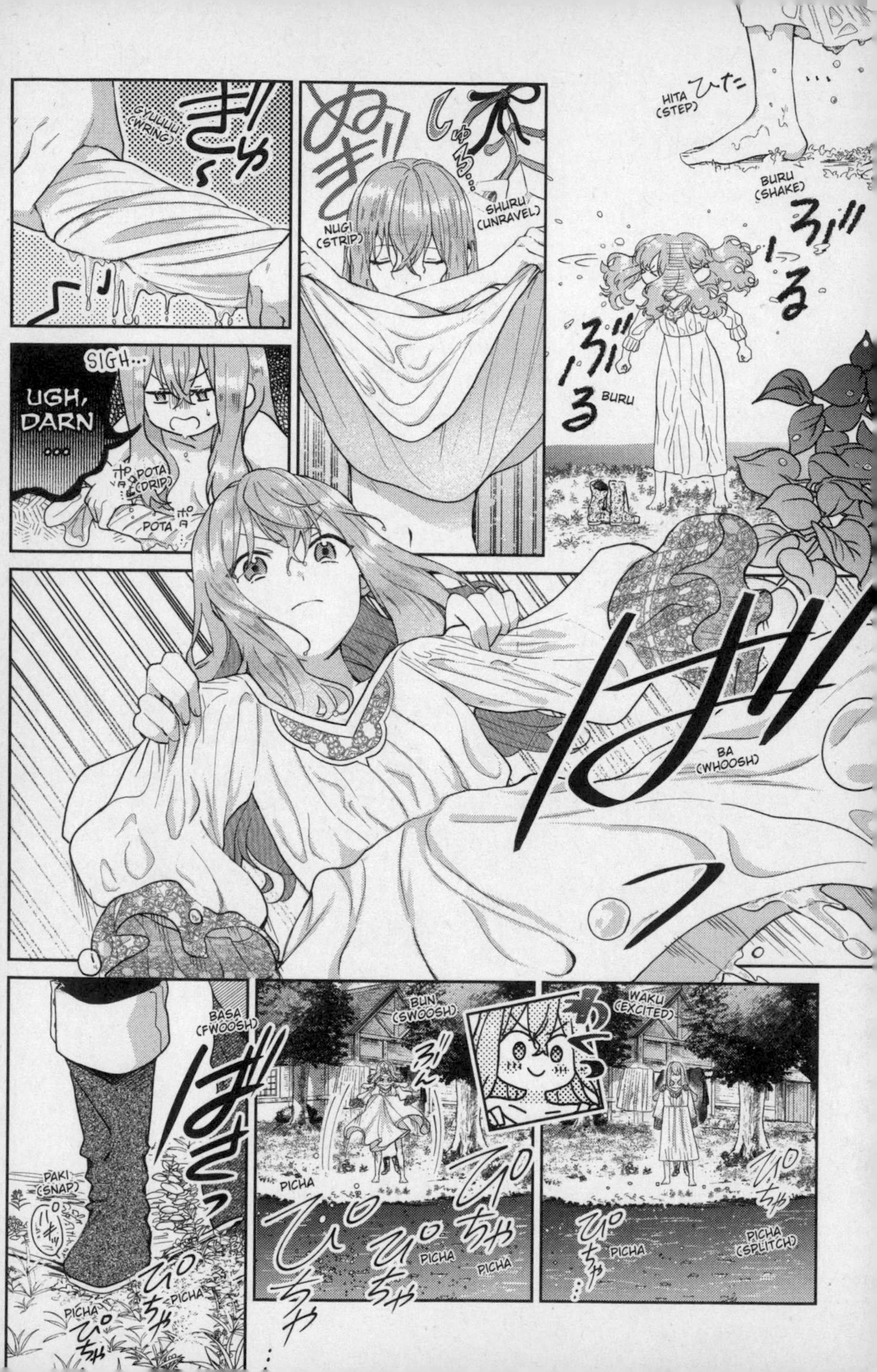

HITA ひた
(STEP)
BURU
(SHAKE)
BURU
NUGI
(STRIP)
SHURU
(UNRAVEL)
GYUUUU
(WRING)
SIGH...
UGH, DARN...
POTA
(DRIP)
POTA
BA
(WHOOSH)
WAKU
(EXCITED)
PICHA
PICHA
(SPLITCH)
BUN
(SWOOSH)
PICHA
PICHA
PICHA
BASA
(FWOOSH)
PAKI
(SNAP)
PICHA
PICHA

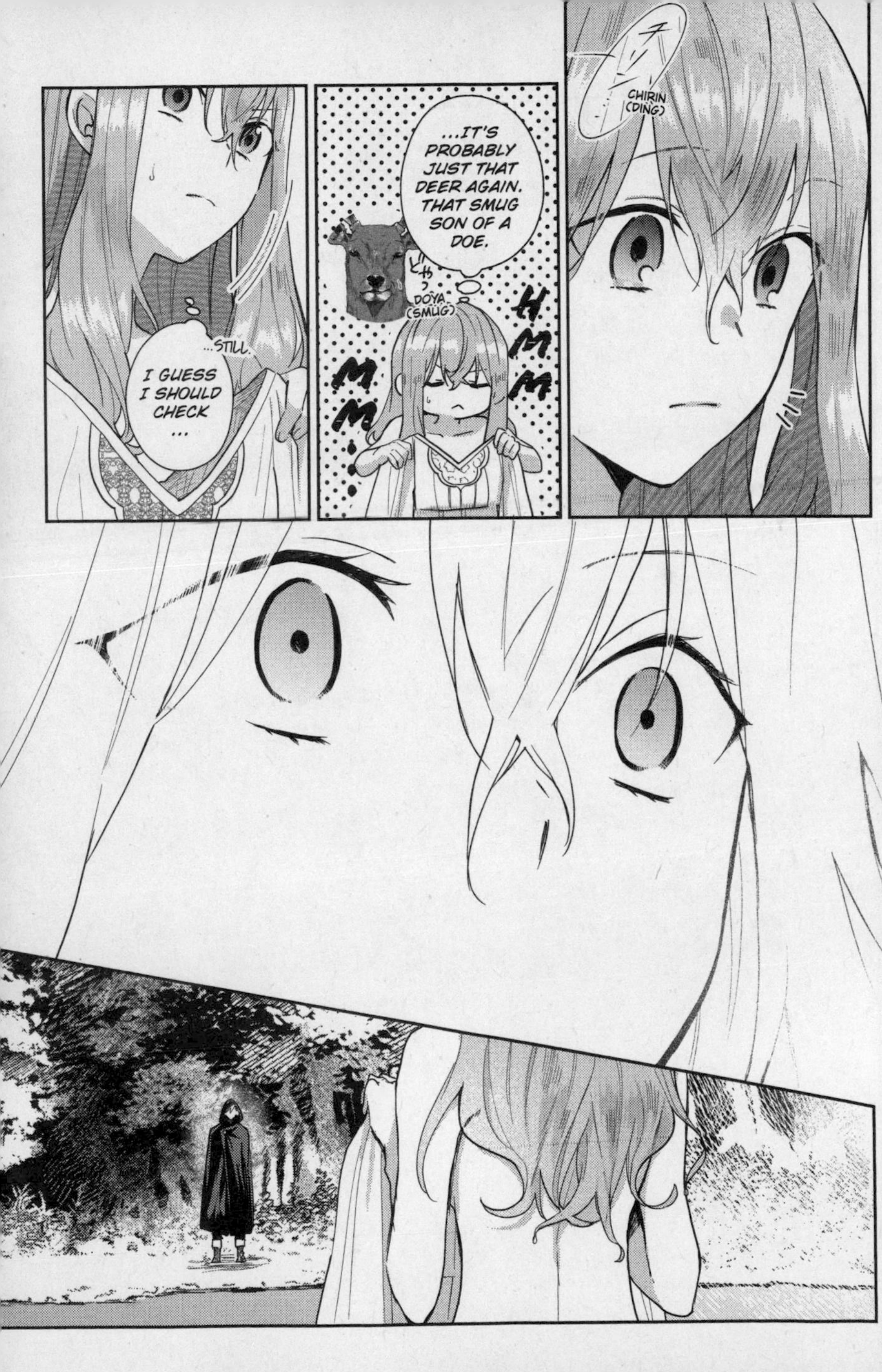
CHIRIN (DING)
...IT'S PROBABLY JUST THAT DEER AGAIN. THAT SMUG SON OF A DOE.
DOYA (SMUG)
HMMM...
...STILL.
I GUESS I SHOULD CHECK...

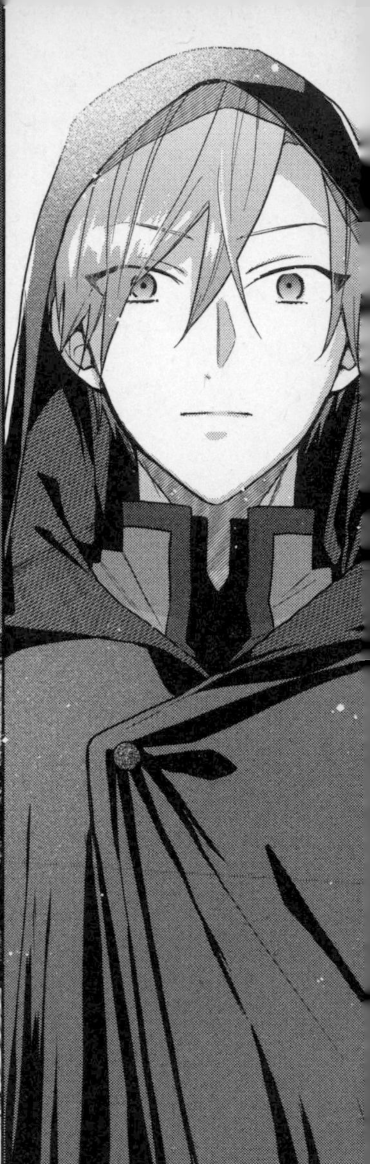
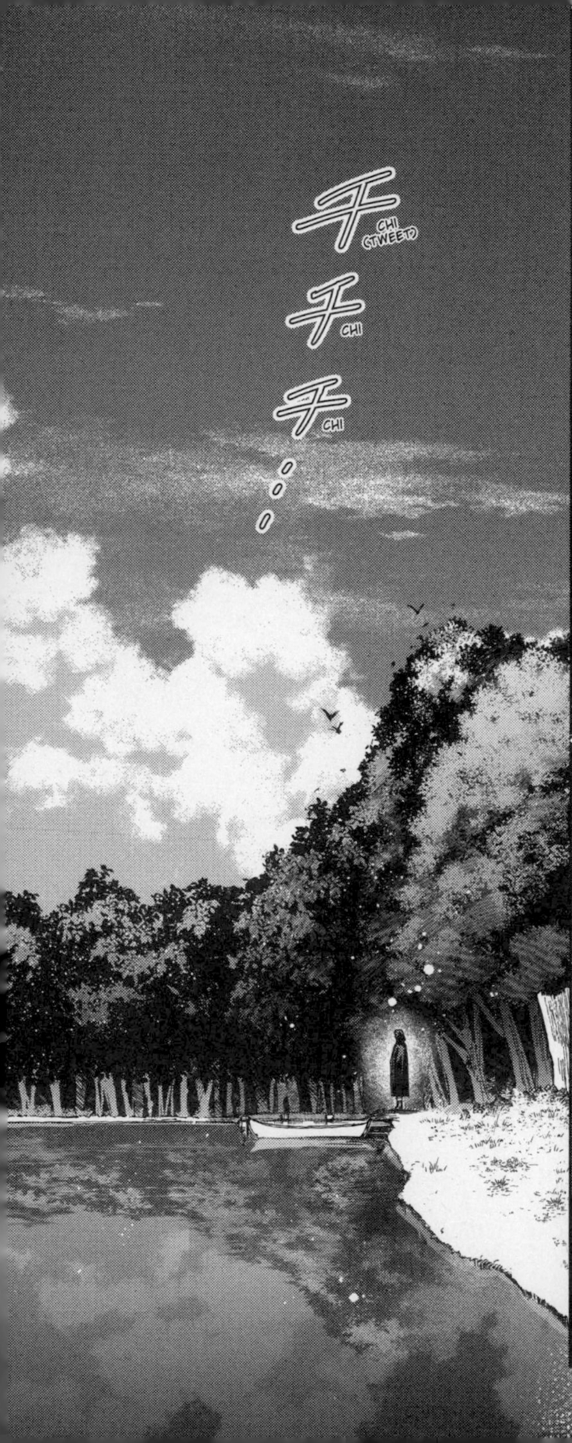
チ
CHI (TWEET)
チ
CHI
チ
CHI
...

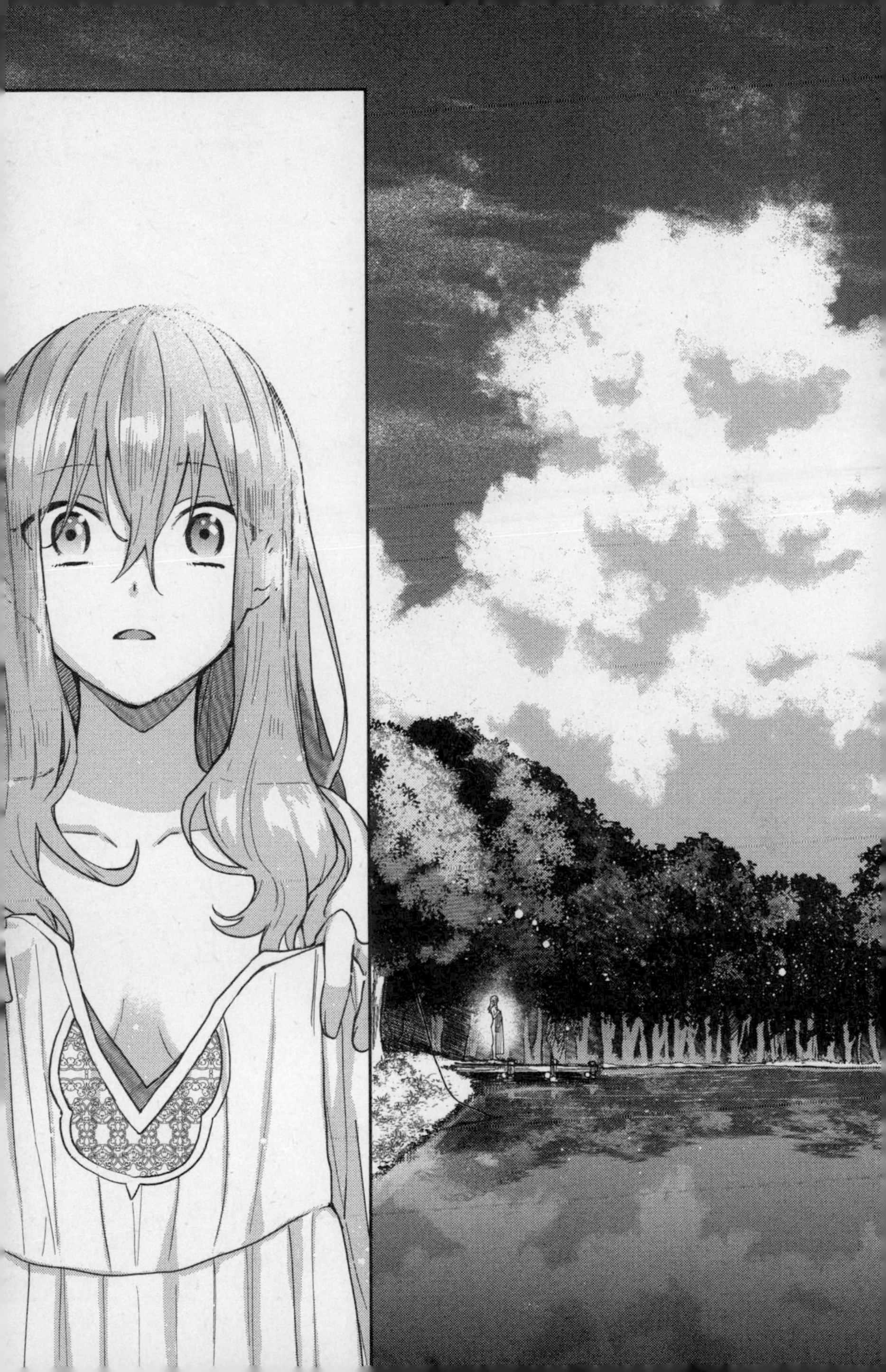

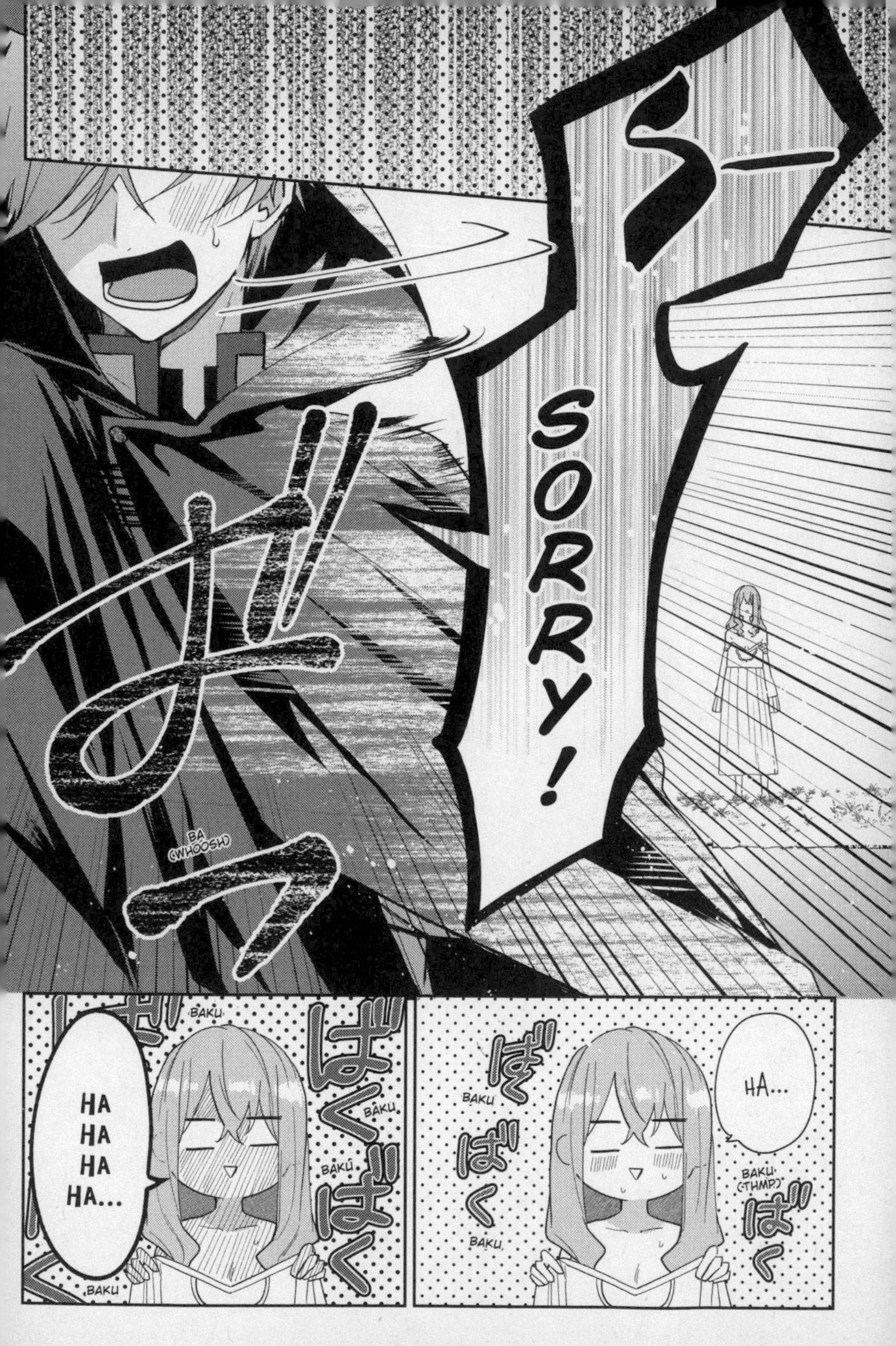
S—
SORRY!
BA
(WHOOSH)
HA...
BAKU
BAKU
(THMP)
BAKU
HA
HA
HA
HA...
BAKU
BAKU
BAKU
BAKU

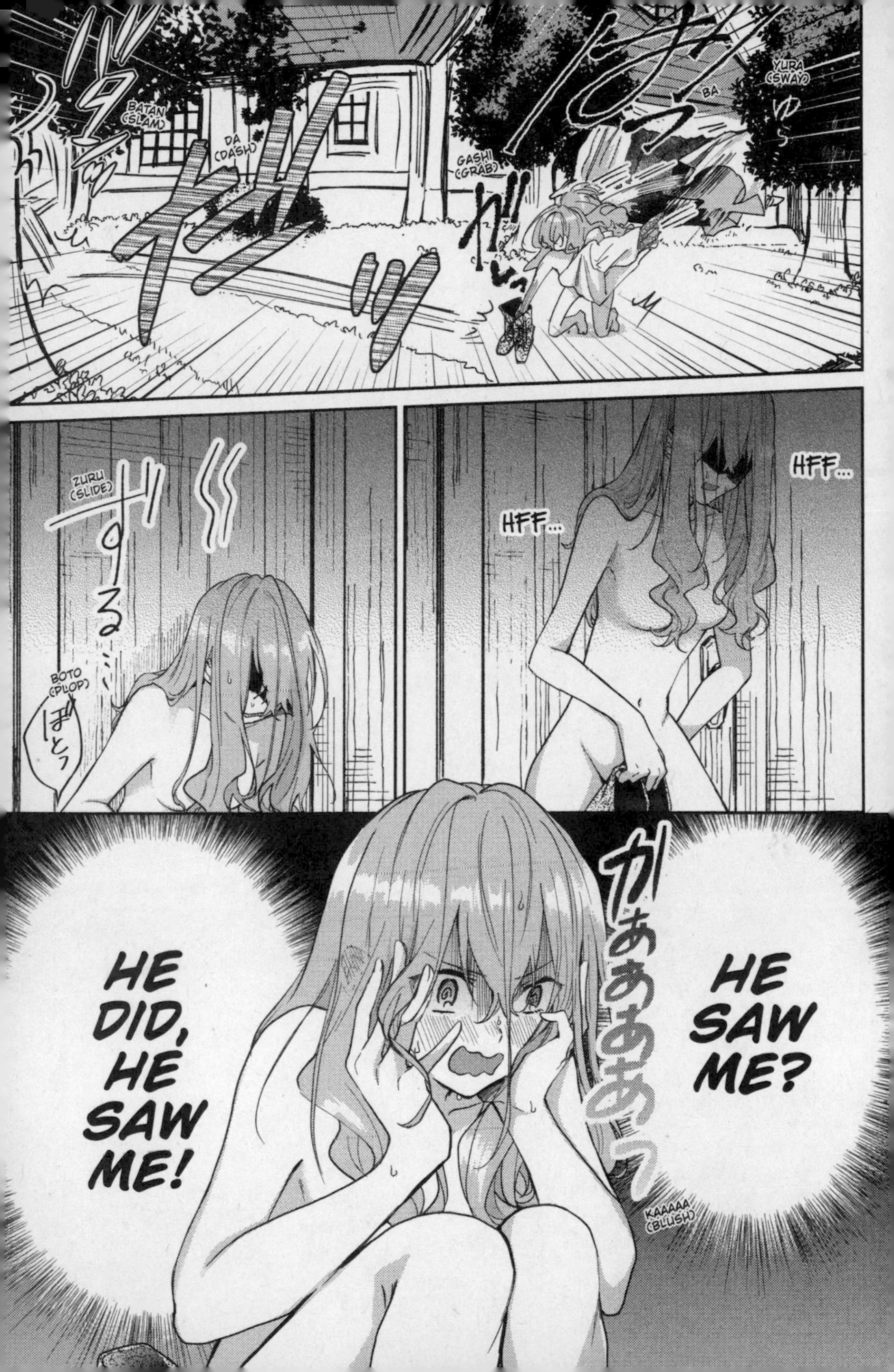

YURA (SWAY)
BA
GASHI (GRAB)
DA (DASH)
BATAN (SLAM)
HFF...
HFF...
ZURU (SLIDE)
BOTO (PLOP)
HE SAW ME?
KAAAAA (BLUSH)
HE DID, HE SAW ME!

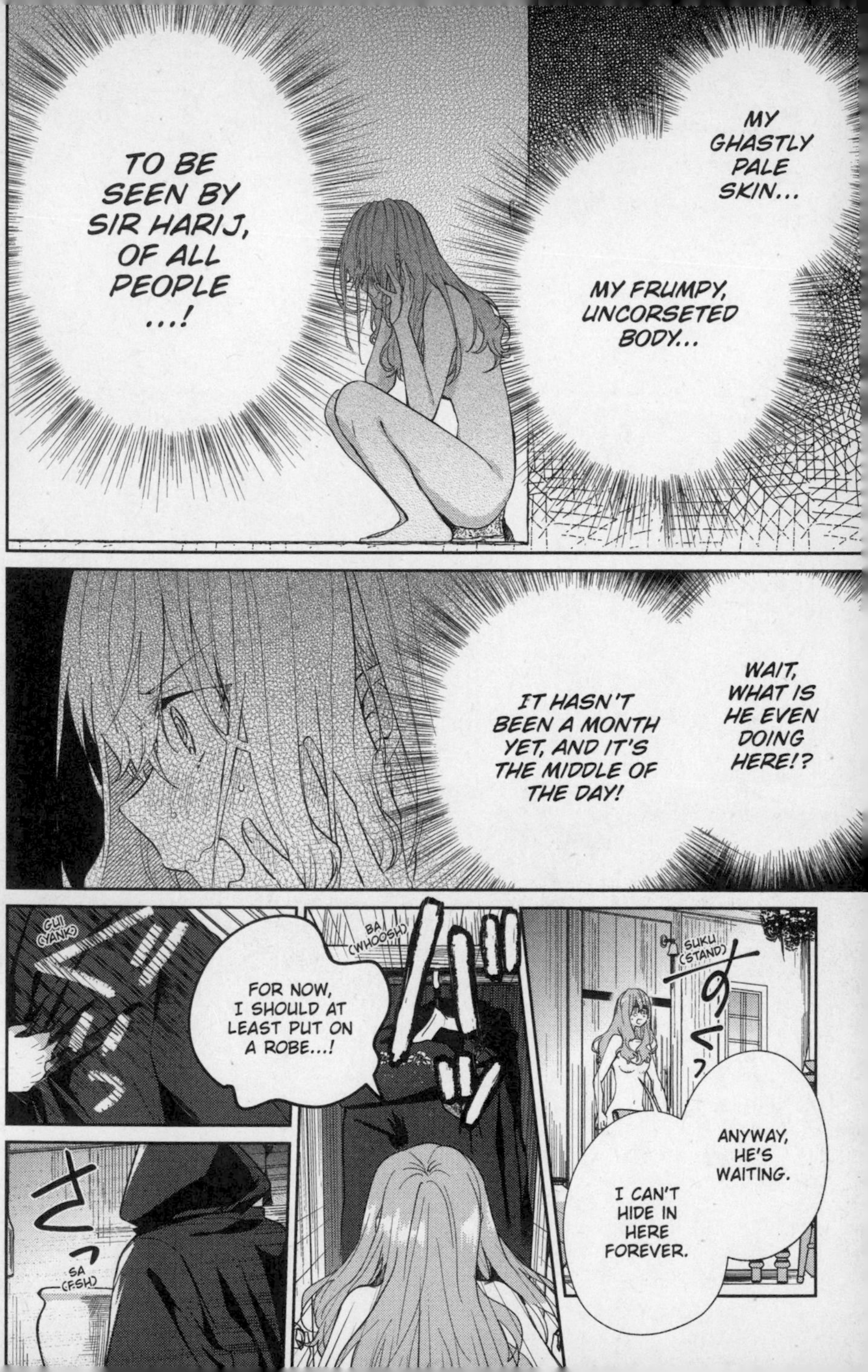
MY GHASTLY PALE SKIN...
MY FRUMPY, UNCORSETED BODY...
TO BE SEEN BY SIR HARIJ, OF ALL PEOPLE ...!
WAIT, WHAT IS HE EVEN DOING HERE!?
IT HASN'T BEEN A MONTH YET, AND IT'S THE MIDDLE OF THE DAY!
SUKU (STAND)
ANYWAY, HE'S WAITING.
I CAN'T HIDE IN HERE FOREVER.
BA (WHOOSH)
FOR NOW, I SHOULD AT LEAST PUT ON A ROBE...!
GUI (YANK)
SA (FSH)

KAAA
(BLUSH)

...LET'S DO THIS.

BECHIN
(SLAP)

I'M SORRY TO KEEP YOU WAITING. YOU MAY CROSS NOW.

GII
(CREAK)

KARAN
(JANGLE)

KARAN

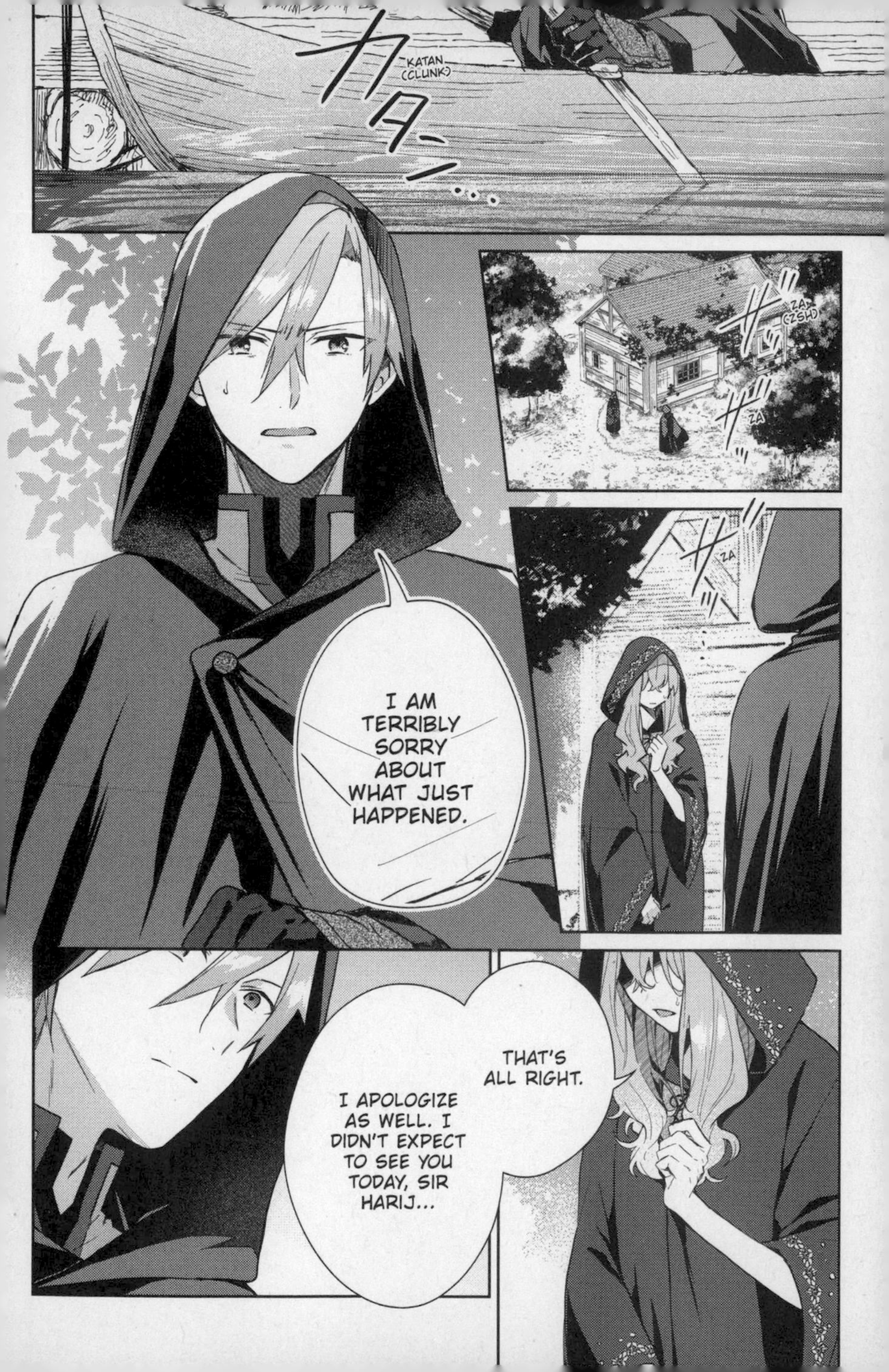

KATAN (CLUNK)
ZA (ZSHD)
ZA
ZA
I AM TERRIBLY SORRY ABOUT WHAT JUST HAPPENED.
THAT'S ALL RIGHT.
I APOLOGIZE AS WELL. I DIDN'T EXPECT TO SEE YOU TODAY, SIR HARIJ...

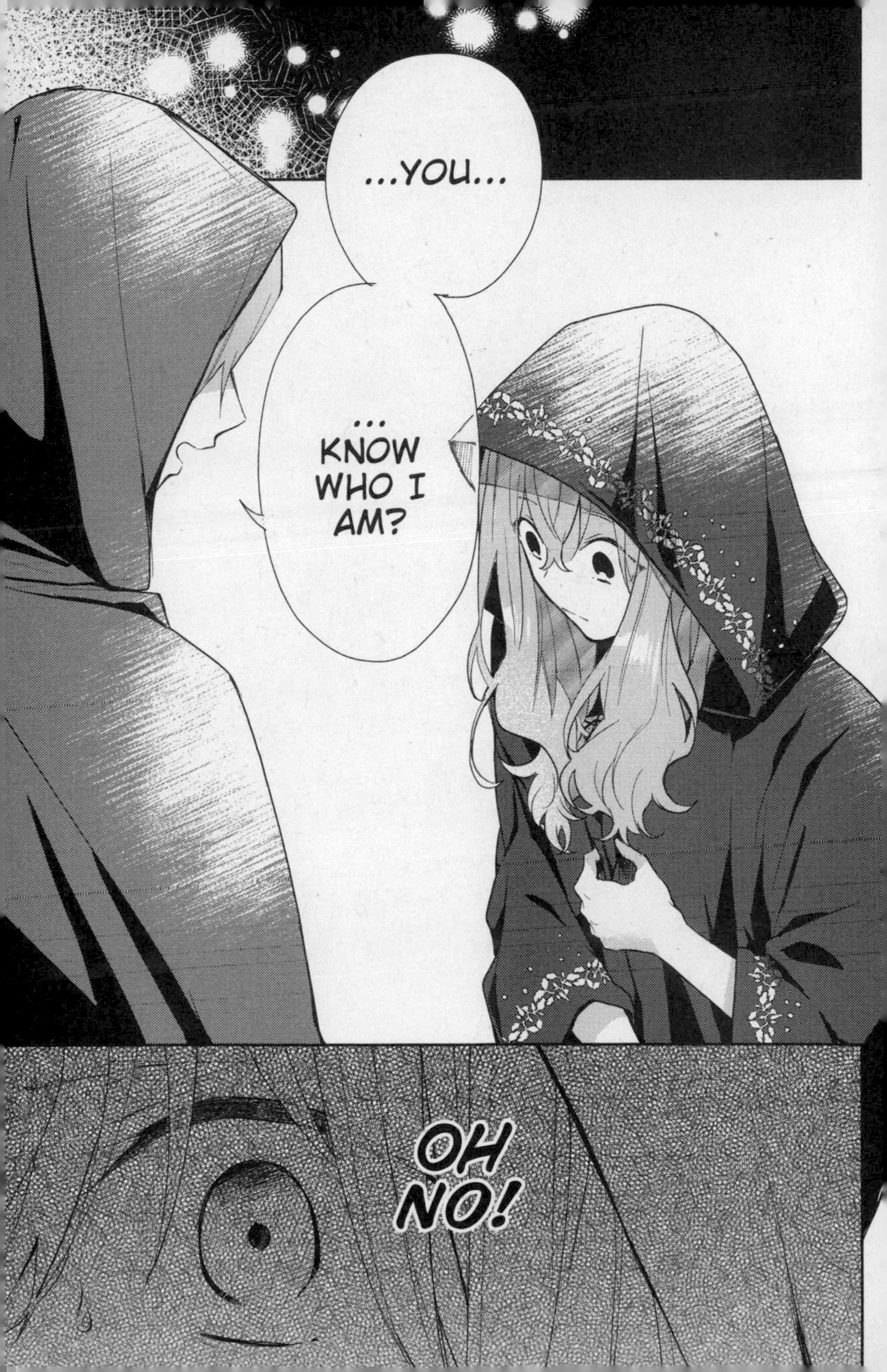
...YOU...
... KNOW WHO I AM?
OH NO!

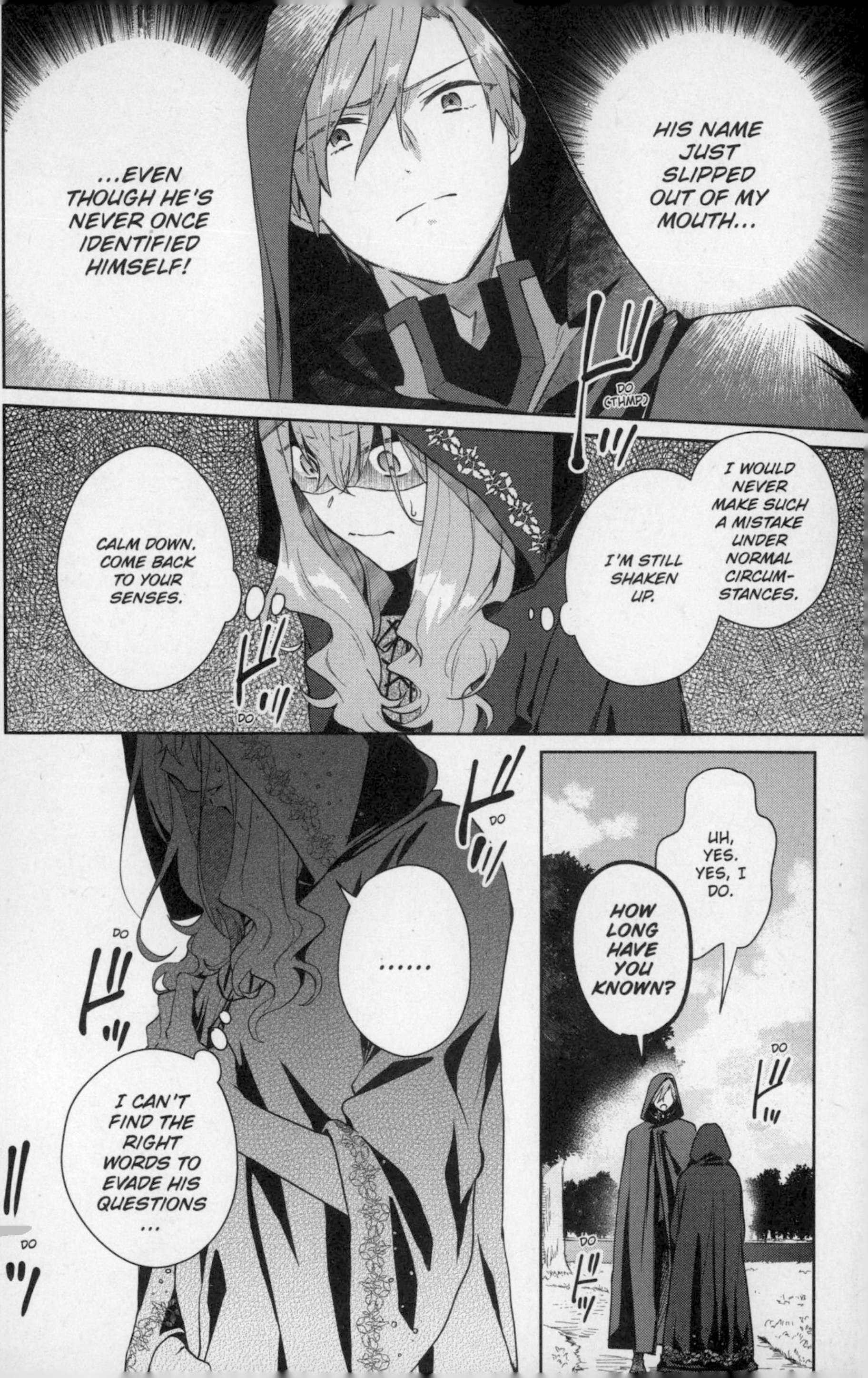
HIS NAME JUST SLIPPED OUT OF MY MOUTH...
...EVEN THOUGH HE'S NEVER ONCE IDENTIFIED HIMSELF!
DO (THMP)
I WOULD NEVER MAKE SUCH A MISTAKE UNDER NORMAL CIRCUM-STANCES.
I'M STILL SHAKEN UP.
CALM DOWN. COME BACK TO YOUR SENSES.
DO
UH, YES. YES, I DO.
HOW LONG HAVE YOU KNOWN?
DO
DO
DO
......
DO
I CAN'T FIND THE RIGHT WORDS TO EVADE HIS QUESTIONS...
DO

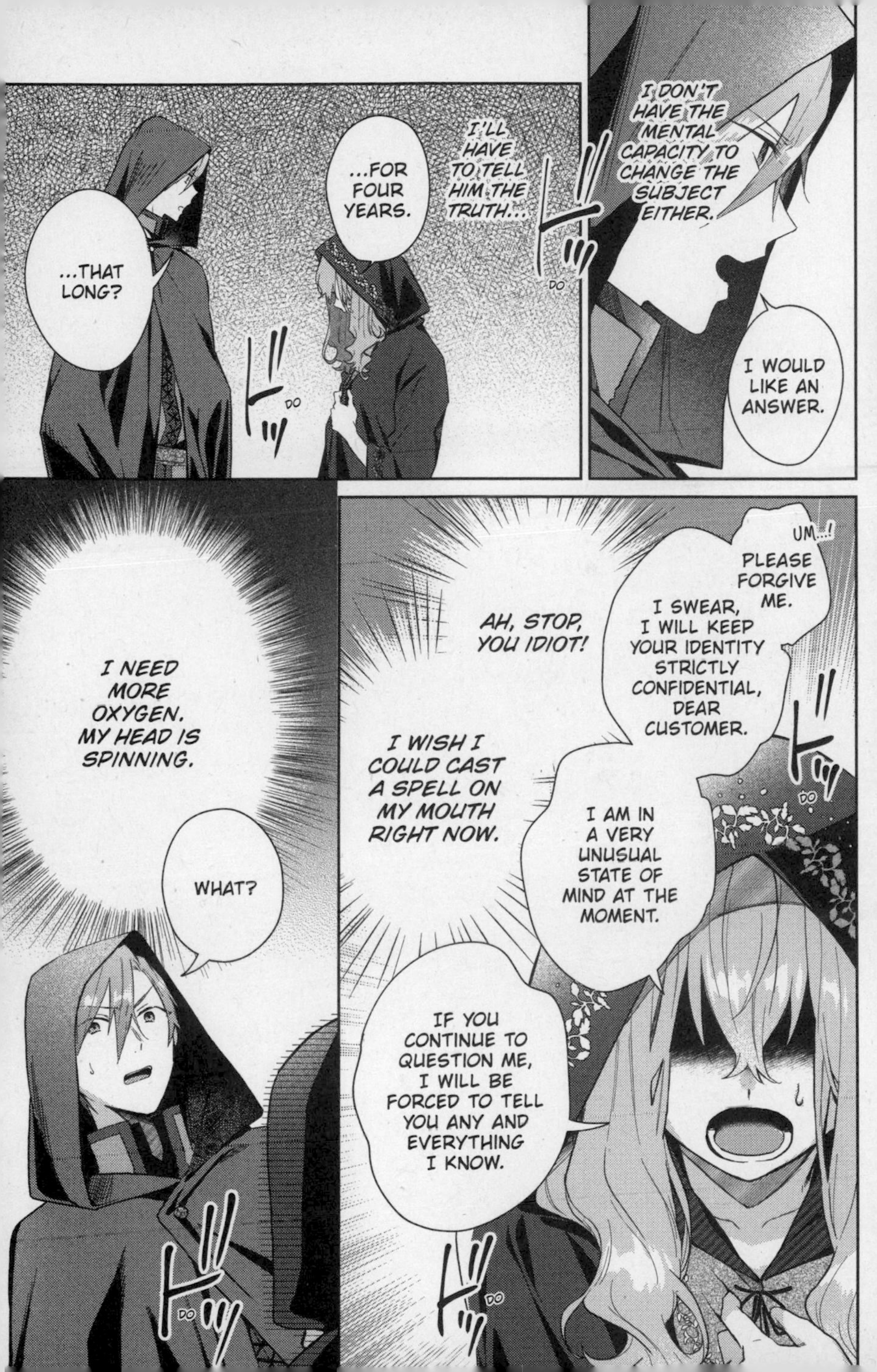
I DON'T HAVE THE MENTAL CAPACITY TO CHANGE THE SUBJECT EITHER.
I WOULD LIKE AN ANSWER.
DO
I'LL HAVE TO TELL HIM THE TRUTH...
...FOR FOUR YEARS.
...THAT LONG?
DO
UM...! PLEASE FORGIVE ME.
I SWEAR, I WILL KEEP YOUR IDENTITY STRICTLY CONFIDENTIAL, DEAR CUSTOMER.
AH, STOP, YOU IDIOT!
DO
I AM IN A VERY UNUSUAL STATE OF MIND AT THE MOMENT.
I WISH I COULD CAST A SPELL ON MY MOUTH RIGHT NOW.
IF YOU CONTINUE TO QUESTION ME, I WILL BE FORCED TO TELL YOU ANY AND EVERYTHING I KNOW.
DO
I NEED MORE OXYGEN. MY HEAD IS SPINNING.
WHAT?
DO

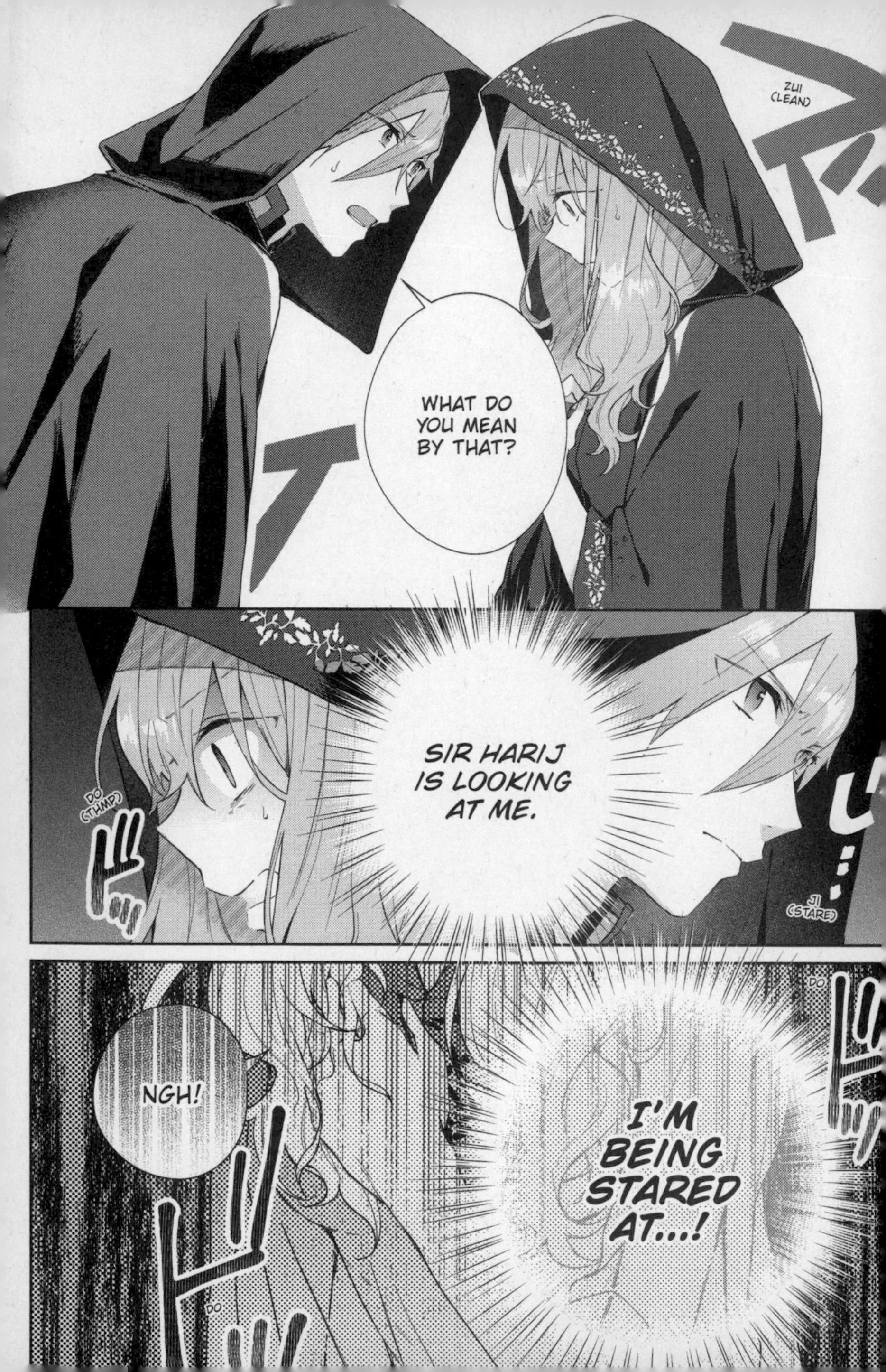
ZUI
(LEAN)
WHAT DO YOU MEAN BY THAT?
JI
(STARE)
SIR HARIJ IS LOOKING AT ME.
DO
(THMP)
DO
I'M BEING STARED AT...!
NGH!
DO

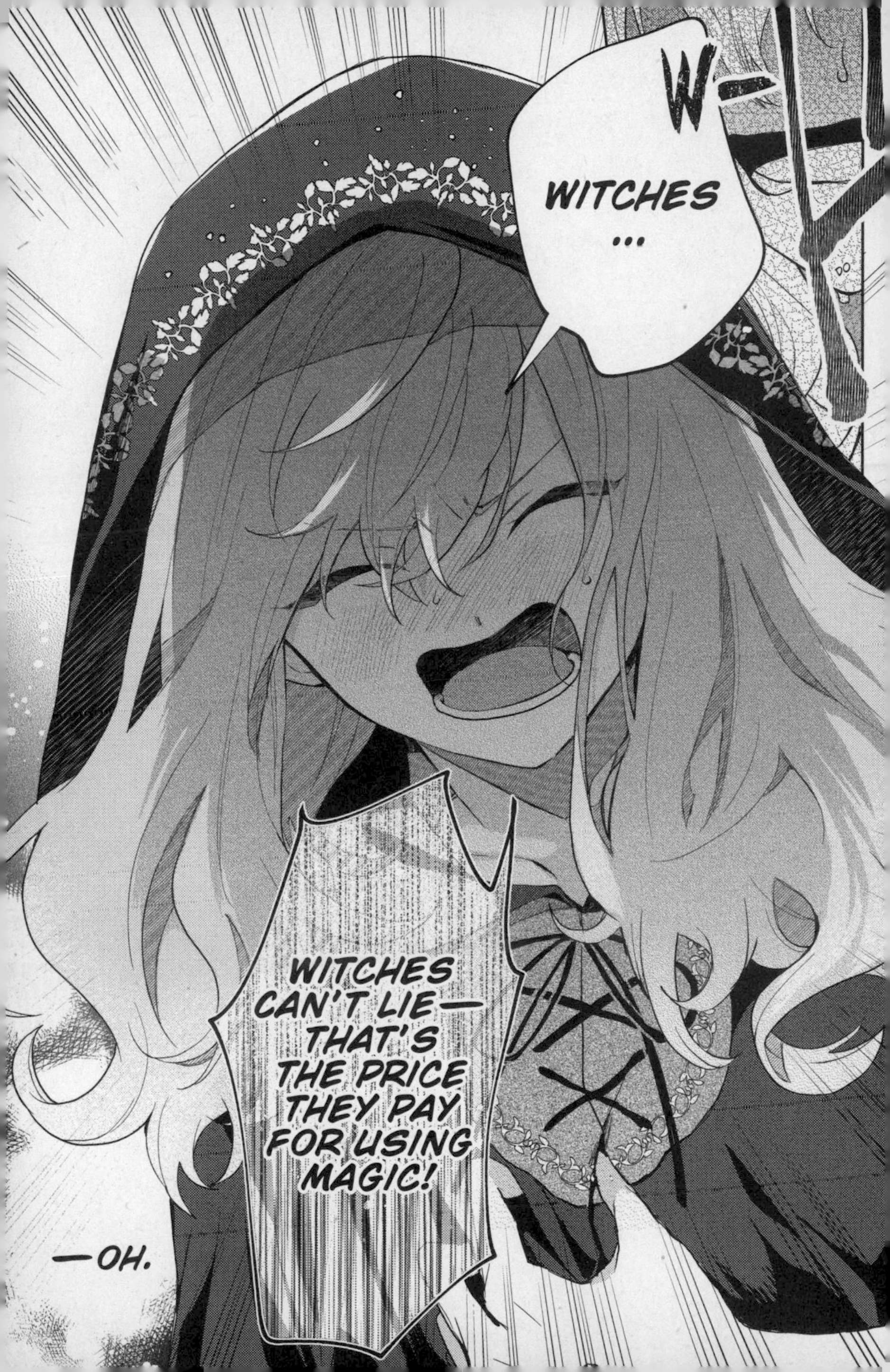
W-WITCHES...
DO
WITCHES CAN'T LIE—THAT'S THE PRICE THEY PAY FOR USING MAGIC!
—OH.

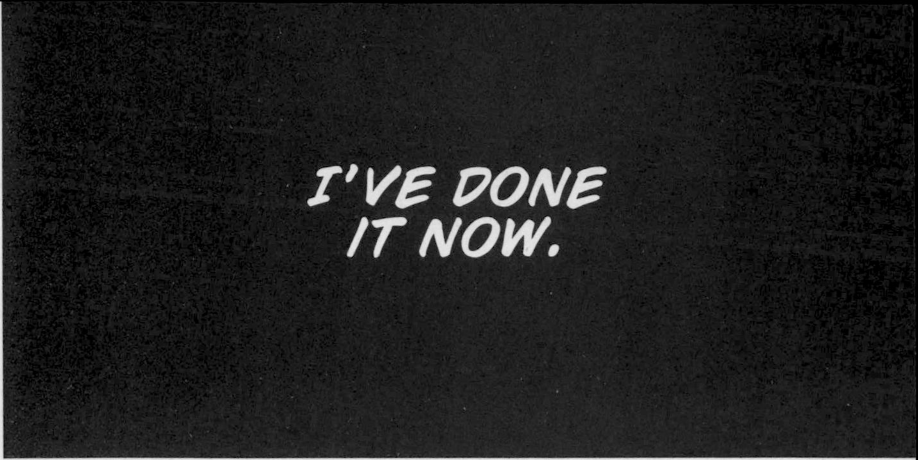
I'VE DONE IT NOW.

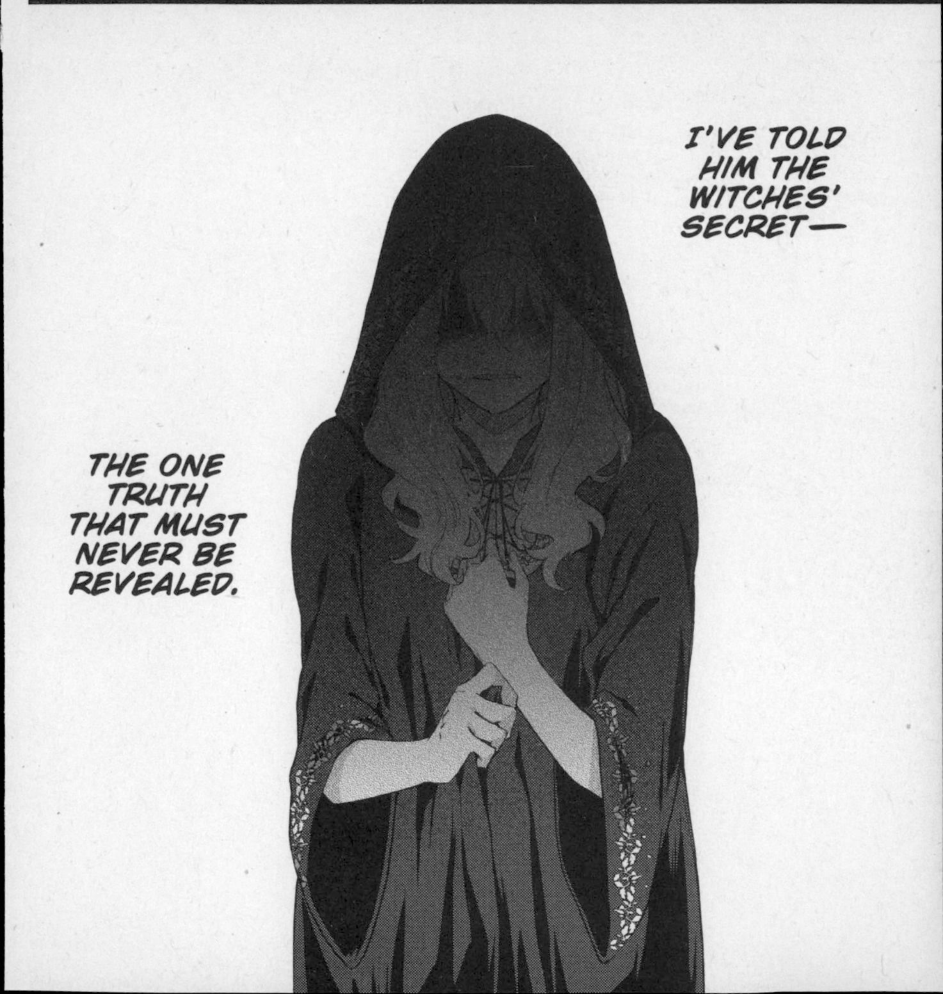
I'VE TOLD HIM THE WITCHES' SECRET—
THE ONE TRUTH THAT MUST NEVER BE REVEALED.

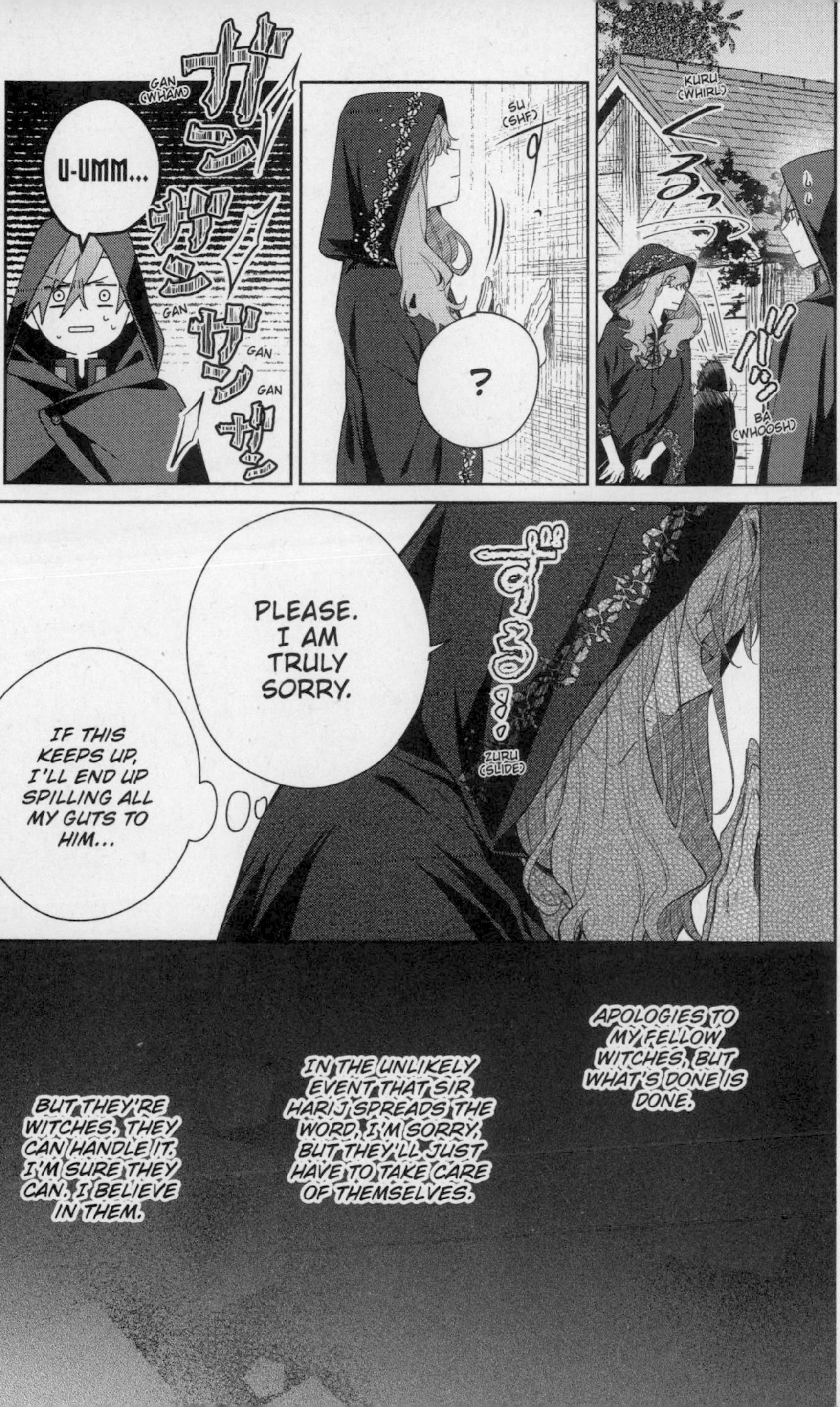

KURU (WHIRL)
BA (WHOOSH)
SU (SHF)
?
GAN (WHAM)
U-UMM...
GAN
GAN
GAN
ZURU (SLIDE)
PLEASE. I AM TRULY SORRY.
IF THIS KEEPS UP, I'LL END UP SPILLING ALL MY GUTS TO HIM...
APOLOGIES TO MY FELLOW WITCHES, BUT WHAT'S DONE IS DONE.
IN THE UNLIKELY EVENT THAT SIR HARIJ SPREADS THE WORD, I'M SORRY, BUT THEY'LL JUST HAVE TO TAKE CARE OF THEMSELVES.
BUT THEY'RE WITCHES. THEY CAN HANDLE IT. I'M SURE THEY CAN. I BELIEVE IN THEM.

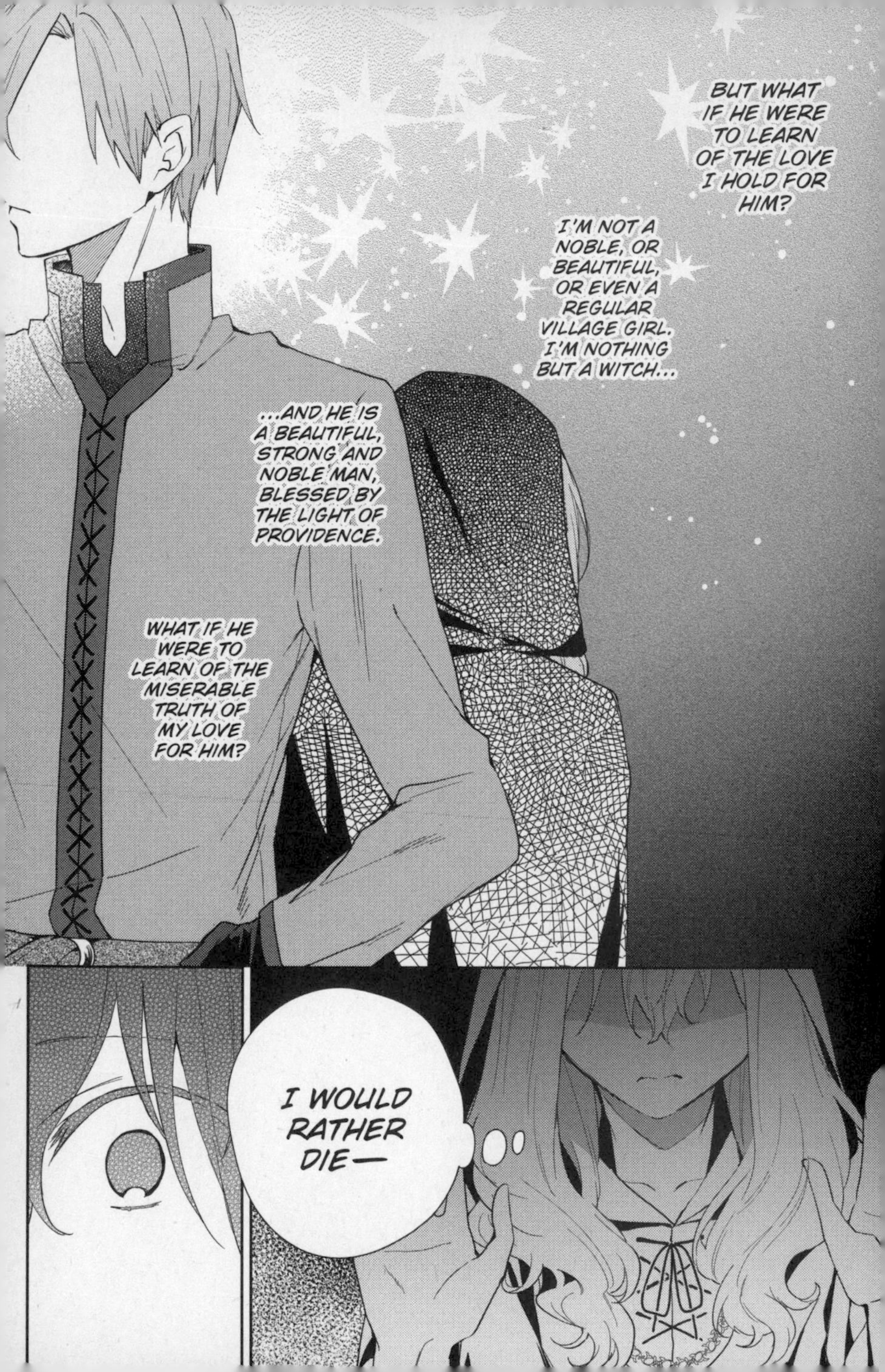
BUT WHAT IF HE WERE TO LEARN OF THE LOVE I HOLD FOR HIM?
I'M NOT A NOBLE, OR BEAUTIFUL, OR EVEN A REGULAR VILLAGE GIRL. I'M NOTHING BUT A WITCH...
...AND HE IS A BEAUTIFUL, STRONG AND NOBLE MAN, BLESSED BY THE LIGHT OF PROVIDENCE.
WHAT IF HE WERE TO LEARN OF THE MISERABLE TRUTH OF MY LOVE FOR HIM?
I WOULD RATHER DIE—

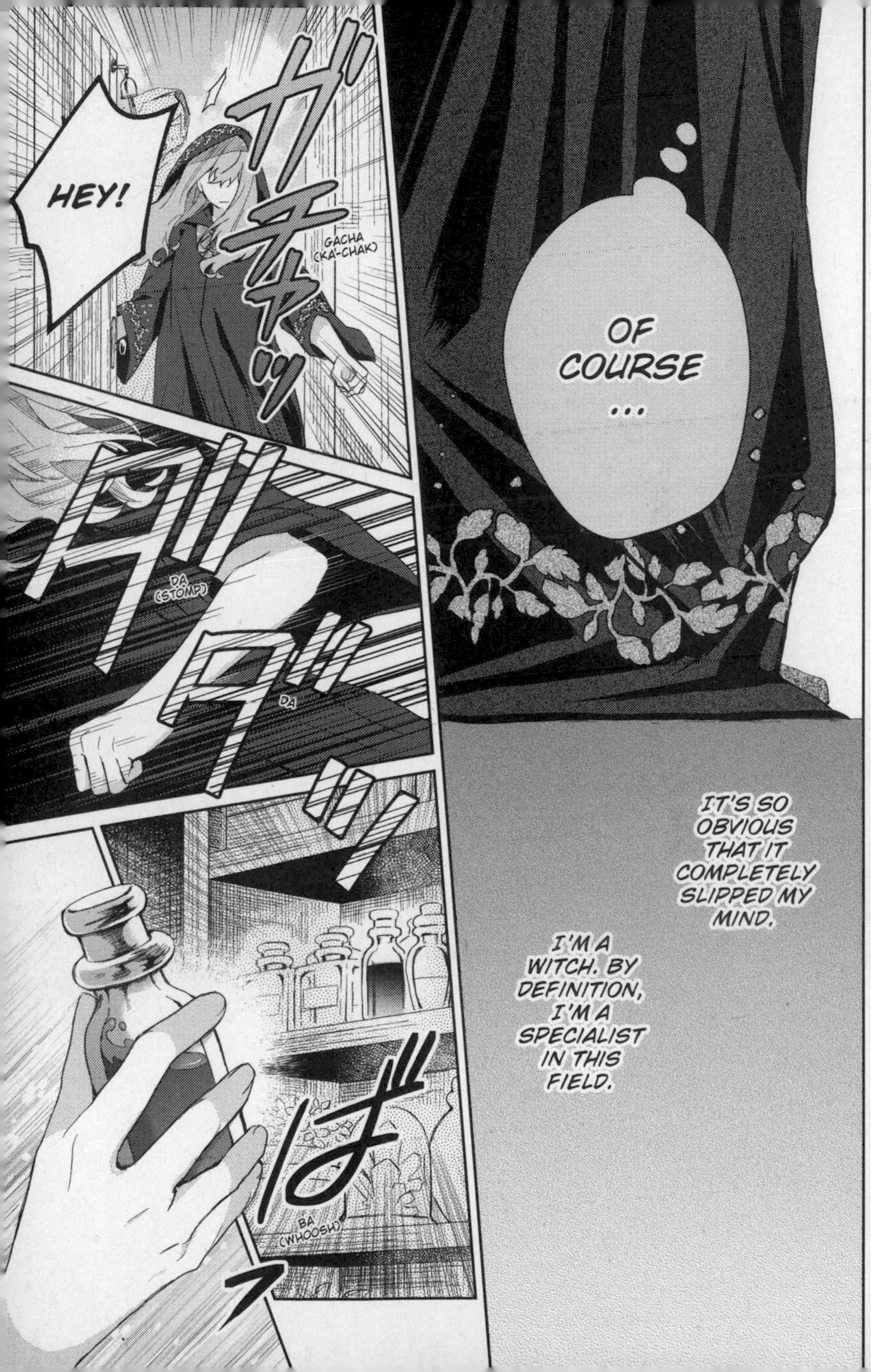
OF COURSE...
IT'S SO OBVIOUS THAT IT COMPLETELY SLIPPED MY MIND.
I'M A WITCH. BY DEFINITION, I'M A SPECIALIST IN THIS FIELD.
HEY!
GACHA (KA-CHAK)
DA (STOMP)
DA
BA (WHOOSH)

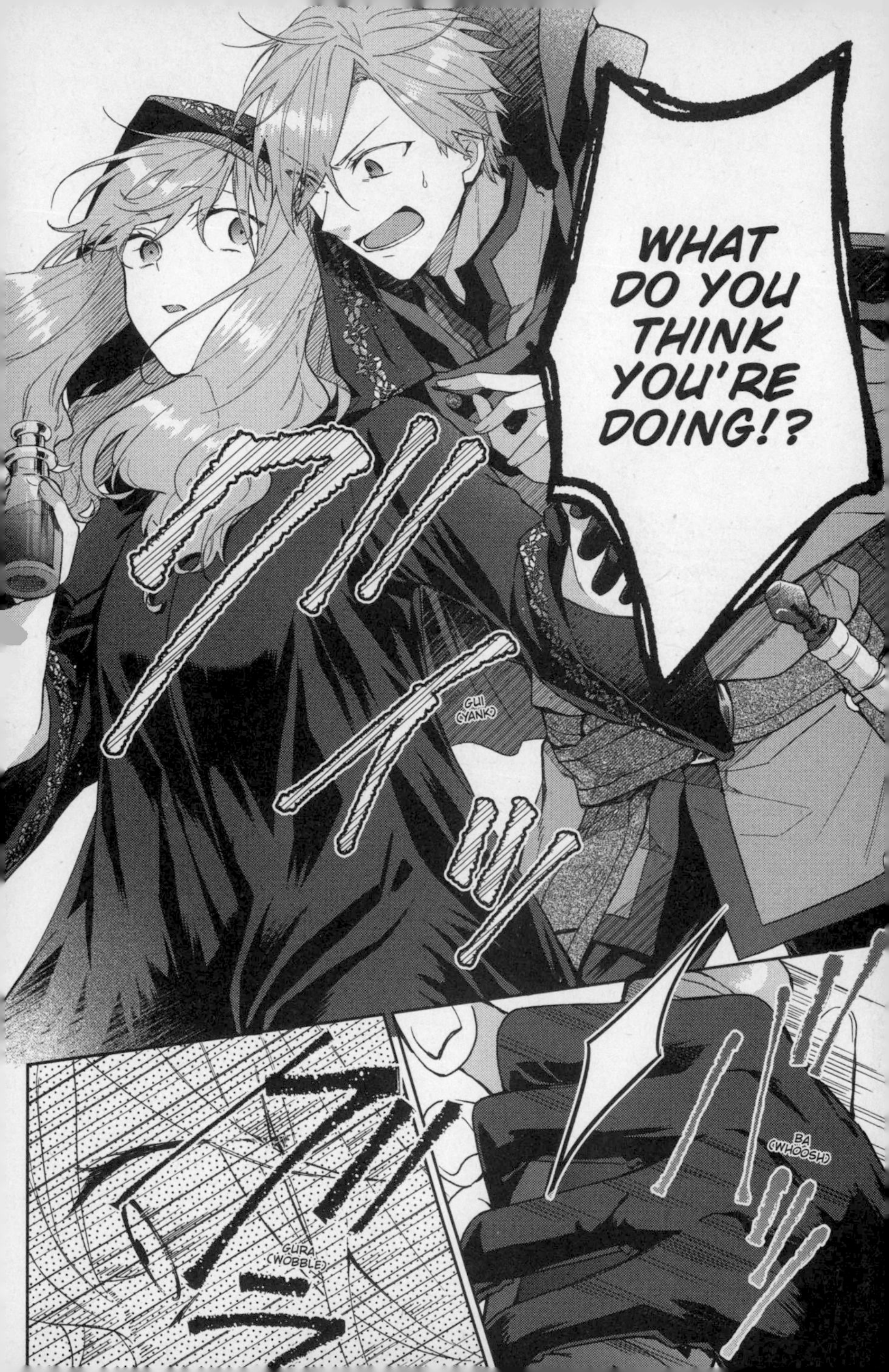
WHAT DO YOU THINK YOU'RE DOING!?
GUI (YANK)
BA (WHOOSH)
GURA (WOBBLE)

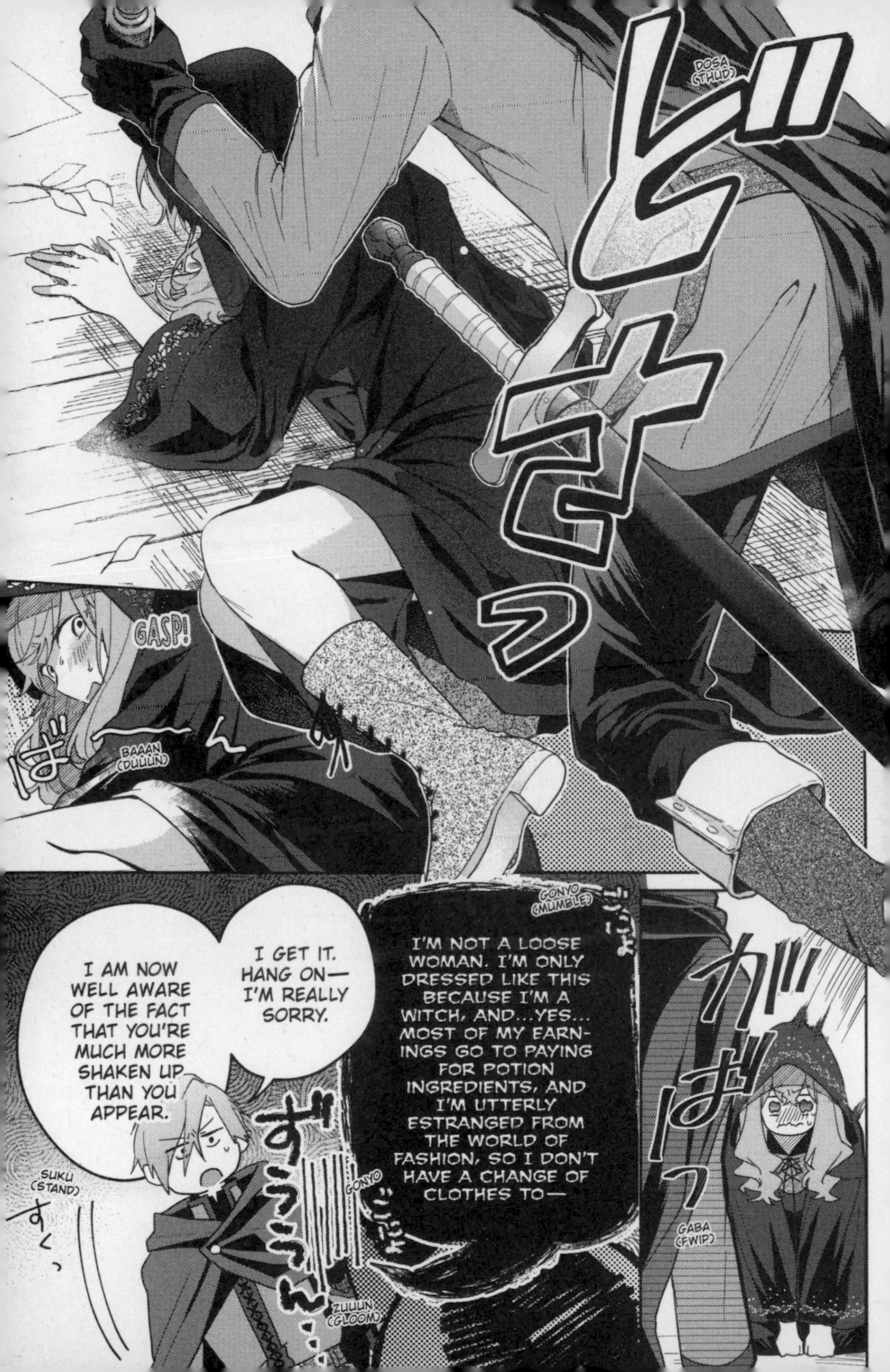
DOSA (THUD)
GASP!
BAAAN (DUUUN)
GABA (FWIP)
GONYO (MUMBLE)
I'M NOT A LOOSE WOMAN. I'M ONLY DRESSED LIKE THIS BECAUSE I'M A WITCH, AND...YES... MOST OF MY EARNINGS GO TO PAYING FOR POTION INGREDIENTS, AND I'M UTTERLY ESTRANGED FROM THE WORLD OF FASHION, SO I DON'T HAVE A CHANGE OF CLOTHES TO—
I GET IT. HANG ON— I'M REALLY SORRY.
I AM NOW WELL AWARE OF THE FACT THAT YOU'RE MUCH MORE SHAKEN UP THAN YOU APPEAR.
ZUUUN (GLOOM)
GONYO
SUKU (STAND)

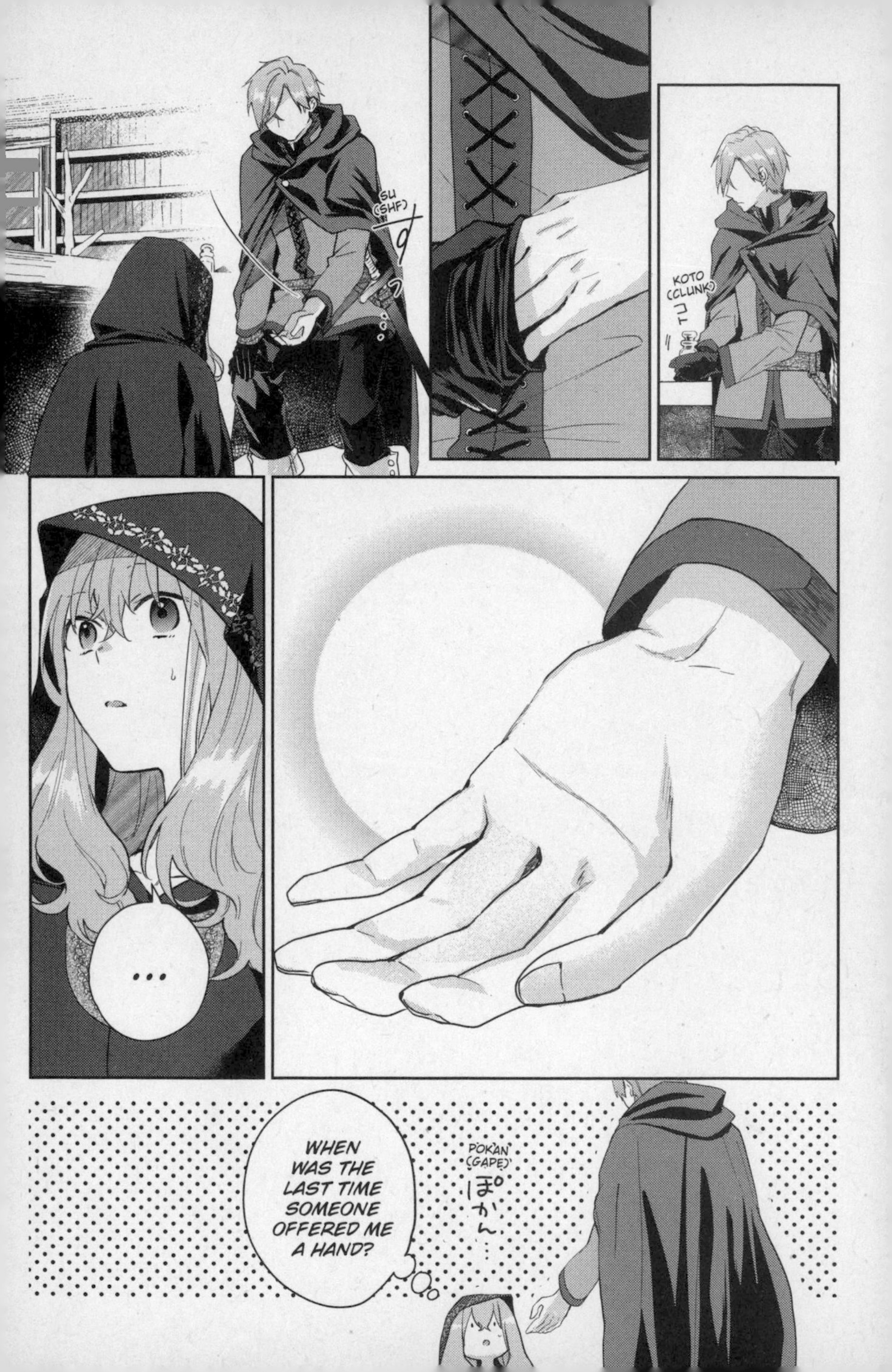
KOTO (CLUNK)
SU (SHF)
...
POKAN (GAPE)
ぽかん…
WHEN WAS THE LAST TIME SOMEONE OFFERED ME A HAND?

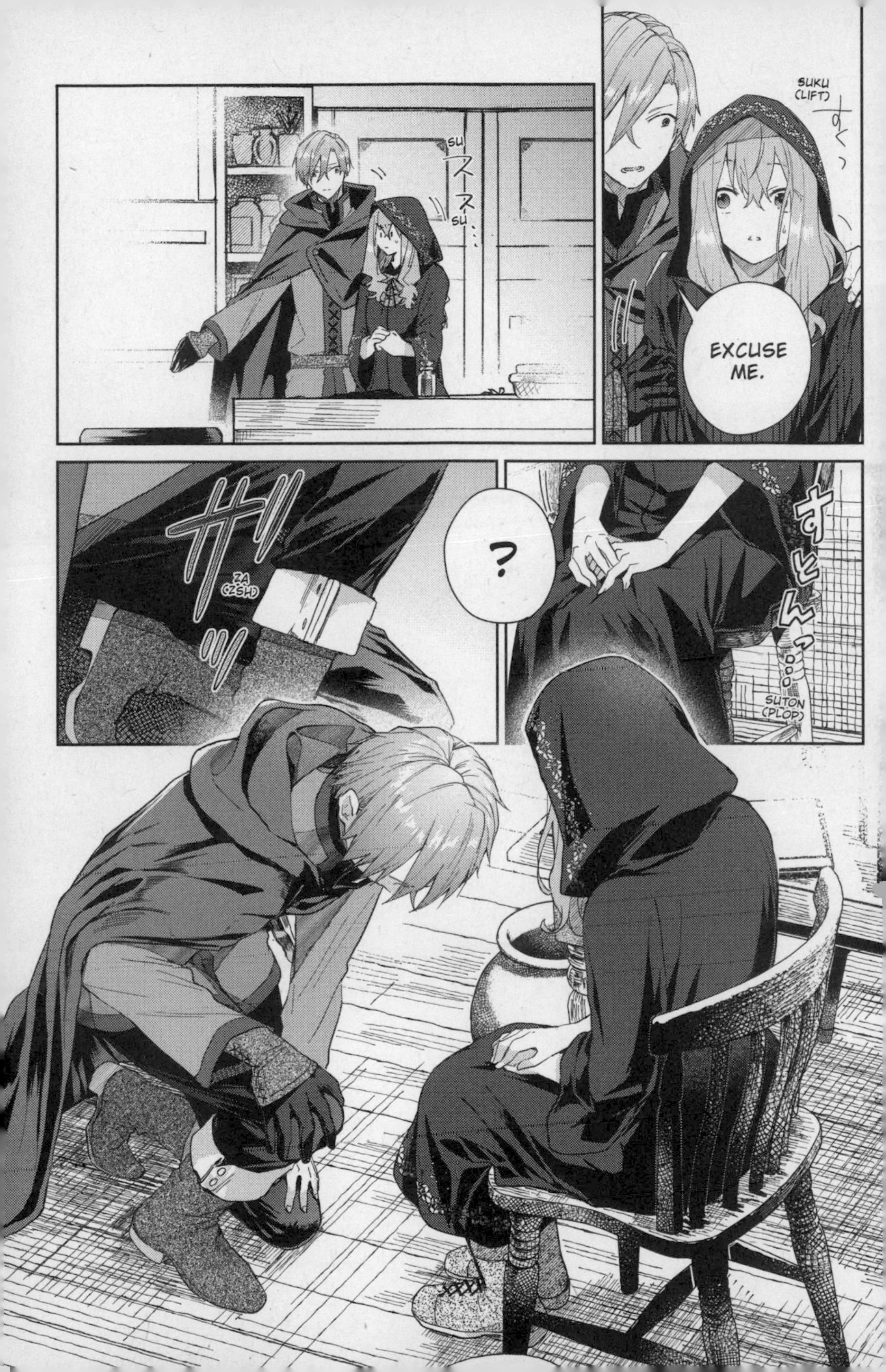
SUKU (LIFT)
すくっ
EXCUSE ME.
SU
スース
SU
すとんっ
SUTON (PLOP)
?
ザッ
ZA (ZSHD)

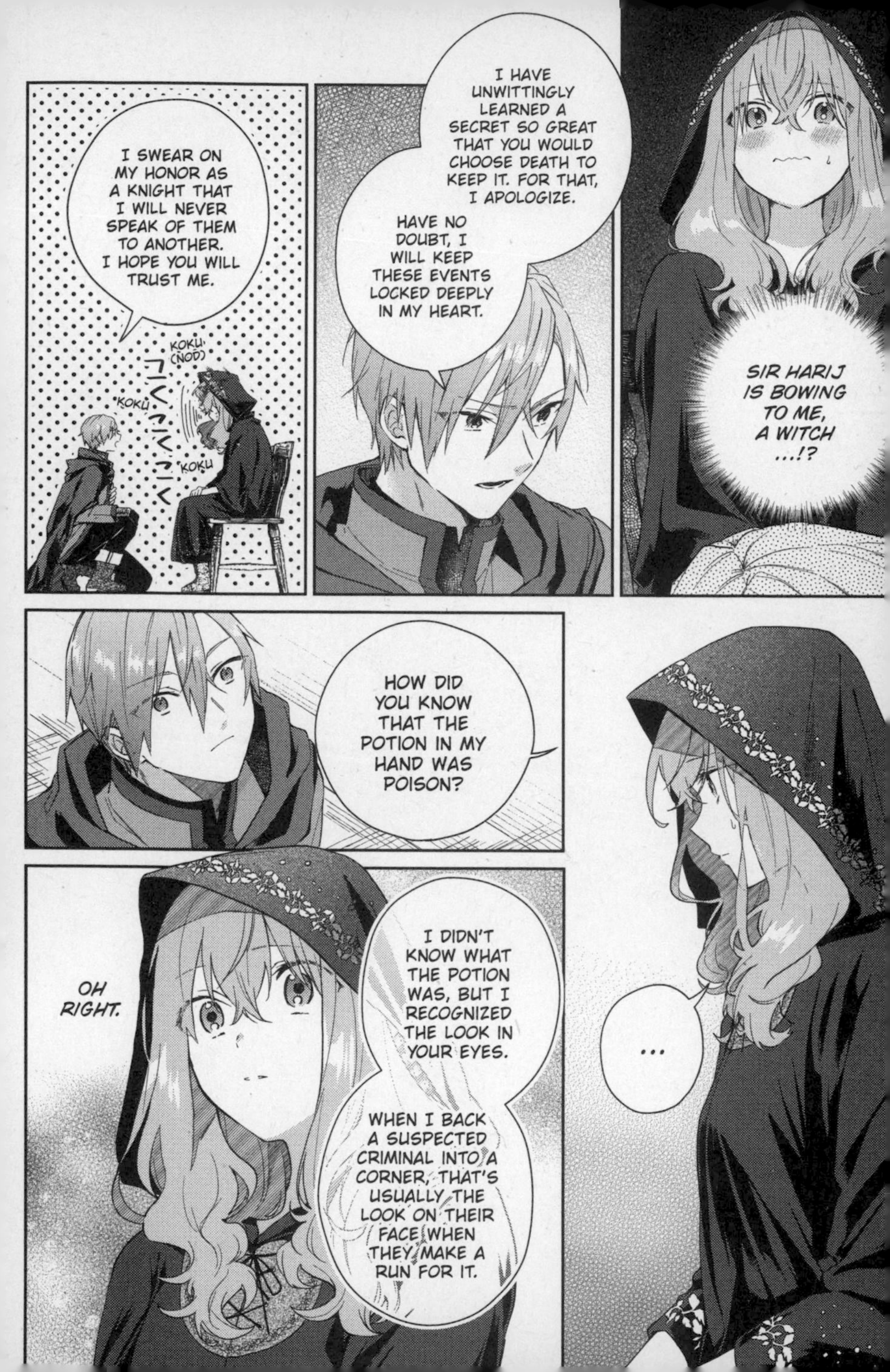
SIR HARIJ IS BOWING TO ME, A WITCH ...!?
I HAVE UNWITTINGLY LEARNED A SECRET SO GREAT THAT YOU WOULD CHOOSE DEATH TO KEEP IT. FOR THAT, I APOLOGIZE.
HAVE NO DOUBT, I WILL KEEP THESE EVENTS LOCKED DEEPLY IN MY HEART.
I SWEAR ON MY HONOR AS A KNIGHT THAT I WILL NEVER SPEAK OF THEM TO ANOTHER. I HOPE YOU WILL TRUST ME.
KOKU (NOD)
KOKU
KOKU
...
HOW DID YOU KNOW THAT THE POTION IN MY HAND WAS POISON?
I DIDN'T KNOW WHAT THE POTION WAS, BUT I RECOGNIZED THE LOOK IN YOUR EYES.
WHEN I BACK A SUSPECTED CRIMINAL INTO A CORNER, THAT'S USUALLY THE LOOK ON THEIR FACE WHEN THEY MAKE A RUN FOR IT.
OH RIGHT.

JI
(STARE)

I'M GLAD I STOPPED YOU IN TIME.

SIGH...

THIS IS THE KIND OF MAN HE IS.

GOSO
(RUMMAGE)

SUKU
(STAND)

GOSO

IF YOU'D GONE THROUGH WITH IT...

...I WOULD HAVE HAD TO EAT ALL THIS BY MYSELF.

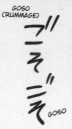

GACHA

GACHA
(KA-CHAK)

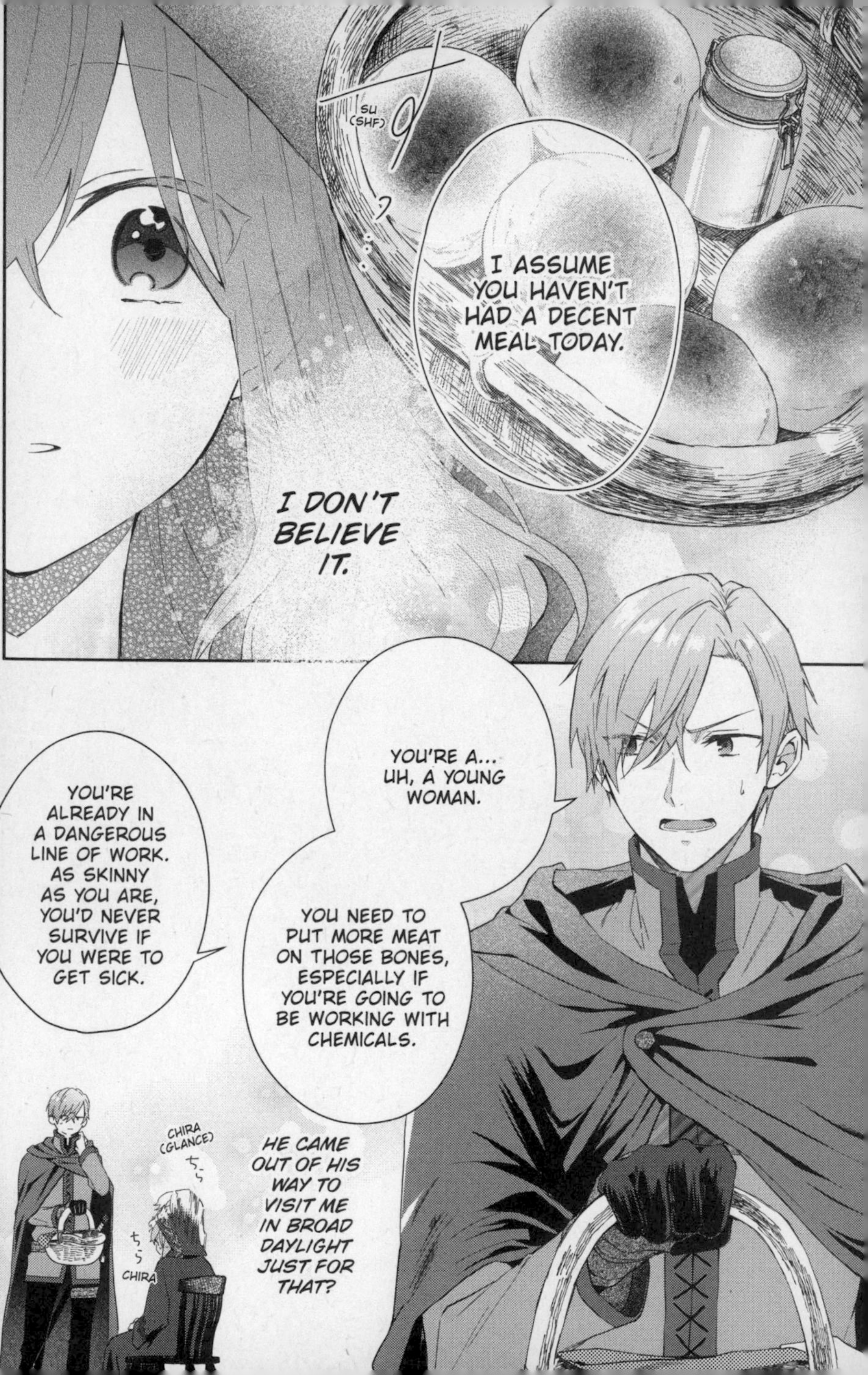
SU (SHF)
I ASSUME YOU HAVEN'T HAD A DECENT MEAL TODAY.
I DON'T BELIEVE IT.
YOU'RE A... UH, A YOUNG WOMAN.
YOU'RE ALREADY IN A DANGEROUS LINE OF WORK. AS SKINNY AS YOU ARE, YOU'D NEVER SURVIVE IF YOU WERE TO GET SICK.
YOU NEED TO PUT MORE MEAT ON THOSE BONES, ESPECIALLY IF YOU'RE GOING TO BE WORKING WITH CHEMICALS.
CHIRA (GLANCE)
CHIRA
HE CAME OUT OF HIS WAY TO VISIT ME IN BROAD DAYLIGHT JUST FOR THAT?

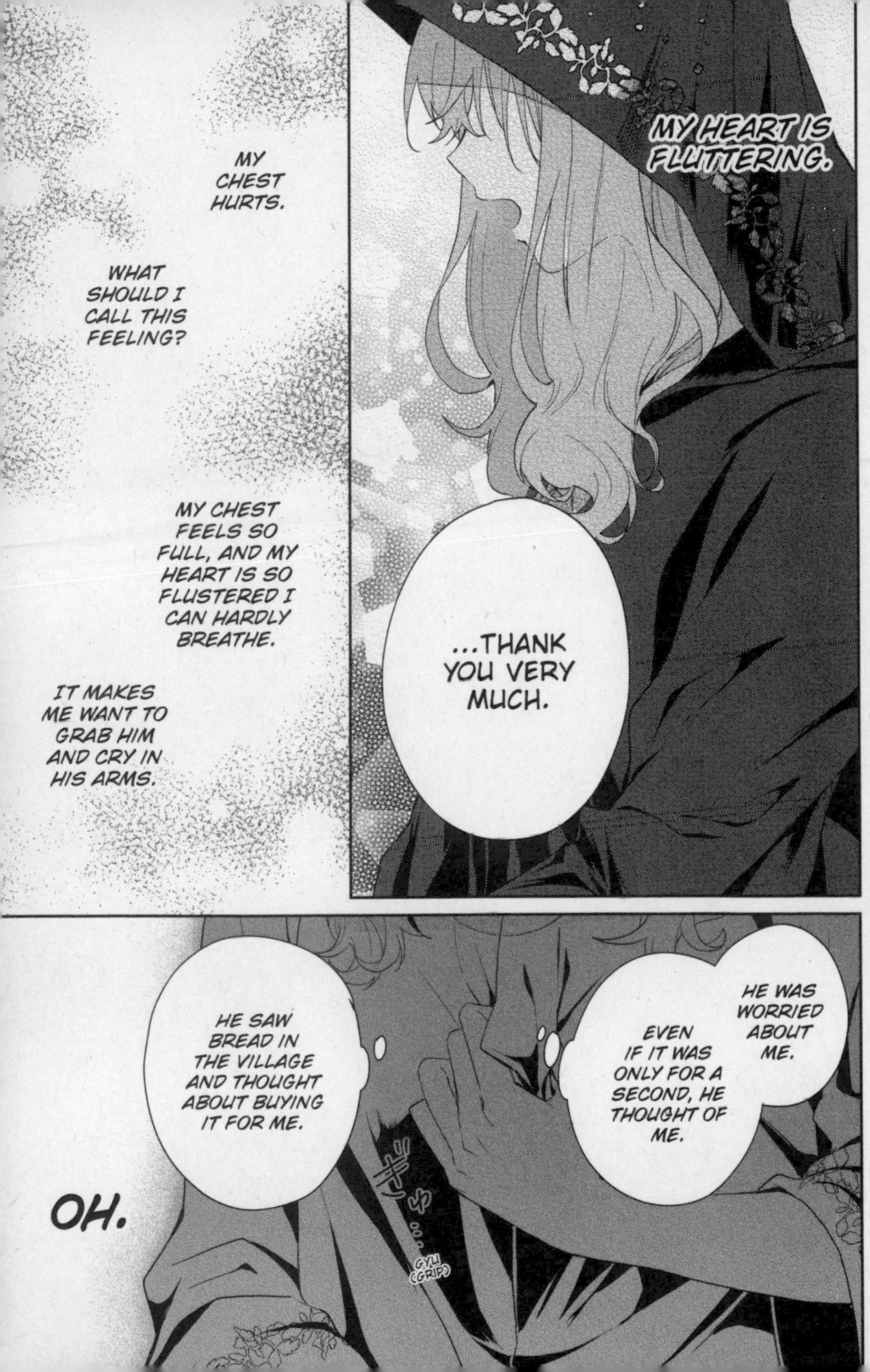
MY HEART IS FLUTTERING.
...THANK YOU VERY MUCH.
MY CHEST HURTS.
WHAT SHOULD I CALL THIS FEELING?
MY CHEST FEELS SO FULL, AND MY HEART IS SO FLUSTERED I CAN HARDLY BREATHE.
IT MAKES ME WANT TO GRAB HIM AND CRY IN HIS ARMS.
HE WAS WORRIED ABOUT ME.
EVEN IF IT WAS ONLY FOR A SECOND, HE THOUGHT OF ME.
GYU (GRIP)
HE SAW BREAD IN THE VILLAGE AND THOUGHT ABOUT BUYING IT FOR ME.
OH.

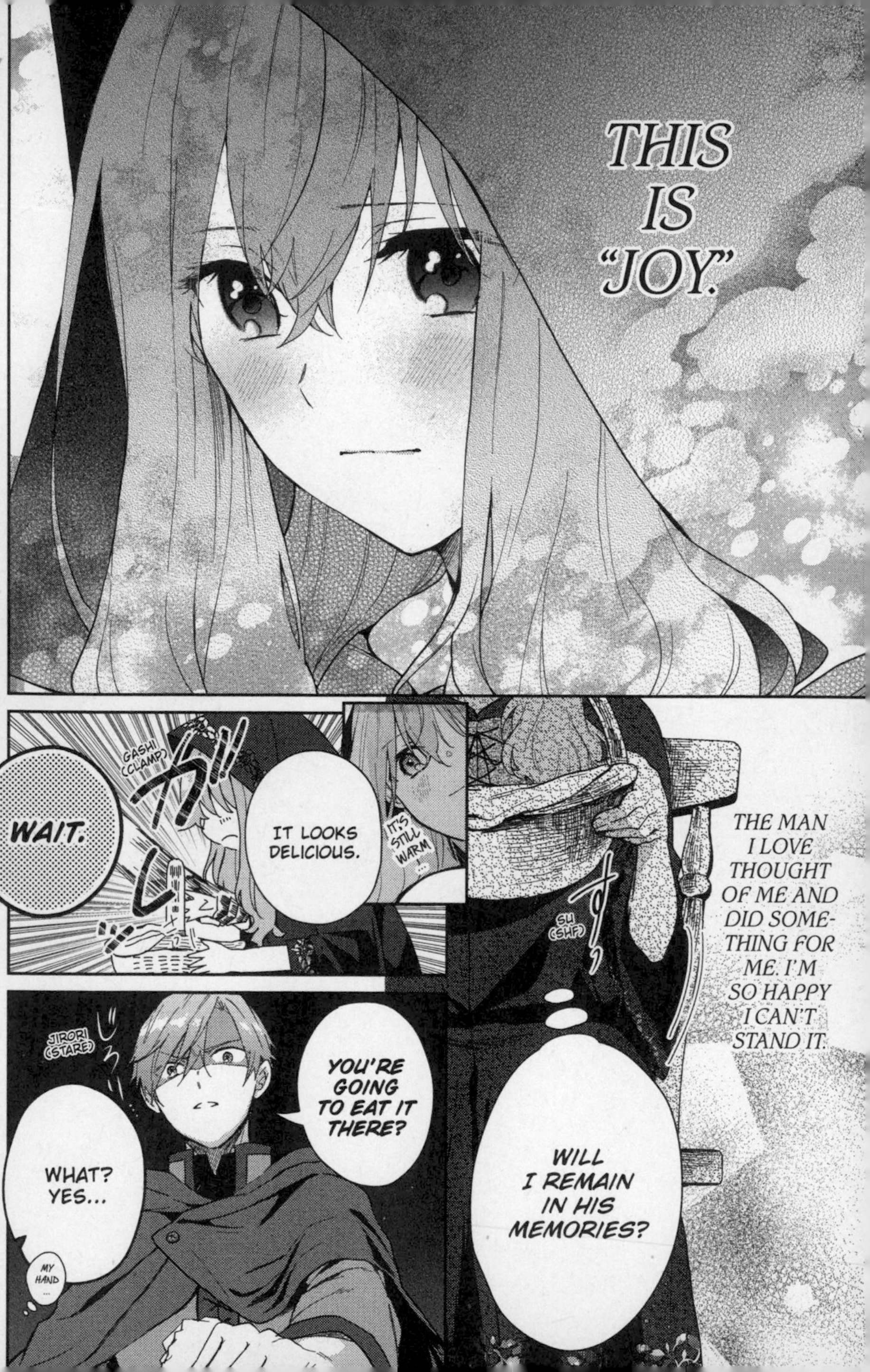
THIS IS "JOY."
THE MAN I LOVE THOUGHT OF ME AND DID SOMETHING FOR ME. I'M SO HAPPY I CAN'T STAND IT.
SU (SHF)
WILL I REMAIN IN HIS MEMORIES?
IT'S STILL WARM...
IT LOOKS DELICIOUS.
GASHI (CLAMP)
WAIT.
JIRORI (STARE)
YOU'RE GOING TO EAT IT THERE?
WHAT? YES...
MY HAND...

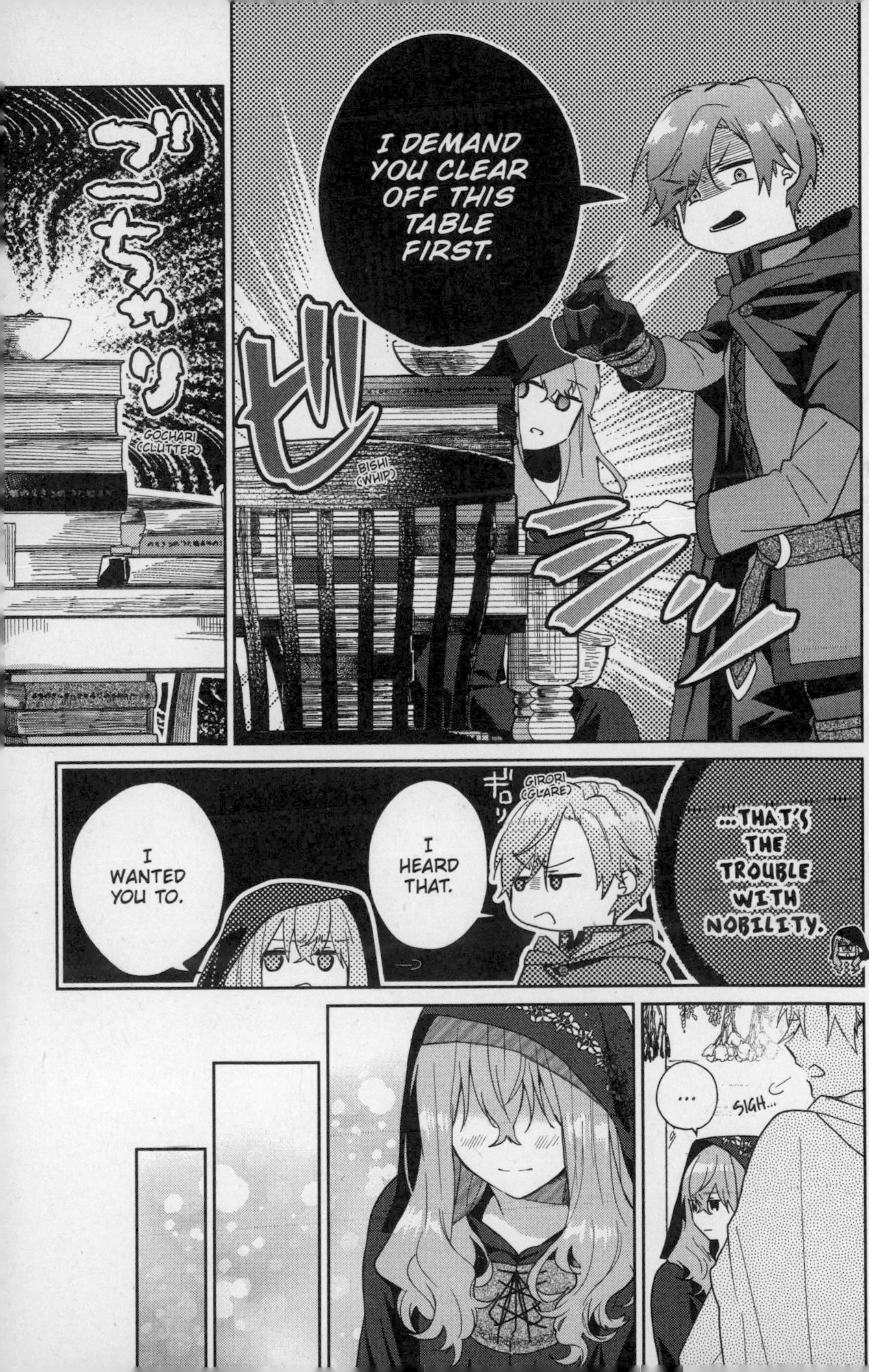
I DEMAND YOU CLEAR OFF THIS TABLE FIRST.
BISHI (WHIP)
GOCHARI (CLUTTER)
...THAT'S THE TROUBLE WITH NOBILITY.
GIRORI (GLARE)
I HEARD THAT.
I WANTED YOU TO.
...
SIGH...

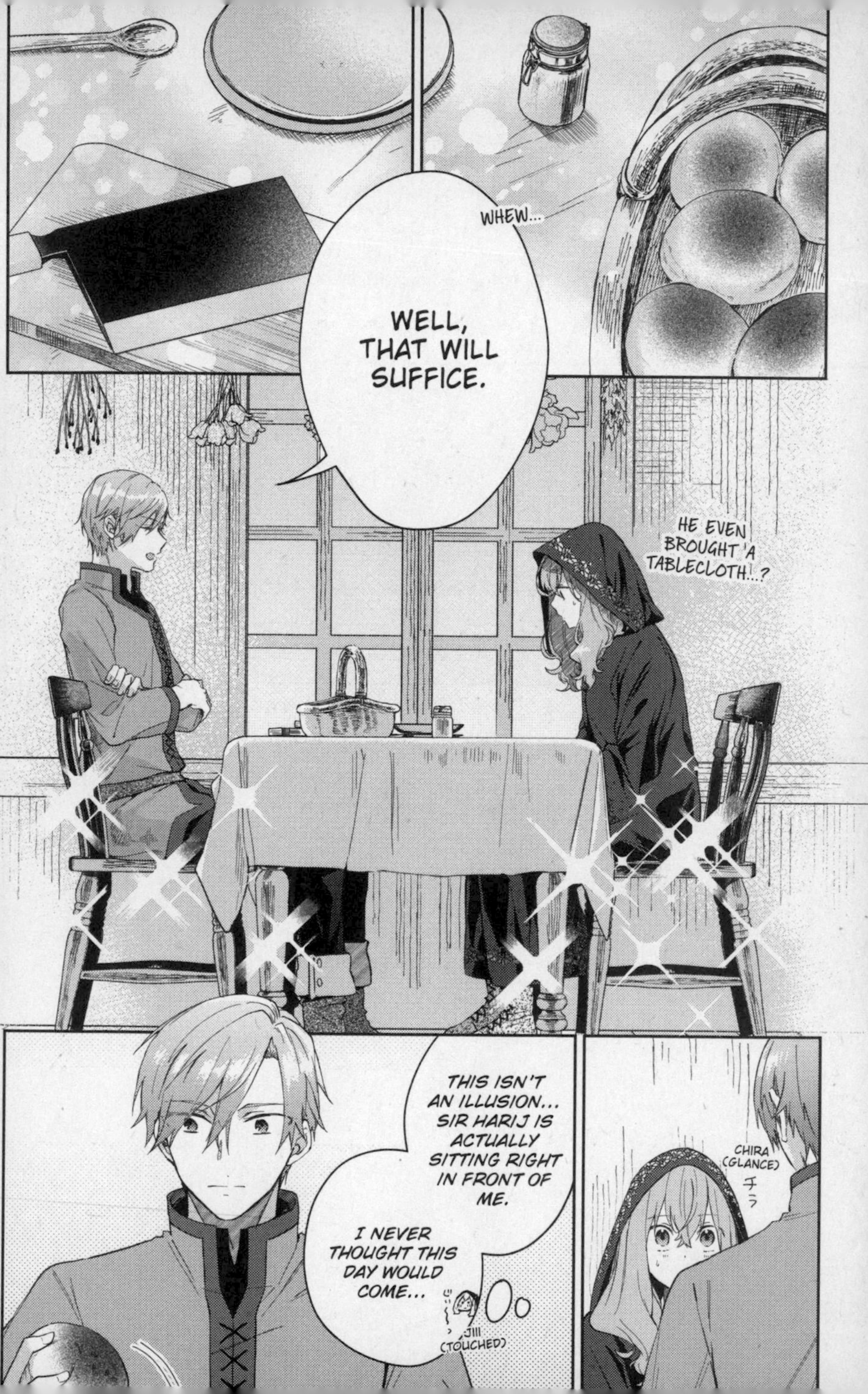
WHEW...
WELL, THAT WILL SUFFICE.
HE EVEN BROUGHT A TABLECLOTH...?
CHIRA (GLANCE)
チラ
THIS ISN'T AN ILLUSION... SIR HARIJ IS ACTUALLY SITTING RIGHT IN FRONT OF ME.
I NEVER THOUGHT THIS DAY WOULD COME...
JIII (TOUCHED)

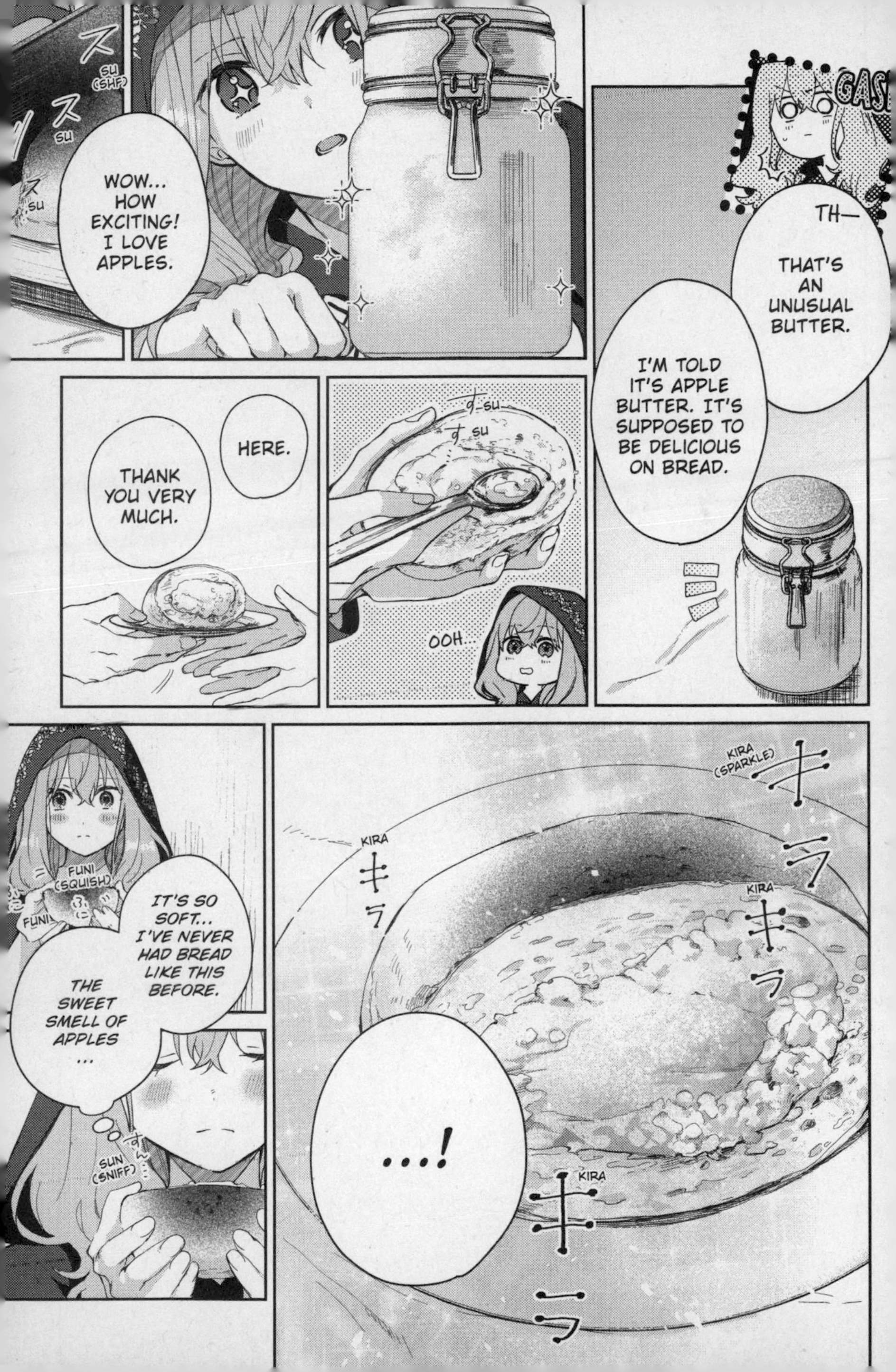

GAS
TH—
THAT'S AN UNUSUAL BUTTER.
I'M TOLD IT'S APPLE BUTTER. IT'S SUPPOSED TO BE DELICIOUS ON BREAD.
SU (SHF)
SU
SU
WOW... HOW EXCITING! I LOVE APPLES.
SU
SU
OOH...
HERE.
THANK YOU VERY MUCH.
KIRA (SPARKLE)
KIRA
KIRA
KIRA
...!
FUNI (SQUISH)
FUNI
IT'S SO SOFT... I'VE NEVER HAD BREAD LIKE THIS BEFORE.
THE SWEET SMELL OF APPLES ...
SUN (SNIFF)

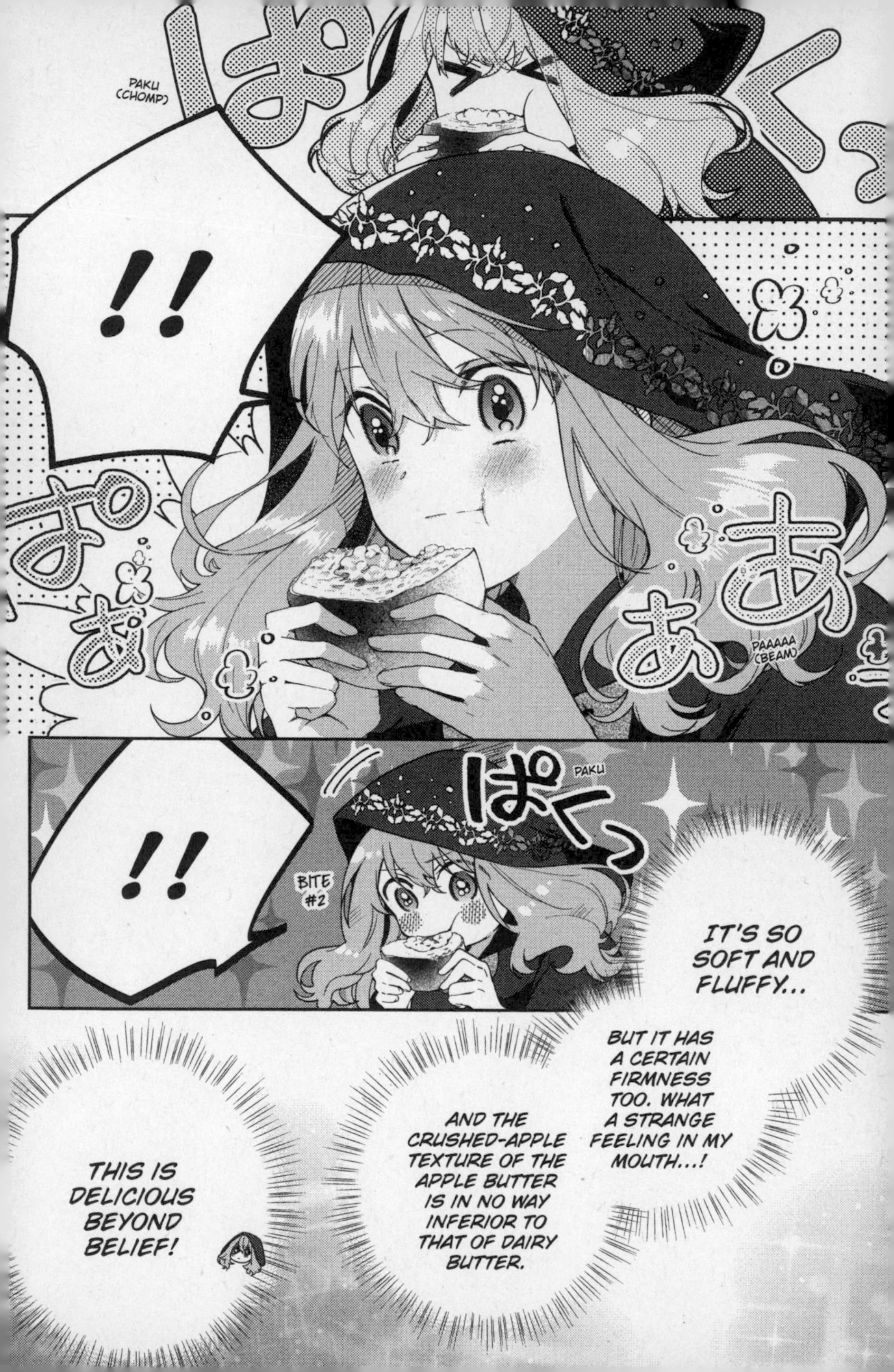
ぱくっ
PAKU (CHOMP)
!!
PAAAAA (BEAM)
ぱくっ
PAKU
BITE #2
!!
IT'S SO SOFT AND FLUFFY...
BUT IT HAS A CERTAIN FIRMNESS TOO. WHAT A STRANGE FEELING IN MY MOUTH...!
AND THE CRUSHED-APPLE TEXTURE OF THE APPLE BUTTER IS IN NO WAY INFERIOR TO THAT OF DAIRY BUTTER.
THIS IS DELICIOUS BEYOND BELIEF!

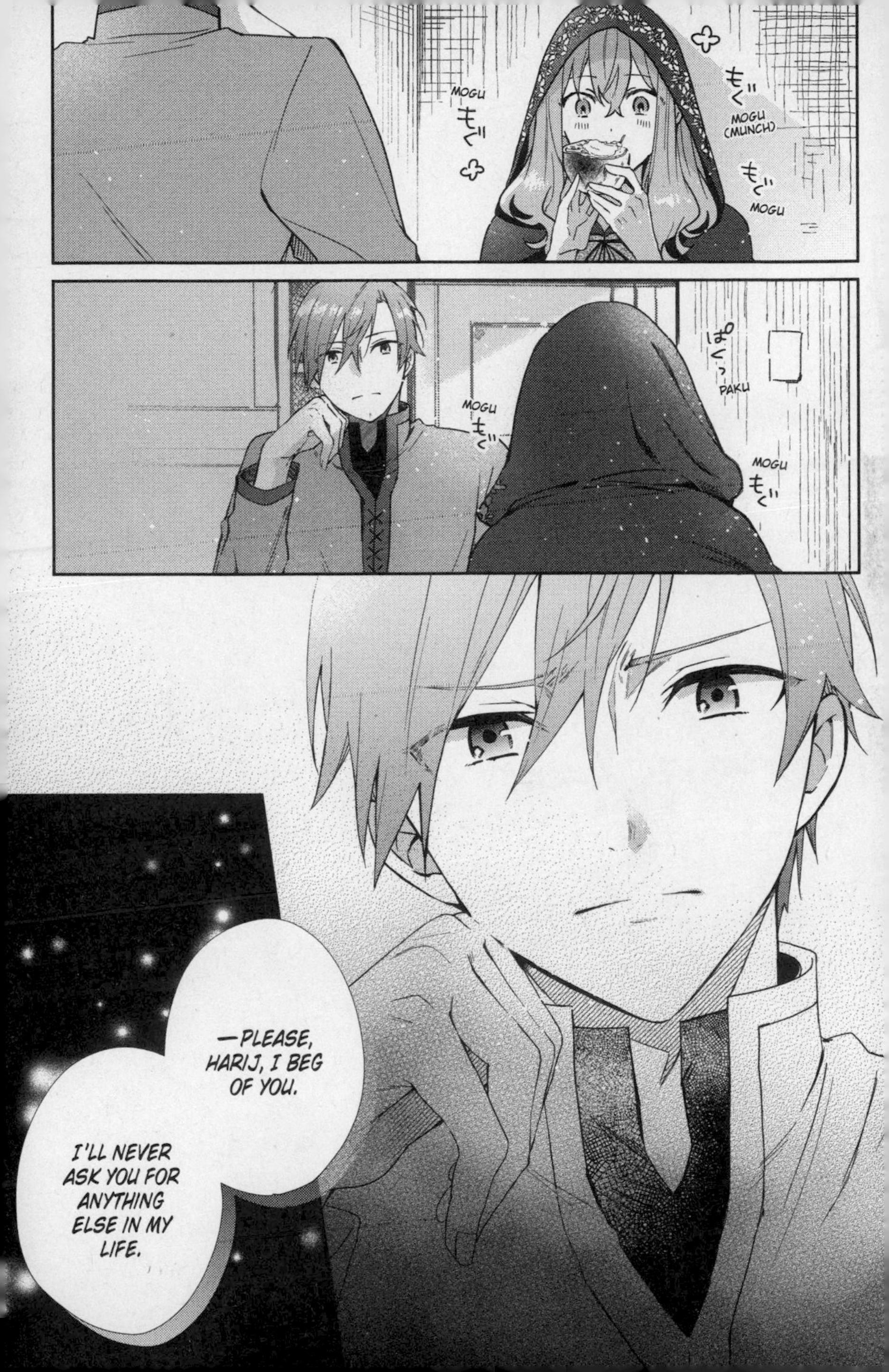
もぐ
MOGU (MUNCH)
もぐ
MOGU
MOGU
もぐ
ぱくっ
PAKU
MOGU
もぐ
MOGU
もぐ
—PLEASE, HARIJ, I BEG OF YOU.
I'LL NEVER ASK YOU FOR ANYTHING ELSE IN MY LIFE.

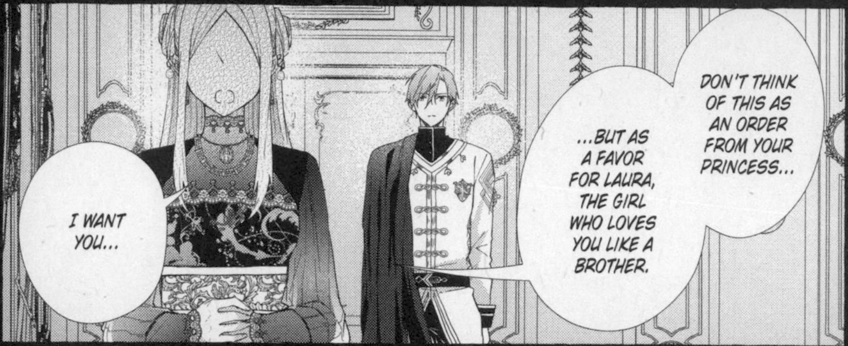
DON'T THINK OF THIS AS AN ORDER FROM YOUR PRINCESS...
...BUT AS A FAVOR FOR LAURA, THE GIRL WHO LOVES YOU LIKE A BROTHER.
I WANT YOU...
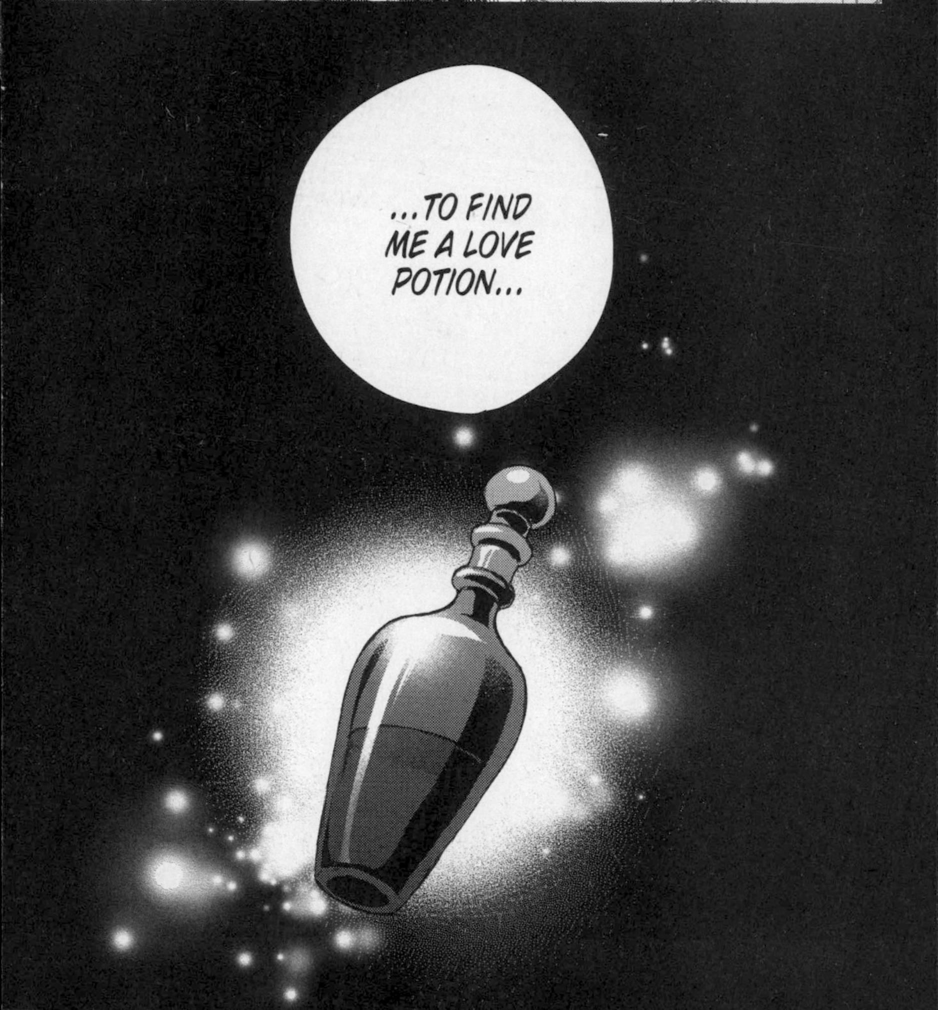
...TO FIND ME A LOVE POTION...

Hi, I'm a

Witch,

and My Crush
Wants Me to Make a
Love Potion

Hi, I'm a Witch, and My Crush Wants Me to Make a Love Potion

CHAPTER 5

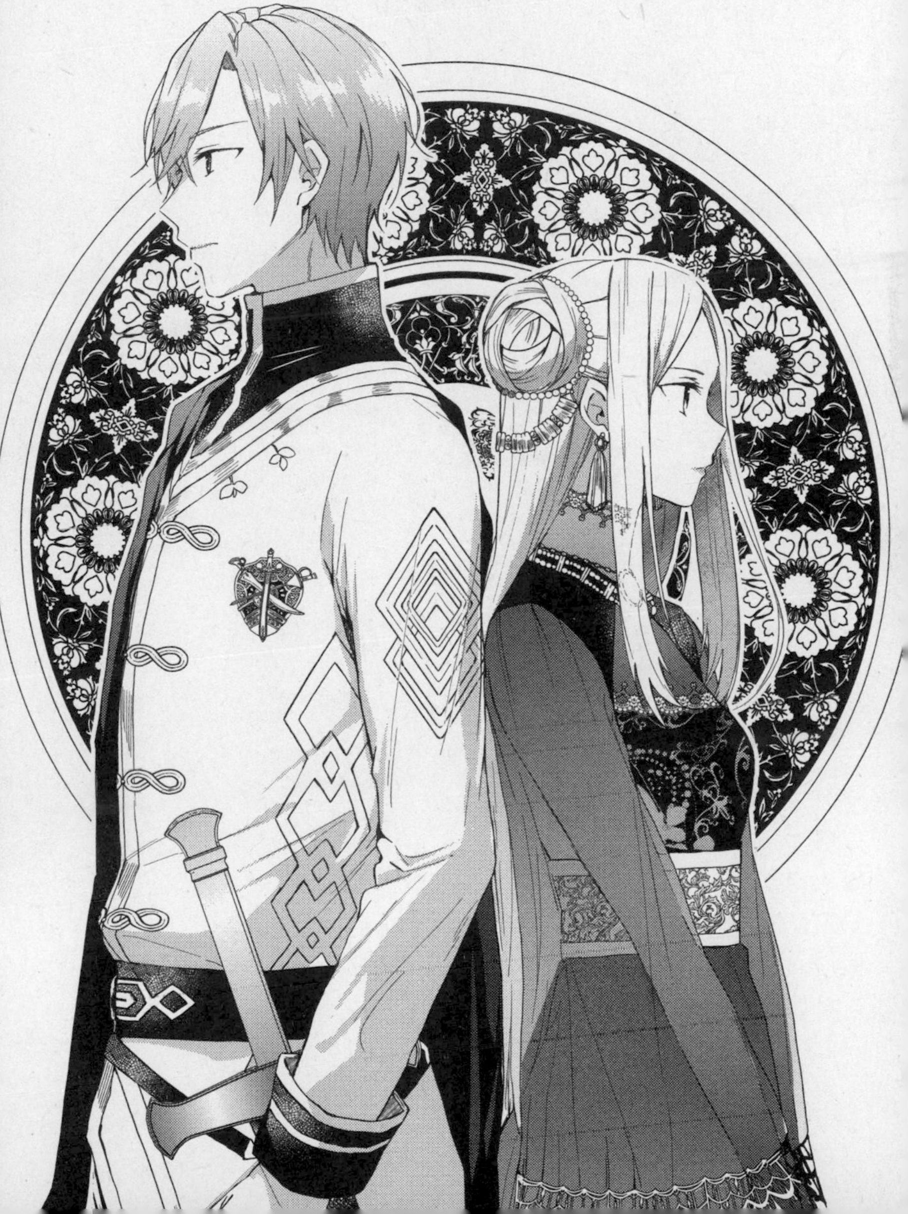

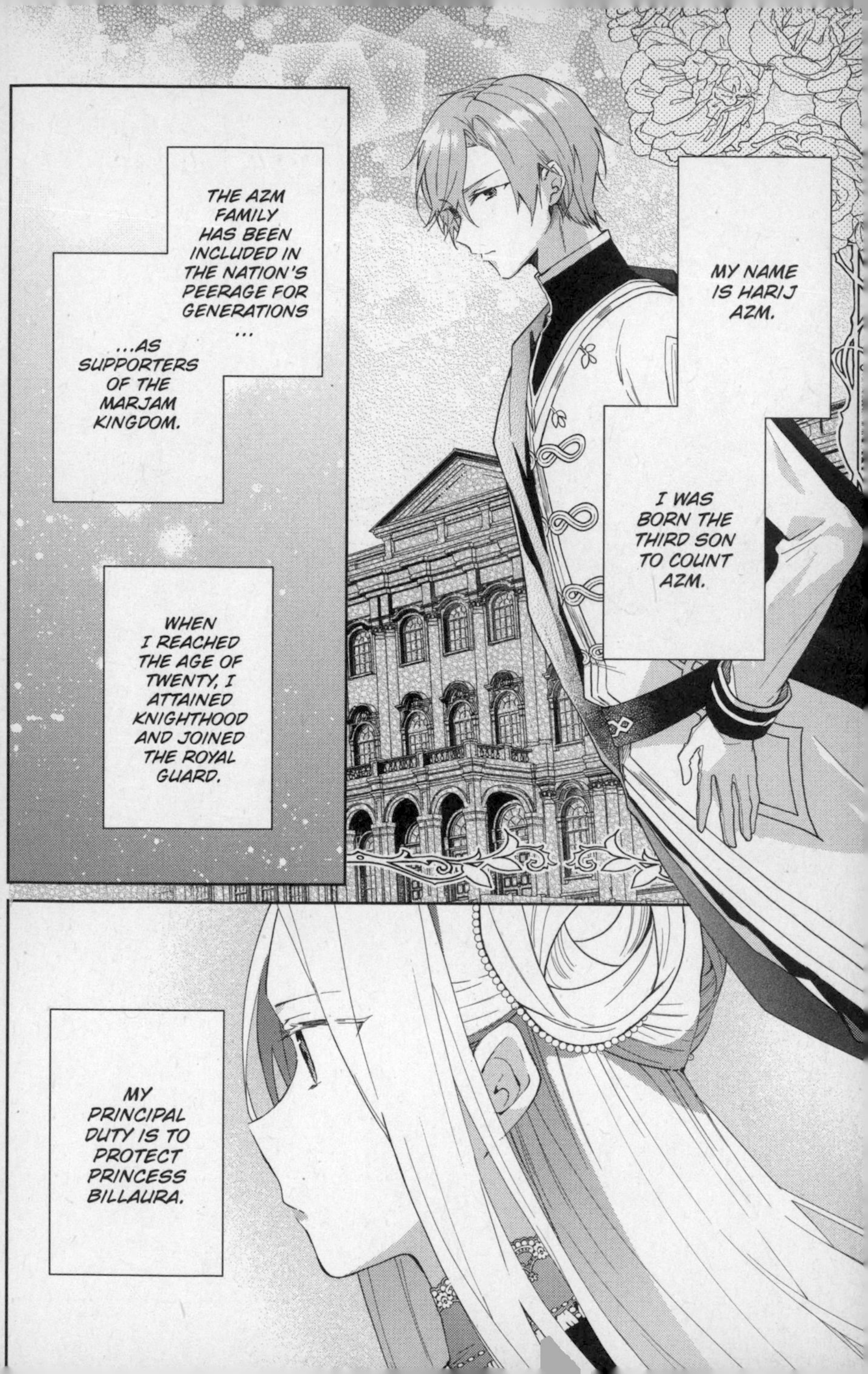
MY NAME IS HARIJ AZM.
I WAS BORN THE THIRD SON TO COUNT AZM.
THE AZM FAMILY HAS BEEN INCLUDED IN THE NATION'S PEERAGE FOR GENERATIONS...
...AS SUPPORTERS OF THE MARJAM KINGDOM.
WHEN I REACHED THE AGE OF TWENTY, I ATTAINED KNIGHTHOOD AND JOINED THE ROYAL GUARD.
MY PRINCIPAL DUTY IS TO PROTECT PRINCESS BILLAURA.

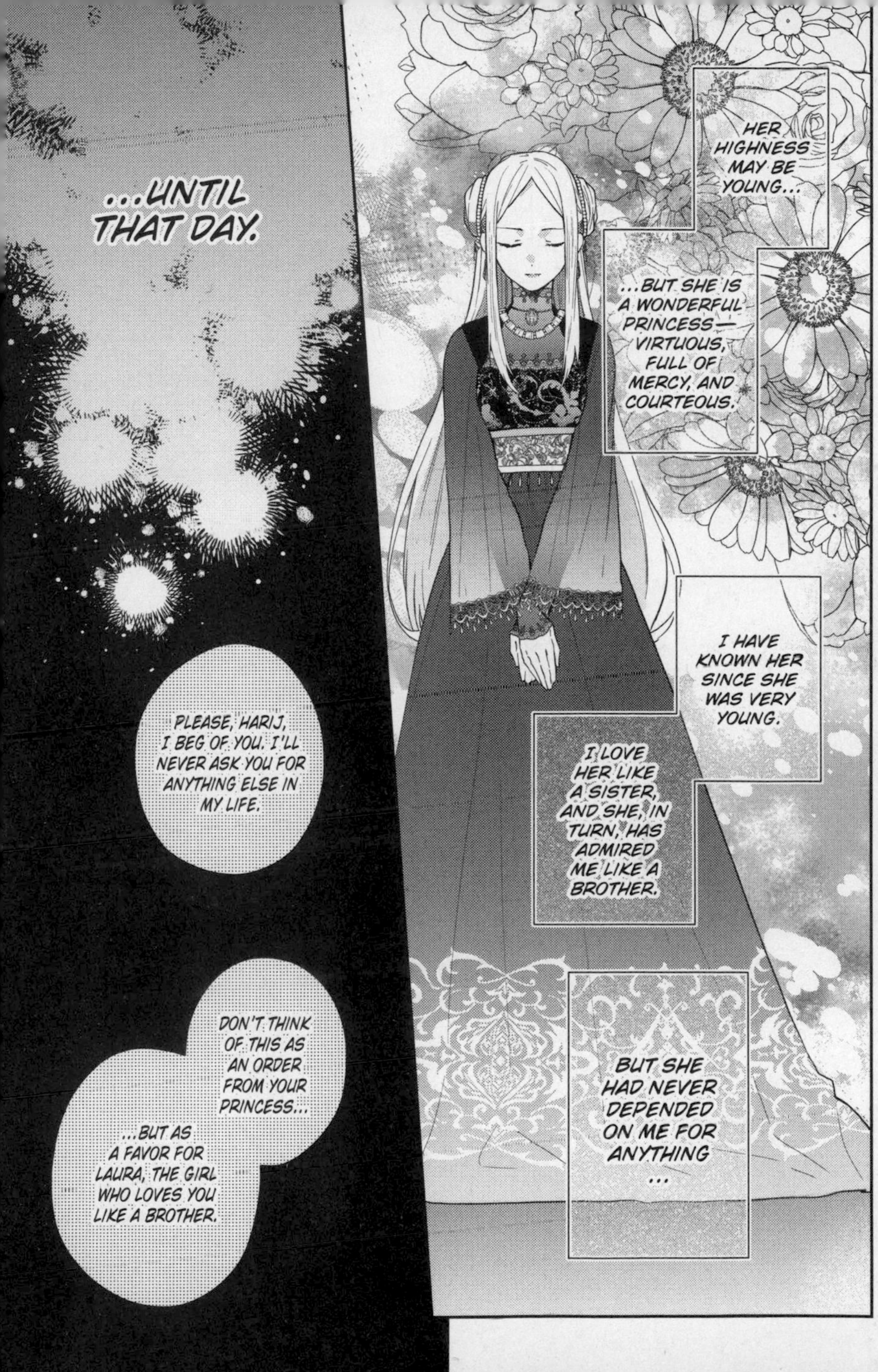
HER HIGHNESS MAY BE YOUNG...
...BUT SHE IS A WONDERFUL PRINCESS—VIRTUOUS, FULL OF MERCY, AND COURTEOUS.
I HAVE KNOWN HER SINCE SHE WAS VERY YOUNG.
I LOVE HER LIKE A SISTER, AND SHE, IN TURN, HAS ADMIRED ME LIKE A BROTHER.
BUT SHE HAD NEVER DEPENDED ON ME FOR ANYTHING...
...UNTIL THAT DAY.
PLEASE, HARIJ, I BEG OF YOU. I'LL NEVER ASK YOU FOR ANYTHING ELSE IN MY LIFE.
DON'T THINK OF THIS AS AN ORDER FROM YOUR PRINCESS...
...BUT AS A FAVOR FOR LAURA, THE GIRL WHO LOVES YOU LIKE A BROTHER.

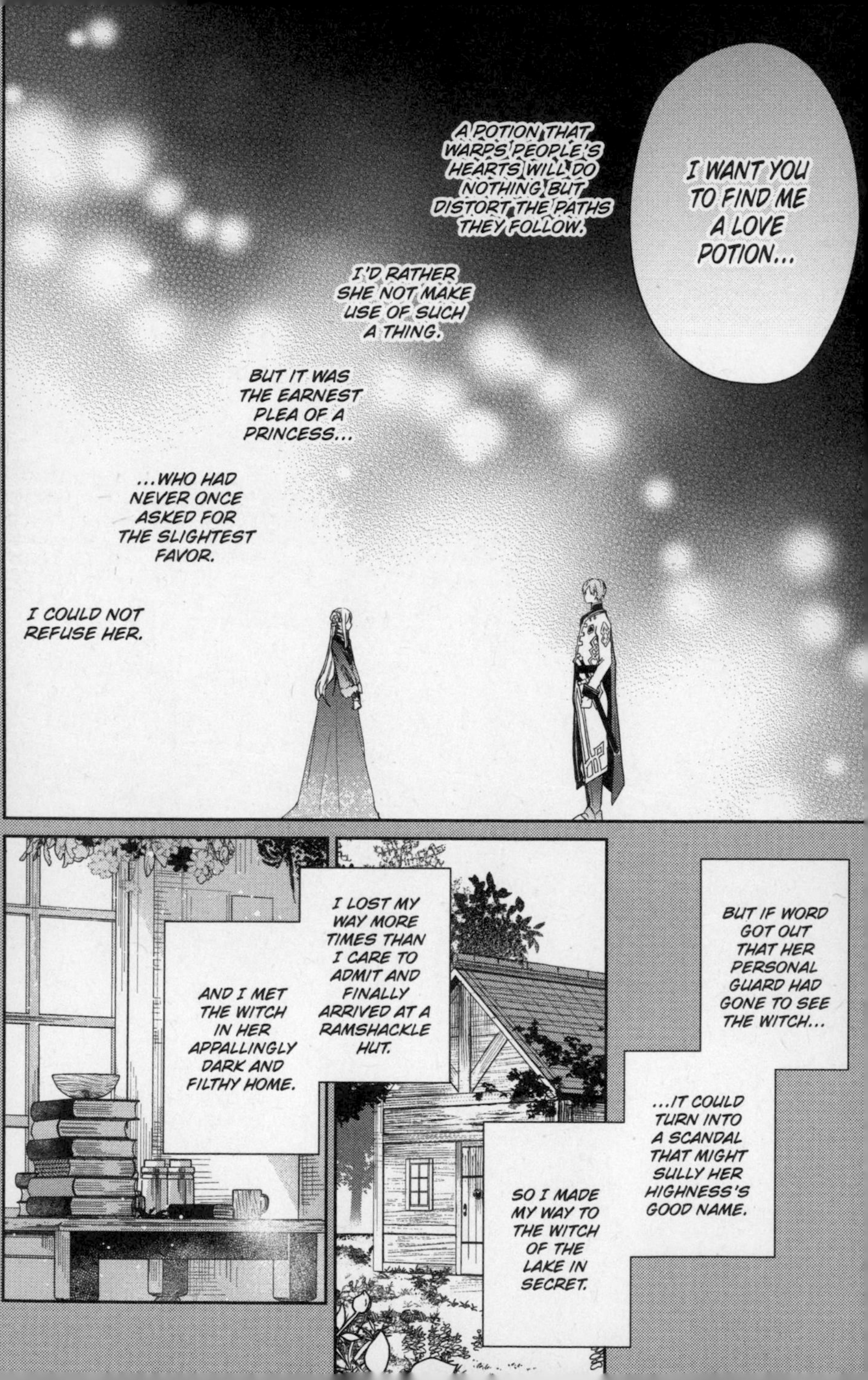
I WANT YOU TO FIND ME A LOVE POTION...
A POTION THAT WARPS PEOPLE'S HEARTS WILL DO NOTHING BUT DISTORT THE PATHS THEY FOLLOW.
I'D RATHER SHE NOT MAKE USE OF SUCH A THING.
BUT IT WAS THE EARNEST PLEA OF A PRINCESS...
...WHO HAD NEVER ONCE ASKED FOR THE SLIGHTEST FAVOR.
I COULD NOT REFUSE HER.
BUT IF WORD GOT OUT THAT HER PERSONAL GUARD HAD GONE TO SEE THE WITCH...
...IT COULD TURN INTO A SCANDAL THAT MIGHT SULLY HER HIGHNESS'S GOOD NAME.
SO I MADE MY WAY TO THE WITCH OF THE LAKE IN SECRET.
I LOST MY WAY MORE TIMES THAN I CARE TO ADMIT AND FINALLY ARRIVED AT A RAMSHACKLE HUT.
AND I MET THE WITCH IN HER APPALLINGLY DARK AND FILTHY HOME.

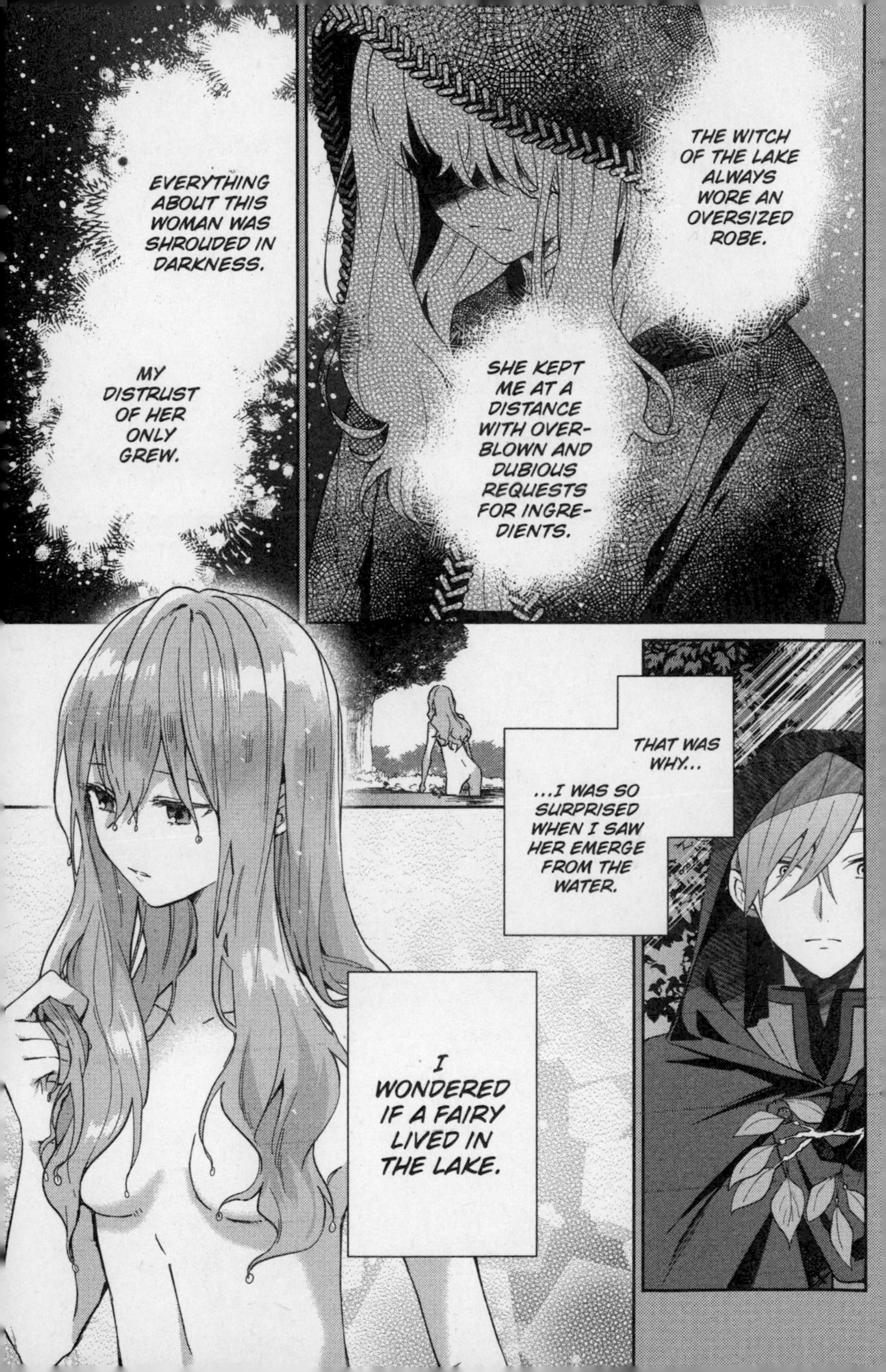
THE WITCH OF THE LAKE ALWAYS WORE AN OVERSIZED ROBE.
SHE KEPT ME AT A DISTANCE WITH OVER-BLOWN AND DUBIOUS REQUESTS FOR INGRE-DIENTS.
EVERYTHING ABOUT THIS WOMAN WAS SHROUDED IN DARKNESS.
MY DISTRUST OF HER ONLY GREW.
THAT WAS WHY...
...I WAS SO SURPRISED WHEN I SAW HER EMERGE FROM THE WATER.
I WONDERED IF A FAIRY LIVED IN THE LAKE.

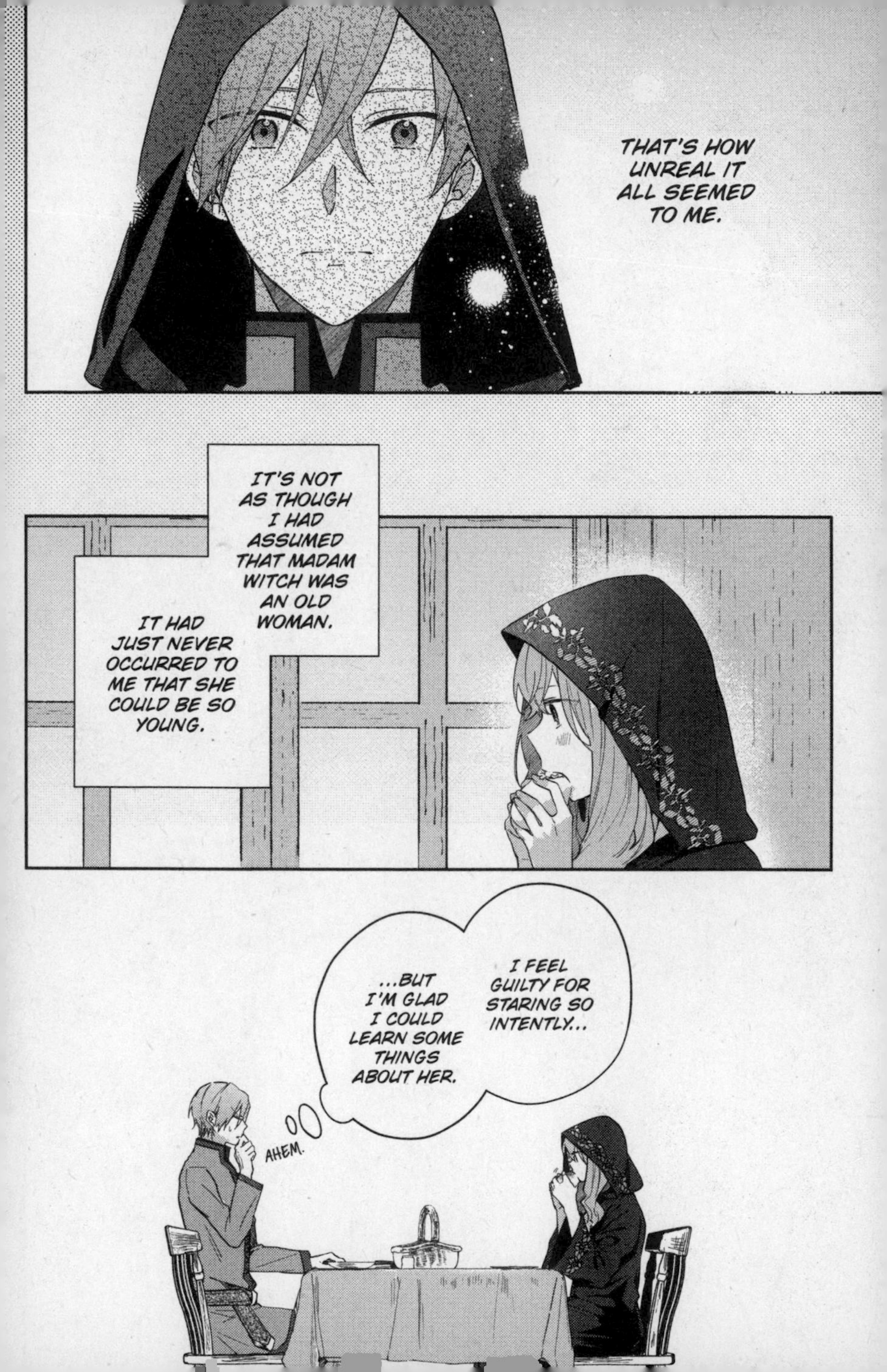
THAT'S HOW UNREAL IT ALL SEEMED TO ME.
IT'S NOT AS THOUGH I HAD ASSUMED THAT MADAM WITCH WAS AN OLD WOMAN.
IT HAD JUST NEVER OCCURRED TO ME THAT SHE COULD BE SO YOUNG.
I FEEL GUILTY FOR STARING SO INTENTLY...
...BUT I'M GLAD I COULD LEARN SOME THINGS ABOUT HER.
AHEM.

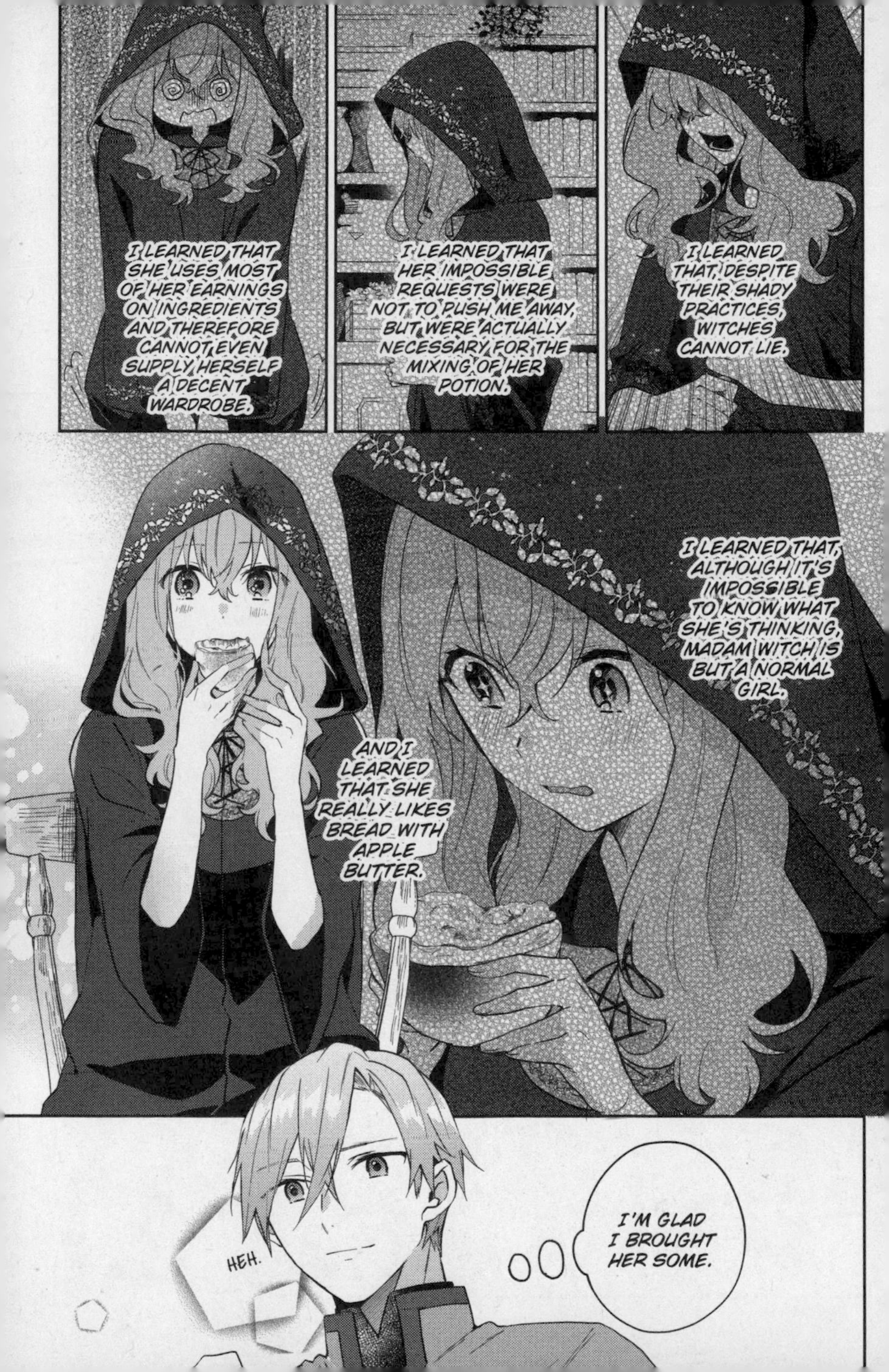
I LEARNED THAT, DESPITE THEIR SHADY PRACTICES, WITCHES CANNOT LIE.
I LEARNED THAT HER IMPOSSIBLE REQUESTS WERE NOT TO PUSH ME AWAY, BUT WERE ACTUALLY NECESSARY FOR THE MIXING OF HER POTION.
I LEARNED THAT SHE USES MOST OF HER EARNINGS ON INGREDIENTS AND THEREFORE CANNOT EVEN SUPPLY HERSELF A DECENT WARDROBE.
I LEARNED THAT, ALTHOUGH IT'S IMPOSSIBLE TO KNOW WHAT SHE'S THINKING, MADAM WITCH IS BUT A NORMAL GIRL.
AND I LEARNED THAT SHE REALLY LIKES BREAD WITH APPLE BUTTER.
I'M GLAD I BROUGHT HER SOME.
HEH.

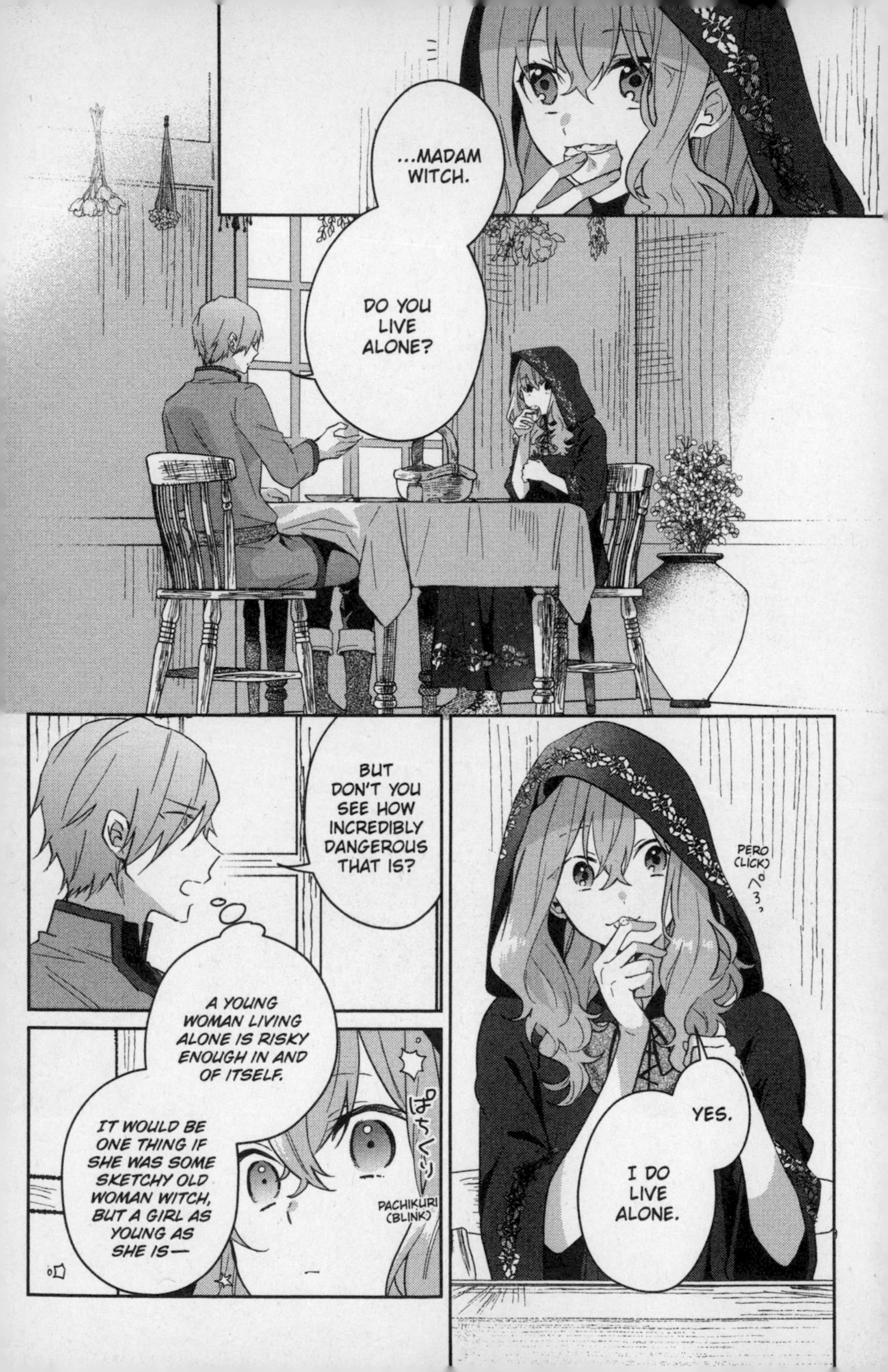
...MADAM WITCH.
DO YOU LIVE ALONE?
PERO (LICK)
YES.
I DO LIVE ALONE.
BUT DON'T YOU SEE HOW INCREDIBLY DANGEROUS THAT IS?
A YOUNG WOMAN LIVING ALONE IS RISKY ENOUGH IN AND OF ITSELF.
IT WOULD BE ONE THING IF SHE WAS SOME SKETCHY OLD WOMAN WITCH, BUT A GIRL AS YOUNG AS SHE IS—
PACHIKURI (BLINK)

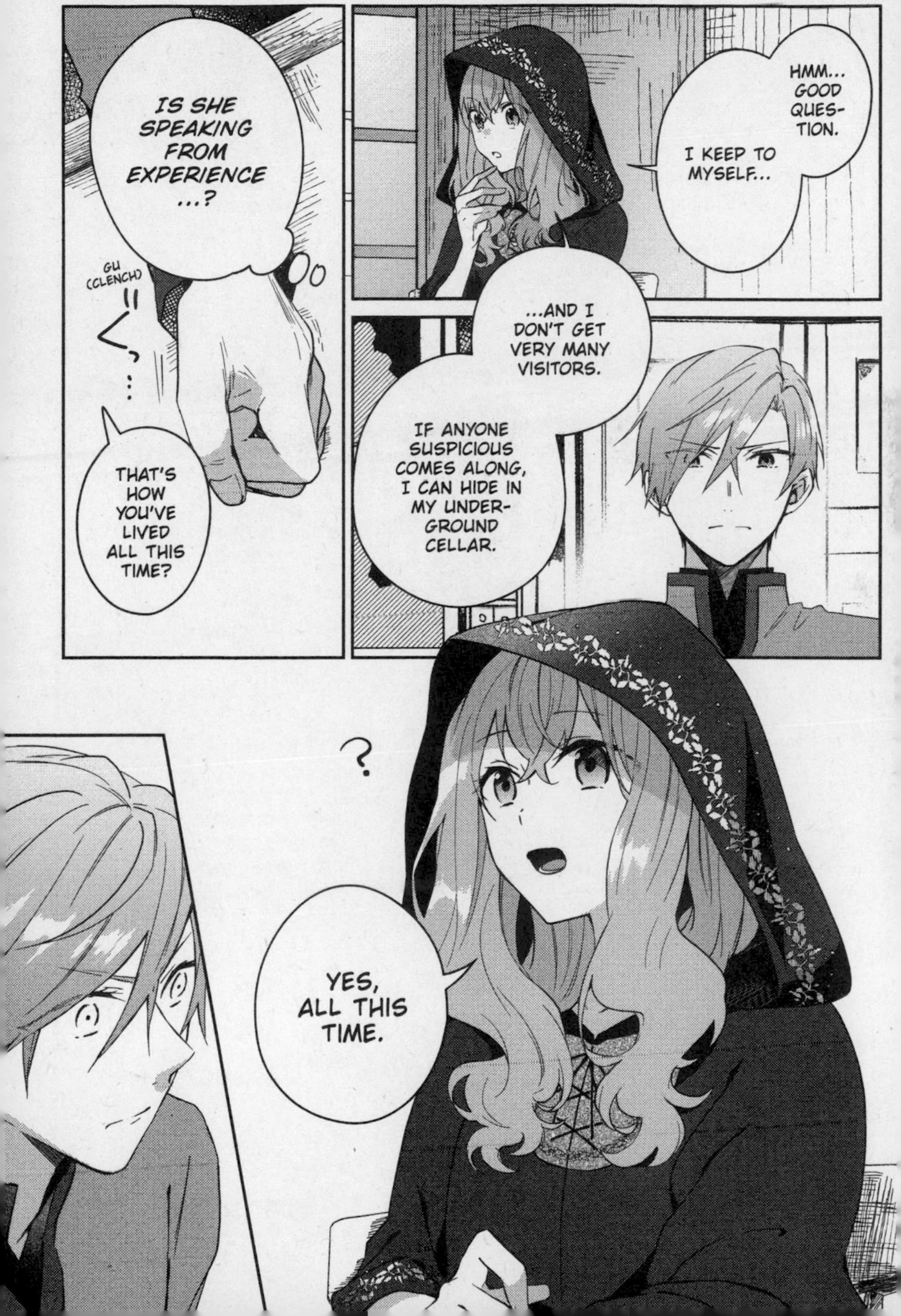
HMM... GOOD QUES-TION.
I KEEP TO MYSELF...
...AND I DON'T GET VERY MANY VISITORS.
IF ANYONE SUSPICIOUS COMES ALONG, I CAN HIDE IN MY UNDER-GROUND CELLAR.
IS SHE SPEAKING FROM EXPERIENCE ...?
GU (CLENCH)
THAT'S HOW YOU'VE LIVED ALL THIS TIME?
?
YES, ALL THIS TIME.

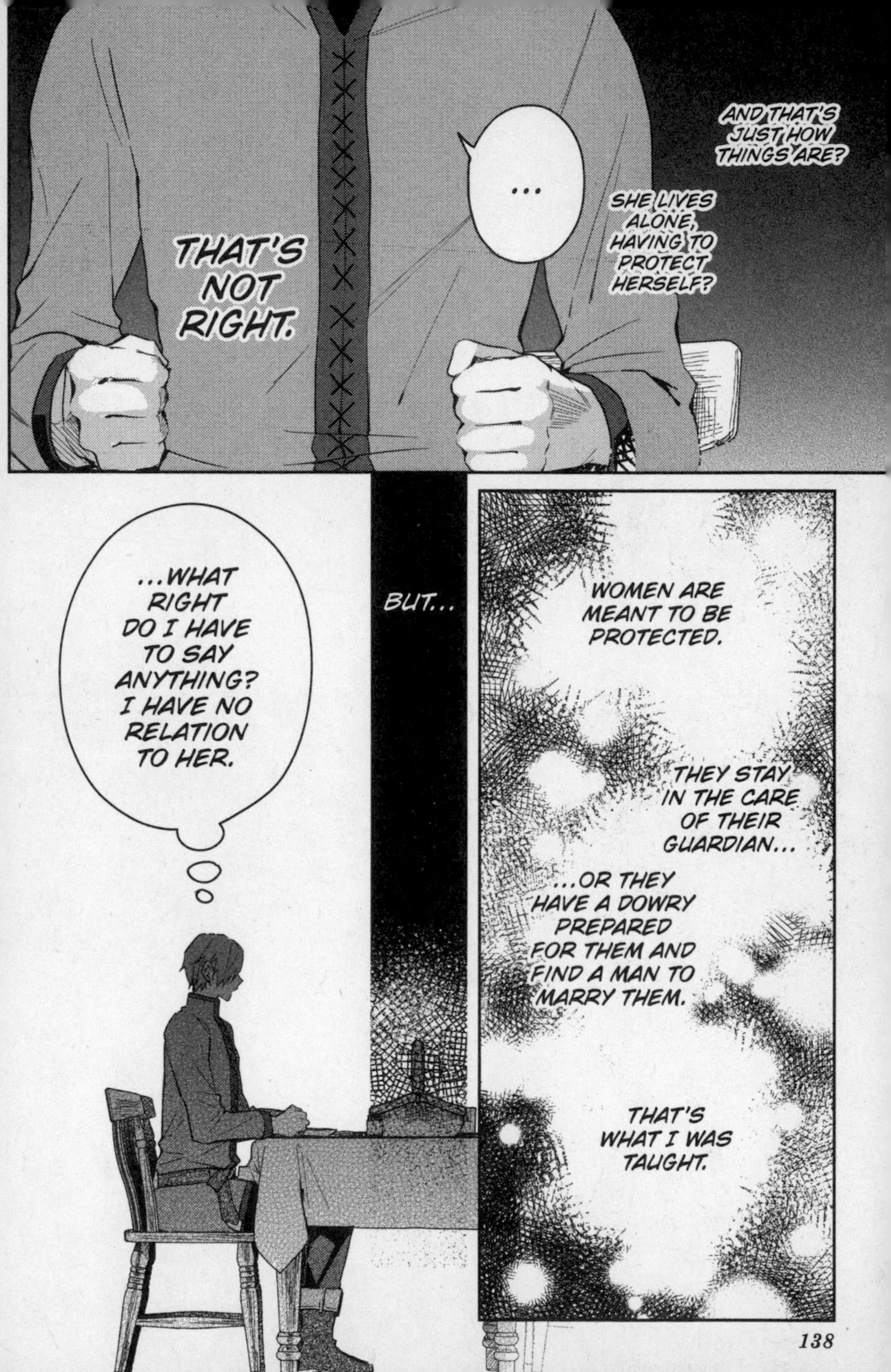
AND THAT'S JUST HOW THINGS ARE?
SHE LIVES ALONE, HAVING TO PROTECT HERSELF?
...
THAT'S NOT RIGHT.
WOMEN ARE MEANT TO BE PROTECTED.
THEY STAY IN THE CARE OF THEIR GUARDIAN...
...OR THEY HAVE A DOWRY PREPARED FOR THEM AND FIND A MAN TO MARRY THEM.
THAT'S WHAT I WAS TAUGHT.
BUT...
...WHAT RIGHT DO I HAVE TO SAY ANYTHING? I HAVE NO RELATION TO HER.

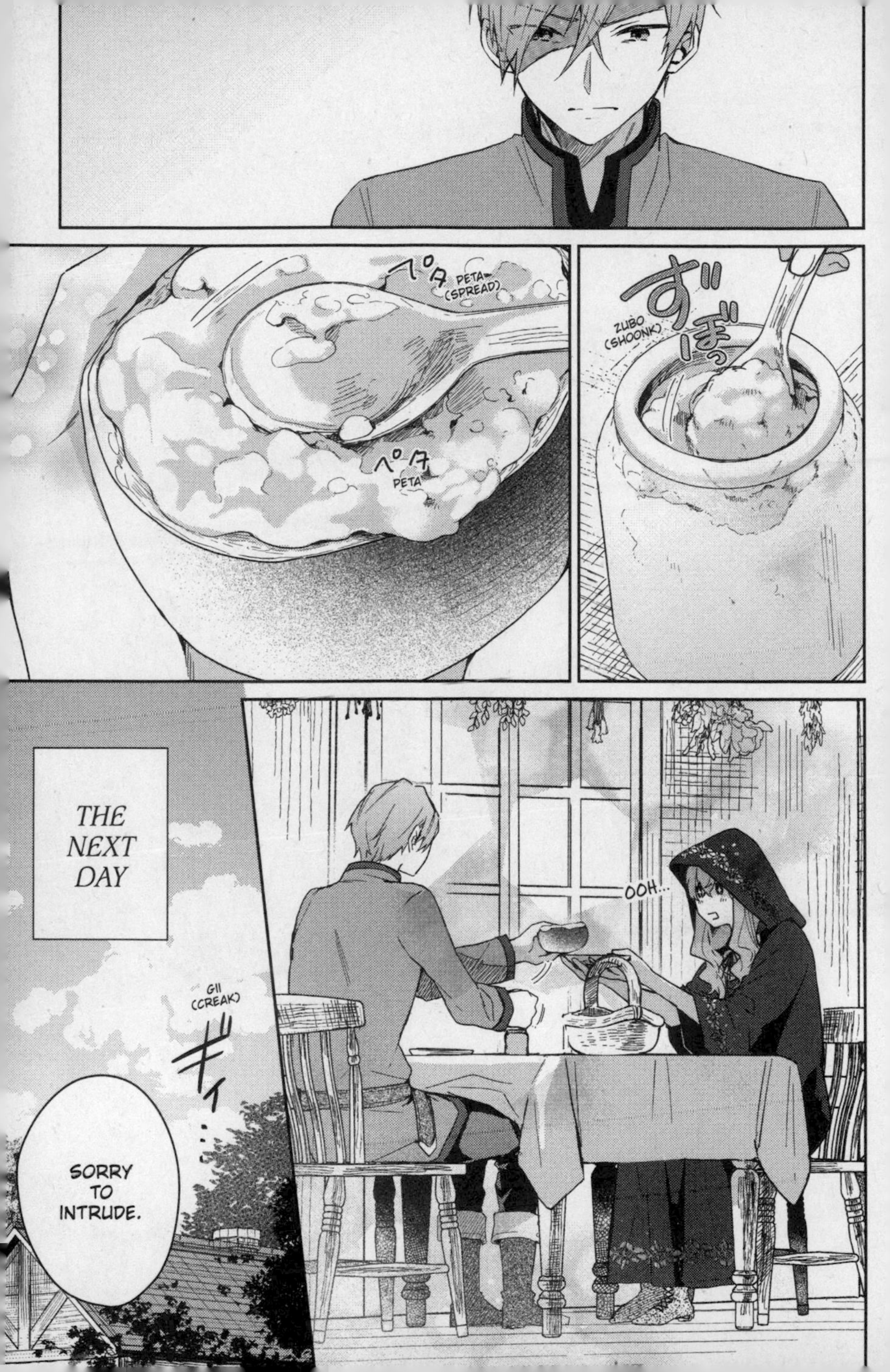
ずぼっ
ZUBO (SHOONK)
ペタ
PETA (SPREAD)
ペタ
PETA
THE NEXT DAY
OOH...
GII (CREAK)
ギィ…
SORRY TO INTRUDE.

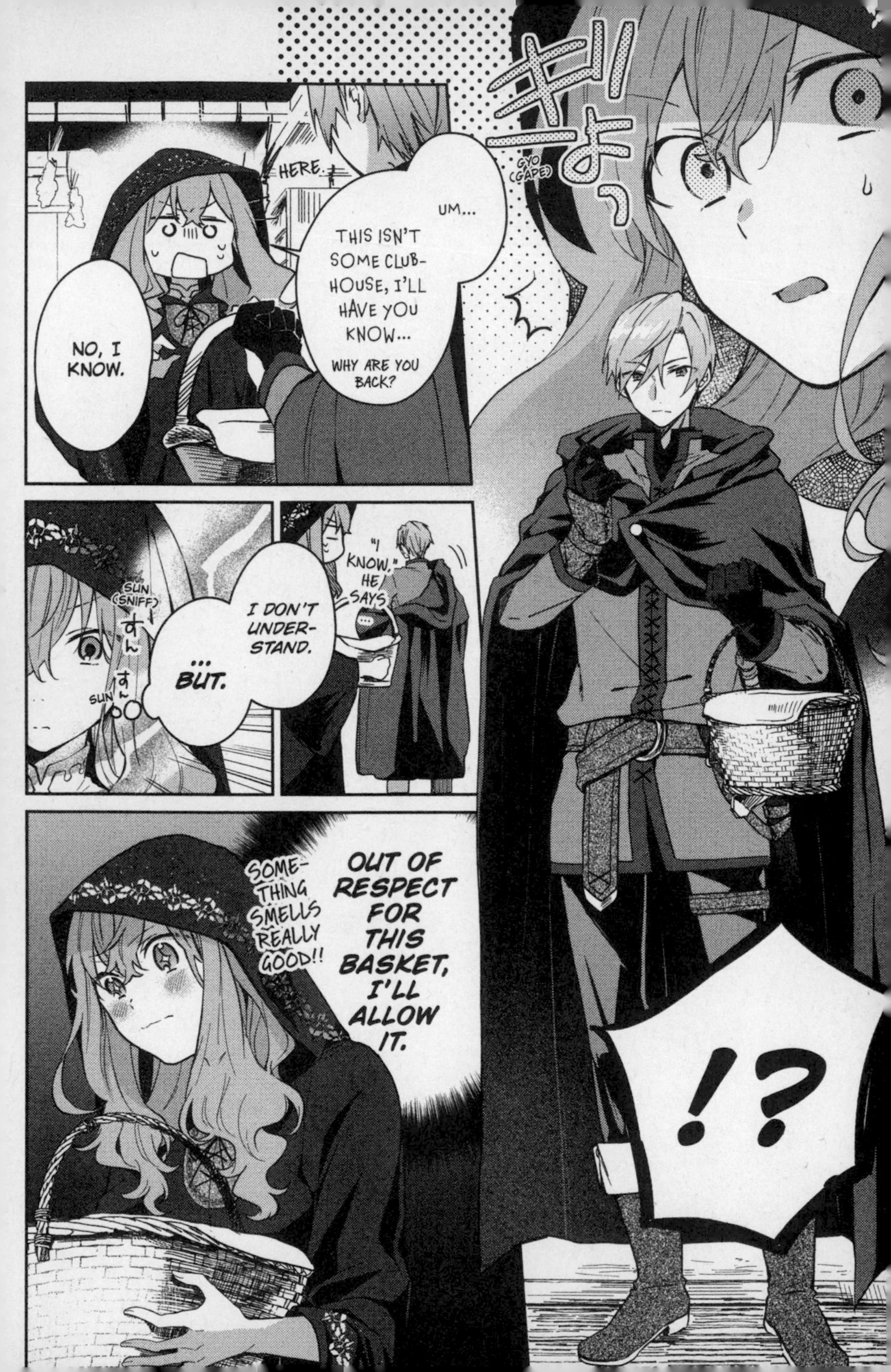ギョっ
GYO (GAPE)
!?
HERE.
UM...
THIS ISN'T SOME CLUB-HOUSE, I'LL HAVE YOU KNOW...
WHY ARE YOU BACK?
NO, I KNOW.
"I KNOW," HE SAYS
...
I DON'T UNDERSTAND.
...BUT.
SUN (SNIFF)
すん
すん
SUN
OUT OF RESPECT FOR THIS BASKET, I'LL ALLOW IT.
SOMETHING SMELLS REALLY GOOD!!

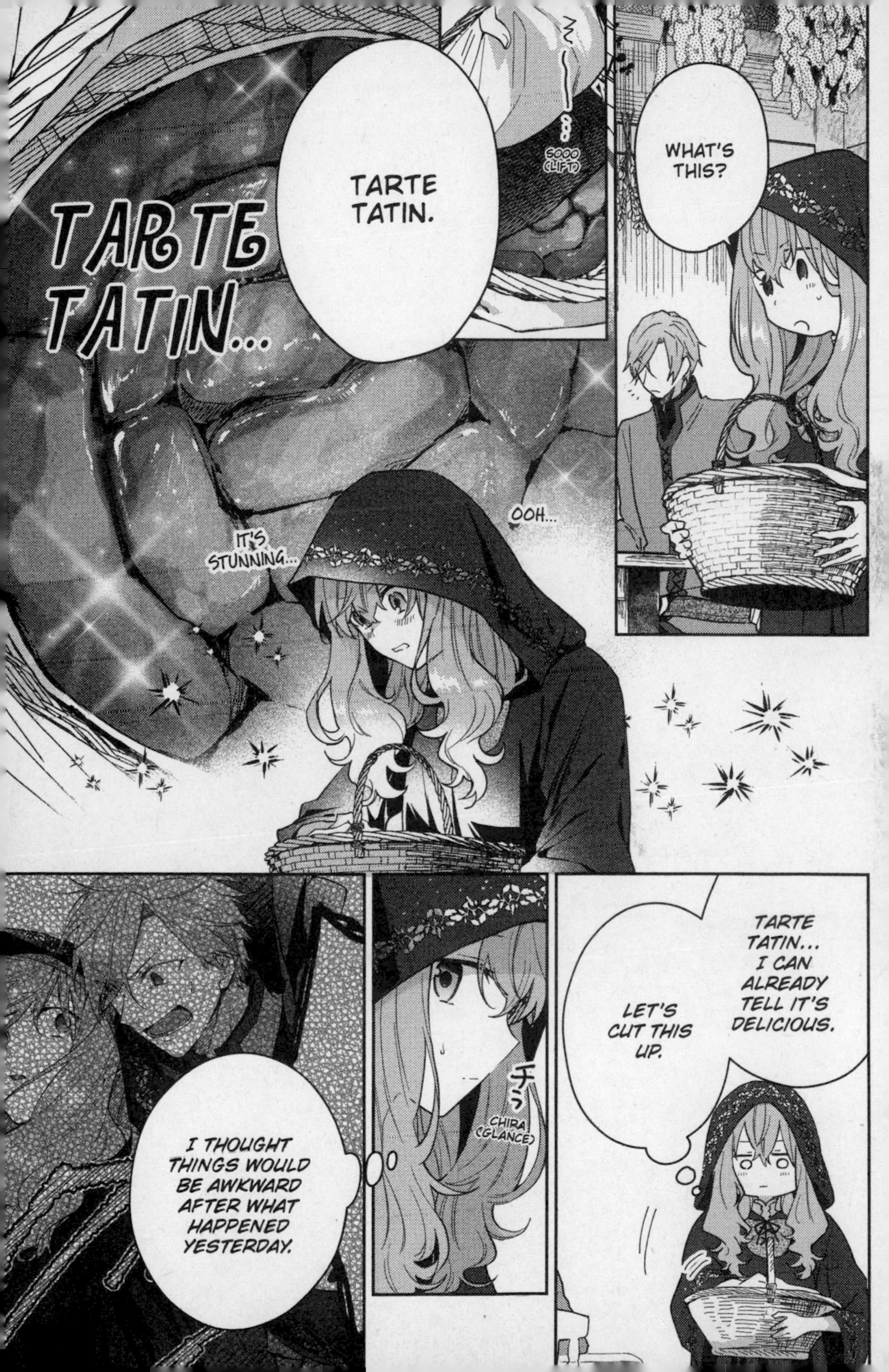
WHAT'S THIS?
SOOO (LIFT)
TARTE TATIN.
TARTE TATIN...
OOH...
IT'S STUNNING...
TARTE TATIN... I CAN ALREADY TELL IT'S DELICIOUS.
LET'S CUT THIS UP.
CHIRA (GLANCE)
I THOUGHT THINGS WOULD BE AWKWARD AFTER WHAT HAPPENED YESTERDAY.

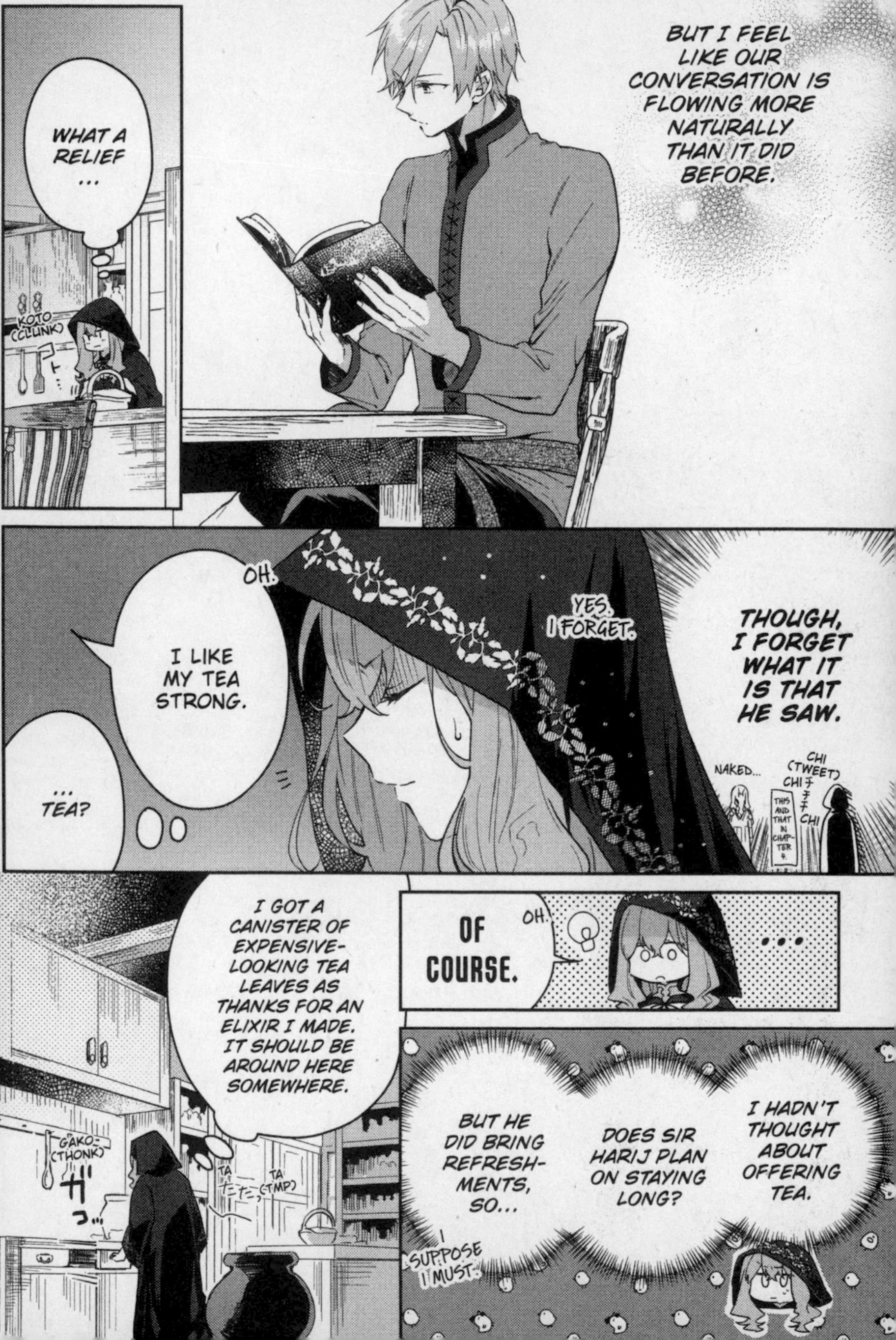
BUT I FEEL LIKE OUR CONVERSATION IS FLOWING MORE NATURALLY THAN IT DID BEFORE.
WHAT A RELIEF ...
KOTO (CLUNK)
THOUGH, I FORGET WHAT IT IS THAT HE SAW.
CHI (TWEET) CHI CHI
NAKED...
THIS AND THAT IN CHAPTER 4.
YES. I FORGET.
OH.
I LIKE MY TEA STRONG.
... TEA?
...
OH.
OF COURSE.
I HADN'T THOUGHT ABOUT OFFERING TEA.
DOES SIR HARIJ PLAN ON STAYING LONG?
BUT HE DID BRING REFRESHMENTS, SO...
I SUPPOSE I MUST.
I GOT A CANISTER OF EXPENSIVE-LOOKING TEA LEAVES AS THANKS FOR AN ELIXIR I MADE. IT SHOULD BE AROUND HERE SOMEWHERE.
TA TA (TMP)
GAKO (THONK)

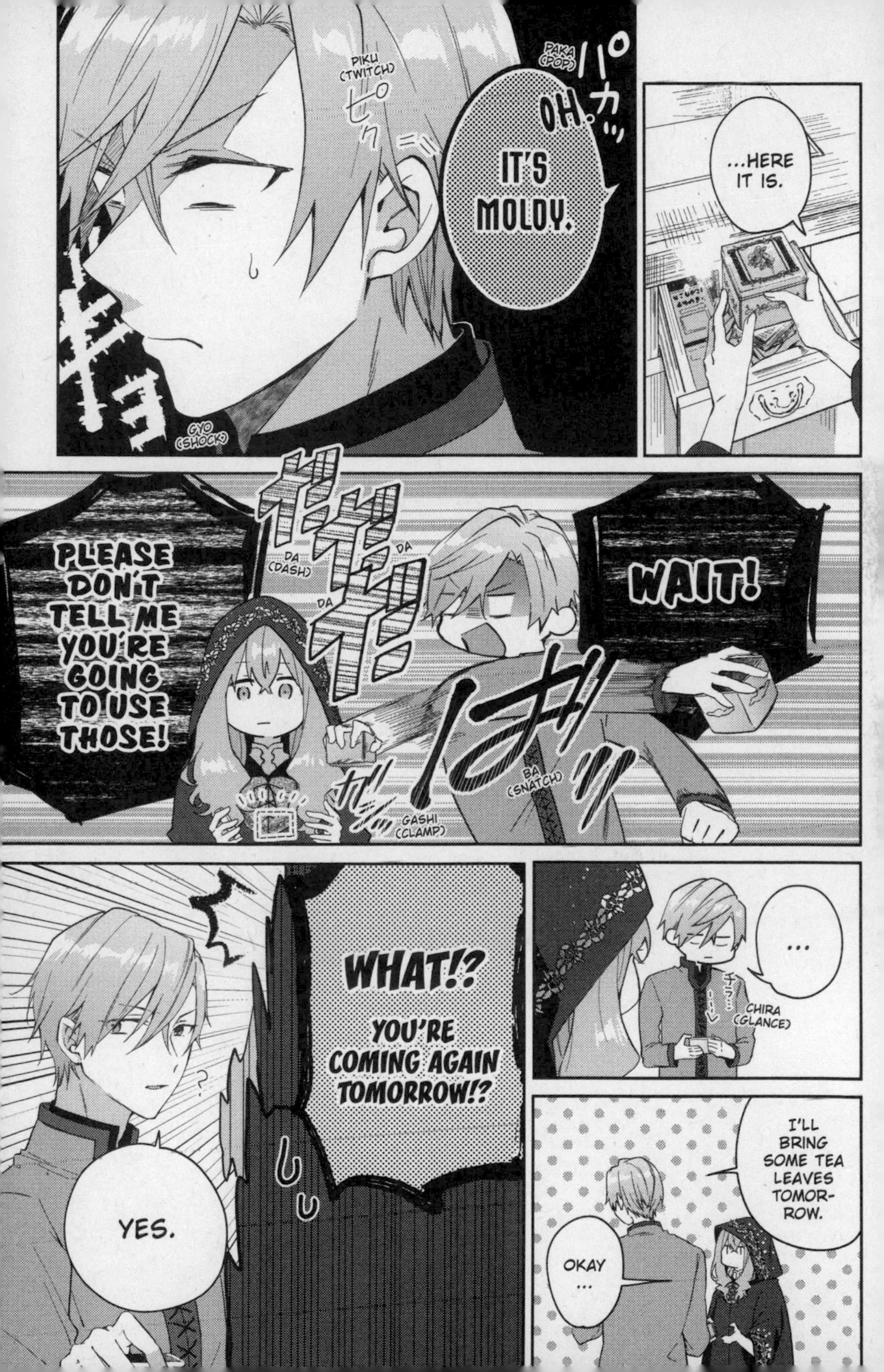
...HERE IT IS.
PAKA (POP)
OH.
IT'S MOLDY.
PIKU (TWITCH)
GYO (SHOCK)
WAIT!
BA (SNATCH)
GASHI (CLAMP)
DA (DASH) DA DA
PLEASE DON'T TELL ME YOU'RE GOING TO USE THOSE!
...
CHIRA (GLANCE)
I'LL BRING SOME TEA LEAVES TOMORROW.
OKAY ...
WHAT!?
YOU'RE COMING AGAIN TOMORROW!?
YES.

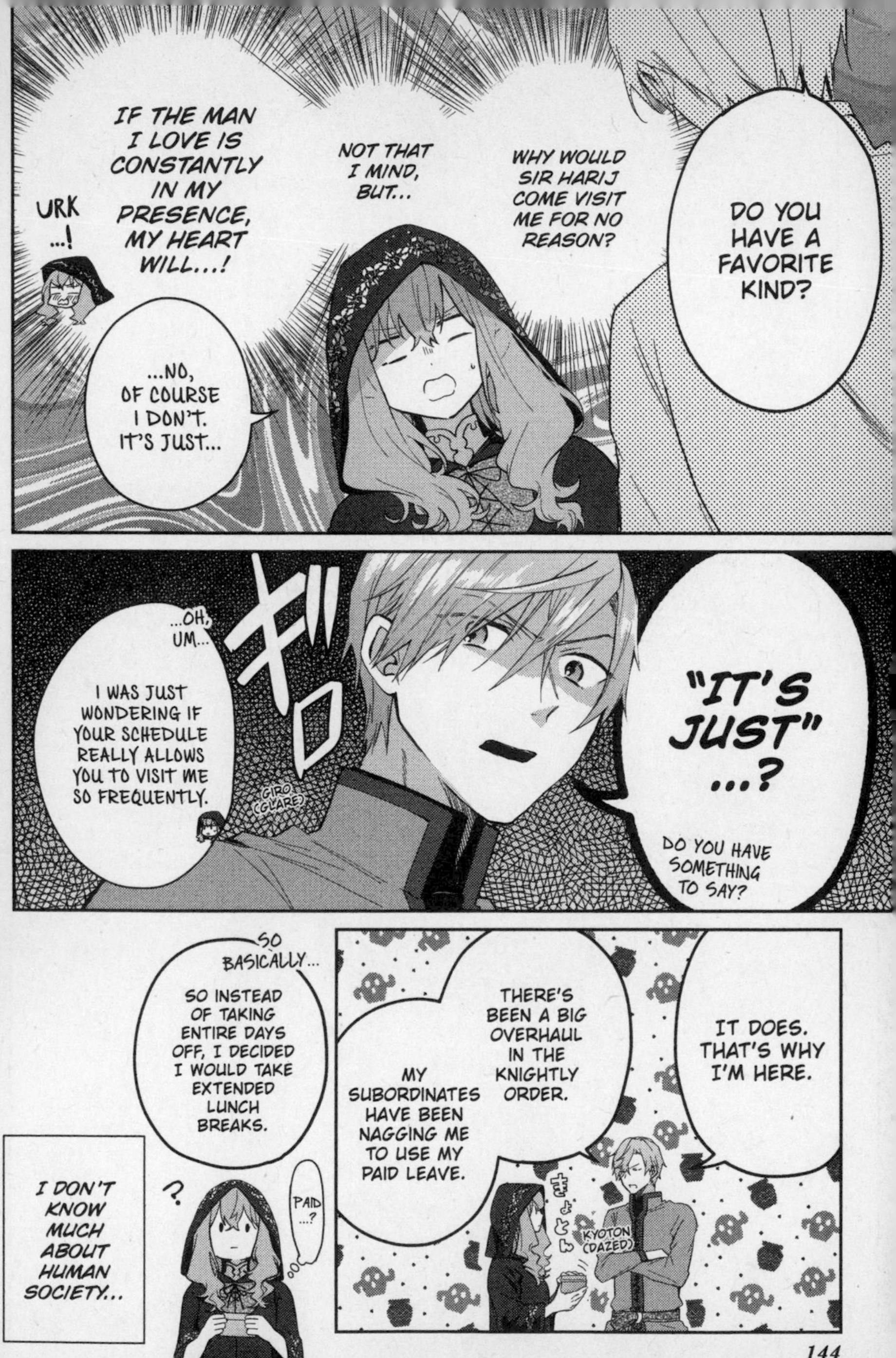
DO YOU HAVE A FAVORITE KIND?
WHY WOULD SIR HARIJ COME VISIT ME FOR NO REASON?
NOT THAT I MIND, BUT...
IF THE MAN I LOVE IS CONSTANTLY IN MY PRESENCE, MY HEART WILL...!
URK ...!
...NO, OF COURSE I DON'T. IT'S JUST...
"IT'S JUST" ...?
DO YOU HAVE SOMETHING TO SAY?
GIRO (GLARE)
...OH, UM...
I WAS JUST WONDERING IF YOUR SCHEDULE REALLY ALLOWS YOU TO VISIT ME SO FREQUENTLY.
IT DOES. THAT'S WHY I'M HERE.
THERE'S BEEN A BIG OVERHAUL IN THE KNIGHTLY ORDER.
MY SUBORDINATES HAVE BEEN NAGGING ME TO USE MY PAID LEAVE.
KYOTON (DAZED)
SO BASICALLY...
SO INSTEAD OF TAKING ENTIRE DAYS OFF, I DECIDED I WOULD TAKE EXTENDED LUNCH BREAKS.
PAID ...?
?
I DON'T KNOW MUCH ABOUT HUMAN SOCIETY...

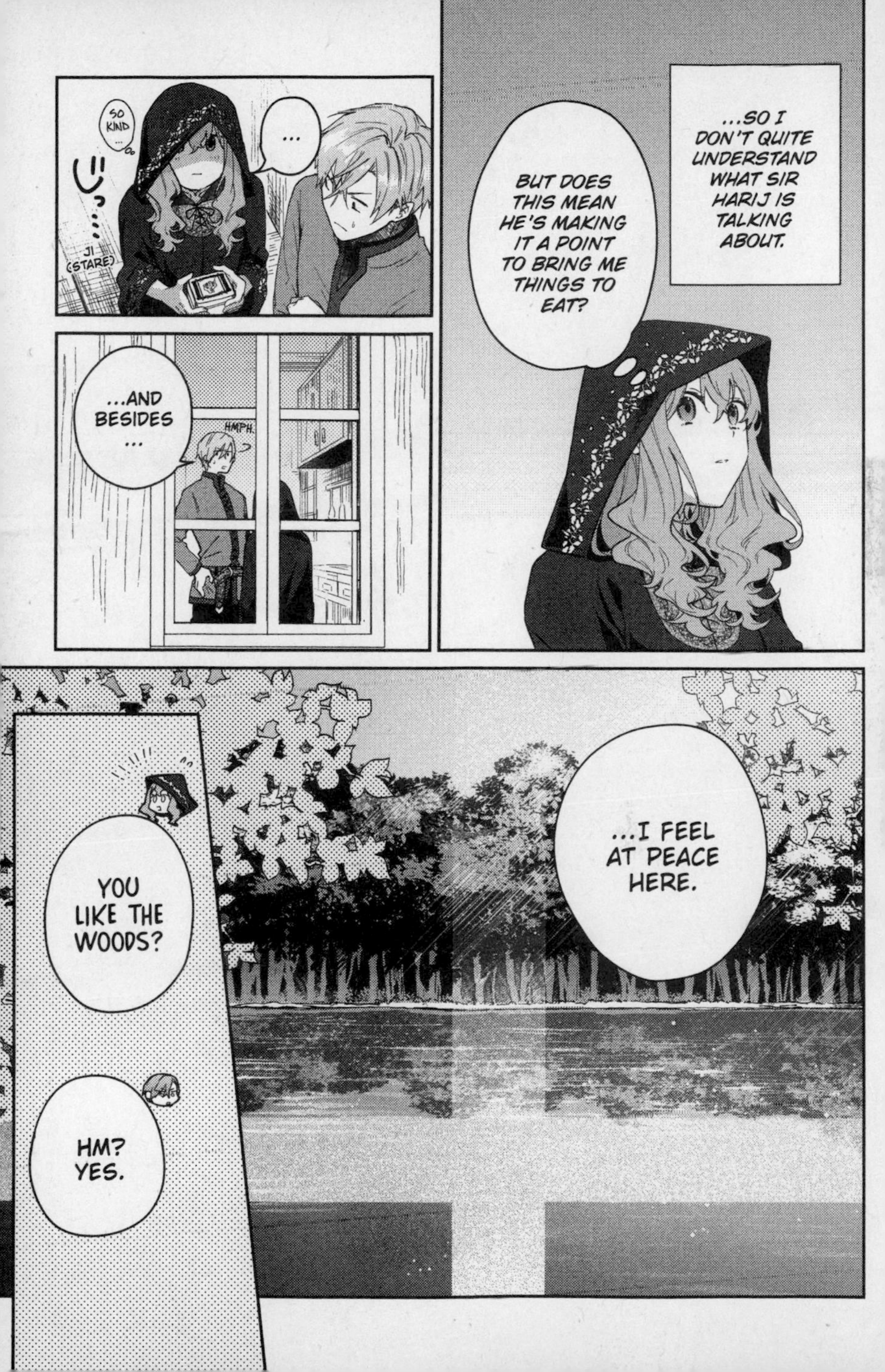
...SO I DON'T QUITE UNDERSTAND WHAT SIR HARIJ IS TALKING ABOUT.
BUT DOES THIS MEAN HE'S MAKING IT A POINT TO BRING ME THINGS TO EAT?
...
SO KIND ...
JI (STARE)
...AND BESIDES ...
HMPH.
...I FEEL AT PEACE HERE.
YOU LIKE THE WOODS?
HM? YES.

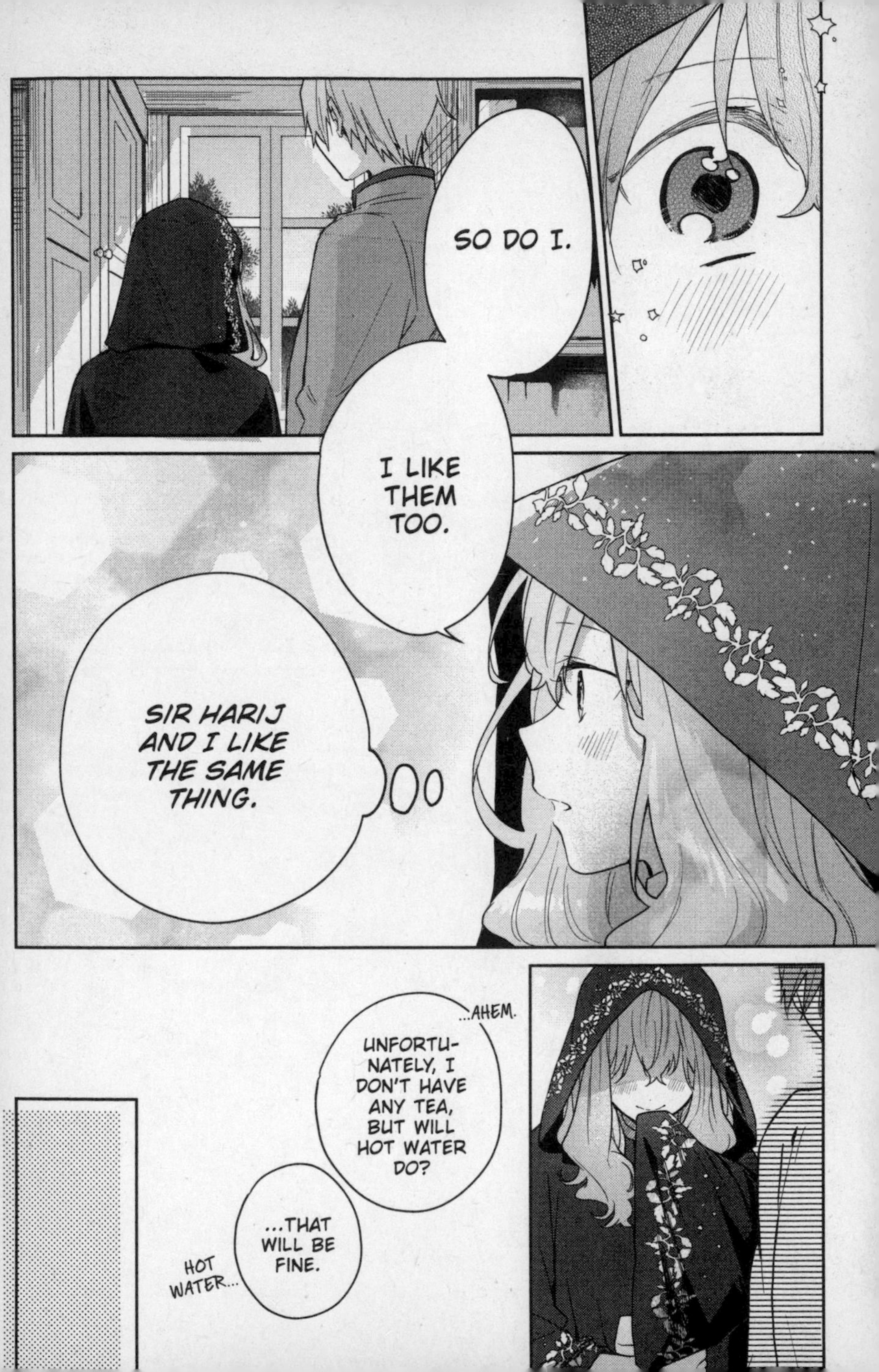
SO DO I.
I LIKE THEM TOO.
SIR HARIJ AND I LIKE THE SAME THING.
...AHEM.
UNFORTUNATELY, I DON'T HAVE ANY TEA, BUT WILL HOT WATER DO?
...THAT WILL BE FINE.
HOT WATER...

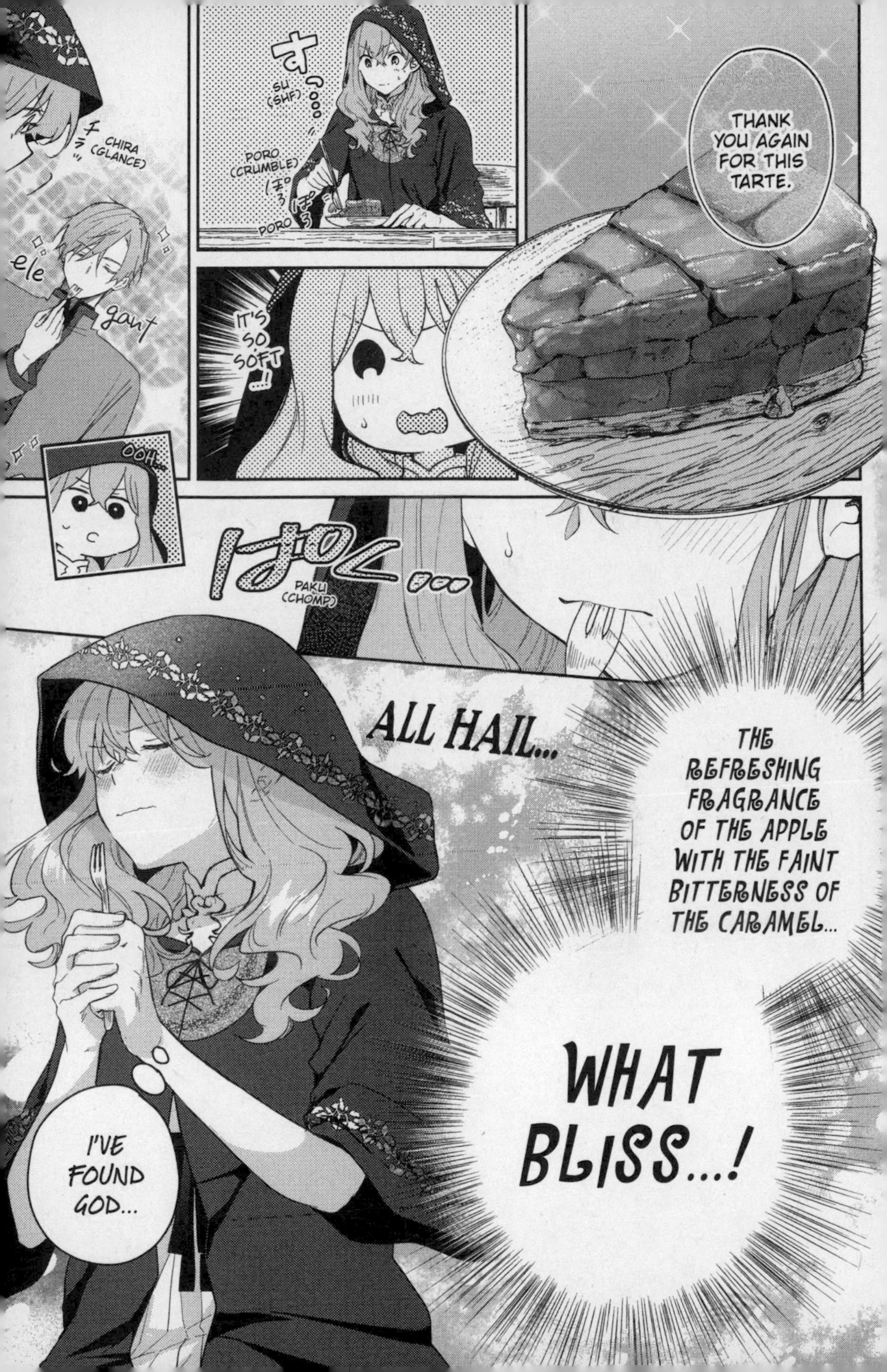
THANK YOU AGAIN FOR THIS TARTE.
SU (SHF)
PORO (CRUMBLE)
PORO
IT'S SO SOFT...!
CHIRA (GLANCE)
ele gant
OOH...
PAKU (CHOMP)
ALL HAIL...
THE REFRESHING FRAGRANCE OF THE APPLE WITH THE FAINT BITTERNESS OF THE CARAMEL...
WHAT BLISS...!
I'VE FOUND GOD...

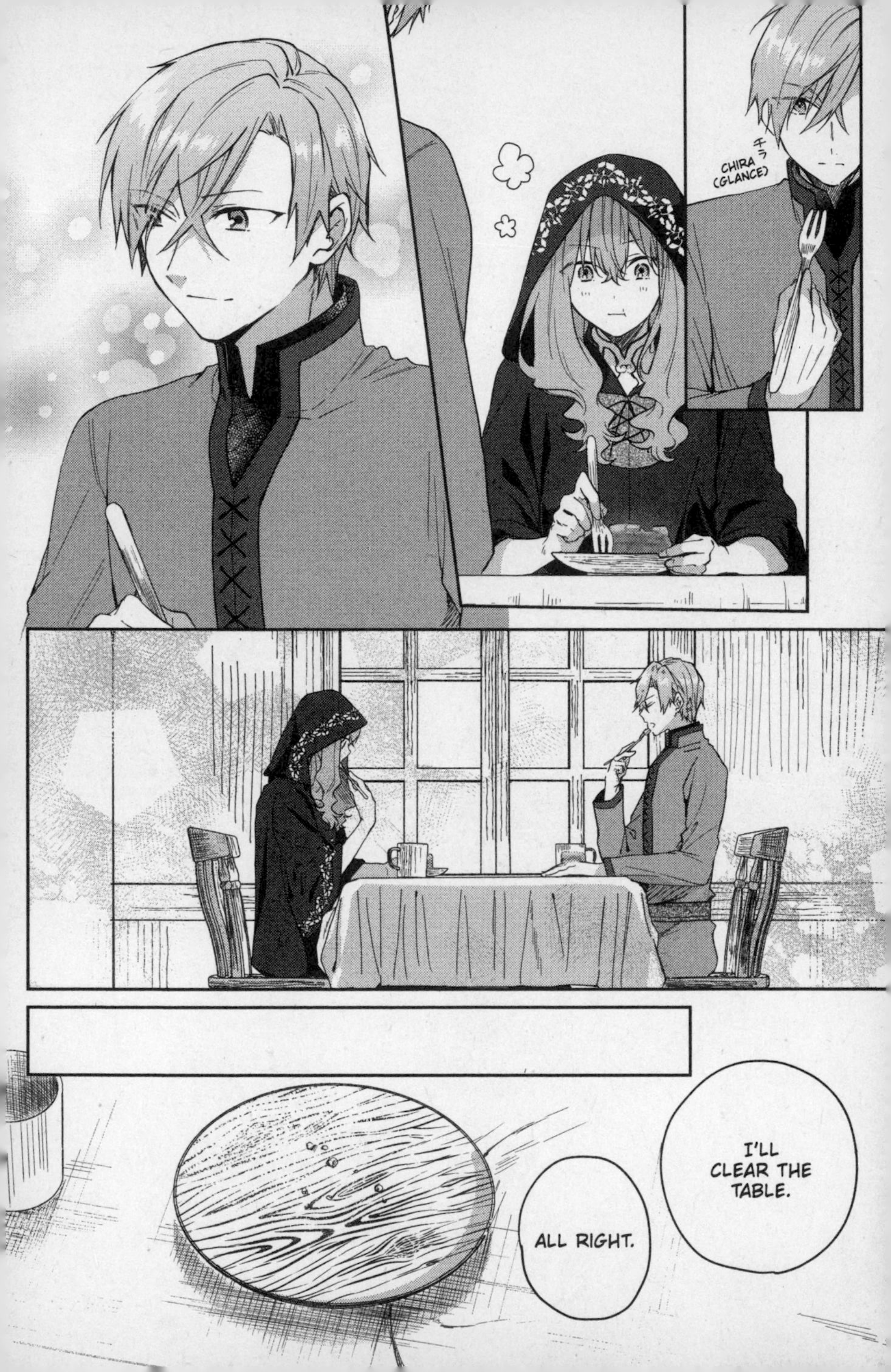
チラ
CHIRA (GLANCE)
I'LL CLEAR THE TABLE.
ALL RIGHT.

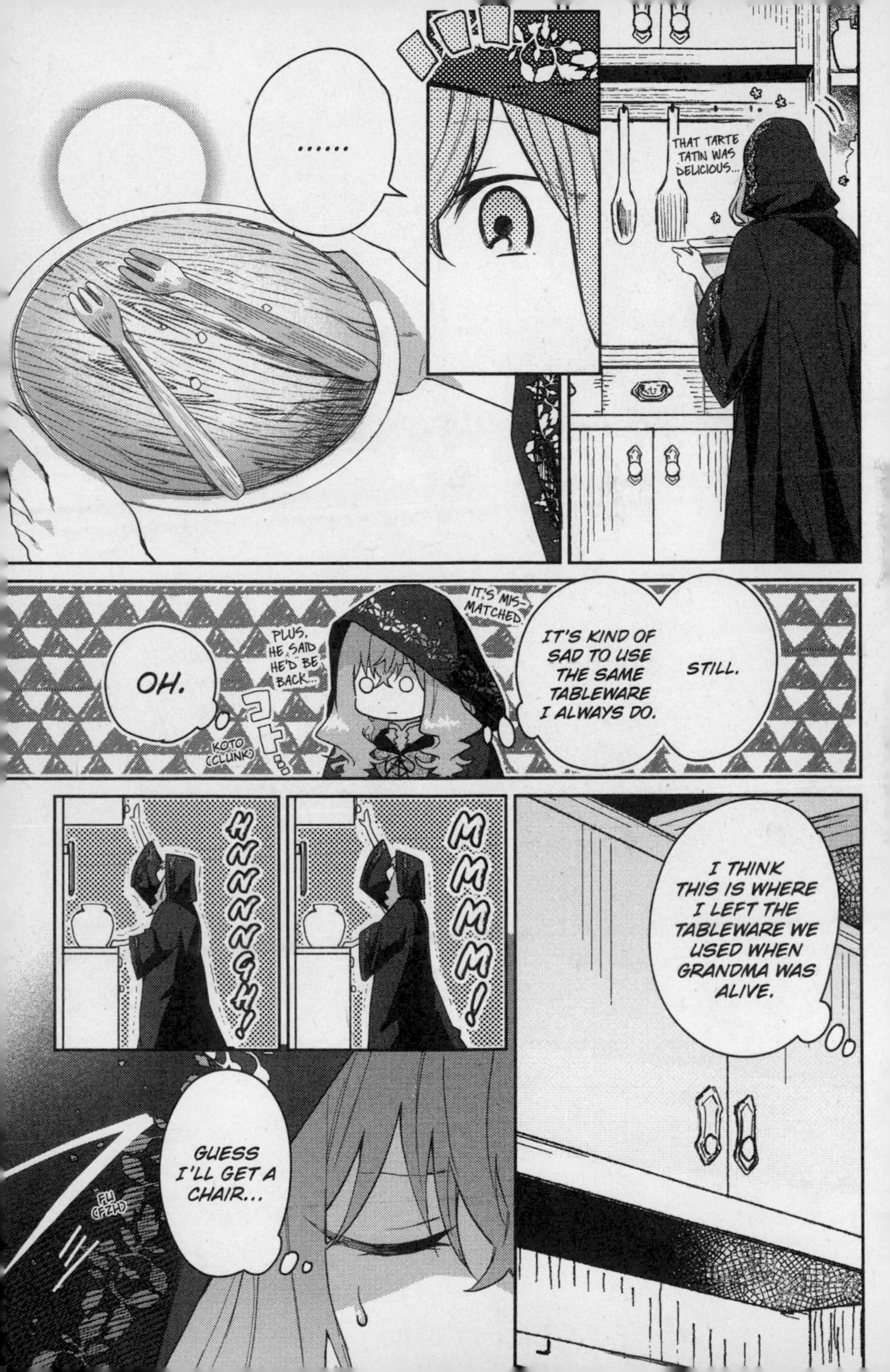
THAT TARTE TATIN WAS DELICIOUS...
......
STILL.
IT'S KIND OF SAD TO USE THE SAME TABLEWARE I ALWAYS DO.
IT'S MIS-MATCHED
PLUS, HE SAID HE'D BE BACK...
コト...
KOTO (CLUNK)
OH.
I THINK THIS IS WHERE I LEFT THE TABLEWARE WE USED WHEN GRANDMA WAS ALIVE.
MMMMMM!
HNNNNGH!
GUESS I'LL GET A CHAIR...
FU (FZHD)

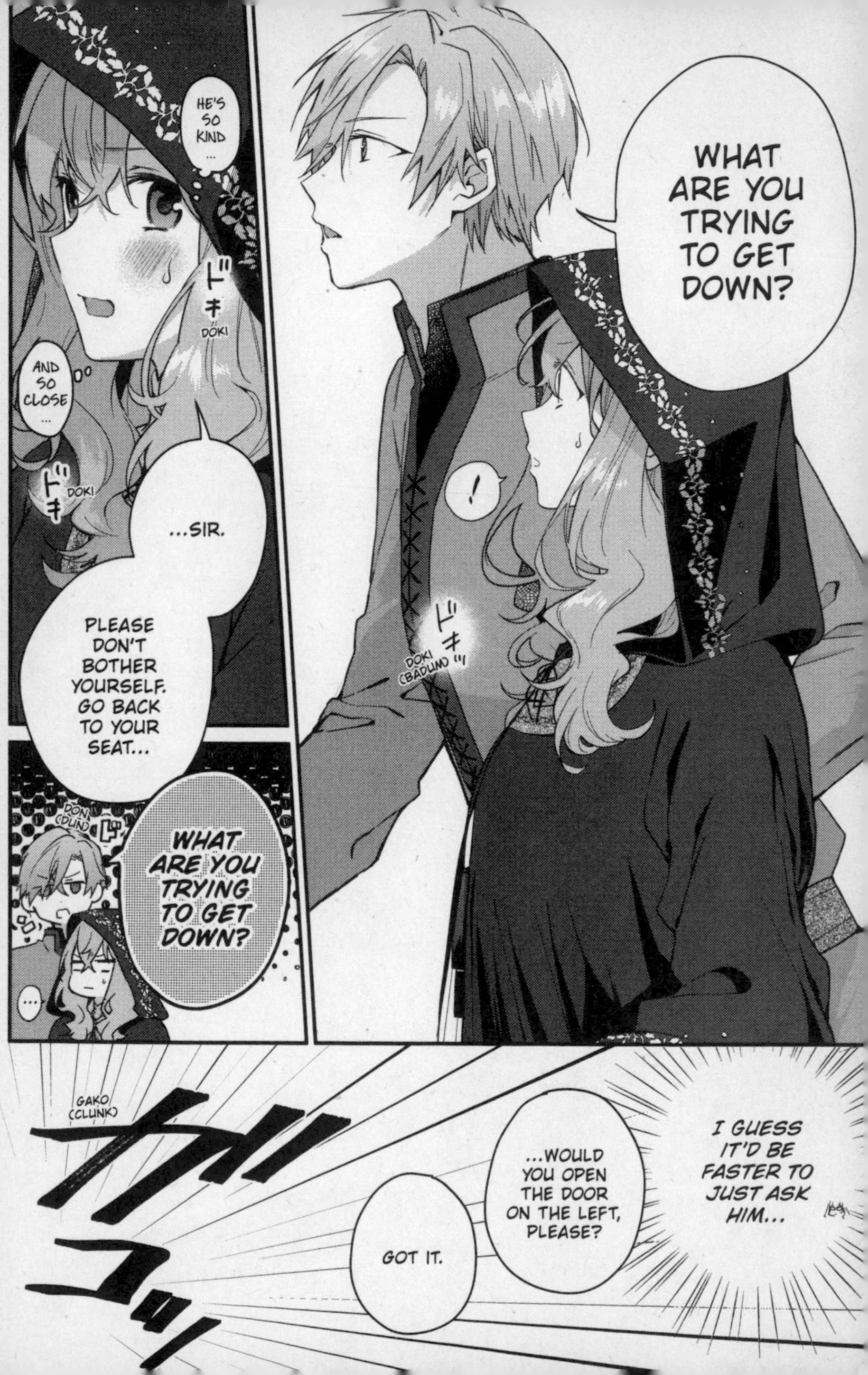
WHAT ARE YOU TRYING TO GET DOWN?
!
DOKI (BADUM)
HE'S SO KIND ...
DOKI
AND SO CLOSE ...
DOKI
...SIR.
PLEASE DON'T BOTHER YOURSELF. GO BACK TO YOUR SEAT...
DON (DUN)
WHAT ARE YOU TRYING TO GET DOWN?
...
I GUESS IT'D BE FASTER TO JUST ASK HIM...
...WOULD YOU OPEN THE DOOR ON THE LEFT, PLEASE?
GOT IT.
GAKO (CLUNK)

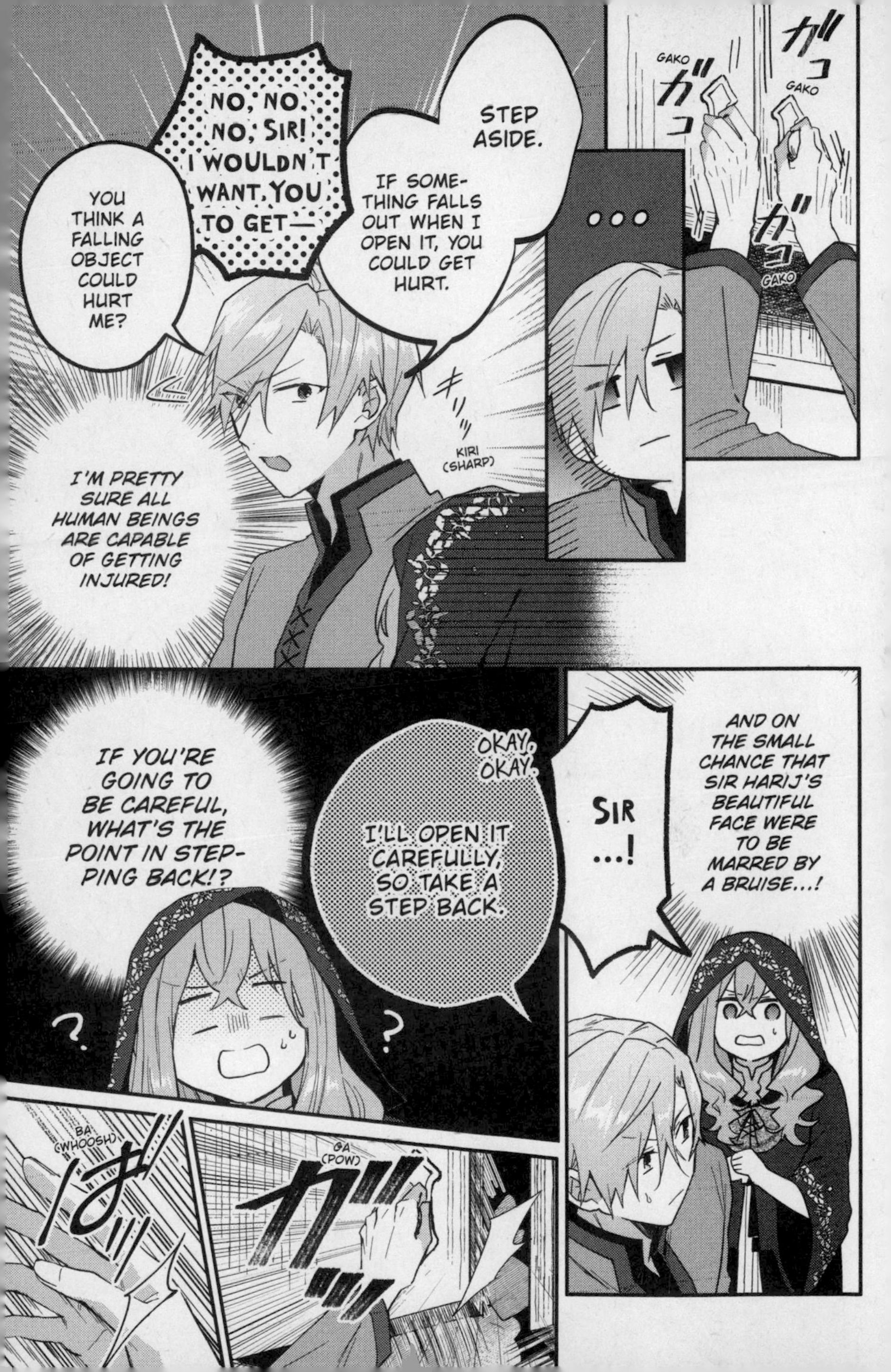

GAKO
GAKO
GAKO
...
STEP ASIDE.
IF SOMETHING FALLS OUT WHEN I OPEN IT, YOU COULD GET HURT.
NO, NO. NO, SIR! I WOULDN'T WANT YOU TO GET—
YOU THINK A FALLING OBJECT COULD HURT ME?
KIRI (SHARP)
I'M PRETTY SURE ALL HUMAN BEINGS ARE CAPABLE OF GETTING INJURED!
AND ON THE SMALL CHANCE THAT SIR HARIJ'S BEAUTIFUL FACE WERE TO BE MARRED BY A BRUISE...!
SIR ...!
OKAY, OKAY.
I'LL OPEN IT CAREFULLY, SO TAKE A STEP BACK.
IF YOU'RE GOING TO BE CAREFUL, WHAT'S THE POINT IN STEPPING BACK!?
GA (POW)
BA (WHOOSH)

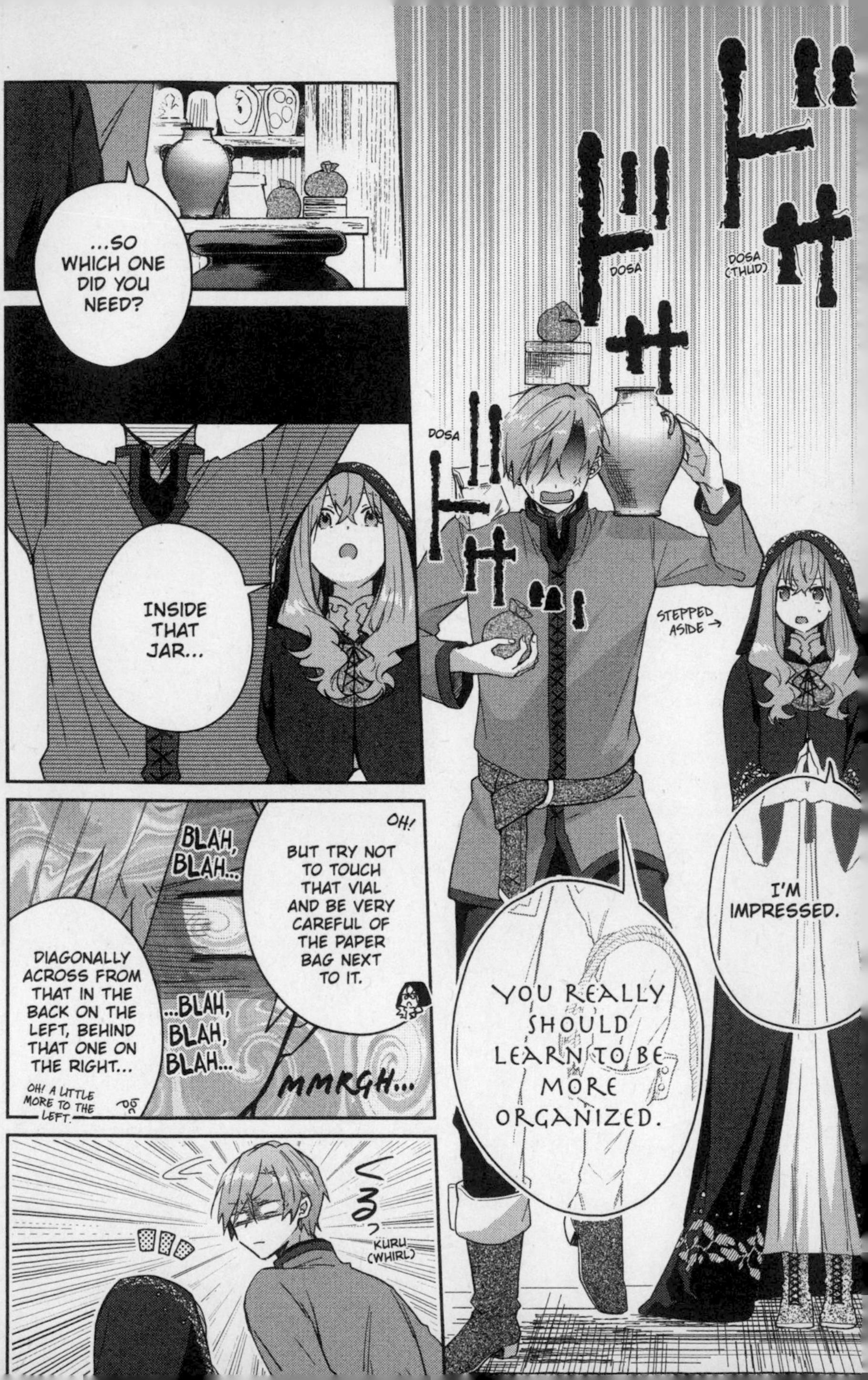
DOSA (THUD)
DOSA
DOSA
STEPPED ASIDE →
I'M IMPRESSED.
YOU REALLY SHOULD LEARN TO BE MORE ORGANIZED.
...SO WHICH ONE DID YOU NEED?
INSIDE THAT JAR...
OH!
BUT TRY NOT TO TOUCH THAT VIAL AND BE VERY CAREFUL OF THE PAPER BAG NEXT TO IT.
BLAH, BLAH...
DIAGONALLY ACROSS FROM THAT IN THE BACK ON THE LEFT, BEHIND THAT ONE ON THE RIGHT...
...BLAH, BLAH, BLAH...
MMRGH...
OH! A LITTLE MORE TO THE LEFT.
KURU (WHIRL)

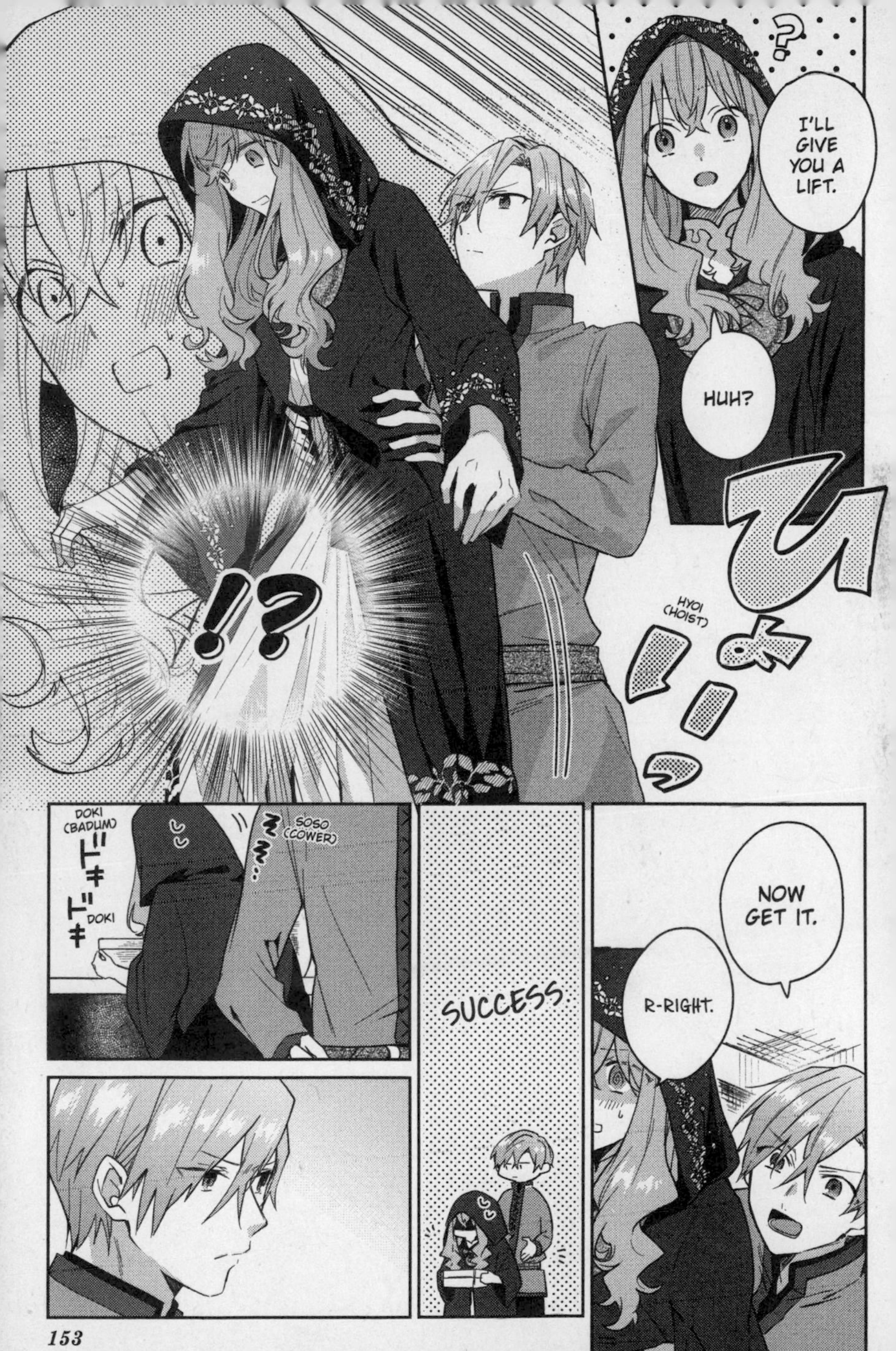
?
I'LL GIVE YOU A LIFT.
HUH?
HYOI (HOIST)
!?
NOW GET IT.
R-RIGHT.
SUCCESS.
SOSO (COWER)
DOKI (BADUM)
DOKI

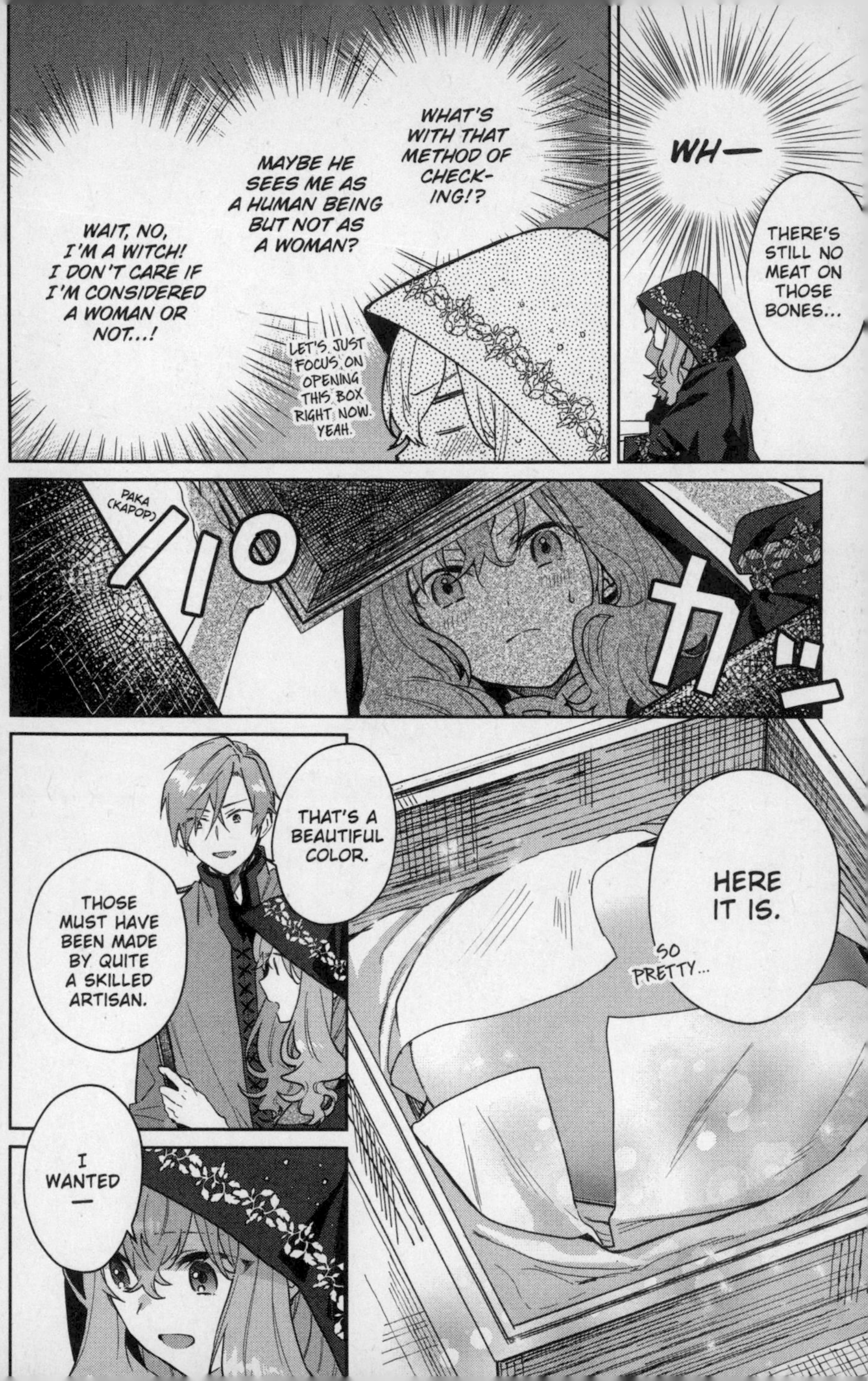
WH—
THERE'S STILL NO MEAT ON THOSE BONES...
WHAT'S WITH THAT METHOD OF CHECKING!?
MAYBE HE SEES ME AS A HUMAN BEING BUT NOT AS A WOMAN?
WAIT, NO, I'M A WITCH! I DON'T CARE IF I'M CONSIDERED A WOMAN OR NOT...!
LET'S JUST FOCUS ON OPENING THIS BOX RIGHT NOW. YEAH.
カッ
パ
PAKA (KAPOP)
HERE IT IS.
SO PRETTY...
THAT'S A BEAUTIFUL COLOR.
THOSE MUST HAVE BEEN MADE BY QUITE A SKILLED ARTISAN.
I WANTED —

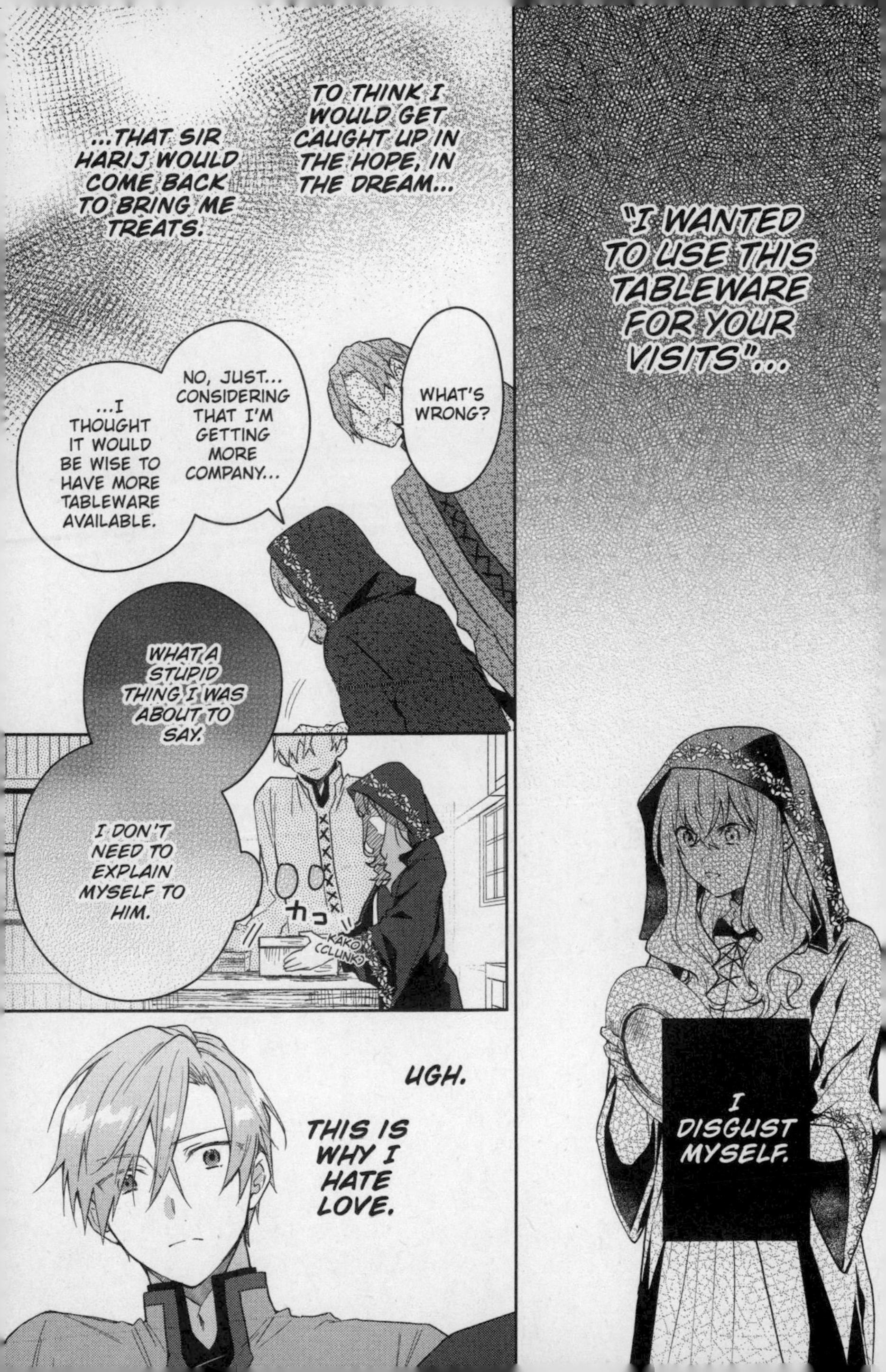

"I WANTED TO USE THIS TABLEWARE FOR YOUR VISITS"...
I DISGUST MYSELF.
TO THINK I WOULD GET CAUGHT UP IN THE HOPE, IN THE DREAM...
...THAT SIR HARIJ WOULD COME BACK TO BRING ME TREATS.
WHAT'S WRONG?
NO, JUST... CONSIDERING THAT I'M GETTING MORE COMPANY...
...I THOUGHT IT WOULD BE WISE TO HAVE MORE TABLEWARE AVAILABLE.
WHAT A STUPID THING I WAS ABOUT TO SAY.
I DON'T NEED TO EXPLAIN MYSELF TO HIM.
カッ
KAKO (CLUNK)
UGH.
THIS IS WHY I HATE LOVE.

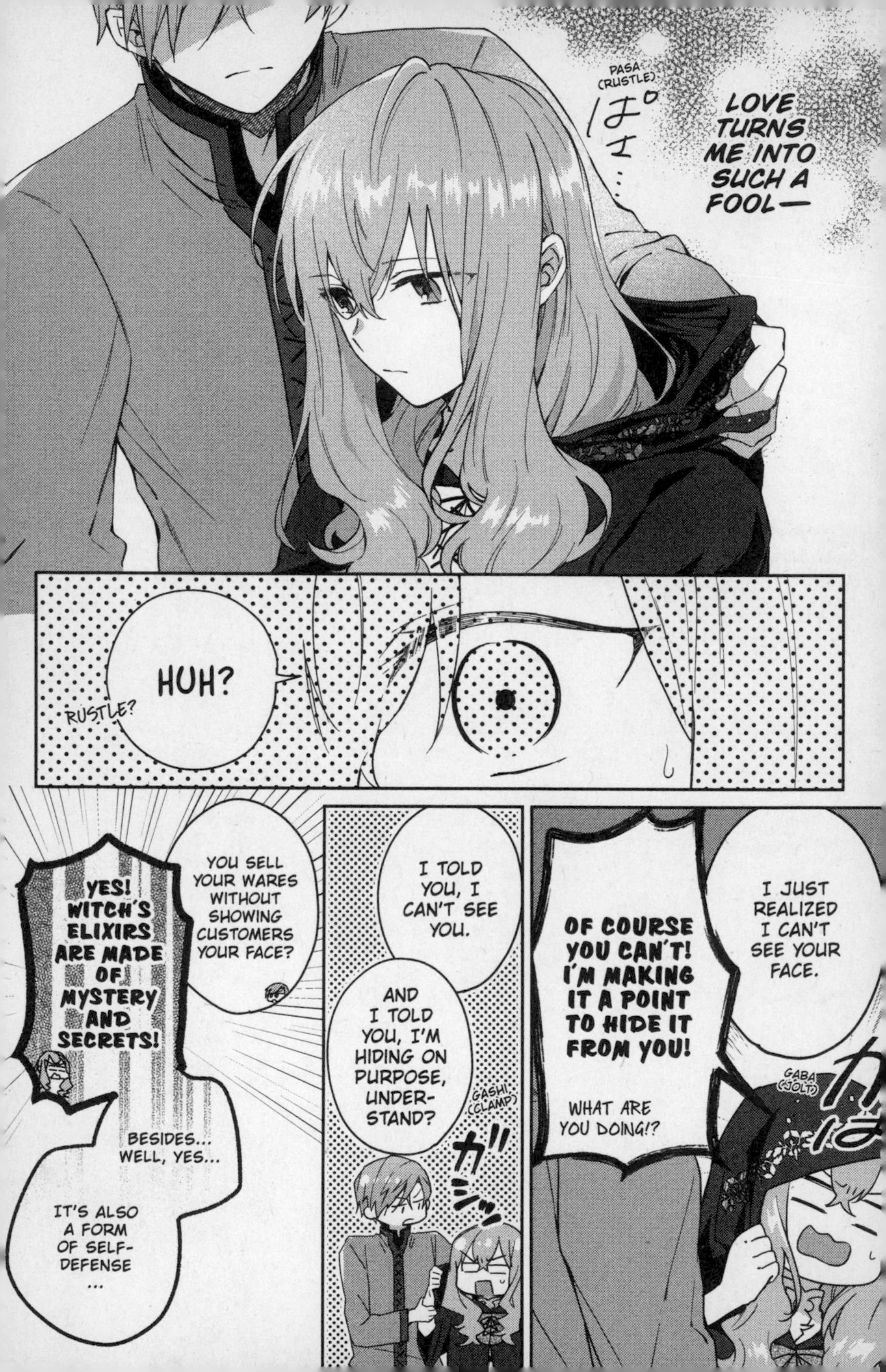
PASA (RUSTLE)
ぱさ…
LOVE TURNS ME INTO SUCH A FOOL—
HUH?
RUSTLE?
I JUST REALIZED I CAN'T SEE YOUR FACE.
GABA (JOLT)
OF COURSE YOU CAN'T! I'M MAKING IT A POINT TO HIDE IT FROM YOU!
WHAT ARE YOU DOING!?
I TOLD YOU, I CAN'T SEE YOU.
AND I TOLD YOU, I'M HIDING ON PURPOSE, UNDER-STAND?
GASHI (CLAMP)
YOU SELL YOUR WARES WITHOUT SHOWING CUSTOMERS YOUR FACE?
YES! WITCH'S ELIXIRS ARE MADE OF MYSTERY AND SECRETS!
BESIDES... WELL, YES...
IT'S ALSO A FORM OF SELF-DEFENSE ...

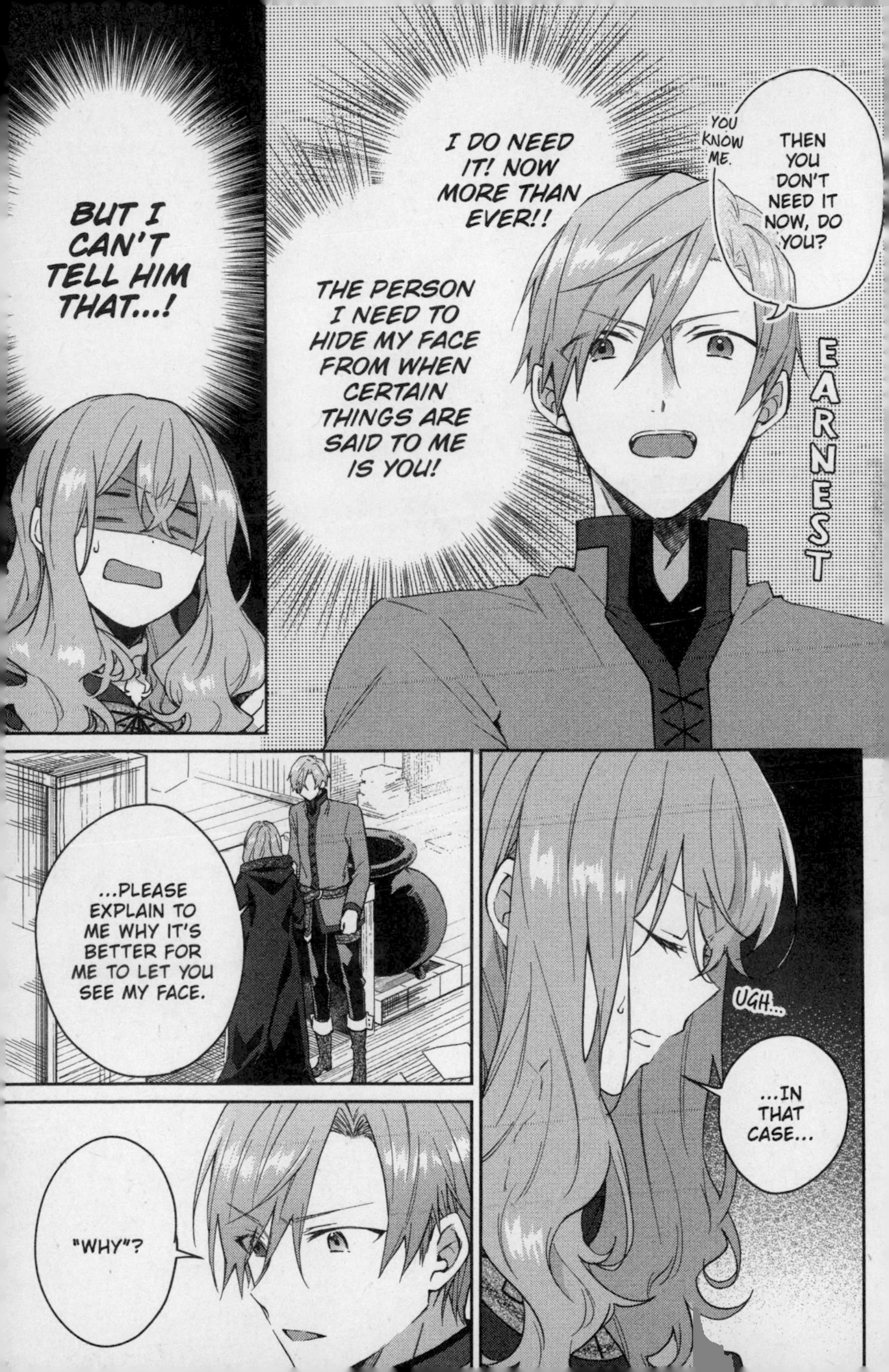

THEN YOU DON'T NEED IT NOW, DO YOU?
YOU KNOW ME.
EARNEST
I DO NEED IT! NOW MORE THAN EVER!!
THE PERSON I NEED TO HIDE MY FACE FROM WHEN CERTAIN THINGS ARE SAID TO ME IS YOU!
BUT I CAN'T TELL HIM THAT...!
UGH...
...IN THAT CASE...
...PLEASE EXPLAIN TO ME WHY IT'S BETTER FOR ME TO LET YOU SEE MY FACE.
"WHY"?

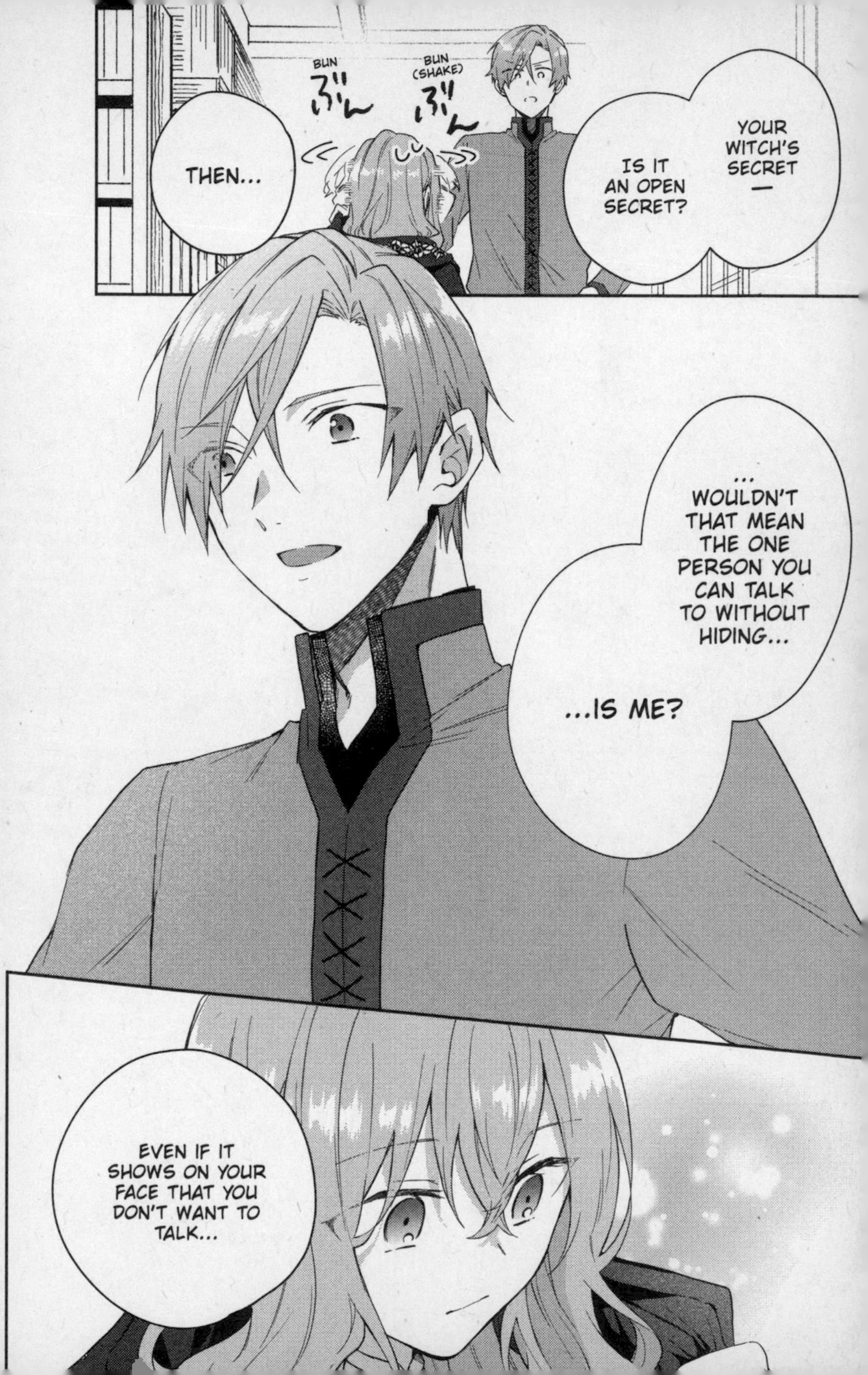
YOUR WITCH'S SECRET —
IS IT AN OPEN SECRET?
BUN (SHAKE)
ぶん
BUN
ぶん
THEN...
... WOULDN'T THAT MEAN THE ONE PERSON YOU CAN TALK TO WITHOUT HIDING...
...IS ME?
EVEN IF IT SHOWS ON YOUR FACE THAT YOU DON'T WANT TO TALK...

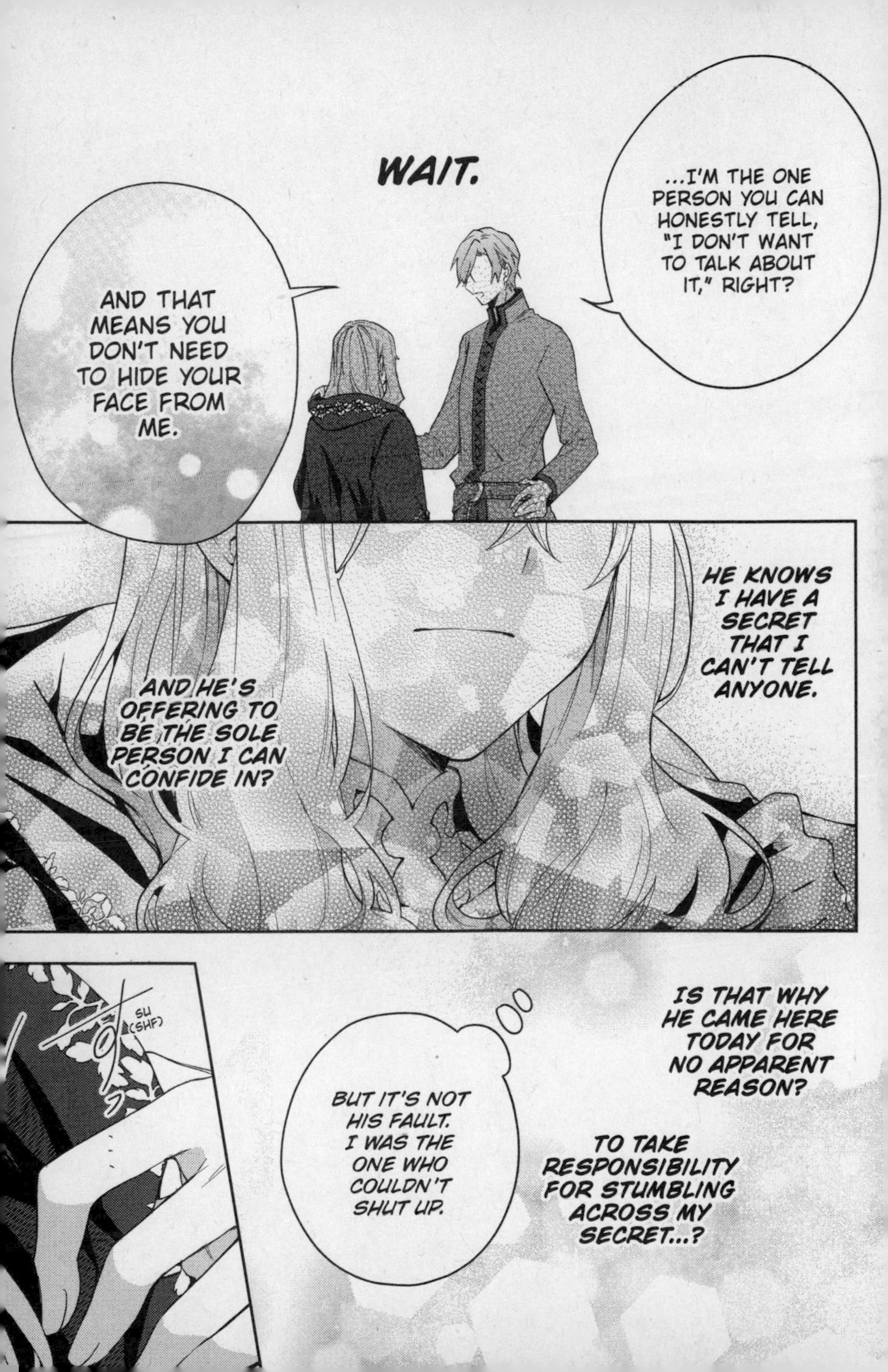
...I'M THE ONE PERSON YOU CAN HONESTLY TELL, "I DON'T WANT TO TALK ABOUT IT," RIGHT?
WAIT.
AND THAT MEANS YOU DON'T NEED TO HIDE YOUR FACE FROM ME.
HE KNOWS I HAVE A SECRET THAT I CAN'T TELL ANYONE.
AND HE'S OFFERING TO BE THE SOLE PERSON I CAN CONFIDE IN?
IS THAT WHY HE CAME HERE TODAY FOR NO APPARENT REASON?
TO TAKE RESPONSIBILITY FOR STUMBLING ACROSS MY SECRET...?
BUT IT'S NOT HIS FAULT. I WAS THE ONE WHO COULDN'T SHUT UP.
SU (SHF)

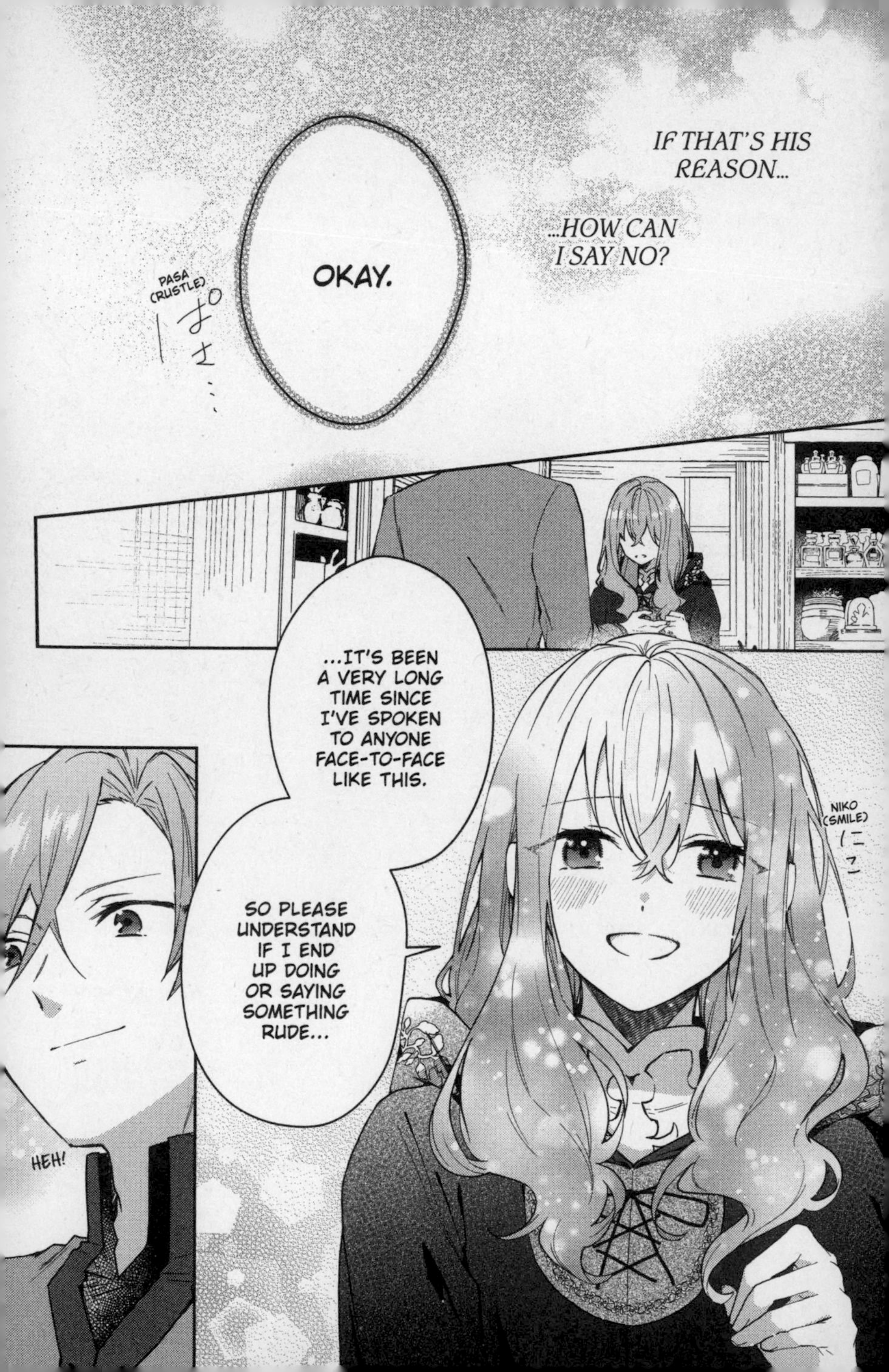
IF THAT'S HIS REASON...
...HOW CAN I SAY NO?
OKAY.
PASA (RUSTLE)
ぱさ…
NIKO (SMILE)
にこっ
...IT'S BEEN A VERY LONG TIME SINCE I'VE SPOKEN TO ANYONE FACE-TO-FACE LIKE THIS.
SO PLEASE UNDERSTAND IF I END UP DOING OR SAYING SOMETHING RUDE...
HEH!

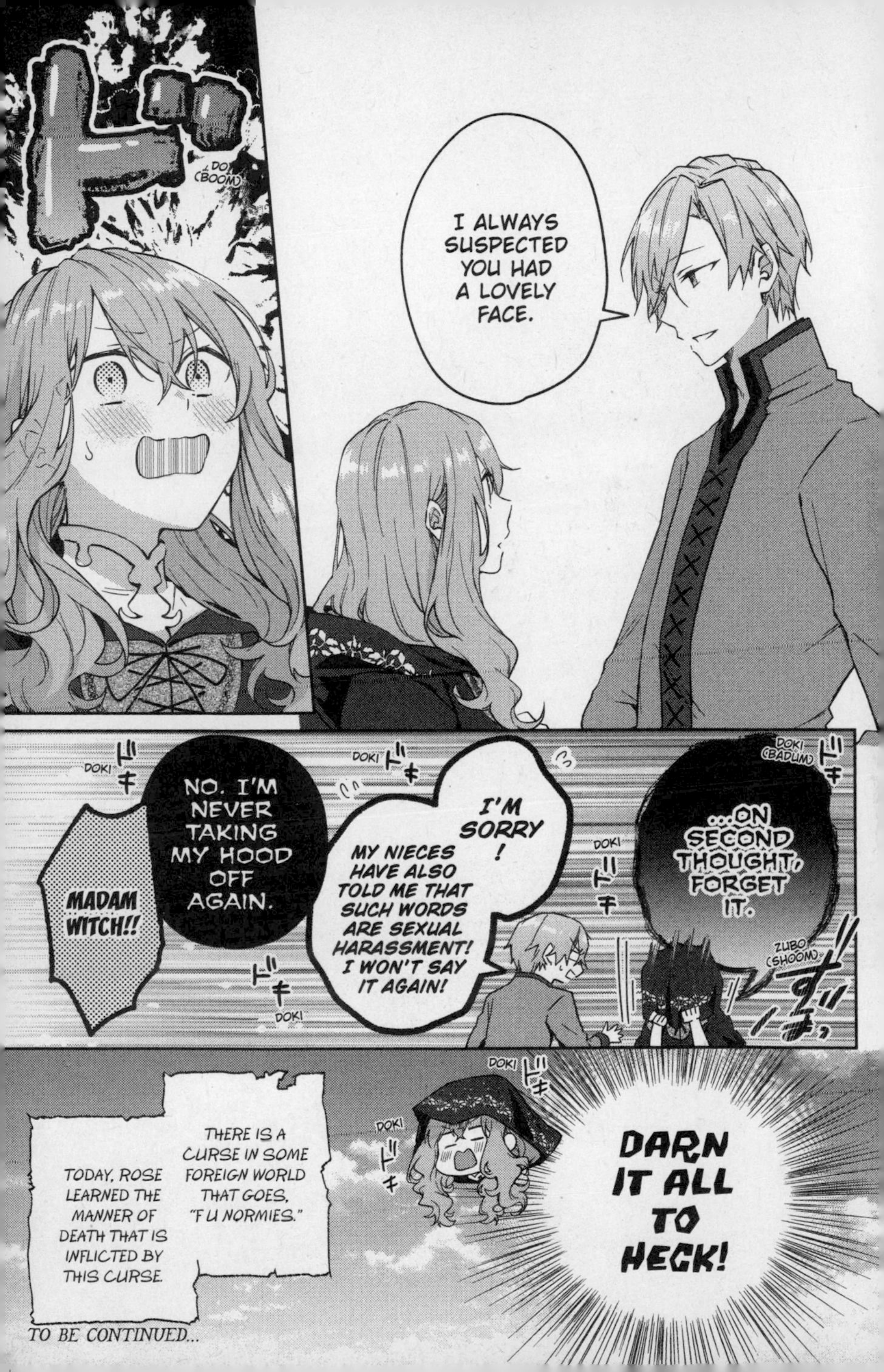
I ALWAYS SUSPECTED YOU HAD A LOVELY FACE.
DOKI (BOOM)
DOKI (BADUM)
...ON SECOND THOUGHT, FORGET IT.
DOKI
ZUBO (SHOOM)
DOKI
I'M SORRY!
MY NIECES HAVE ALSO TOLD ME THAT SUCH WORDS ARE SEXUAL HARASSMENT! I WON'T SAY IT AGAIN!
DOKI
NO. I'M NEVER TAKING MY HOOD OFF AGAIN.
DOKI
MADAM WITCH!!
DOKI
DOKI
DARN IT ALL TO HECK!
THERE IS A CURSE IN SOME FOREIGN WORLD THAT GOES, "F U NORMIES."
TODAY, ROSE LEARNED THE MANNER OF DEATH THAT IS INFLICTED BY THIS CURSE.
TO BE CONTINUED...

AFTERWORD

Hello, nice to meet you.
I'm Kamada, the artist for the manga version of *Hi, I'm a Witch, and My Crush Wants Me to Make a Love Potion*.
Thank you very much for reading.

I had the pleasure of reading the original novel, and the interactions between this couple in their constant agony were just so cute I couldn't put it down.
I'm very honored to be able to turn it into a manga!

Rose shows very little on her face but is a mess on the inside...and it's so much fun to draw. In volume one specifically, I liked drawing the tarte tatin! I tried tarte tatin and apple butter for the first time after being accepted into the world of *Witch's Love Potion*, and they're both so delicious that I was just as impressed as Rose was...Ha-ha!

I will do my very best to make sure the delicate emotions of the couple and the gentle world depicted in Mutsuhana's original novel are conveyed faithfully in the manga!
I hope you read the next volume, too!

Kamada

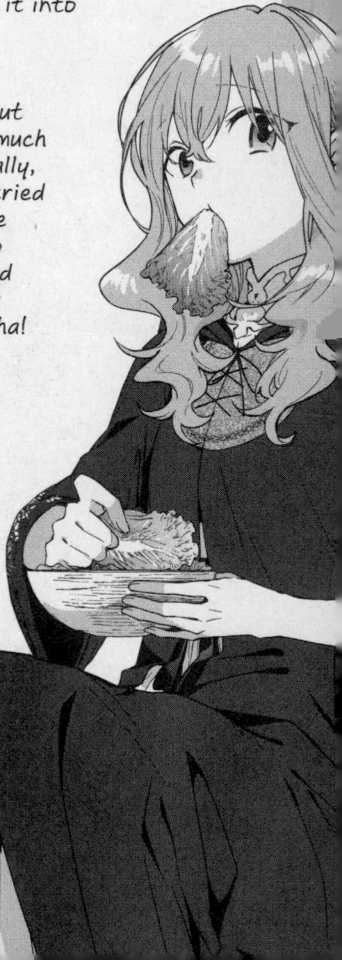

Thank you very much for picking up the manga version of *Hi, I'm a Witch, and My Crush Wants Me to Make a Love Potion*, or *Witch's Love Potion* for short! I'm Mutsuhana, the author of the original novel.

When they came to me about turning the story into a manga and told me that this manga would be drawn by Kamada, of whom I'm a big fan, I was so happily surprised my eyes nearly fell out of their sockets, my heart nearly jumped out of my mouth, and a *botamochi* confectionary nearly fell off my shelf.

Adorable facial expressions, detailed backgrounds that let you feel like you're there, and bold but easy-to-read panel layouts. I get to read the drafts and completed manuscripts a little ahead of the rest of the world, and every time I do, I feel just like Rose on page 147 when she says, "I've found God..."

I am extremely honored to have so many readers enjoy this series in so many different forms—a web novel, a print novel, and now a manga. I hope you will continue to enjoy *Witch's Love Potion*.

Eiko Mutsuhana

Hi, I'm a Witch, and My Crush Wants Me to Make a Love Potion

1

Kamada

Original Story
Eiko Mutsuhana

Character Design
vient

TRANSLATION ❦ **Alethea Nibley & Athena Nibley** LETTERING ❦ **Rachel J. Pierce**

DOMO, SUKI NA HITO NI HOREGUSURI O IRAI SARETA MAJO DESU. Vol. 1
© Kamada 2020
© Eiko Mutsuhana, vient 2020
First published in Japan in 2020 by KADOKAWA CORPORATION, Tokyo.
English translation rights arranged with KADOKAWA CORPORATION, Tokyo and Yen Press, LLC through Tuttle-Mori Agency, Inc.

Yen Press
150 West 30th Street, 19th Floor
New York, NY 10001

Visit us at yenpress.com
facebook.com/yenpress ❦ twitter.com/yenpress
yenpress.tumblr.com ❦ instagram.com/yenpress

First Yen Press Edition: June 2022
Edited by Yen Press Editorial: Won Young Seo, JuYoun Lee
Designed by Yen Press Design: Liz Parlett

Yen Press is an imprint of Yen Press, LLC.
The Yen Press name and logo are trademarks of Yen Press, LLC.

The publisher is not responsible for websites (or their content) that are not owned by the publisher.

Library of Congress Control Number: 2022934293

ISBNs: 978-1-9753-3864-0 (paperback)
978-1-9753-3865-7 (ebook)

10 9 8 7 6 5 4 3 2 1

WOR

Printed in the United States of America